Epictetus's *Encheiridion*

Also available from Bloomsbury:

Epicurus and the Singularity of Death, by David B. Suits
Marcus Aurelius: A Guide for the Perplexed, by William O. Stephens
Nietzsche and Epicurus, edited by Vinod Acharya and Ryan J. Johnson
Skill in Ancient Ethics, edited by Tom Angier and Lisa Raphals
Stoic Ethics: Epictetus and Happiness as Freedom, by William O. Stephens
Straw Man Arguments, by Scott Aikin and John Casey
The Ethics of Epicurus and Its Relation to Contemporary Doctrines,
by Jean-Marie Guyau and edited by Keith Ansell-Pearson and Federico Testa

Epictetus's *Encheiridion*

A New Translation and Guide to Stoic Ethics

Scott Aikin and William O. Stephens

BLOOMSBURY ACADEMIC
LONDON · NEW YORK · OXFORD · NEW DELHI · SYDNEY

BLOOMSBURY ACADEMIC
Bloomsbury Publishing Plc, 50 Bedford Square, London, WC1B 3DP, UK
Bloomsbury Publishing Inc, 1359 Broadway, 12th Floor, New York, NY 10018, USA
Bloomsbury Publishing Ireland, 29 Earlsfort Terrace, Dublin 2, D02 AY28, Ireland

BLOOMSBURY, BLOOMSBURY ACADEMIC and the Diana logo
are trademarks of Bloomsbury Publishing Plc

First published in Great Britain 2023
Reprinted 2025

For legal purposes the Acknowledgements on p. xi constitute an
extension of this copyright page.

Cover design by Louise Dugdale
Cover image: The Artist Moved by the Grandeur of Antique Fragments,
Henry Fuseli, 1778–79.

Bloomsbury Publishing Inc does not have any control over, or responsibility for, any
third-party websites referred to or in this book. All internet addresses given in this
book were correct at the time of going to press. The author and publisher regret any
inconvenience caused if addresses have changed or sites have ceased to exist,
but can accept no responsibility for any such changes.

A catalogue record for this book is available from the British Library.
Library of Congress Control Number: 2023939199

ISBN: HB: 978-1-3500-0950-9
         PB: 978-1-3500-0951-6
         ePDF: 978-1-3500-0953-0
         eBook: 978-1-3500-0952-3

Typeset by Integra Software Services Pvt. Ltd.
Printed and bound in Great Britain

For product safety related questions contact productsafety@bloomsbury.com.

To find out more about our authors and books visit www.bloomsbury.com
and sign up for our newsletters.

SA dedicates this book to his students over the years, for their searching questions and their refusal to accept bad answers.
WOS dedicates this to his wife, Kathy; his mother, Mary Irene; and his brother, John, for their boundless, loving support.

Contents

Preface

With this translation and commentary, we are out to accomplish several overlapping objectives. First, we want to show how Epictetus's *Encheiridion* is part of a larger story of a philosophical school's inception, development and reception in the ancient world and beyond. Much of that story is about the Stoic tradition that antedates Epictetus with philosophers like Socrates and Diogenes, who were inspirations to the later Stoics. We turn to focus on Zeno, Cleanthes and Chrysippus as they formulated the core ideas of their school. We also believe an under-appreciated figure, Musonius Rufus, deserves focused attention for his story, given his role in Epictetus's introduction to the Porch. Furthermore, we wish to highlight the starkness and clarity that define the Stoic programme, which we believe is best served by discussing Cicero's catalogue of Stoic paradoxes (with one we add for good measure). Our remarks on these set the stage for a picture of Epictetus the philosopher and the story of his *Encheiridion*, compiled and distributed by his student Arrian. We trace the high points of the *Encheiridion*'s influence on philosophy and literature in the Western tradition to its contemporary impact.

Our translation is inspired by the thought that the *Encheiridion* was written in Koinē Greek, the accessible language of everyday people, not the technical Greek of the philosophers. Consequently, the translation aims in like fashion to meet progressors and readers where they are.

Our commentaries on the chapters are posited on the view that Stoic philosophical practice is underwritten by one reasoning to and endorsing precepts about the nature of the world and what is good. Consequently, we have endeavoured to provide maximally argumentative interpretations of each chapter, providing whatever background considerations or suppressed reasons one needs to see what is intellectually compelling about Epictetus's case. Moreover, we often pause to note the points in the progress of the *Encheiridion* where new complications arise or questions demand answers. One take-away is that we see the *Encheiridion* as a developmental work, one with exercises and arguments for progressively more advanced students in later chapters, along with challenges for these advanced progressors to address in light of their progress. That is, new kinds of challenges for practitioners of Stoic philosophy will arise because of their improvement as philosophers. We will call these instances *progressors' temptations*; they are difficulties Epictetus is particularly intent on observing and answering towards the end of the *Encheiridion*.

We conclude this *Guide* with a collection of what we take to be the most widely posed and most challenging objections to Stoicism generally and Epictetus's statement of it specifically. Many are old problems for the philosophy, familiar to and addressed in different ways by the ancients. Others are newer but equally troubling challenges informed by developments in logic, physics, psychology and critical reflections on contemporary culture. To each objection, we present what we think the most promising Stoic responses are. We hope this work shows that Stoicism is a living philosophical tradition well worth critically defending and developing.

Finally, we wish to note that a commentary on a book with sections commonly called 'chapters' creates a challenge for internal reference if the commentary itself has sections that must be referenced. Calling all these sections 'chapters' causes confusion, so we've opted to continue using 'chapter' for the sections of Epictetus's work and 'parts' to refer to sections of our own work on the *Encheiridion*.

Acknowledgements

SA is grateful for the regular and insightful feedback on this project from his colleagues at Vanderbilt University: Matthew Congdon, Emanuele Costa, Idit Dobbs-Weinstein, Lenn Goodman, Diana Heney, Michael Hodges, John Lachs, Alyssa Lowery, Karen Ng, Isabella Reinhardt, Robert Talisse, Paul C. Taylor, Jeffrey Tlumak and Julian Wuerth. In addition, there have been many students over the years who have given Aikin significant reason to think critically about the Stoics. These include most prominently Erin Bradfield, Fiacha Heneghan, Emily McGill, Tempest Henning, Glenn Trujillo and Lucy Alsip Vollbrecht. A final thanks goes to William O. Stephens for his scholarly judgement and the depth of his knowledge.

For three decades countless students at Creighton University responded with enthusiasm, candour and ambivalence to the efforts of WOS to present Epictetus on his own terms. He thanks them for planting the seeds that grew into these pages. For various contributions to his Stoic education WOS credits Michael A. Brown, Randy and Barb Feezell, Greg Bucher, Christina Clark, Claire Climer, Alyssa Ellerbusch, Piotr Stankiewicz, Krzysztof Łapiński, Scott Rubarth, John Sellars and Tony Long. WOS is also grateful to Rebecca Zawistowski for her collaboration on the initial translation. Sean Erwin, too, deserves thanks for encouraging words on the translation. Most thanks go to Aikin, the Heracles to Stephens's Iolaus.

Both authors appreciate Bloomsbury's six anonymous reviewers for warmly welcoming the idea for this project. In Part Two, some material from Stephens's 'The Stoics and Their Philosophical System' is used, from *The Routledge Handbook of Hellenistic Philosophy*, K. Arenson (ed.), pp. 25–37, Copyright © 2020 by Routledge. Reproduced by permission of Taylor & Francis Group.

Finally, we wish to thank the editorial staff at Bloomsbury for their patience in the production and delivery of this book. In particular, we wish to thank Suzie Nash and Becky Holland for their consistent work encouraging us to meet deadlines, and Colleen Coalter and Andrew Wardell for their guidance in formulating the initial project.

Abbreviations

Const	Seneca, *De Constantia Sapientis* (*On the Firmness of the Wise Man*)
De Fin	Cicero, *De Finibus Bonorum et Malorum* (*On the Ends of Good and Evil*)
Disc	*Diatribai, Dissertationes, Discourses* of Epictetus as reported by Arrian
DL	Diogenes Laertius, *Lives of the Eminent Philosophers*
Ench	*Encheiridion, Handbook* or *Manual*
Ep	Seneca, *Epistulae Morales ad Lucilium* (*Letters on Ethics to Lucilius*)
Helv	Seneca, *De Consolatione ad Helviam* (*To Helvia, on Consolation*)
M	Sextus Empiricus, *Adversus Mathematicos* (*Against the Mathematicians*)
Med	Marcus Aurelius, *Meditations*
Parad	Cicero, *Paradoxa Stoicorum* (*Stoic Paradoxes*)
PH	Sextus Empiricus, *Pyrrhoniae Hypotyposes* (*Outlines of Pyrrhonism*)
SVF	*Stoicorum Veterum Fragmenta* (*Fragments of the Ancient Stoics*) edited by Hans von Arnim, 4 vols, 1903–5
Tusc	Cicero, *Tusculan Disputations*

Part 1

An Introduction to Ancient Stoicism

Stoicism was an ancient philosophy with many proponents and practitioners over hundreds of years in the Greek and Roman periods of Mediterranean history. Part One offers a short history of that tradition from its forebears and its originators to its most famous writers and adherents in the Roman imperial period. We survey six of its core themes and discuss the famous 'paradoxes' of Stoicism. Our objective here is to set a philosophical baseline for interpreting Epictetus's *Handbook*. In light of these themes and paradoxes, in Part Five we aim to clarify where Stoicism's critics have a point and where Stoics have replies.

1.1 Stoicism before the Stoa

Socrates (*c.* 469–399 BCE) was the first Stoic. At first glance, this claim is a bald-faced anachronism: Socrates was executed by his fellow Athenians in 399 BCE, and Zeno of Citium didn't begin to propound his philosophy in the Painted Stoa[1] until a century later. Yet many of the most important ethical ideas discussed by Socrates and defended by a character of that name in Plato's early dialogues inspired the philosophizing of that of Zeno and his followers. The first idea is that reason is the most valuable tool available to human beings for living a good life. Knowing the good, then, is doing the good. Second, is that the perfection of reason is wisdom. Third, all the virtues are unified, so that wisdom, justice, self-control, courage, piety, generosity, etc., are all inter-entailing: if you lack one, you lack them all. Fourth, wickedness (vice) guarantees misery no matter how much physical strength, physical health, wealth, prestige, political power and pleasure you manage to pile up. The corollary to this complex of ideas is that virtue is necessary and sufficient for the good life.

Socrates' bravery in the face of threats of punishment by the Athenian lawcourt in the *Apology* particularly inspired Epictetus's admiration. As a husband, father, law-abiding citizen, military veteran and pious gadfly stationed by the god(s) in Athens with the mission of prodding his fellow citizens to philosophically examine their lives and to value virtue above all else, Epictetus upholds Socrates as a heroic role model for Stoics to emulate. Central to Socrates' wisdom, as Epictetus sees it, is his strong grasp of what is good, what is bad and what is neither good nor bad. Socrates knew that imprisonment, confiscation of property, exile and death were not evils. He knew that if he were executed while loyally performing his divine mission as the gadfly, he would be killed at his post stalwartly doing his greatest duty. As such, he knew that his wife becoming a widow and his children becoming orphans would not be bad. Rather, he was convinced that it would be bad and impious to disobey his superior, the god, who, like a general who has tasked him, the philosopher-foot soldier, with battling Athenian injustice, hubris, greed, hedonism and complacency. Socrates knew that to be good meant dedicating one's life to becoming as wise, self-respecting, (epistemically) humble, loyal and obedient to the gods as possible. For these reasons Epictetus praises Socrates for knowing how to play ball skilfully (*Disc.* ii.5.18–20). This means doing your best to assent to only true beliefs, form only sound judgements, make consistently wise decisions, have only noble motives, act always honourably and to dare to do your duty without fail. Socrates concentrated on 'the things up to him' while confidently accepting that 'the things not up to him' would unfold as the gods willed and so would turn out just fine.

If ideas like these associated with Socrates arguably identified him as a proto-Stoic, then it can be argued that the second proto-Stoic of ancient Greece was the flamboyant Diogenes (*c.* 404–323 BCE). Diogenes was an exile from Sinope, a city on the coast of the Black Sea. Like a 'faithful hound', Diogenes dogged the steps of Antisthenes, an austere philosopher who was one of the young men who closely attended to the discussions Socrates held in public.

Diogenes famously 'debased the currency' by scorning conventional norms and embracing the norms of nature in their place. His fellow ancient Greeks believed that happiness requires income, comfortable clothing, a nice house to live in, marriage, friends, civic participation and political privileges. Diogenes ridiculed this belief. He insisted that one should strive to need (and so have) as little as possible and demonstrate virtue in action, not blab about it. So, when he saw a boy drinking water from his hands, Diogenes threw away his one bowl as unnecessary. Like Socrates, Diogenes went barefoot, but he took austerity to a higher level. Instead of sheltering under a roof, he occupied an abandoned *pithos* – a ceramic jar as big as a coffin used to store grain, oil or wine. To toughen his body, on hot days he rolled naked in the burning sand of a beach. On cold days he stripped and hugged bronze or stone statues. He lived off the land and begged for food. He owned only three possessions. He had a cloak he would wrap up in to sleep. He carried a sack to hold whatever edibles he scavenged. Third, he carried a walking stick he used to fend off aggressive curs.

When he lacked a willing partner, Diogenes believed that the easy way to relieve his sexual desires was to masturbate, no matter where he was. He joked that he wished his desire for food could go away by merely rubbing his belly. Similarly, when nature called, he thought it entirely natural, and so acceptable, to urinate and defecate anywhere, even in public. When hungry, he would eat outdoors too, a practice considered unsanitary and uncouth by his fellow Greeks. His defiance of social norms of decency earned him the nickname Diogenes 'The Dog' or *kynos* (*kyōn*) in Greek. It was from the adjective *kynikos*, meaning 'of or like a dog', that followers of Diogenes were called *Cynics*.

Captured by pirates and sold into slavery, Diogenes promulgated his lessons in austere, no-nonsense living to his so-called 'masters', treating them as a schoolmaster treats ignorant pupils. Slavery, Diogenes meant to show, often involves shackles on the mind at least as much as chains on the body.

Diogenes' tough physical training, *askêsis* in Greek, is the origin of the term 'ascetic'. By fending for himself as much as humanly possible, Diogenes demonstrated nearly Herculean self-sufficiency (*autarkeia*). He fearlessly spoke his custom-busting truths to authority figures, not giving a damn what people thought or said about him. His frankness (*parrhesia*) targeted all *tuphos* (vanity). *Tuphos* means being full of oneself, literally being puffed up and full of hot air, and so flatulent. Being 'civilized' was what made people this way, and so Diogenes saw enculturation, particularly mindless conformity to baseless societal norms and customs and the pursuit of material comforts, as a big problem. Disdainful of the conventional notion that people need political standing to thrive, Diogenes proclaimed himself a 'citizen of the world' (*cosmopolitês*), a cosmopolitan, at home everywhere on Earth.

After settling in Corinth, Diogenes handed down his dog-like way of life to Crates, the second Cynic. Crates set out to be a confirmed bachelor like his master Diogenes. But a woman named Hipparchia, undeterred by Crates' discouragement and her parents' protests, insisted on marrying the penniless Cynic and adopting his way of life.

1.2 The Stoics

Zeno of Citium (334–262 BCE)[2]

Zeno was born on the island of Cyprus in the town of Citium (today's Larnaca). One report has it that his father, a merchant, brought back from his trips to Athens many books about Socrates, stirring his son's passion for philosophy. According to another story, Zeno's ship from Phoenicia wrecked and he lost all his cargo. Arriving bedraggled in Athens, Zeno went to a bookstore, read about Socrates and asked where he could find such a man. The bookseller directed him to Crates, who became Zeno's teacher. Crates' Cynic way of life made a strong impression on Zeno's developing philosophy taught in Athens' famous painted colonnade, the *Stoa Poikilê*. The school Zeno founded thus came to be known as *the Stoa*, after that colonnade, and his followers were named *Stoics*.

Zeno was said to have shown great endurance against heat, cold, rain and pain. He rejected the belief that pain was a bad thing because he valued the ability to calmly endure it. This Stoic doctrine that pain is not a terrible thing that necessarily makes you worse off while pleasure is not a true good that always improves your life finds expression in the maxim of the U.S. Marine Corps that 'pain is weakness leaving the body'. Zeno was no masochist. He habituated himself to take discomfort in stride to grow more resilient. He trained himself to be very frugal. He wore a thin cloak. He ate raw food and bread to become temperate in his appetites. He was consistently content and dignified no matter his circumstances. Zeno may have been the first to divide philosophical discourse into logic, physics and ethics. He declared that nothing is more unbecoming than arrogance, especially in the young, who should walk and dress with perfect propriety. To honour him, the Athenians erected a bronze statue of him.

Cleanthes of Assos (331–232 BCE)

When Zeno died, his student Cleanthes became the second scholarch (head) of the Stoa. A boxer from Assos (modern-day Behramkale) in northwest Asia Minor, Cleanthes arrived in Athens with a pittance of four drachmas (perhaps roughly the pay for four days of work by a skilled worker or a foot soldier). Too poor to buy paper, Cleanthes took notes from Zeno's lectures on oyster-shells and the blade-bones of oxen. To eke out a living he did hard manual labour. It was said that by day he studied arguments and by night he hauled up water from wells. Asked in court to explain how so burly a man as he made a living, Cleanthes produced as witnesses the gardener he drew water for and the woman who paid him to mill grain into flour. For his toils and brawn, Cleanthes was called a second Heracles. Of his writings, one long fragment of his *Hymn to Zeus* survives. The hymn allegorizes the active principle of Stoic physics, praising Zeus as the giver of every gift and the sovereign ruler of the heavens, the earth and all its creatures. Those obedient to God's universal law, Cleanthes writes, can obtain the true wealth of a noble life. The wicked unwittingly chase the evils of fame, gain, folly or carnal pleasures.

Aristo of Chios (c. 320–c. 240 BCE)

Aristo the Bald was from the island of Chios in the eastern Aegean Sea. He attended the lectures of Zeno. Aristo was dubbed 'the Siren' for his great eloquence. Chrysippus would later establish a Stoic orthodoxy, including the doctrine that virtue is the only good, vice is the only bad, and all other things are termed 'indifferent' since, by themselves, they bring neither happiness nor misery. The orthodox doctrine distinguished 'preferred indifferents' (e.g. life, health, wealth and good reputation) from 'dispreferred indifferents' (e.g. death, illness, poverty and ill repute). The former can be selected, and the latter avoided, so long as virtue is preserved above all.

Aristo challenged this doctrine of Chrysippus. Aristo argued that the goal of action is a life of complete indifference to everything that is neither virtue nor vice. To defend his rejection of distinctions among indifferents he cited the example of the alphabet. When writing names, we sometimes place some letters first and at other times other letters, adapting our choices to varying circumstances. We thus select some letters over others not by nature, but to fit each situation. Similarly, in the things between virtue and vice there is no natural preference of some over others, but rather circumstances dictate our selections. Aristo further illustrated this idea by comparing the wise man to a good actor who, when cast to act the role of a brute like Thersites or a king like Agamemnon, plays either role equally well.

In addition to disagreeing with Chrysippus, Aristo rejected Zeno's belief in a plurality of virtues, affirming instead their unity. His independence of thought included the position that ethics is the only legitimate subject of philosophy. He rejected logic and physics entirely, claiming that physics was beyond us and logic did not concern us. Regarding logic, Aristo likened dialectical arguments to spiders' webs whose workmanship is impressive but nonetheless useless. Aristo declared that the wise hold no opinions. Practical rules of advice he dismissed as useless to those lacking wisdom. He defended the virtuous person's infallible discernment of what to do in each case.

Chrysippus of Soli (c. 280–c. 205 BCE)

Born in the town of Soli in Cilicia, on the southern coast of Asia Minor, Chrysippus was a long-distance runner of slight build. Chrysippus succeeded his teacher Cleanthes as the third scholarch of the Stoa. The famous saying among scholars of philosophy 'Had there been no Chrysippus, there would have been no Stoa' (DL vii.183) is hardly an exaggeration. He assimilated the doctrines of his predecessors, crafted an arsenal of original arguments to support them, and constructed a sophisticated, unified philosophical system that would establish Stoic orthodoxy. More than 705 books are credited to him. An extensive catalogue of the titles lists dozens on logic. Chrysippus's prodigious writings survive only as fragments preserved by non-Stoic authors. His brilliance in dialectic was said to be dear to the gods (DL vii.180), so it is unsurprising that many considered him arrogant.

Our knowledge of the views of the Stoics of the first three centuries BCE derives entirely from fragments quoted by authors often determined to distort or criticize them. The first two centuries CE, on the other hand, provide texts written by actual Stoic authors or their students living during the early Roman empire.

Seneca the Younger (c. 4 BCE–65 CE)

The philosopher Lucius Annaeus Seneca was born into a wealthy family in Corduba, Spain. His father was an equestrian (*eques*) who wrote and taught rhetoric in Rome. Equestrians were the aristocratic class ranked second only to senators. From childhood Seneca learned literature, grammar, rhetoric and philosophy in Rome. Throughout his life Seneca suffered from asthma and poor health, including possibly tuberculosis. His brilliance in oratory so offended the megalomania of the emperor Caligula that only the assurance that the sickly Seneca would soon die saved his life. In 41 CE he was accused of adultery with the emperor Claudius' niece and exiled to Corsica. A few weeks earlier his only son had died. Recalled to Rome in 49, Seneca became praetor in 50, married the younger, wealthy Pompeia Paulina, and was made tutor to the future Emperor Nero. The powerful friends Seneca made included Sextus Afranius Burrus, the prefect of the Praetorian Guard. In 54 Claudius was murdered. As advisers to Nero from 54 to 62, Seneca and Burrus wielded great clout. By making high interest loans throughout Italy and the provinces, Seneca amassed vast personal wealth and properties. When Burrus died in 62, Seneca retired from public life. In 65 his enemies accused him of complicity in Calpurnius Piso's plot to kill

Nero. Though his guilt is doubtful, Nero ordered Seneca to kill himself. The historian Tacitus reports that Seneca met his end calmly, despite his suicide being painfully protracted.

Seneca's works, written in Latin, are by far both the most diverse in genre and double the size of the extant writings of the other Roman Stoics combined. Seneca wrote nine tragedies, a satire on the apotheosis of the emperor Claudius, and a kind of scientific treatise, *Natural Questions* (in seven books). His nine shorter essays treat assorted ethical topics. Each of three other essays consoles a loved one who had suffered a loss. *On Mercy* (in three books) exemplifies Seneca's attempt to pacify the young Emperor Nero. The seven books of *De Beneficiis* explain how to give and receive favours. And his essay *On Anger* is an argument that there is no room in the well-managed mind for even moderate anger, which he takes to be a sickness of the soul. Seneca also composed 124 letters of varying length, addressed to a friend named Lucilius. These letters conduct an interpersonal philosophical exchange centring on the moral improvement of both the addressee and the author.

Musonius Rufus (c. 20 to 30–c. 80 to 100 CE)

Gaius Musonius Rufus was a Roman equestrian from Volsinii, an Etruscan city of Italy. When Emperor Nero banished his friend Rubellius Plautus around 60 CE, Musonius accompanied him into exile in Asia Minor. After Rubellius died in 62 Musonius returned to Rome, where he taught and practised Stoicism. On discovery of the Pisonian conspiracy in 65, Nero exiled Musonius to the desolate island of Gyaros in the Aegean Sea. He returned to Rome under the reign of Galba in 68 and tried to advocate peace to the Flavian army approaching Rome. In 70 Musonius secured the conviction of the philosopher Publius Egnatius Celer, who had betrayed Rubellius' friend Barea Soranus. Musonius was exiled a second time, by Vespasian, but returned to Rome in the reign of Titus. Highly respected and a renowned teacher, Musonius had a considerable following, including Epictetus. Because of his direct influence on Epictetus and because his work is not as widely available or discussed as Epictetus's work, we will devote considerably more time to Musonius's views than to the Stoic forebears.

Either Musonius wrote nothing himself, or what he did write is lost, because none of his own writings survive. His philosophical teachings survive as thirty-two apophthegms (pithy sayings) and twenty-one longer discourses, all apparently preserved by others and all in Greek, except for Aulus Gellius's testimonia in Latin. For this reason, it is likely that he lectured in Greek.

Musonius favoured a direct and concise style of instruction. He taught that teachers of philosophy should not present many arguments but rather should offer a few, clear, practical arguments oriented to their audience and couched in terms known to be persuasive to that audience.

Musonius believed that (Stoic) philosophy was the most useful thing of all because it rids us of fear. Stoic philosophy persuades us that neither life, nor wealth, nor pleasure is a good, and that neither death, nor poverty, nor pain is an evil. Consequently, the latter are not to be feared. Virtue is the only good because it alone keeps us from making errors in living. Moreover, Musonius held it is only the philosopher who seems to make a study of virtue. The person who claims to be studying philosophy must practice it more diligently than the person studying medicine or some other craft, because philosophy is more important, and more difficult to understand, than any other pursuit. This is because, unlike other crafts, people who study philosophy have been corrupted in their souls with vices and thoughtless habits by learning things contrary to what they will learn in philosophy. Philosophy is a kind of cultural re-programming focused on virtue. But the philosopher does not study virtue just as theoretical knowledge. Rather, Musonius insists that practice is more important than theory, as practice more effectively leads us to action than theory. He held that though everyone is naturally disposed to live without error and can be virtuous, someone who has not actually learned the skill of virtuous living cannot be expected to live without error any more than someone who is not a trained doctor, musician, scholar, helmsman or athlete could be expected to practice those skills unerringly. Musonius's insistence on philosophy as a way of life that must be put into practice and exercised daily like an athlete's muscles informs Epictetus's *Ench.* chapters 29 and 51.

In one lecture Musonius recounts the advice he offered to a visiting Syrian king. A king must protect and help his subjects, so a king must know what is good or bad, helpful or harmful, useful or useless for people. But to diagnose these things is precisely the philosopher's job. Since a king must also know what justice is and make just decisions, a king must study philosophy. A king must have self-control, frugality, modesty, courage, wisdom and magnanimity. A king must be able to prevail in speech over others and endure pain. A king must be free of error. Philosophy, Musonius argued, is the only art that provides all these virtues and abilities. To show his gratitude the king offered him anything he wanted, to which Musonius asked only that the king adhere to the principles he set forth.

Musonius held that since a human being is made of body and soul, we should train both, but the soul demands more attention. This dual training (*askêsis*) requires becoming accustomed to cold, heat, thirst, hunger, scarcity of food, a hard bed, abstaining from pleasures and enduring pains. This training strengthens the body, inures it to suffering and makes it fit to do every task. He believed that the soul is similarly strengthened by developing courage through enduring hardships, and by making it self-controlled through abstaining from pleasures, including culinary pleasures. Thus, Musonius criticized cooks and chefs but defended farming as a suitable occupation for a philosopher and no obstacle to learning or teaching essential lessons. Musonius's call to toughen up the body is echoed in Epictetus's advice in *Ench.* chapters 10, 33.7, 34, 39, 41 and 47.

Musonius taught that exile, poverty, physical injury and death are not evils and that a philosopher must scorn all such things. Epictetus repeats this lesson about death in *Ench.* chapters 3, 7, 11, 14, 21 and 26. Musonius declared that a philosopher denies that being beaten, jeered at or spat upon are either injuries or shameful, so would never litigate against anyone for any such acts. This resonates with Epictetus's advice about handling insults and abuse in *Ench.* chapters 10, 20, 28, 30 and 42. Musonius argued that since we acquire all good things by pain, the person who refuses to endure pain all but condemns himself to being unworthy of anything good.

What and how we eat are very much ethically charged, according to Musonius. He believed that mastering one's appetites for food and drink is the basis for self-control, a vital virtue. He argued that the purpose of food is to nourish and strengthen the body and to sustain life, not to provide pleasure. Digesting our food gives us no pleasure, he reasoned, and the time spent digesting food far exceeds the time spent consuming it. It is digestion which nourishes the body, not consumption. Therefore, he concluded, the food we eat serves its purpose when we're digesting it, not when we're tasting it. Musonius believed that the proper diet was the least expensive, so it includes only the most readily available lacto-vegetarian foods like raw fruits that are in season, certain raw vegetables, milk, cheese and honeycombs. He judged cooked grains and some cooked vegetables to be suitable for humans, but meat to be too crude for humans and more suitable for wild animals. Those who eat lots of meat Musonius considered slow-witted.

We are worse than nonhuman animals when it comes to food, he thought. Why? Because we obsessively embellish our food's presentation. We fuss about what we eat and how it is prepared merely to amuse our palates. Too much rich food harms the body. So Musonius concludes that gastronomic pleasure is without question the most difficult pleasure to combat. He roundly rejected indulging in gourmet cuisine and delicacies as a hazardous habit. (*Ench.* 33.2 cautions us not to chatter about which bars and restaurants to wine and dine at, so Epictetus was moved by these thoughts.) Musonius judged gluttony and craving gourmet food to be shamefully intemperate. He was convinced that those who eat the least expensive food can work harder; are the least fatigued by working; become sick less often; tolerate cold, heat and lack of sleep better; and are stronger than those who eat expensive food. He concluded that responsible people opt for foods that are easy to get over those that are difficult to obtain, meals that involve no trouble to prepare over those that require lots of preparation, and edibles that are available over those that aren't. These preferences promote self-control and goodness. (Cf. *Ench.* 15 on patiently waiting to take a modest serving of food as and when it is offered to you.)

Similarly austere scruples about clothes were promoted by Musonius. The purpose of our clothes and footwear is strictly protection from the elements. So, he reasoned, clothes and shoes should be modest and inexpensive, not attract the attention of the foolish. One should dress to strengthen and toughen the body, not to bundle up in many layers so as never to feel cold or hot. Pampering the body makes it soft and overly sensitive. Musonius advised dressing to feel a little cold in the winter. He called for going shoeless when possible and avoiding shade in the summer.

The purpose of houses is similarly to protect us from the elements, so Musonius thought our dwelling should protect us and our food the way a cave would. Money should be spent both publicly and privately on people, not on elaborate buildings or fancy décor. Beds or tables of ivory, silver or gold, hard-to-get textiles, cups of gold, silver or marble are all totally unnecessary, shameful extravagances. Items that are expensive to acquire, hard to use, troublesome to clean, difficult to guard or impractical are inferior to inexpensive, useful and practical items made of cast iron, plain ceramic, wood and the like. Ignorant people covet expensive furnishings they wrongly believe are precious. Musonius said he would rather be sick than live in luxury, because illness harms only the body, whereas living in luxury harms both the body and the soul. Luxury makes the body weak and soft and the soul undisciplined and cowardly. Musonius judged that luxury fosters unvarnished injustice and greed, so it must be eradicated (and Epictetus echoes this at *Ench.* 33.7).

The ancient Roman philosophers followed their Greek predecessors in regarding the beard as the badge of the philosopher ever since Socrates. Musonius said that a man should cut the hair on his scalp the way he prunes vines, by removing only what is useless and bothersome. But the beard must not be shaved, he insisted, because (1) nature provides it to protect a man's face, and (2) the beard is the emblem of manhood, the human equivalent of the cock's comb and the lion's mane. Hair should never be trimmed to beautify oneself or to please women or boys. Hair is no more trouble for men than feathers are for birds, Musonius said. Consequently, shaving or fastidiously trimming one's beard were acts of emasculation. Epictetus shares these same scruples about beards and cutting hair (see *Disc.* i.16.9–14; ii.23.21; iii.1; iv.8.12–15).

Musonius presented many reasons to think that it is just as appropriate for women to study philosophy, and thereby to consider how to live honourably, as it is for men. A woman who studies philosophy would be just, a blameless partner in life, a good and like-minded co-worker, a careful guardian of husband and children, and completely free from the love of gain and greed. She would regard it worse to do wrong than to be wronged, and worse to take more than one's share than to suffer loss. No one, Musonius insisted, would be more just than she. Moreover, a philosophical woman would love her children more than her own life. She would not hesitate to fight to protect her children any more than a hen that battles predators much bigger than she is to protect her chicks. The philosophical woman would have the same virtues and hold the same beliefs as the Stoic man: she would have noble thoughts, would not judge death to be an evil, nor life to be a good, would not shrink from pain, nor would pursue lack of pain above all else. Musonius thought it likely that this kind of woman would be self-motivated and persevering, would breast-feed her children, serve her husband with her own hands and do without hesitation tasks which some regard as only suitable for slaves. Thus, he judged that a woman like this would be a great advantage for her husband, a source of honour for her kinfolk and a good example for other women.

When it comes to certain tasks, on the other hand, Musonius was less egalitarian. He believed that males are physically stronger than females, and so the most suitable tasks ought to be assigned to each sex accordingly. Generally, men should do heavier work, like gymnastics and outdoor chores, while women should do lighter tasks, like spinning yarn and indoor chores. Sometimes, however, certain circumstances like a person's health condition would warrant men doing some of the lighter tasks and women taking on some of the heavier chores. Thus, Musonius concluded that no chores have been exclusively reserved for either sex. Both boys and girls must receive the same education about what is good and what is bad, what is helpful and what is harmful. Shame towards everything base must be instilled in both sexes from infancy on.

Musonius's philosophy of education dictated that both males and females must be accustomed to endure toil, and neither to fear death nor to become dejected in the face of any misfortune.

Musonius condemned all recreational sex acts. He insisted that only those sex acts aimed at procreation within marriage are right. He decried adultery as unlawful and illegitimate. He judged homosexual relationships to be contrary to nature. He argued that anyone overcome by shameful pleasure is sordid in his lack of self-control. So, Musonius faulted the man, whether married or single, who has sex with his own female slave as much as the woman, whether married or single, who has sex with her male slave.[3]

Musonius advocated companionship and mutual care of husband and wife in marriage since its chief end is to live together and have children. Spouses should consider all things as common possessions and nothing as private, not even the body itself. But since procreation can result from sexual relations outside of marriage, he reasoned that childbirth cannot be the sole motive to marry. He admired as beautiful a marriage in which each spouse competes to surpass the other in giving complete care. But when a spouse considers only his or her own interests and neglects the other's needs and concerns, it ruins their marriage. Such a couple either splits up or they suffer a misery worse than solitude. Neither wealth, nor beauty, nor noble birth promotes partnership or harmony, according to Musonius, nor do they facilitate procreation. He judged most fit for marriage bodies that are healthy, normal in form and able to function on their own, and souls that are naturally disposed to self-control, justice and virtue.

Wild animals, Musonius believed, spare nothing they can devour. They have no companions, never work together and have no share in anything just. He supposed that human nature is very much like that of bees, who cannot live alone and die when isolated. Bees work together. The wicked are unjust and savage and have no concern for neighbours in trouble. Good people are just, kind and show love for their fellows and concern for their neighbours. Marriage is the way for a person to create a family to provide the well-being of the city. Therefore, Musonius judged that anyone who opposes marriage destroys family, city and the entire human race. He reasoned that this is because humans would cease to exist if there were no procreation, and there would be no just and lawful procreation without marriage.

Musonius loved kids. He taught that the bigger a family is, the better. He thought having lots of kids benefitted cities while having few or none harmed them. He denied that poverty is a legitimate excuse to have smaller families. Musonius decried the affluent who refused to raise children who were born later so that their older children would inherit more wealth. Musonius argued that it is far better to have many siblings than to have many possessions. Possessions invite plots from greedy neighbours, so possessions need protecting. Siblings, he deduced, are one's greatest protectors.

Should you always obey your parents? Musonius taught that refusing to do what you ought not to do deserves praise, not blame. The disobedient person disobeys orders that are right, honourable and beneficial, and so acts shamefully. But to refuse to obey a shameful, blameworthy command of a parent is blameless. The obedient person obeys only his parent's good, appropriate advice.

Musonius taught that the best thing to have on hand during old age is living in accord with nature. Human nature, he thought, is better understood by contrasting with the natures of other animals. Horses, dogs and cows are all inferior to human beings, in his view. We do not think a horse reaches its potential by simply eating, drinking and mating without restraint while doing none of the things suited to a horse. Nor do we think a dog achieves its potential if it merely indulges in many pleasures while doing none of the things for which dogs are thought to be excellent. Nor would any other animal reach its potential by being glutted with pleasures but failing to function in a manner appropriate to its species. Hence, no animal comes into existence for pleasure. The nature of each animal determines the virtue characteristic of it. Nothing lives in accord with nature except what demonstrates its virtue through the actions which it performs in accord with its own nature. Therefore, Musonius concluded, the nature of human beings is to live for virtue; we did not come into existence for the sake of pleasure. Those who live for virtue deserve praise; can justifiably respect themselves; and can be courageous, cheerful and joyful. This lesson about nature, pleasure and excellence learned from Musonius Epictetus teaches throughout the *Discourses*.

The human being, Musonius taught, is the only creature on earth that is in the image of the divine. Since we have the same virtues as the gods, he reasoned, we cannot imagine better virtues than intelligence, justice, courage and self-control. Therefore, a god, since he has these virtues, is stronger than pleasure, greed, desire, envy and jealousy. A god is magnanimous and both a benefactor to, and a lover of, humans. Consequently, Musonius reasoned, since a human is a copy of a god, a human must be considered to be like a god when he acts in accord with nature. The life of a good person is the best life, and death is its end. Musonius denied that wealth defends against old age because wealth lets people enjoy food, drink, sex and other pleasures, but never brings contentment nor banishes grief.[4] Thus, money cannot buy happiness. But the good person, Musonius concluded, lives without regret and according to nature by living honourably, and so happily, till the end, fearless of death. This lesson of the good, godly life and the calm, fearless death is a frequent refrain in Epictetus's *Discourses* and *Handbook*.

Musonius seems to have acted as an advisor to his friends the Stoic martyrs Rubellius Plautus, Barea Soranus and the Roman senator Thrasea Paetus. Musonius's pupils and followers include the Roman senator Gaius Minicius Fundanus, Timocrates of Heracleia, Athenodotus, the golden-tongued orator Dio of Prusa (*c.* 40–died after 110 CE) and Euphrates of Tyre (*c.* 35–*c.* 118 CE). Euphrates was a highly respected Stoic famed for great eloquence (see *Ench.* 29.4) whom Epictetus commended for an exemplary life of putting philosophical theory into practice.

Musonius was widely admired by philosophers and theologians alike. The Stoic Hierocles (second century CE) and the Christian apologist Clement of Alexandria (*c.* 150–*c.* 215 CE) were strongly influenced by him. Roman emperor Julian the Apostate (331–363 CE) said that Musonius became famous because he endured his sufferings with courage and sustained with firmness the cruelty of tyrants. Dio of Prusa judged that Musonius enjoyed a reputation greater than any one man had attained for generations and that he was the man who, since the time of the ancients, had lived most nearly in conformity with reason. The Greek sophist Philostratus (*c.* 170–*c.* 245 CE) declared him unsurpassed in philosophic ability.

Epictetus (c. 55–c. 130 CE)

Born into slavery as the son of a slave woman in Hierapolis, Phrygia in central Asia Minor, his name means 'Acquired'. Epictetus was lame, possibly because his master broke his leg. The story was that his master wished to punish him by twisting his leg, and Epictetus warned him that another twist would break it. When the master turned it one more time, the leg broke. Epictetus then said that he had told the master that it would break. Epictetus later travelled to Rome. There, as a slave of Epaphroditus, a freedman and administrative secretary of Nero, Epictetus was permitted to study with the great Stoic teacher Musonius Rufus. After he was freed, Epictetus taught in Rome until he and other philosophers were expelled from the city by the emperor Domitian (in 89 or 92 CE). Epictetus moved to northwest Greece where he established a school in the town of Nicopolis. There he taught Stoicism to Roman adolescents preparing for public service and other visitors. Epictetus never married. Late in life he adopted a child in need of parental care and raised it with the help of a nanny.

Other than a few fragments in later authors, his teachings survive in four books of *Discourses* and the short compendium called the *Handbook*, both recorded by his student Arrian of Nicomedia. His experience of harsh treatment as a slave surely fuelled his philosophical reflections on rough treatment of the body, coercion and the mind's power to liberate itself from fear through self-mastery. Though his biggest hero was Socrates, Epictetus, like his teacher Musonius, also greatly admired Diogenes the Cynic for his heroic life of freedom, autonomy, austerity, frugality and self-sufficiency. Epictetus was one of the greatest teachers of Stoicism in antiquity. Part 2 will provide a fuller overview of Epictetus's life and the history of the *Encheiridion*'s influence.

Marcus Aurelius (121–180 CE)

Marcus was said to be austere, solemn, modest, reserved and yet friendly. The Emperor Hadrian nicknamed him *Verissimus*, meaning 'Truest'. Marcus studied philology, literature, history, rhetoric, law and philosophy. His devotion to Stoicism was won when he was loaned a copy of Epictetus's *Discourses*. Marcus gave no title to his sole surviving philosophical work, traditionally called the *Meditations*. In the first of its twelve books he thanks all his relatives, teachers and mentors for the traits of character each gifted him. The remaining eleven books rehearse a set of philosophical themes, echoing Heraclitus and Epictetus, designed to console, spur mindfulness and exhort noble conduct. Marcus reminds himself of how to think about time, change, the self, virtues, vices, the cosmic law and the roles every person, animal and insect plays in the world. The mortality of all living things, including loved ones, is a common refrain. Marcus affirms that Stoicism can dispel all fears, including the fear that one's child will die (clearly influenced by Epictetus's *Ench.* chapters 3, 7, 11, 14 and 26), with the reminder that all generations of human beings are leaves the wind predictably blows to the ground (*Med.* x.34). He investigates the significance of a thing by viewing it as a whole composed of lesser parts, or as a constituent part of a greater whole. Affirming Heraclitus's cosmology, Marcus sees the world as a dynamic, eternal whole that endlessly recycles every fleeting part it spawns and inevitably reclaims. From this cosmic perspective, material wealth, fame and bodily pleasures are transient, trivial and empty. What is precious, in stark contrast, are the wisdom and dignity of a righteous mind that acts with kindness and love, never hesitating to do its duties day in and day out. One must live harmoniously both locally with the fellow citizens of our community and globally with all rational beings sharing the same universe as home.

1.3 The System

The Stoics created the most systematic of all ancient philosophies. They divided philosophical discourse into three parts: logic, physics and ethics. This tripartition was illustrated by several analogies. If philosophy is like a living being, then logic corresponds to the bones and sinews, ethics to the flesh and blood, and physics to the soul. If philosophy is compared to an egg, then logic is the shell, ethics is the white and physics the yolk. If philosophy is like an orchard, then logic is the surrounding fence, physics the land and trees, and ethics the fruit. The organicism of these analogies is significant. The Stoic system functions like a self-sustaining animal in which none of its organs or cells are unambiguously prior to any others and all are inseparably interconnected.

How do the Stoics conceive of this organic interconnection between logic, physics and ethics? Stoics think that humans derive their rationality from the same *logos* embodied in the well-ordered universe (*cosmos*). Cosmic events and human events (including actions) are thus consequences of the same *logos*. Human *logos* enables us to ascertain facts about Nature (*phusis*) and to reason from those facts to discover further truths through rules of inference (logic). This process yields knowledge (science). Full recognition of the implications of our relationship to cosmic Nature inspires us to live up to the excellence of our human potential by living in agreement with cosmic Nature. Thus, Stoics believe that events in Nature (physics) are so causally related to one another that a set of propositions can be supported by argument (logic) which will enable a person to plan a life entirely in harmony with Nature or God (ethics).

1.3.1 Logic

'Logic' derives from the Greek word *logos*, which has the root meaning 'rational utterance'. The Stoics divided the logical part of philosophical discourse into rhetoric and dialectic. Rhetoric is the science of speaking well on matters presented in plain narrative. Rhetoric involves the invention, expression, arrangement and delivery of arguments. Mastery of rhetoric was very important for Stoics, whether they were lecturing to pupils, making public addresses or debating opponents.

The Stoics divided dialectic into subjects of discourse and language. The subject of language, both spoken and written, comprises the parts of speech, errors in syntax and in single words, poetical diction, verbal ambiguities, euphony and music. The elements of discourse are 'impressions' (*phantasiai*), 'sayables' (*lekta*) and their constituent subjects and predicates, genera and species, moods, arguments, syllogisms and fallacies. An impression is a sensory stimulus, a thought or a memory that appears to a perceiving subject, making a (temporary) imprint on her soul. The Stoics were physicalists who believed that only physical bodies exist. Since one's soul causally interacts with one's body, they reasoned that body and soul are both physical and so both destructible. An impression either originates from a real object or does not. For the Stoics, assent to impressions is the locus of human freedom. The Stoics believed that causal determinism is compatible with human freedom. Though all events are fated, some acts of adults are free. A free act is one an agent assents to that is also fated, thereby making it co-fated. If an agent withholds assent from a fated event, then she is like a dog tied to a moving wagon that drags her along behind it despite her futile effort to resist. Note how fate (a key aspect of physics) connects to ethics (wisdom) here.

The Stoics likened the mind at birth to a blank sheet of paper. Impressions stamp themselves on the mind, and the goal is to assent only to those that proceed from real objects or facts. Such reliable mental stamps are called 'apprehending' (*kataleptikê*) impressions. They always result from real objects or facts and cannot ever come from what is false. So, apprehending impressions are always distinguishable from false impressions. But though the mind of a newborn baby is like a blank page, even that page has inherent characteristics the Stoics called 'common conceptions' (*koinai ennoiai*). These common conceptions are unconscious generalizations everyone with the same human physiology shares. From these common conceptions and myriad impressions, we do our best to acquire the skill of assenting only to sayables that reflect apprehending impressions. When we succeed, we gather true beliefs. When we fail, we get false beliefs. Ordinary people (non-sages) are fallible, so they are lucky if they have more true beliefs than false beliefs. But since only the reason (*logos*) of the sage has been perfected into wisdom, only the sage has genuine systematic knowledge. Note how logic (epistemology) connects to ethics (the ideal of the sage) here.

In sum, the 'logical' part of Stoic doctrine treated all parts of language, including the causal powers of words, propositions, concepts, meaning, truth, argument and thought. Their system of propositional logic was more flexible and more sophisticated than Aristotle's categorical logic. Stoic dialectic comprised not only epistemology and etymology but also literary criticism and the allegorical interpretation of myths.

1.3.2 Physics

The physical part of philosophical doctrine describes the totality of physical reality, causation, the elements of the universe and its governing principles. The Stoics assert that the universe contains two indestructible, incorporeal principles: the active and the passive. The passive principle is substance without quality, that is, matter. The active principle is the seminal reason that shapes matter. The Stoics call the active principle God, Zeus, Providence, Fate, Destiny, Nature and Seminal Reason (*spermatikos logos*). This principle transformed matter into four elements: air (cold), water (wet), earth (dry) and fire/aether (hot). These elements combine to form objects. God can be conceived of as either the designer, or the orderliness, of the cosmos.

The Stoics argued that (a) animate is better than inanimate; (b) nothing is better than the cosmos; and (c) hence, the cosmos is animate. They held that the cosmos is a finite, spherical, living, intelligent, rational being endowed with soul, with fire as its ruling principle. The cosmos plus the infinite, incorporeal void they called the All, that is, the totality of things. Time, the measure of the motion of the cosmos, is also incorporeal on their view. They reasoned that the cosmos must end because it began. They argued that (a) that which has perishable parts is a perishable whole; (b) the parts of the cosmos transform into each other and so perish; and (c) ergo, the whole cosmos must perish. The Stoics describe the world and the heavens as God's substance. They ascribe to God only three anthropomorphic qualities: being alive, rational and beneficent. God is immortal, perfectly happy, devoid of evil (see *Ench.* 27), and provides for everything in the cosmos.

Nature (*phusis*) refers to either that which holds the cosmos together or that which causes earthly things to grow. Nature is a force moving by itself, producing and preserving in being its offspring in accord with seminal principles, within set periods, and effecting results homogeneous with their sources. The Stoics describe nature as artistic fire (*pur technikon*) equivalent to fiery or creative breath (*pneuma*). Because *pneuma* pervades every corner of the cosmos, all its parts are intimately interlinked. This ubiquitous causal interlinkage is so seamless that all events are fated. Fate (*heimarmenê*) is thus an endless chain of causation whereby things exist. Consequently, most Stoics judged credible the forecasting of future events from present clues known as divination (*mantikê*). The intensity of the tension (*tonos*) of the *pneuma* determines an object's qualities. Stones have the lowest level of cohesion (*hexis*). Next up is the vegetative nature (*phusis*) in plants. Above that the tension of *pneuma* in animate soul (*psuchê*) is found in animals with sensation and impulse. The highest level is rational soul (*logikê psuchê*) in adult humans. (Note how physics and logic interconnect here.)

Body (*sōma*) is finite substance (matter) that can act or be acted upon. Soul (*psuchê*) is an animating body consisting of fine breath (*pneuma*) that enables locomotion and perception. The human soul has eight parts: vision, hearing, smell, taste, touch, the powers of reproduction and speech, and reason or the 'ruling part' (*hêgemonikon*). The *hêgemonikon* processes impressions, triggers impulses (*hormai*) and issues assents. Chrysippus located it in the heart, others in the brain.

The Stoics held that individual souls of animals are parts of the soul of the cosmos and are perishable, whereas the soul of the cosmos is indestructible. According to the doctrine of the world-conflagration (*ekpurōsis*), creative fire consumes the entire cosmos, whereupon elemental fire and the other elements re-coalesce into a new cosmos. Epictetus and Marcus Aurelius believed that when death separates souls from bodies, nature recycles both.

1.3.3 Ethics

Stoic ethics is the most influential legacy of this ancient tradition. It is first and foremost a theory of the good life. Ancient Greek philosophers agreed that the goal (*telos*) of all human effort is *eudaimonia*, an enduring state of happiness, well-being or flourishing. The Stoics, Epicureans and Sceptics of the Hellenistic period often identified *eudaimonia* with a smooth flow of life or imperturbability (*ataraxia*). The Stoics believed that the purpose of philosophy is to attain this goal by mastering the art of living. Stoicism educates us in this art. But mastery of Stoicism is not a matter of merely learning theories that serve only to expand our minds. Rather, the art of living demands consistent application of Stoic insights to daily life. This can only be achieved through rigorous training that replaces bad habits with good ones. A lifetime of such arduous effort, when successful, transforms the self.

According to their doctrine of *oikeiōsis* ('appropriation' or 'affinity'), what nature makes dearest to every animal is itself and its own constitution. This natural self-love leads to self-preservation. Self-preservation motivates an animal to seek what benefits it and avoid what harms it (see *Ench.* 31.3 for this example). For plants and non-rational animals, self-preservation is achieved simply by meeting biological needs for water, food and bodily protection. But when a pre-rational child matures into a rational adult human being, self-preservation becomes more complex. Reason discerns both what is good for a person and how to get it, and what is bad for her and how to avoid it. So, the rationality of an adult becomes dearest to her, rather than, say, her infected toe or a morsel of food. Rationality *is* most of all the self of a rational being. Thus, her rational mind is what a fully realized human being seeks to preserve above all.

The Stoics define the goal (*telos*) as 'living in agreement with nature'. This formula is rich in meaning. As a living organism, it agrees with one's biological nature to use one's perceptual abilities to sustain the good functioning of one's body. But human beings also naturally associate with others of their kind. So, it agrees with one's social nature to build relationships with others, make friends, create a family and participate in society. This social dimension of human nature expresses the social theory of *oikeiōsis*. Recognizing the affinity we have with our neighbours, fellow citizens and all human beings, we establish justice as the basis of societal concord.

For a rational being, living in agreement with nature requires living in agreement with reason. Reason perfected is virtue. Virtue, the Stoics famously insisted, is the only good because it alone is necessary and sufficient for *eudaimonia*. Conversely, the only thing that is bad and that guarantees misery is the corruption of reason, called vice. All else is counted neither good nor bad but in the class of 'indifferents'. Indifferents are neither beneficial nor harmful because they can be used either well, in which case they bring happiness, or badly, in which case they cause misery. Within the class of indifferents orthodox Stoics distinguished the 'preferred' from the 'dispreferred'. Preferred indifferents usually promote one's physical well-being, so selecting them is *usually* commended by reason. Preferred indifferents include life, health, pleasure, beauty, strength, wealth and good reputation. The dispreferred indifferents are their opposites. It is usually appropriate to avoid the dispreferred indifferents, but in rare circumstances it can be virtuous to select them. The virtue or vice of the agent is determined not by the possession of an indifferent, but by how it is used.

Epictetus likens indifferents to game equipment (*Disc.* ii. 5. 1–5 and 15–17). A ball or set of dice lacks intrinsic value. Thus, the equipment itself is indifferent. But how well a player *uses* the ball or dice displays her excellence in the game. Thus, the *use* of the equipment, how one *plays* the game, matters a lot. Therefore, virtuous and skilful use of indifferents makes a life happy, whereas vicious, inept use ruins it. Fair play, sportsmanship and being a good teammate matter a lot. Cheating, boasting and pettiness are always disgraceful. Playing as well as we can is always up to us and so must always be our sole concern. The conduct of the other players, the referee's calls and the game's final score are ultimately not up to us, so they are never anything to worry about.

The Stoics divided virtue into four main types: wisdom, justice, courage and temperance. Wisdom was subdivided into good sense, good calculation, quick-wittedness, discretion and resourcefulness. Justice was subdivided into piety, honesty, equity and fair dealing. Varieties of courage they identified as endurance, confidence, high-mindedness, cheerfulness and industriousness. Types of temperance they named good discipline, seemliness, modesty and self-control. Similarly, they divided vice into foolishness, injustice, cowardice, intemperance and the rest. The Stoics argued that the virtues are inter-entailing and constitute a unity: to have one is to have them all. The Stoics argued that, just as one person is a poet, an orator and a general, so too the virtues are unified but apply to different spheres of practice.

The Stoics understood wisdom to be knowledge of what is good, bad and neither. Wisdom is the self-transforming characteristic of the wise person or sage. The sage recognizes that living in agreement with nature entails living in agreement with the whole cosmos. The sage is a mortal microcosm whose way of living and acting harmonizes with the providential macrocosm of the universe. Harmony with Providence means that the sage astutely embraces all events and affirms their meaning, purpose and holistic necessity. Over the course of a lifetime of rigorous training, the sage has finally freed herself of all violent, disturbing passions (*pathê*). These passions (*pathê*) are pathological in that they are mental illnesses. These illnesses include fear, anger, hatred, resentment, envy, jealousy, greed, grief, pity and lust. These passions either are, or result from, false judgements about which things are good, bad or indifferent. In contrast, the sage experiences three 'good feelings' (*eupatheiai*): joy (*khara*), caution (*eulabeia*) and rational wish (*boulêsis*). Joy is expressed as delight, mirth or cheerfulness. Caution is displayed in reverence or modesty. Rational wish is shown in benevolence, friendliness, respect or affection.

The Stoics believed that the sage is as rare as the phoenix. Some suggested that Socrates, Zeno of Citium or Cato the Younger may have been sages. All non-sages the Stoics regarded as fools. Within the class of fools, one progressing towards virtue is a 'progressor' (*prokoptōn*). A progressor can perform a 'prescribed action' (*kathêkon*) or duty, like exercising to be fit, taking care of your parent or returning an item borrowed. But only the sage performs actions wisely, comprehending how they harmonize with the cosmic whole. The sage, thus, performs 'perfect actions' (*katorthōmata*). The early Stoics asserted that the sage was infallible. The idea of the flawless, infallible sage served as a prescriptive ideal Stoic progressors aspired to approximate. The sage was said to participate in politics if nothing hinders it.

The final stage of *oikeiōsis* occurs when a person realizes affinity with not only her family members, friends, and neighbours, but also her fellow-citizens. Thus, the final stage of social *oikeiōsis* explained the origin of justice. Stoics saw themselves both as citizens of their country and as citizens belonging to the cosmic realm of rational beings of all species everywhere. Because of this very influential doctrine of cosmopolitanism, the Stoics dismissed exile as affecting merely the location of their bodies. Their idea of twin citizenship conferred upon Stoics dual roles with corresponding dual sets of duties. As citizens of specific locales they had civic duties to the inhabitants of the immediate communities they occupied or visited. As citizens of the cosmos they had duties of solidarity with all persons, human and divine, throughout the universe, regardless of race, ethnicity, class, creed, age, ancestry, gender, gender expression or disability. The Stoics were stalwart friends, no matter the risk of violence, imprisonment, banishment or death.

1.4 Six Core Themes

Six themes constitute the core of Stoicism. First, Stoics stress the necessity of self-control. Second, Stoics insist on seeing things as they are. Third, living according to nature is vital to Stoics. Fourth, your virtue depends on doing your duties, which are defined by your roles. Fifth, having virtue depends on knowing. Sixth, Stoicism is an aspirationalist ethics. Let's explicate each theme in turn.

1.4.1 Self-control

If you cannot control yourself, the Stoics reason, you have no hope of controlling anything in your life. If you do not master your desires, your desires will master you. If you do not improve yourself, it is unreasonable to think that others will improve you. Freedom, paradoxically, comes from mastering yourself. Failure to work on yourself, on making progress towards your self-mastery, will inevitably result in inertia, failure to progress towards freedom. Complacency will serve only to strengthen the chains of dependency on unreliable, fickle frills. Complacency hardens the bonds enslaving you to dangerous desires, namely, desires for and about things not up to you.

One danger of desiring what is not up to you is that you thereby enslave yourself to whoever or whatever controls those things. You make yourself a puppet on the strings manipulated by a puppet-master who can all too easily coerce you. A worse danger of desiring what is not up to you is that it fools you into desiring the wrong things. Physical beauty, physical gratification, wealth, fame and power over others are not things that can win self-respect. Without self-respect, happiness is impossible. Stoics are convinced that you only respect people who are decent, kind, fair, generous, helpful, strong, loyal and loving. Thus, you can gain self-respect only by becoming good, grateful, just, temperate and wise. Virtues are up to you to cultivate. Virtues are up to you to *want*. By contrast, wanting things that are not virtues inevitably leads to compromising your moral integrity for shiny baubles and fleeting frills and thrills. Fancy flowers wilt. Luxurious rugs fade. Priceless vases shatter. Mansions crumble. Fortunes are stolen. Applause dies out. Virtues are the true treasures that can last a lifetime.

1.4.2 See things as they are

Stoics are uncompromising realists. One bit of realism is the crucial division between the things that are up to you and the things that are not up to you. We term this 'the Fundamental Divide' in the commentary to underscore its enormous, continentally enormous, import. For greater precision, we can distinguish (a) things completely up to you, (b) things you have some power to affect but that also depend on causal factors that are not up to you and (c) things not at all up to you. Our minds are up to us and belong to group (a). We are responsible only for what is up to us and we are completely responsible for what is up to us. The minds of others are not up to us, but, in the right circumstances, it is not unreasonable to try to influence others even though we know that ultimately they make up their own minds. Thus, the minds of others belong to group (b). Epictetus knows full well that it is up to him to try to impart wisdom to his students; he can try to teach them. But whether and what they learn is ultimately up to them, not him.

Institutions, corporations, bureaucracies, social classes, economies, financial markets, governmental structures, insurrections and geopolitical conflicts are not up to us. Earthquakes, tsunamis, volcanic eruptions, the weather, erosion, floods, landslides, droughts, wildfires, solar storms, asteroids, meteors and climate are not up to us. Disease, epidemics and famine are not up to us. All such things belong in group (c). Wanting to control things that remain stubbornly not up to us is futile and foolish.

The limitations built into the furniture of the world are also not up to us. Because of entropy, things break down over time. Entropy is not up to us. The limitations of our bodies are not up to us. All living things age. Ageing is not up to us. Disease is ultimately not up to us. All living things suffer injuries or illness. Seneca suffered grievous attacks of asthma. Epictetus was lame. Marcus Aurelius struggled with poor health throughout his life and may have become addicted to a medicine prescribed by his physician. All living things die sooner or later. Mortality is not up to us. Change is constant in the cosmos. Global, cosmic change is not up to us. For Stoics, logic dictates that understanding how things are teaches us to accept how things are. In contrast, wishing that things not up to you were up to you is a recipe for misery. Trying to bend the unalterable features of reality to your desires is crazy. Hoping for the impossible is lunacy. Human beings all too often see only what they want to see and believe what is comforting to believe. Stoicism disabuses us of wishful thinking. They believe that pleasant delusions are toxic. The Stoics challenge us to be realists. The Stoics are also convinced that, seen from their relentlessly realistic and global perspective, the world is a beautiful home we can learn to live in happily.

1.4.3 Live according to nature

Nature equips us with the power of reason and reflection. Nature gives us the ability to examine our beliefs. We can assess whether our beliefs align with the world the way it is or we can instead choose to believe what is comforting, what inflates our self-love, what helps blind us to the way things are. It is up to us whether we commit to believing only what is warranted and most likely to be true or spurn all unpleasant facts. We can either embrace reality or conjure up fantasies. Living in agreement with nature involves embracing our natural cognitive abilities to think, consider, reflect, evaluate, assent or withhold assent, contemplate, deliberate, decide, intend and attempt. We must use these abilities properly and hone them. Living in agreement with nature means to train ourselves how to reason, in every situation, the best we possibly can. It means committing oneself to becoming a mental athlete, an intellectual Olympian. It means dedicating oneself to becoming a lover of wisdom, a philosopher. Taking up this challenge is entirely up to us. Doing what it takes to progress at it is up to us and us alone. Nature gives us all the tools we need to transform our lives for the better, Stoics reassure us. What are we going to do with these natural gifts? Each of us answers this by living our lives as we do.

1.4.4 Know your roles, do your duties

The Stoics believe that we are what we do. Our myriad activities collectively constitute our personal identity. Our activities flow from our roles. We each have many roles. Some roles we are born into and have our whole lives. Others we choose and have for mere minutes or hours. Others we retain for years, whether others assign them to us or we choose them for ourselves.

The moment we are born, we land into our first role: to be a child. We discover that we are either an orphan or a member of a family. The role of an orphan often requires learning how to share with other orphans. The role of a family member requires sharing with one's closest kin, siblings, parents, perhaps cousins and perhaps grandparents. Epictetus emphasizes that our role as children in a family requires that we obey our parents. He insists that our role as a sibling demands that we not fight with our sibling(s).

Another role we are born into is that of being social. The role of social beings necessitates associating with, collaborating with and peacefully abiding with the other members of our community. Like all ancient philosophers, Stoics believe that human beings are social and political animals. Our natural gregariousness rules out eremitism. Bellicose behaviour directly conflicts with human nature's norm of peaceable harmony. Concord is the basis of justice and social well-being. So, our role as citizens of the local community requires us to be lawful, courteous, help our neighbours in need, contribute to the good of the whole, preserve communal bonds and protect our community from threats. Our role as cosmopolitan 'citizens of the cosmos' requires us to affiliate with all rational beings everywhere in the universe, regardless of their ethnicity, nationality, political party, socio-economic class, gender, sexual orientation, religion or species.

The ancient Stoics believed that all human beings and gods in the universe were fellow members of the same cosmic city. For us today, the concept of Stoic cosmopolitanism should arguably include not only all nonhuman animals on this planet, but also all extra-terrestrial life forms who count as 'rational', however that is to be understood. As adults, our most important role requires that we not only *preserve* our rationality but strive throughout our lives to *perfect* it. The perfection of reason is wisdom (or virtue). The role of rationality calls us to reason, reflect, collect evidence, contemplate, consider, judge, evaluate, deliberate and learn. Our role as rational beings also requires us to communicate well with our fellow rational beings. If reason dictates that the right thing to do is to sacrifice ourselves for a family member, a friend, a fellow-traveller, a neighbour, our city or our country, then preserving our rationality necessitates ending our life.

A very incomplete list of roles follows:

- Child, parent, sibling, cousin, spouse, companion, partner, friend.
- Worker, employee, employer, supervisor, manager, colleague, assistant.
- Host, guest, visitor, resident, renter, owner, clerk, neighbour.
- Pedestrian, cyclist, skater, skier, surfer, motorist, crew member, captain, pilot.
- Traveller, guide, porter, driver, passenger, operator.
- Teacher, student, writer, reader, researcher, orator.
- Athlete, professional, amateur, hobbyist, intern, volunteer.
- Competitor, teammate, coach, trainer, referee, umpire, spectator.
- Officer, organizer, commander, soldier, first responder.
- Caretaker, conservator, curator, custodian, guardian, ward.
- Caregiver, patient, doctor, midwife, surrogate, therapist, counsellor.
- Chef, server, diner.
- Buyer, seller, trustee, beneficiary, benefactor, donor.
- Attorney, client, judge, juror, defendant, advocate, mediator.
- Citizen, voter, legislator, councillor, mayor, governor, senator.
- Director, thespian, conductor, musician, performer, audience member.
- Leader, follower, mentor, mentee, advisor, advisee.
- Layperson, philosopher.

This last pair of roles is a second kind of Fundamental Divide for Epictetus. He believes that deciding to undertake the role of a philosopher dramatically transforms one's life in a way that other roles do not. The layperson or private citizen (*idiōtês*) does not aspire to self-perfection, according to Epictetus. Laypersons are comfortable with their character flaws. The vast majority of people live by conventional norms, believing that money, status, popularity, fame, power, physical gratification and physical beauty lead directly to happiness. Thus, most people are laypersons who seek happiness from outside sources rather than from within themselves. For Epictetus, this grievous misunderstanding leads laypersons to be susceptible to lying, cheating, stealing and betrayal of friends when others dangle external temptations (a promotion, a bribe, sex, flattery, etc.) in front of them as carrots. Their failure to grasp the incomparable value of virtue similarly leads laypersons to be susceptible to coercion by means of blackmail, threats to take away or destroy their external possessions, or physical harm. At the end of *Ench.* 29 the Greek word *idiōtês* is translated *schlub*. Schlubs are ethically and intellectually lazy. Philosophers, in contrast, make ethical self-improvement and enquiry their paramount goals in life. The role of the philosopher and the role of the schlub can pair with any of the other roles listed above. But one cannot possibly embrace both the role of a philosopher and the role of a schlub, according to Epictetus. This is strictly an either/or choice.

Successfully performing each role involves completing a range of tasks. Each task requires its own set of skills. Learning skills takes time, ability, effort and resources. Since different people have different abilities, talents and weaknesses, each of us is naturally better suited to some roles than others. Moreover, people like and dislike different activities. A big challenge is being truly thoughtful when choosing roles, exercising care about which roles to take up, when to do so and for how long, and which roles to set aside and when. This requires knowledge both about oneself and the tasks that must be done. Stoics emphasize that we are responsible for fulfilling all of our roles, both those nature and circumstances impose on us and those we freely select. Failing to do a duty dictated by a role is a grave failure.

1.4.5 Virtue depends on knowing

Whether an act is virtuous or not depends on what we know about the situation and what we are supposed to do. For example, if someone does something that seems very brave, but she did not know about the danger, that ignorance undercuts our evaluation of that person's action as properly brave. Or take someone who happens to equitably distribute some goods among those who need it. She has done so justly only if she knew what equitable distribution she was trying to achieve and saw it as a just distribution. If it just happened to be a lottery or she didn't care how things came out but just randomly happened to make this distribution, we wouldn't see her acts as properly just. Furthermore, our knowledge that something is the right thing must be the reason why we do it, too, for our actions to be virtuous. So, if someone were to know that repaying a debt is right, but they are motivated to repay only by threat of force, their repayment, though rightly done and alongside knowledge that one should do it, is nevertheless not virtuous, either. This is because that knowledge of what's right to do must be part of why one does what is right. Knowledge is an essential part of being a good person, and it's not just ethical knowledge that is required for this, but knowledge of the world and how it works. Given our roles as people on whom others depend and who must effectively manage our tasks in the world, we must have a wide knowledge of how things work and what to expect. So, part of our duties to ourselves and others is to have knowledge. Call this broad collection of commitments *ethical intellectualism*. To live right, one must see the world right. In seeing the world right, we see our paths clearly. Not only can we identify our duties and what the norms of justice, bravery and piety demand of us, but we can see what's worth worrying about and what's not.

The intellectualist programme extends to our emotions. Once we see things for what they are, we know better how to handle ourselves and our reactions. On the cognitivist theory, our emotions are determined by how we view the things happening around us. If we judge something as bad, we will then feel bad if it happens to us. If we judge something as good, we will feel good when it is ours. The problem for living well, then, is about controlling our judgements in a way that mitigates all the ways the world can make us feel bad. So, a person might feel jealous resentment when a peer gets a promotion or award and she does not. This is because she judges that a bad thing has befallen her – that she has been overlooked for a good thing. The solution is, first, to prepare for these events so that you are not surprised by them, and second, to see them in the right lights. These intellectual exercises cut negative reactions out. So, you know that the world is full of inappropriately distributed honours – why would you expect that your own case will be any different? And what are honours and promotions, anyway? More often than not, they are accolades from people who aren't knowledgeable or good, but merely powerful and rich. Seeing things clearly, then, can even out our emotions. But it's also useful to see that knowledge also produces positive emotions. Seeing living things bloom, appreciating the interconnectedness of the world, understanding oneself and one's fellows – these can be sources of deep, abiding joy and placidity.

1.4.6 Stoicism as aspirationalism

One way to understand aspirationalism in ethics is to see it in the context of its denial. Immanuel Kant, the great German philosopher and ethicist, proposed that the principle *ought implies can* binds moral theories. That means that any rule or norm of action should be one that people can reasonably be expected to follow. So, ethics is not only practical but practicable. In contrast, aspirationalism demands of us more than we might reasonably be able to do. Its principle is *ought implies aspire to*. The aspirationalist view puts the highest good out of our reach, a perfection we can only strive towards. Aspirationalism posits an ethical North Star as our point of orientation but something we may never reach. (To continue the analogy, the principle of *ought implies can* makes the ultimate goal more like the North Pole, which not only is orienting but reachable.)

Aspirationalism was common in antiquity, and it persisted in Christian religion. To start, Plato's programme of perfecting the harmony in one's soul and putting it in touch with timeless truths was one that could only imperfectly be implemented. Diogenes the Cynic proposed that one should strive to be fully independent of distorting culture, despite the fact that he largely lived in town, begged for scraps from townspeople, spoke Greek and wore clothes. The programme of *imitatio dei* in the Christian tradition, that of trying to make oneself like Christ, is bound to failure, given our sinful natures as non-gods. These aspirationalist programmes put the goal of our lives outside of our capacities, but they do so precisely because we are deeply flawed and limited creatures. What is more, we have so far to go to perfect ourselves. But putting the goal beyond our grasp, the reasoning goes, stretches our reach. We vie with the gods, and in so doing, we improve in ways that we would otherwise not be able to (Aikin 2017). This is partly because we see our failures so starkly and also because we are striving to be the best we can be. Stoics acknowledge that though Stoicism doesn't require much to get started (one only needs a mind capable of distinguishing between what's up to it and what's not), it requires so very much to perfect one's practice.

Seeing Stoicism through this aspirationalist lens is useful in a few ways. One is that Stoicism calls for a radical break with so many of our habits of thought and practice. It is a critique of what passes for 'common sense', which is really, from a Stoic perspective, a culture of confusion. Consequently, Stoic practitioners must be aware of how 'paradoxical' or counter-intuitive their substantive views are. They must be regularly reminding themselves that their principles diverge from how most people think. We will see how this kind of 'paradoxical' thinking works in the next section, but it is important to underline that the Stoics, as aspirationalists, are holding themselves to standards that are not standard measures of good enough to pass for being called excellence by the mob.

Another consequence of the Stoics' aspirationalist perspective is that of a deep modesty. Despite the fact that the Stoics must (as just noted) think of themselves as exceptional in comparison with the *idiōtês* (as we've translated 'schlubs' and 'fools'), they cannot be full of themselves. This is because they are very far from having perfected what they have set out to improve, namely, themselves. Stoic practitioners will pay more attention to how far there is to go to manifesting a complete virtue than how they have outdone non-Stoics. But this will be an ongoing temptation for those who are not yet wise. We will later call this progressor's temptation, and it is an ironic consequence of progress towards virtue for those who are not yet virtuous. The key, though, is that the primary Stoic objective is not to outdo others, but to improve oneself. And given the ultimate standard, Stoics should always be humble with regard to themselves, since it is clear that they will always have further skills to master and principles to learn.

1.5 The Stoic Paradoxes

The Roman writer, orator and statesman Marcus Tullius Cicero (106–43 BCE) was not a Stoic but displays great respect for Stoicism in his philosophical writings. Those writings provide valuable, detailed accounts of the Stoics' teachings. One such work, *Paradoxa Stoicorum*, treats six key counter-intuitive doctrines the Stoics staunchly defended. These 'paradoxes' are:

(1) Virtue is the only good.
(2) Virtue suffices for happiness.
(3) All good actions are equal, as are all bad actions.
(4) All non-sages are insane; only the sage is sane.
(5) All non-sages are slaves; only the sage is free.
(6) All non-sages are poor; only the sage is rich.

A seventh paradox, not included in Cicero's list but worth comment, is:

(7) All non-sages are ugly; only the sage is beautiful.

Reviewing the paradoxes is useful since they mark Stoicism as a revisionary programme in ethics. The Stoics freely admitted that their core views are *paradoxai*, meaning counter-intuitive commitments. They break with what passes for common sense. Thinking them through as brazen divergences from what often looks like wisdom among those who have not thought carefully about things highlights Stoicism's unique contribution as an ethical system. They also highlight what a challenge Stoicism is for those who practise it.

1.5.1 Virtue is the only good

Fools are not stupid, in the sense that they cannot understand things. Fools simply lack education. That education results from close study of Stoicism, which guides all of one's desires, aversions, attitudes, actions and reactions. Yet from the crib, fools are spoon-fed anti-Stoic propaganda. This propaganda includes the widely popular belief that all sorts of things are good, desirable and worth pursuing at any cost. All kinds of wealth, from material possessions, real estate, automobiles, private jets, yachts, corporate holdings and financial portfolios, are believed to be good and desirable by fools. Pleasure, whether from food, alcohol, drugs, massages or sex, fools believe is good and desirable. Physical health, use of all five senses, use of one's arms and legs, strength, agility, fitness and stamina fools believe are good and desirable. Myopia, blindness, hearing loss, loss of smell or taste, fibromyalgia, damage to one's limbs, paraplegia, quadriplegia and all manner of physical disabilities fools believe are bad under all circumstances. Popularity, fame and political power fools believe are always good and desirable. Disenfranchisement, incarceration, deportation, exile, poverty and being a refugee are believed by fools to be miserable conditions that make happiness impossible (Stephens 2020). Ageing, grey hair, wrinkles, arthritis, aches, pains and death fools believe are awful and to be resisted at all costs. Youth and life fools believe are goods to admire and prolong as much as possible.

Stoics reject all this popular propaganda. Stoics argue that for something to be a good, it must always be beneficial in all circumstances. The rationale for that criterion is that if something requires circumstances to be good, then it is the circumstance that is good. The thing identified is not the contributing factor. What the Stoics see as the contributing factor in all the cases of benefit is that the person is made better. So, the only thing that always benefits a person is virtue, the perfection of reason. Wisdom, courage, temperance, justice, generosity, kindness and all other admirable traits are the same unitary psychological state (virtue) applied in different situations. Virtue(s) cannot ever be harmful, yet all the supposed goods fools cherish can be undesirable in certain circumstances. For that reason, only virtue is good and only its opposite vice (wickedness, sleaziness) is bad. An admirable death is therefore always better than stooping to something despicable to save your life. A gruelling struggle to achieve a noble end is always better than indolent capitulation to injustice. Hard work to reach a respectable goal is always better than lazing about in comfort. Fools chase what they falsely believe will bring them happiness, but all those empty baubles inevitably fail to make fools into better persons. And thereby, they are not truly benefitted or made better. Only virtue(s) make you a better person. It is possible to have all the things fools treasure and still be a nasty, selfish, petty, mean, greedy, dishonest, cowardly, abusive, hateful, disgusting jerk. Conversely, infamy, exile, poverty, disenfranchisement, disease, pain and death are not bad because all of them are consistent with being a good, decent, kind, loving, admirable person.

Death and the rest are not bad. Living badly is bad. Bad living results from bad actions and disturbing emotions. Bad actions result from bad choices. Bad choices and disturbing emotions result from poor judgements and false beliefs. False beliefs invite disturbing emotions, like fear, anger, jealousy, resentment, lust, vanity, pettiness, spite and hatred. These disturbing emotions afflict fools. In contrast, a wise person (a sage) has, over the course of a lifetime of arduous self-improvement, daily training and disciplined practice, achieved the complete integrity of character that is comprehensive wisdom, that is, virtue. All material goods, fame, political power and physical gratifications can fade away, be stolen, ruined or destroyed. A virtuous character, in contrast, is impervious to assault, erosion or loss caused by human beings, storms, floods, fires, mayhem, war, economic upheaval or time.

In *Paradoxa Stoicorum* Cicero presents four arguments for the thesis that virtue is the only good. First, he denies the claim that money, real estate, political power, resources and pleasure are goods for this reason: appetite for these *indifferents*, as the Stoics term them, has a thirst that is never fully satisfied. The more wealth you get, the more you want. The more power you wield over others, the more you want. The more pleasure you get, the more you want, and so forth. Non-Stoics (fools or schlubs) are thus tortured not only by the ceaseless craving to increase their possessions, properties, power and pleasures but also by the fear of losing those things (*Parad.* 6). Indifferents are ultimately beyond one's control, so you can never hold onto them indefinitely, so non-Stoics inevitably fear losing them. In contrast, a person's virtue cannot be stripped away by any hurricane, tornado, tidal wave, wildfire, earthquake, building collapse, bullet or blade. One's virtue is thus securely in one's own control, and so immune to chance. Therefore, virtue is the only true, reliable, unconditional good.

One way to interpret Cicero's first argument is to see it as also a case against the deficient or popular non-Stoic use of terms such as 'benefit' and 'harm' and the like. So, on a non-Stoic view, 'goods' are things like pleasures and status, and 'harms' are things like pain and financial ruin. So, on this reasoning, we now can see how something can be a 'harm' to a virtuous person – perhaps a Stoically virtuous person's health can fail, so they suffer from chronic pain. That would, as non-Stoically interpreted, be a harm. And we now can see how things that a vicious person might delight in (perhaps duping a neighbour into a bad trade of goods or exercising capricious power over an underling) would be something that brings a virtuous person no pleasure (and so, no 'benefit'). Analogously, a vicious person may find pleasure in being given an award she knows she does not deserve, but it would offend the sensibilities of a virtuous person. To repeat, given the background principle that good things will be uniform in their benefits (and bad things in their harms), we can see how this argument shows that non-Stoic values fail the test of reflection.

Cicero's second argument can be reconstructed like this:

1. If X is a good for one person, then X cannot be an evil or harm for another.
2. Indifferents can harm, and so are evils for, virtuous persons.
3. Therefore, indifferents are not goods for vicious persons (or anyone else).

Unfortunately, Cicero gives no example of an indifferent harming a virtuous person in this context. Perhaps we could imagine a virtuous person becoming corrupted by great wealth or political power. Perhaps we could imagine a virtuous person being distracted by pleasure so much that she fails to do her duty. The second premise in this argument is problematic if by 'virtuous persons' Cicero means sages. According to Stoic orthodoxy, the sage retains her virtue even when drunk or ill, so it is not at all clear how any indifferent could harm a sage in any way whatsoever. A sage could accidentally be crushed to death by a heavy object, but such an accident would not harm the sage's virtue in the slightest. So, this argument presented by Cicero is troublesome on Stoic grounds.

The third argument Cicero gives can be reconstructed like this:

1. Anyone amidst an abundance of goods must herself be good.
2. Bad people possess indifferents and remain bad.
3. Therefore, indifferents cannot be good.

This argument reflects the belief of Stoics, Platonists and other ancient philosophers that good things must *benefit* those who have them. A mean, nasty person can be stinking rich. A selfish jerk can be popular and politically powerful. A gluttonous coward can wallow in all types of pleasures. Since the indifferents these individuals enjoy fail to transform them into good, admirable human beings, those indifferents cannot be goods. Cicero calls the indifferents non-Stoics desire and stockpile 'toys of fortune' (*lubridia fortunae*) (*Parad.* 9).

Cicero's fourth argument targets pleasure. He concedes that pleasure may be a good for cattle (or, more generally, mere animals without capacity for reflection or reason), but intellect is the most excellent and most divine thing that exists. So, pleasure cannot be a good for human beings endowed with intellect. He reasons as follows:

1. Any good thing makes its owner better and more praiseworthy.
2. Feeling pleasure does not make a person better.

3. Feeling pleasures does not make a person praiseworthy.
4. Therefore, pleasure is not a good thing.

Indeed, pleasure actually *hinders* the mind from clear thinking, good judgement and the pursuit truth. Cicero says that the greater the pleasure, the more it dislodges the mind from its abode and station. Pleasures entice the lowly beast in us by drawing us away from our most exalted, godlike aspect – our intellects. Pleasures, consequently, dehumanize us, and so cannot be good. Wisdom, justice, courage, temperance, etc., are aspects of a single perfected mind. Thus, what makes us the most mindful is our true good, and that one thing is virtue.

1.5.2 Virtue suffices for happiness

Call this the *sufficiency thesis,* that virtue is sufficient for happiness. Aristotle believed that though virtue is the most important part of happiness, it is not sufficient for it. One must have at least a modest amount of money, a good reputation, a good family, friends, decent looks, and so on. Otherwise, Aristotle reasoned, our happiness is marred (*Nicomachean Ethics* i.1099b). In contrast, Stoics insist that virtue, that is, moral integrity or nobility of character, all by itself suffices for happiness. One way into this thought is to ask the question: if a person is already happy, what does adding an external contribute? Stoics wonder how wealth could add to the happiness of an admirable person. How could good reputation boost the happiness of a moral paragon? How could physical health increase the happiness of a person with sound character, the sanest, mentally healthiest person there is? The Stoics argue that since happiness is a mental state, no bodily condition, no material possession and nothing non-mental can heighten happiness. Consequently, if these externals do not contribute to happiness, they are not components of happiness (otherwise, by adding them, we would have made these people happier). It is again worth highlighting just what a deviation from what passes for common sense this is, since so many of the ways that people reason about how to have a good life is overturned. This is what it is for the Stoics to be committed to *paradoxa.*

The first response to the Stoics here runs: don't severe illness, grinding destitution and brutalizing slavery make happiness impossible? If not, do Stoics have a completely bizarre conception of happiness that is totally alien to non-Stoics? The Stoics announce that they have a revisionary programme in ethics, but is this revision so great that their product is hardly recognizable as an ethical theory?

One way to understand the Stoics' challenging notion of happiness is to conceive of it as a kind of satisfaction that comes only from self-respect. Stoics do not respect wealth, fame, physical beauty, bodily strength or health, or anything that depends, even partly, on luck. Stoics respect only virtue, whether in the form of a person, intention or action. So, to earn self-respect, a Stoic knows she must become a good, virtuous person. A good person whose home burns down loses none of her integrity. A good person who loses her job loses no nobility of character. A good person who is maimed in a car accident loses no worthiness of admiration from others. How can a person who is out of work, homeless, penniless, maimed and in agony be said to be happy? Doesn't this strain the meaning of *happiness* beyond the breaking point? The Stoics notoriously maintained that the sage was happy even when being tortured on the rack. If real happiness is possible only when coupled with self-respect, then we can understand why Stoics believed that the self-respecting sage retains every bit of her self-respect, and so the satisfaction that comes with that self-respect, even under excruciating circumstances. So, it may be plausible to think of this contentment that comes exclusively from self-respect, that is, absolutely certain awareness of one's own virtue, as the kind of happiness Stoics believe all human beings want – or what they should want. Stoics challenge the non-Stoic construal of *happiness* as painless, titillating, gratification and revelry in material consumption and vanity. Villains know they are miserable, according to Stoics, because they see their own vice. Moreover, no cheater, no coward, no glutton, no sleazeball, no thug and no villain can gain self-respect. They may try to mask it with money, achievements or pleasure, but they cannot escape themselves. To know one's own abiding faults is to know unhappiness. Self-deception has no power to win a wicked person self-respect. Thus, the tiniest bit of self-deception is incompatible with what Stoics regard as real, secure, virtue-guaranteeing happiness. Since there is no substitute for virtue, and only virtuous people can truly respect themselves, virtue alone is necessary and sufficient for happiness.

To support the Stoic paradox that the possession of virtue is sufficient for happiness, Cicero cites the example of Marcus Regulus. The story goes that Regulus was taken prisoner during the First Punic War with Carthage. The Carthaginians sent him back to Rome as a prisoner of war to arrange peace with the agreement that only if he succeeded in a peace resolution could he be freed. But Regulus knew that the Carthaginians were weakened by the war, so Rome would win in the next engagement. Accordingly, Regulus instead advised his countrymen to reject the offer of peace to Carthage. Having vowed to do so, he returned to Carthage, since he did not arrange peace. The Carthaginians rewarded him for honouring his vow by torturing him to death. Cicero argues that the tortures of the Carthaginians had no effect on Regulus's magnanimity, dignity, loyalty, constancy or any of his other virtues. His sound mind was impregnable to assaults on his body (*Parad.* 16). No one can fail to be supremely happy, Cicero argues, who relies solely on himself and who counts as his own only possessions within himself. In stark contrast, people whose hope, purpose and thought hang entirely on fortune and external factors beyond their control can possess nothing certain, nothing they can count on keeping for a single day. Externals will always be fickle and temporary. Only internals – character traits – are firm fixtures free from fate and foe. Lack of contentment with what you have and fear of losing it guarantee misery. The virtuous, in contrast, fear no one and nothing. The good are content with whatever comes to them. Their happiness is safe from circumstance. Cicero contends that whereas no wicked, foolish or idle person can have well-being, so the good, courageous and wise cannot be wretched. So, what makes a life wretched? Non-Stoics think that poverty, disrepute, illness and pain make a life wretched. But Stoics argue that fear, anger, resentment, regret, envy, lust, greed and grief cause unhappiness both to yourself and to everyone around you. How can one banish fear, anger, resentment, regret, envy, lust and greed from one's life? By sacrificing everything for the sake of decency, honesty, kindness, loyalty, justice and honour. By never compromising your moral integrity. A good person never fears becoming a bad person, and so lives without anxiety, frustration, disappointment, regret or sadness. No one who worries, resents or envies has peace of mind. No one who lacks peace of mind is happy. Consequently, nothing adds to the happiness of the person who already enjoys the complete peace of mind that virtue, and virtue alone, brings.

What about friends? Don't friends make a good person happier? Again, Aristotle's common-sense view of virtue and happiness runs that it does. In fact, Aristotle holds that supreme happiness depends on having excellent friends (*Nicomachean Ethics* ix.1170b.20). Here we meet perhaps the sharpest edge of this paradox. Stoics believe that precisely what draws us to befriend (or love) others is their virtue. So, the goodness in others that attracts us to them is the same goodness in ourselves that suffices for our happiness. When a Stoic's friend moves away, disappears or dies, it subtracts nothing from the Stoic's own virtue. What made the friend valuable (namely, her virtue) is not reduced when the friend is gone, since our Stoic is, by hypothesis, virtuous, too. But that also suggests that a friendless sage is just as happy as a sage with many friends. Nothing is added to the happiness of the sage when she makes a new friend. The solution the Stoics offered to this quandary was to argue that all sages everywhere (and perhaps even the gods!) are friends of one another, even if they never meet. This 'solution' is not very persuasive. This may be because Epictetus and other Stoics emphasize self-sufficiency (*autarkeia*) as a key trait of the sage which heightens the tension with the importance of social, familial and communal relationships in a good life. We will discuss the problem of friendship, mutual dependence and self-sufficiency in section 5.3 as what we call 'the Ruin Problem'.

1.5.3 All good actions are equal, as are all bad actions

Above we explained that failing to perform a duty dictated by a role one has is a grave failure, according to Stoics. All such failures are equally grave, according to this paradox. This means that what non-Stoics regard as a very minor error, like arriving late for an appointment, is just as bad as clipping a pedestrian when driving a car. The syllogism that leads to this conclusion goes like this:

1. To err is to fail to do as one ought.
2. One does as one ought or not; there are no degrees.
3. Therefore, no errors (or correct actions) come in degrees.

Stoics reject the tactic of making excuses for one's mistakes. When the person late for an appointment describes her tardiness as a trivial error, she is trying to excuse herself and duck responsibility. But showing up late for an appointment disrespects the person(s) who attended on time. Tardiness is thus a kind of insult. All insults are offensive in the core form of not respecting someone's dignity or interests. It's in that core disrespect that the badness of insults lies, and this commitment isn't gradable. One either respects another's dignity or not. Therefore, being tardy is just as offensive as calling someone a nasty name or slapping them in the face. One may be more overt or cause more pain, but they are all at bottom the same kind of disrespect. So, to try to excuse yourself for acting carelessly by saying that you did not do something far worse is in fact to admit you screwed up but to deny that you should be held to account. When Ann wrongs Barb, and Ann makes an excuse, Ann is trying to forgive herself. But only Barb can forgive Ann for Ann's wrongdoing. (If Barb is a magnanimous Stoic, then she would most likely dismiss Ann's wrongdoing as having done her no real harm rather than forgive Ann for having truly hurt her.)

The point is that Stoics insist that people are responsible for all their actions. Every circumstance gives us the opportunity to act well or badly. We act well when we fulfil all our roles and perform all of the duties that follow from those roles. We act badly when we shirk any duty dictated by any of our roles. Every act of omission and commission counts. An analogy may be useful to see this. If a single note of music is off, it ruins the whole melody. If a single line uttered by a stage actor is botched, it spoils the entire drama. When playing tennis, the ball you hit lands in or out. Whether the ball lands out by half an inch or it sails over the fence forty yards from the court, you lose the exact same point – no more, no less. Perfection does not admit of degrees, and virtue is the perfection of reason, the Stoics contend. The wise are not even a little bit foolish, not even on rare occasions. Dichotomous thinkers that they are, Stoics apply a strict pass/ fail grading standard for evaluating right and wrong action, virtuous and vicious character, and good and bad living.

Cicero explains that transgressions are not to be measured by their results but by the character defects (vices) of the transgressor. Whether the ship is loaded with a thousand bars of gold bullion or a hundred bales of hay, the incompetence of the helmsman who capsizes the ship is equal. The recklessness of the motorist responsible is equal whether she causes a chain reaction collision mangling twenty people in smashed cars or just the honking of horns and curses by those twenty endangered motorists. All acts of reckless driving are equally culpable even though not all acts of reckless driving cause accidents, injuries or fatalities. Fortunate consequences never exonerate negligent conduct.

Cicero argues that to fail to repay a loan is wrong regardless of the size of the loan. Hence, defaulting on a fifty-dollar loan is just as wrong as defaulting on a fifty-thousand-dollar loan. Why? Because all virtues are equal, as are all vices. He reasons:

1.   Good actions are actions done correctly.
2.   Nothing is more correct than that which is correct.
3.   Hence, all good actions are equally good.
4.   Good actions proceed from the virtues.
5.   Virtues are valuable in terms of the good actions they ground.
6.   Hence, all virtues are equally good.
7.   Bad actions are actions done incorrectly.
8.   Actions are either correct or incorrect – there are not grades.
9.   Bad actions proceed from the vices.
10. Vices are bad in terms of the bad actions they ground.
11. Hence, all bad actions are equally bad.
12. Hence, all vices are equally bad.

A single misdeed can be regarded as committing multiple transgressions, according to Cicero. What matters to Stoics is the motive behind the action, not its consequences. Consequentialism is a normative theory rejected by Stoics. Stoics favour a form of virtue ethics deontology according to which our duties (from the Greek word *deon*, meaning 'fit to be done') derive from our roles. Ascertaining our duties enables us to act properly, practise good habits, build good character and thereby live well. On this view, motives (intentions) reveal one's character to be moral or immoral, admirable or shameful, laudable or deplorable. Consequences are entangled in the causal nexus of factors not up to us.

Consider four examples: a cook, a motorist, a pilot and a barber. The careless cook who leaves on a stove's burner is as much to blame whether a pot is charred or an entire house burns down.[5] The motorist who gets drunk and recklessly drives home from a bar Tuesday night without leaving in his wake any injuries, fatalities or damaged property is lucky, but every bit as culpable as he is on Friday evening when he gets drunk, drives recklessly and causes an accident which both cripples himself and smashes a safely driven minivan, killing its passengers: a mother, father, their three daughters and their dog. The incompetent pilot whose airplane crashes with its two passengers surviving commits no smaller a wrong than the airplane pilot whose incompetence crashes a plane carrying two-hundred passengers and crew members, all of whom die. Both transgressions are equally inexcusable. The distracted barber who, with his straight razor, puts a tiny nick in the earlobe of his customer is as much to blame as if he were to distractedly slash a deep, blood-spurting gash in that customer's throat. What makes the misdeeds equal is the irresponsibility of failing to pay attention. The negligence is the same because what makes the actions wrong is the same, regardless of whether the harms that ensue are minor, moderate, severe or catastrophic.[6]

Bear in mind that the pedagogical lesson contained in this Stoic paradox that all good actions are equal, as are all bad actions pertains to the Stoic's self-improvement, not penology. Thus, this tenet is neither a principle for judges assigning punishments to convicted criminals, nor a guide for parents disciplining their naughty children, nor a policy for employers penalizing employees guilty of misconduct. To maintain that all bad actions are equally bad does not entail that all liars, shoplifters, bank robbers, embezzlers, frauds, tax cheats, schoolyard bullies, muggers, thugs, drug dealers, pimps, prostitutes, adulterers, graffiti artists, vandals, arsonists, child abusers, poisoners, rapists, traitors and assassins ought to receive the same punishment for their misdeeds. Punishments serve more roles than that – they can give recompense to those harmed or serve as deterrence for others. So there will be variance with punishment given other factors. Nor does this paradox imply that all good deeds deserve the same recognition or rewards. These will vary given other objectives with rewards, too. Rather, the point of this paradox is that no one committed to making progress as a Stoic is permitted excuses. All mistakes count. All mistakes are equally bad, equally shameful. All mistakes are proof positive that the Stoic in training must be more vigilant, work harder and more urgently dedicate herself to self-improvement.

1.5.4 Only the sage is sane

One is either sane or insane. This dichotomy strictly separates the sage, who has wisdom, from everyone else. All who lack wisdom suffer from false beliefs. False beliefs trigger anger, fear, worry, jealousy, regret, schadenfreude and all other disturbing emotions that destroy peace of mind. To lack peace of mind is to be confused, troubled and disturbed. Thus, false beliefs guarantee mental disorder. The wisdom of a sage banishes all mental upset from her life. The foolishness of non-sages makes their minds messes. So, according to this strict bifurcation, everyone is either a sane sage or an insane fool.

The Greek term for being insane in this paradox is *mainetai*. This term is used in Homer's *Iliad* to describe Achilles' rage at being denied what he considered his proper rewards. His overpowering fury at being overstepped by a man he regarded as his lesser (Agamemnon) not only caused him to lose control of himself, but it precipitated his withdrawing from the Trojan War, leaving his countrymen to fight without him. He was supposed to be the best of the Greeks, but he flies off the handle over being slighted. This failure nearly ruins the army's chance of success. Not only is Achilles' reaction unseemly and self-indulgent, it is also destructive and drives him to turn his back on those depending on him. The lesson, then, is that those who live without Stoic wisdom are all essentially in Achilles' position. They are buffeted by overpowering emotions triggered by even the smallest of disappointments. This is what it is to be overcome by *mania*. The only cure for it is Stoic wisdom.

What is so special about the wisdom of the sage? Why can't wisdom be acquired in degrees, incrementally? Why think the possession of wisdom is an all-or-nothing affair? Doesn't this commit the informal fallacy known as false dilemma? To defend this paradox, Stoics famously appeal to the analogy of a ship passenger cast overboard and plunged into the sea. It does not matter whether the man overboard is a foot underwater or a hundred fathoms deep – he drowns all the same. This underscores the urgency of our situation. The only way to keep from drowning in our (equally serious) failures and (equally bad) character flaws is to swim as hard as we can, every minute, straight up towards the surface. We must do all we possibly can to get our heads above water before we die. Only above water can we breathe the life-giving air of virtue. Missing by an inch offers no more comfort than missing by a mile.

The sage is described by Cicero as having a mind walled and fortified with grandeur of purpose, endurance of fortune and contempt of human affairs (*Parad.* 27). By the last he means having no worries about what others do. The sage focuses only on her own judgements, decisions and reactions, not on anything that is not up to her. The sage acts with confidence, whereas fools hesitate and then are lost. The mind of a sage cannot be banished to a foreign land, and when her body is exiled, it does not disturb her mind in the least. In contrast, fools complain that exile is an unendurable punishment. In essence, the fool's mind is so attached to the contingencies of his body that his mind is dragged along into whatever exiles or imprisons his body. The fool falsely believes that if his body is harmed, then his mind is too. The sage knows better. The sage knows that nothing belongs to her but her mind. That is the sober truth. The fool, on the other hand, is deluded enough to believe that he owns his clothing, money, dog, bicycle, house, reputation and any other external possessions he has bought and keeps nearby. All such things can be stripped from him by fate. Stoics believe it is deluded to think that things that are not up to you are up to you. This madness makes for misery.

1.5.5 Only the sage is free

Before presenting Cicero's reasoning for this paradox, it is worth pausing to note that he does not mean that non-Stoics are literally enslaved people. Rather, the usage is metaphorical, in the sense that one might say that another is a *slave to his passions*. But there is an important depth to this metaphorical usage in that control over one's life, even in the metaphorical senses, is not located in one's own judgement, but in the variances of others and circumstances. If one values, for example, the acclaim of others, there is a distinct sense that one really is a servant of others' desires, and one caters to their whims and tastes, instead of pursuing things as one sees fit. Or think of someone who cannot control himself around some temptation (be it food, drink or sexual pleasure). There is a real sense that this person's autonomy has been compromised by these attachments and habits. Here we see the force of Cicero's metaphorical use of 'slave', since it seems you can damage your own self-control by the kinds of things you value and how you think about the things you want. Let us call those who have made this error and then have consequently damaged their capacity for autonomy *psychological slaves.*

Cicero's reasoning in this paradox can best be presented reasoning first from the second part (that only the sage is free), and then to the first (that fools are psychological slaves). Here is the argument:

1. Freedom is the power to live as you want.
2. The Stoic sage desires to live in accord with what Fate has determined and to do her duty. Those are within her power.
3. Therefore, the Stoic sage is free.
4. The person who is not wise wants to live with money, status and other external goods that are not under her control.
5. Therefore, the person who is not wise is not free.
6. The psychological slave is a person whose life is not under her own control.
7. Therefore, the person who is not wise is a psychological slave.

The Stoic sage is someone who lives as she wants. She follows the things that are right, she enjoys doing her duty, she has mapped out a carefully considered way of life, and she obeys the law not out of fear but out of respect, having judged that doing so is most conducive to health. The sage lives such that her every utterance, act and thought is voluntary and uncoerced. All her undertakings and courses of conduct originate from herself and likewise culminate in herself, and nothing has more influence with her than her own will and judgement. The Stoic sage, then, does nothing against her will, nor with regret, nor by compulsion. Consequently, only the Stoic sage is free, and those who do not live in this fashion are slaves. Cicero's insight behind this part of the Stoic paradox is that (psychological) slavery means the obedience of a broken and abject spirit that has no volition of its own. All people who put the goods of their lives in things not up to themselves suffer from broken, abject spirits that have no volition of their own. Therefore, all non-sages are (psychological) slaves. All fear, then, is psychological slavery, as Cicero declares (*Parad.* 40). The least fret or trepidation is enough to constrain the mind. So, only the sage, who is fully fearless, is free.

Freedom is paramount to Epictetus. Since he was born into slavery and earned his freedom only as an adult, it is no surprise that his many years in bondage left a deep impression on his philosophy. What Epictetus learned about slavery is that it is not a simple matter of being legally owned as the chattel of someone else. Rather, he insists that anyone who has power over your desires has chains on you. Anyone who can impose on you what you dislike, or take away something you cherish, becomes your master. Anyone who can manipulate you, blackmail you or otherwise coerce you into doing a deed that disgusts you enslaves you. Your body need not be the legal property of another to be held hostage psychologically. Anyone who desires or is averse to what is not up to her but up to someone else can be made into a puppet yanked around by the strings held by that person, your puppet master. Moreover, impersonal circumstances, the weather and cosmic forces exert enormous influence over our ability to get what we want and avoid what we dislike. Consequently, those who are foolish enough to want or fear things subject to impersonal forces beyond anyone's control are slaves to circumstance (or fate).

How can we liberate ourselves from slavery to fate or people? Our salvation, Epictetus teaches, is found in education. This education is provided by Stoic philosophy. Only by learning the truths Stoics teach, applying those lessons in every situation, and training ourselves to live as Stoics every single day can we be free. The fundamental lesson in Epictetus's curriculum is to understand what is good, what is bad and what is neither. The fundamental challenge is then to adapt your desires accordingly. Once you grasp that only virtue is good, nothing bad can happen to you. Once you grasp that only vice is bad, you never covet what is not up to you. Once you grasp that the externals or 'indifferents' that non-Stoics crave are neither good nor bad, you rise above the vicissitudes of circumstance. You inoculate yourself from any possible coercive poisoning by others. Stoic wisdom most fundamentally consists in always knowing what is good, what is bad and what is indifferent. Fools can never be free so long as they believe that happiness comes from things not up to them, from other people, from luck or fate. Fools doom themselves to servitude by accepting non-Stoic propaganda. Fools are slaves to their own false beliefs because those beliefs underpin misguided desires and fears. Misguided desires and fears guarantee complaint, frustration, regret and misery. Lack of wisdom about what to desire, what to avoid and what to take calmly in stride shackles fools to unhappiness. Therefore, only those wise in Stoic understanding are free. All who are blind to Stoic truths grope in vain in the dark for the key to unlock them from their wretched prisons.

Everyone who fusses or worries is a non-sage. Everyone who feels disappointment, dread, regret or resentment is a non-sage. Everyone who gets anxious, nervous, impatient or bored is a non-sage. Everyone who gets annoyed, irked or vexed is a non-sage. Everyone who feels envy, jealousy or lechery is a non-sage. Everyone who is smug, vain, lazy or apathetic is a non-sage. Everyone who is boastful, arrogant, rude or domineering is a non-sage. Everyone who is pessimistic, hostile, aggressive, judgemental, malicious, selfish or petty is a non-sage. Everyone who makes excuses, procrastinates or exercises too little is a non-sage. Sages never eat or drink to excess. Sages never eat or drink at the wrong time or place. Sages never chew tobacco, smoke, toke, vape, use drugs to recreate, gamble or harbour any other unhealthy habits. Everyone who wastes time or money is a non-sage. Everyone who whines, gossips, flatters, lies or cheats is a non-sage. Everyone who blames others or pities herself is a non-sage.

Sages are magnanimous, benevolent, careful, calm, cheerful, confident, courageous, courteous, cooperative, diligent, friendly, helpful, kind, fair, faithful, frugal, generous, loyal, modest, patient, polite, punctual, reliable, resourceful, self-sufficient, temperate, thoughtful, trustworthy and loving. Sages lack all the mental maladies that grip and grind down non-sages. Since sages are free *from* all disturbance and distress, they are free.

Sages probably don't exist and perhaps never have, Stoics admit, but they serve perfectly well nonetheless as shining role models for Stoics in training to emulate. The concept of the sage functions for Stoics as a prescriptive ideal, not a fanciful, fruitless figment. This, again, is a point about Stoic aspirationalism we addressed earlier. In this case, total freedom belongs only to sages, but greater partial freedom is still better than less partial freedom or none. Consequently, it is not only possible to approach the target of sagehood, but also as worthwhile as any aspiration can be. Stoics are convinced that it is wise to strive, as vigorously and urgently as one can, for sagehood.

Epictetus praises several figures as heroic role models in the *Discourses*, but Socrates is his favourite.[7] For guidance in coping with difficult situations he suggests his students ask themselves 'What would Socrates do?' This is essentially to ask oneself 'What would a Stoic sage do?' The objection could be raised that there was only one Socrates. So, by idealizing Plato's depiction of Socrates into a superhero, Epictetus erects a superhuman target that is useless as a guide for real, thoroughly imperfect human beings. We reply that the tacit message contained in this Stoic paradox is that all mentally competent adult human beings are free to work on improving themselves. Progress in self-improvement is patently possible even if perfection may not be. What is unquestionably foolish is not even to aim for wisdom by making the excuse that you don't know whether you or anyone can or will ever reach it. Real failure consists in giving up trying. In contrast, it brings no shame to do your level best, over decades of effort, inching forward, becoming a better person incrementally and then dying short of the goal of achieving fully transformative wisdom. What is shameful is sitting out the race – that eliminates even the slightest chance of winning it. The race to freedom is a lifelong marathon. Anyone who gets anywhere near the finish line deserves admiration. So, it doesn't matter whether a single racer breaks the tape at the end. Here winning consists in *progressing*. Only those who energetically compete for wisdom can shed any of the wrong-headed beliefs holding their happiness hostage. Fools convince themselves that they are powerless to loosen and discard even a few of the chains of their misery. Paradoxically, fools freely choose to remain slaves because they cling to their familiar, dreadfully debilitating, foolish beliefs.

1.5.6 Only the sage is rich

Stoics carefully analyse common concepts non-philosophers rarely question. We saw this earlier with Cicero's metaphorical use of 'slavery' to extend to what we've called here *psychological slavery*. In this case, the core idea is that of *wealth*. Many unthinkingly take for granted how to construe the notion of being rich or wealthy. This popular understanding is rejected as confused by Stoics in this paradox. They observe that wealth must be measured by the causal power it bears in one's life. Specifically, wealth consists in having the resources one needs. That is, to be rich is to possess abundant means of living happily. What are those means? Recall that in his *Hymn to Zeus* the early Stoic Cleanthes explains that those who obey God's universal law can obtain the true wealth of a noble life. Nobility of character is the means of living well. In other words, virtue is the resource (necessary and) sufficient for happy living.[8]

As seen earlier in our comments on his life and work, the Stoic conception of wealth struck Musonius Rufus as eminently intuitive and unparadoxical. He saw no reason to relax his exceptionless prohibition against all luxurious food, drink, clothing, shoes, shelter and hairdressing in old age. Musonius argued that wealth allows for the enjoyment of food, drink, sex and other pleasures. But wealth never brings contentment nor banishes grief. Therefore, wealth provides no balm in old age or at any age, for that matter. So, money cannot buy a wicked person happiness. Yet a good, honourable person lives without regret, fear or grief. Nobility funds her happiness. Real riches, then, are the virtues of the wise.

The term 'wealthy' (*plousios*) in the ordinary sense of owning property occurs in *Ench.* 44. There Epictetus analyses the concept of wealth thus: if I am wealthier than you, then my property is better than yours. But he points out that it is illogical to infer from this conditional that I am better than you. Why? Because, he declares, *you* are not property. Epictetus conceives of you not as your property or your body or your reputation. He insists that you are your volition (*prohairesis*), your power of assent (*sunkatathesis*), your integrity of character. On this view, a pauper can have great ethical and intellectual assets. A pauper can have a princely spirit.

Cicero concludes his explanation of the paradox that only the sage is rich with a clever argument.

1. The wealthy person has what she needs to live so that she is easily contented, and desires nothing more than what she has.
2. Hence, if a person lacks nothing, troubles about no other resources, and is fully satisfied with her possessions, then she is wealthy.
3. The sage's mind is rich with virtues.
4. The sage thinks her virtues are all she needs, and she lacks nothing.
5. Hence, the sage is fully satisfied with her precious possessions.
6. Therefore, the sage is wealthy.

In contrast the minds of non-sages are poor in virtues. And wealth does not satisfy them in the way they expect it would. Non-sages thus suffer from empty coffers inside them no matter how many vast estates, herds of cattle, stables of horses, limousines, yachts, private jets, cellars full of rare vintages, galleries full of artworks, halls decked with finery and chests brimming with jewels surround them. This is because they not only now need goods of equal or greater opulence to satisfy them in the future, but they will always want more. By contrast, if you require little, then you *make* yourself rich. But if you desire something beyond your reach, then you are needy. If you believe you need something you lack, then poverty grips you. Since virtue is the most precious, most valuable thing, the person with that is the richest. Only the sage is virtuous, so only the sage is wealthy. Cicero writes that not to be covetous is equivalent to having cash, not to love buying things is itself a kind of income (*Parad.* 51). The goodness and self-sufficiency of the sage are her fortune. Always wanting more than they have keeps non-sages forever in arrears. Fools suffer the debt of their foolish cravings for things not up to them. Virtue is the only asset that cannot be lost to earthquake, fire, storm, flood, shipwreck or market crash. The sage cannot be robbed or cheated out of her abundant virtue. But greed drives non-sages to invest all their pennies in chance, gambling on externals (indifferents). Whatever jackpots they occasionally luck into necessarily remain insecure. Consequently, non-sages always feel needy, want more and remain poor.

1.5.7 Only the sage is beautiful

The final paradox we shall discuss is not included in Cicero's *Paradoxa Stoicorum*. Other sources attest that the ancient Stoics declared that beauty belongs only to the sage (Čelkytė 2020). They argue:

1. The soul is incomparably better than the body.
2. Hence, the beauty of the soul is incomparably greater than the beauty of the body.
3. The beauty of the soul consists in virtue.
4. Only the sage is virtuous.
5. Therefore, only the sage is beautiful; all non-sages (because they lack virtue and are, instead, vicious) are ugly.

Socrates was depicted as bald, with a snub nose, bulging eyes, thick lips and a broad forehead. Judged by ancient Greek aesthetic standards, he was quite ugly. Yet the exceedingly handsome, charismatic, talented and ambitious young Alcibiades was so enamoured with Socrates' soul that he tried mightily yet in vain to seduce the ugly, old, barefoot gadfly of Athens![9] This story no doubt inspired this seventh Stoic paradox. To a Stoic's eye vices look like warts, corns, blisters, boils, eczema, psoriasis, melanoma and carcinoma peppering the souls of fools. Stoics see that pretty faces and shapely bodies fail to veil disgusting souls. A repulsive soul makes a repulsive human being.

One way to think about this paradox is to consider the ways knowing that someone is a terrible person makes her less attractive or that knowing a person is excellent makes her more attractive. That is a familiar enough phenomenon, but for the Stoics, this propensity is magnified. The primary way it happens is that one's attention as a Stoic is directed only to the things that matter, and in this case, only virtue matters. One might be impressed with the paint job or cool gadgets on a car, but it is how the car functions that makes it impressive and excellent. Similarly, with people, so much of their appearance is just that – an appearance. Appearances are often illusions created by makeup, flattering lighting, tailored clothes and too often our desires. But what makes them really beautiful is not how they seem, but how they are. From this orientation, we can see many other coordinate paradoxes that Stoics held in like fashion. Only the wise can be friends, since those who are not wise cannot appreciate what's really valuable in the friendship. Only the wise are pious, since they honour the gods out of their knowledge of what they are and never for the sake of their own gain. Moreover, only the wise are knowledgeable of what is right and wrong, since even if those who are not wise hold a correct view about a particular act or principle, they still lack a systematic view of the good. The result of the Stoic programme, seen through the paradoxes, is a revisionary ethical vision which calls its practitioners to overcome what passes for common sense and adopt a radical view of the good life. Epictetus's *Handbook* is an entrée into this system. It is framed as a set of exercises to clarify one's vision so as to not only recognize the Stoic principles and paradoxes as true, but to in turn live by them.

Part 2

The *Encheiridion* and Its Context

In this part we trace two lineages. The first begins with Epictetus the man. Putting his life into perspective requires telling the story of his early experiences as a slave, his education in Rome, his time as a teacher of philosophy in Nicopolis, and his connection to the influential Roman statesman, historian and general, Arrian. The *Encheiridion* and *Discourses* are Arrian's literary products, so we need to tell the story of how this came to pass and why it matters. The second lineage is that of the books themselves and their impact on philosophy and literature afterwards. The *Encheiridion* is a powerful work. It has had many admirers and commentators over the centuries since its first circulation. Here we put the new translation and commentary on it into this context as carrying on a rich tradition.

2.1 Epictetus and His Philosophical Influence

Epictetus, whose name means simply 'Acquired', was born into slavery as the son of a slave woman in the city of Hierapolis in the province of Phrygia in Asia Minor between 50 and 60 CE. At some point he travelled to Rome, where he was owned by Nero's freedman and administrative secretary Epaphroditus, who allowed him to study with the acclaimed Stoic teacher Musonius Rufus. After he was manumitted, Epictetus taught Stoicism for a few years in Rome. Philosophy in the Roman empire was largely conceived as therapy, as a way to burnish the character flaws from one's personality and to find peace of mind amidst the surging tides of worldly misfortune. This philosophical therapy cut across school and class divisions, as everyone from the lowliest slave to the emperor himself could benefit from a proper understanding of the emotions (Ahbel-Rappe 2006, 530). Philosophers, as freethinkers often outspoken in their criticisms of despots, occasionally provoked the ire of less tolerant rulers. So, when emperor Domitian banished all philosophers from the Italian peninsula (presumably in 89 or 92 CE), Epictetus travelled southeast to the province of Epirus in northwest Greece. There, in the large and sumptuous city of Nicopolis (just outside modern-day Preveza), he set up his own school. In Greek, Nicopolis means 'city of victory' because it was founded by Augustus to commemorate his victory over Marc Antony at nearby Actium in 31 BCE. Epictetus's choice of location was sensible. Comfortable lodgings for his students would have been available there. Nicopolis lay on a major commercial and cultural route. To the northwest, across the Adriatic Sea, this route connected the important port city of Brundisium (in the heel of Italy's boot) to Rome along the Via Appia. To the east the route crossed the Greek mainland to Athens and, across the Aegean Sea, connected to Anatolia and the eastern provinces of the Empire.

We know that Epictetus was lame (*Disc.* i.16.20). Two different causes of his lameness are given by sources. One is that he contracted rheumatism or the like in old age. The far more dramatic account originates from Celsus, the second-century pagan philosopher whose comprehensive criticisms of Christianity are targeted in the Christian work *Against Celsus*. On this account, as his master was abusing him, the boy Epictetus said, 'You're going to break my leg.' When the leg broke, the boy calmly replied, 'Told you so.' If this story is true, it is easy to imagine that his master took pleasure in such cruel punishment and that no care was taken to set the broken bone, leaving the boy to limp severely the rest of his life (Samuelson 2018, 146).

Epictetus's style of living was meagre. In Rome he never locked the doors of his dwelling, and his only furniture was said to be a pallet and a rush mat (Epictetus 1925, x). His disdain for material possessions is shown in a story told in his lesson about not getting angry with wrongdoers. In Nicopolis a thief once entered his house through a window and stole an iron lamp kept in front of his household gods. Epictetus surmised that to do such a thing, the thief must have been driven by a powerful motive. So, unfazed, he opted to replace his iron lamp with a plainer earthenware lamp, reminding himself that you can only lose what you have (*Disc.* i.18.15–16). Epictetus chalks up the loss of his lamp to the thief being better at keeping awake than he was. But the thief, he observes, paid a high price for the lamp because to get it, he became a thief, a man of bad faith and a wild beast (*Disc.* i.29.21).

Above all else Epictetus dedicated himself to others. In old age, he saved a baby that would otherwise have been exposed to death by adopting it. To help him raise the child, after decades of celibacy, he took into his humble home either a wife or a female servant. The sympathy, concern and affection Epictetus had for children is clear (*Disc.* i.11.1–26; i.23.1–10; i.24.20; i.29.31; ii.1.15–16; ii.22.12; iii.24.60; iv.4.141; iv.7.1–5). He relishes joining in playing their simple games, crawling on all fours with them and baby talking with them (*Disc.* ii.24.18). He admires their creativity (*Disc.* iii.13.18). This evidence must be kept in mind when children are discussed in *Handbook* 3, 7, 14 and 16. Epictetus died between 120 and 135 CE. The equanimity with which he coped with poverty, pain, lameness, exile and loss provides vital context to his remarks in the *Handbook* about such challenges.

At his school Epictetus taught Stoicism to wealthy Roman youths preparing for public service. A typical day in Epictetus's class, which was conducted in public, 'began with an oral recitation of one of the old Stoics. In the afternoon Epictetus extemporized from the day's reading' (Ahbel-Rappe 2006, 535). The school became famous, drawing many students and visitors travelling between Rome and Athens. For philosophers of the imperial period, philosophy was conceived as a sacred rite: learning, teaching and belonging in the transmission of wisdom were interlocking parts of a larger vision of philosophic activity as a way of life in harmony with the cosmos (Ahbel-Rappe 2006, 539).

Like his hero Socrates, Epictetus devoted himself not to writing philosophy, but to oral philosophizing. He taught his students Stoicism as a programme for transforming their lives by freeing their minds from fear, anger, grief and greed. Fortunately for us, one of those students was the historian, public servant and military commander Flavius Arrianus of Nicomedia, that is, Arrian (*c.* 86/89–*c.* after 146/160 CE). Arrian is the author of eight extant works. In his *Anabasis of Alexander* (in seven books), he borrows from Xenophon's account of the March of Cyrus and imitates the Attic style of Thucydides and Xenophon. In his work on India he uses the Ionic dialect. A third work is titled *On Hunting with Hounds*. More importantly to us, Arrian conveyed the impact Epictetus's instruction had on him by recording and compiling Epictetus's lectures and classroom conversations into eight volumes, or books, of *Diatribai* in Greek, *Discourses* in English. Only four of these books survive. Arrian abridged these lengthy *Discourses* into a short compendium called the *Encheiridion*, a *Manual* or *Handbook* containing pithy extracts easier to digest by less patient readers. 'In a letter to Massalenus, referred to by Simplicius, Arrian states that in composing the *Encheiridion* he picked out the most vital and necessary elements of Epictetus's philosophy, which would most strongly influence the souls of the readers' (Boter 1999, xiii). Arrian probably composed the *Handbook* no earlier than 107–110 CE.[1] Additional evidence comes from Simplicius, who reports that Arrian dedicated the *Handbook* to a person named Messalenos. This presumably refers to C. Prastina Pacatus Messalinus, *consul ordinarius* in the year 147 CE. The supposition that Arrian produced the *Handbook* around 130 CE agrees with the assumption that he produced the *Encheiridion* after he had already recorded the *Discourses*. At that time Arrian lived in Athens, where he held honorary political posts and wrote his historical works.

How faithful to Epictetus's actual teachings are these writings of Arrian? We have no way to know for certain since we lack independent means of verification. Yet confidence that the works we have reflect Epictetus's thought rather than Arrian's appears justified for two reasons. First, the *Discourses* and *Handbook* are written in *koinē*, the common Greek rather than the sophisticated literary language of Arrian's other writings. Second, the brusque, economical phrasing, dialogical structure, precise philosophical vocabulary and argumentative rigour of the *Discourses* and *Handbook* stand in stark contrast with Arrian's style in his other works.

The genre of the diatribe ('discourse') and the handbook through which Arrian portrayed the philosophy of Epictetus was already well established in the Hellenistic period, centuries before Epictetus and Arrian. The Cynics, Epicureans and Stoics publicly touted their respective philosophies as competing accounts of the art of leading the good life. Their didactic activities and attempts to win adherents found expression in the letter, in the collection of maxims, in the diatribe and in the handbook. Examples include Epicurus' letters to Herodotus, Menoeceus and Pythocles; Epicurus' *Kuriai Doxai* ('Principal Doctrines'); and the diatribes of the early Stoics Zeno, Aristo and Cleanthes. Most scholars suppose that Epictetus adopted the form of the diatribe, like his teacher Musonius did, from the Cynic tradition of Bion of Borysthenes and Teles of Megara. This seems plausible given the great admiration for the Cynics Musonius and Epictetus each show in their *Discourses*.

An *encheiridion* means literally 'a little thing easily held in the hand'. Originally this term was used to designate a hand weapon, especially a dagger or short sword. This is how it is customarily used by Herodotus, Thucydides and Plato. The term is first used to designate a textual genre rather than a hand weapon by the Epicurean Demetrius of Lacona in the second century BCE, who uses it in the title of a synopsis of problems in ethics and physics. So, the concept of an *encheiridion* as a short instruction manual was already familiar in the first and second centuries CE. Previously Theophrastus used the term *encheiridion* not specifically for a hand weapon but more generally for a grip, handle or aid in grabbing and holding onto something. The use of the expression in this sense expanded so that the word *encheiridion* could designate any aid or tool that is manageable, handy and ready for use. This expanded usage continued into the third century CE when Philostratus applied it to a document. Texts which imparted a given technique or a doctrine in a handy form come down to us under the title *encheiridion*. Examples of such texts offering technical instruction and introduction include the *Harmonikon Encheiridion* of the Neoplatonic mathematician Nicomachus of Gerasa of the first century CE and the *Encheiridion Peri Metrōn* of Hephaistion of the second century CE commented on by Longinus. Once *encheiridion* no longer referred to a weapon but to a text, it seems very likely that it supplemented a *biblion* (book) as was the case with the handbook of Nicomachus. In his commentary on the handbook of Hephaiston, which was written in the first century CE, Longinus refers to the *Encheiridion* of the metrist Heliodorus. From this we can conclude that the term *encheiridion* denotes a hand***book*** even without the postscript *biblion*.

Nonetheless, even without the postscript the title of Epictetus's *Handbook* remains ambivalent. On the one hand, *Encheiridion* refers to the little booklet compiled by Arrian that presents Epictetus's philosophical principles in a *handy* way. On the other hand, *Encheiridion* refers to the practical aim of the ethical instruction conveyed in the booklet, that is, to the *handling* of the Epictetan principles. The aim is to have these principles continuously on hand so as always to be armed against every kind of challenge, to be on guard against every impression (*phantasia*) one encounters, with the goal of perfecting one's technique in the art of living. In the sixth-century CE Simplicius uses *To Epiktetou Encheiridion Epigegrammenon* as an established title and states that in the case of the Epictetan instruction manual, it is apt to associate *encheiridion* with the original meaning *dagger*. It is worth noting that Epictetus's *Handbook* is handed down to us not only with the title *encheiridion* but also under the title *Gnomologion*.

Our commentary stands in a very long tradition of elucidating Epictetus's *Encheiridion* dating back to Simplicius in the sixth century CE. But Simplicius was no Stoic. His commentary contorts Epictetus's ideas to fit within his Neoplatonist framework. (Think of hammering square pegs into round holes.) After Simplicius traditional remarks on the *Encheiridion* increase in number, for example by Hieronymus Verle (Antwerp 1543), Thomas Naogeorgus (Strassburg 1554), Hieronymus Wolf (Basel 1561) and Christian Francken (Klausenberg 1585). In 1798 (Leipzig) Johann David Büchling composed a school-commentary that formed the basis of the first critical edition of the *Encheiridion* by Johann Schweighäuser (Leipzig 1798). All the editions published in the nineteenth and twentieth centuries rely on Schweighäuser's edition, which was superseded by the magisterial, painstaking critical edition of Gerard J. Boter (Leiden 1999). He establishes that there are over one hundred manuscripts of the Greek text of the *Encheiridion* (Boter 1999, xvi).

The commentary by Ulrike Brandt (Heidelberg 2015) focuses on the literary form of the *Handbook*. Rejecting the prevailing judgement that the *Encheiridion* is a second-rate excerpt and mere summary of the *Discourses*, she contends that nearly half of the chapters of the *Handbook* relate either not at all, or only loosely, to the textual content transmitted in the *Discourses*. Brandt scrutinizes the Greek text of the *Encheiridion* in detail, attends closely to the terminology, and comments on its peculiar synthesis of rhetorical and argumentative presentation. She demonstrates the significance of the *Encheiridion* in its own right, independent of Epictetus's *Discourses*, as one of the first philosophical handbooks ever.[2]

2.2 The Historical Influence of the *Encheiridion*

From the second to the sixth centuries CE Epictetus was admired as a virtuous pagan by many influential Christians. His *Encheiridion* is referred to by the church fathers Clement of Alexandria, Ambrose of Mailand, Basil of Caesarea, John Chrysostom and Synesius of Cyrene. Christian authors transmitted anecdotes and composed verses in praise of Epictetus's excellence and 'free' character, unhampered as he was by his poverty, lameness and slavery (Long 2002, 260). The high esteem for Epictetus by the great Christian ascetic and prolific scholar Origen is clear from a striking contrast he drew between Epictetus and Plato. 'Whereas Plato, he writes, "is only in the hands of those reputed to be scholars, Epictetus is admired by ordinary people who have the urge to be benefited, and who perceive improvement from his words" (*Against Celsus* VI.2). The "words" Origen mentions are likely to have been largely confined to the *Manual*' (Long 2002, 260). In addition to its content, the format of the *Encheiridion* shaped Christian teachings, as is evident in Augustine's *Enchiridion ad Laurentium*. In the fifth century Stobaeus, the compiler of extracts from many Greek authors, quotes passages from the *Encheiridion* twenty-one times.

Content from the *Encheiridion* finds its way into other philosophers' writings without mention of their source. In their commentaries on Plato's *Alcibiades I*, the Neoplatonists Proclus and Olympiodorus help themselves to Epictetus's trichotomy of those uneducated in philosophy, those progressing in their education and those fully educated, without reference to *Handbook* 5. In his commentary on Plato's *Gorgias* Olympiodorus mentions Epictetus by name, as does Damascius. The Byzantine scholar Procopius of Gaza and the Christian monk Dorotheus of Gaza refer to *Handbook* 8. Another work that resembles Epictetus's *Handbook* due to its function as a vade mecum is the *Strategikon*, a manual on military and household affairs composed *c.* 1078 by the Byzantine scholar Kekaumenos. Moreover, the tradition of philosophical handbooks is evident in the *Encheiridion* of the Syrian scholar Jacob of Edessa (*c.* 640–708). In the ninth century, a consolatory letter by the great Arab philosopher and polymath Al-Kindi contains references to *Handbook* 2, 5, 7–8 and 11. Yet the most significant contribution for understanding the indirect tradition is Simplicius's sixth-century commentary on Epictetus's *Encheiridion*.

The impact of the *Encheiridion* on monasticism was so strong that it was adopted to suit the needs of Christian ascetics three different times. One way the *Handbook* was specifically modified for the use of monks was to replace the name of Socrates – Epictetus's favourite exemplar for Stoics in training to emulate – with that of St Paul. The first Christian adaptation is usually associated with St Nilus Ancyranus (*c.* 400 CE), though its authorship is debated. This adaptation was first edited by J. M. Suarez, along with other works by Nilus, in 1673 in Rome. The second adaptation is the *Enchiridii Paraphrasis Christiana*, which was first edited by M. Casaubon, along with his edition of the authentic *Encheiridion*, published in 1659 in London. The third Christian adaptation of Epictetus's *Encheiridion* was discovered by the patristics scholar Michel Spanneut in the manuscript named *Vaticanus graecus* 2231 written between 1317 and 1338.

The *Encheiridion* was first translated into Latin by Niccolò Perotti in 1450. In 1479 Angelo Poliziano's Latin translation supplied the individual chapters with titles by placing programmatic sections taken from Simplicius's commentary above the *Encheiridion* passages. Poliziano (Politian) published the first printed edition (*editio princeps*) of his Latin translation in Bologna in 1497. While Perotti's translation did not gain much popularity, Poliziano's translation has been endlessly reprinted. The first edition of the complete Greek text was published by Gregor Haloander in 1529. Since then, editions of the Greek text and translations into English, French, German and Italian have been plentiful. Hieronymus Wolf published the *Handbook* as an appendix to his edition of the *Discourses* in 1561. The popularity of the *Encheiridion* peaked between 1550 and 1750. It was translated into most European languages, and there were multiple translations in English, French and German. 'Most of the early translators of the *Manual* were Protestants who typically read and corrected Epictetus through the medium of their religion, and there were poetic summaries of the work' (Long

2002, 261). These include Christian paraphrases by Matthias Mittner, Ellis Walker, Zacharias Hemminger, Edward Ivie and Ludwig Ernst von Faramond. James Sandford used a French translation to compose the first English translation in 1567. This was followed in 1610 by John Healey's English translation from the Greek. The brilliant orator, lawyer, statesman and Neostoic Guillaume du Vair (1556–1621) translated the *Encheiridion* into French in 1586 and popularized it in his *La Philosophie morale des Stoiques*. Another Neostoic, the Flemish Catholic philologist Justus Lipsius (1547–1606), was familiar with Epictetus's philosophy and quotes *Handbook* 38 in his *Manuductio ad Stoicam Philosophiam* (1604). In the *Book of Twenty-Five Paragraphs* published in 1605, the Jesuit missionary Matteo Ricci partly translated the *Encheiridion* into Chinese convinced that its affinity with Confucianism readied its readers for conversion to Christianity.

By the seventeenth century, the *Handbook* had become the better known of the Epictetan writings; it was usually read rather than the *Discourses*. Epictetus was admired by the philosopher, mathematician, physicist and fervent Jansenist Christian Blaise Pascal (1623–62). In his short essay *Discussion with Monsieur de Sacy on Epictetus and Montaigne*, Pascal contrasts Epictetus the Stoic with Michel de Montaigne, whom he considers a Pyrrhonian Sceptic. Pascal quotes from *Handbook* 1, 8, 11, 17 and 21 to illustrate Epictetus's superior understanding of 'man's duties' and his 'seeing God as his principal aim' (Long 2002, 263). But whereas Pascal also criticizes Epictetus for prescribing 'wickedly proud principles', in his *Discourse on Method* the other great French philosopher and mathematician of the day René Descartes (1596–1650) discerns what Pascal misses, namely, how Epictetus's understanding of human limitations informs his aspirational programme of education. 'Descartes offers an extraordinarily accurate and appreciative synopsis of Epictetus's philosophy' (Long 2002, 266). Moreover, it is credible, as is supposed, that the *Encheiridion* belonged to the library of the eminent Dutch philosopher Baruch de Spinoza (1632–77), given that Stoicism is the fundamental historic and systematic reference of his philosophy (DeBrabander 2007; Miller 2015).

Despite his being more famously a Pyrrhonian Sceptic, Michel de Montaigne (1533–92) himself embraces a famous dictum of the *Encheiridion*. The fourteenth essay of the first book of his *Essays* opens quoting 'an old Greek maxim', namely the first sentence of *Handbook* 5: 'What disturbs people is not things, but their judgements about the things.' The lasting impact and popularity of this single dictum of the *Handbook* cannot be overstated, as it is found in a variety of works from the sixteenth to the early nineteenth centuries. It resurfaces in Shakespeare's *Hamlet* (1602) as 'there is nothing either good or bad but thinking makes it so'

(Act 2, Scene 2. 268). The motto is quoted by the Anglican cleric Laurence Sterne (1713–68) in his novel *The Life and Opinions of Tristram Shandy, A Gentleman* (1759). The German philosopher and poet Johann Gottfried Herder (1744–1803) quotes it in his treatise *This Too a Philosophy of History for the Education of Humanity* (1774). The maxim also appears in the German-French edition of the *Essay on the Metamorphosis of Plants* (1790) by the botanist, anatomist, poet, playwright and novelist Johann Wolfgang von Goethe (1749–1832), the giant of all German writers.

The importance of Epictetus continued into the Enlightenment period in England. This is evident in the writings of Anthony Ashley Cooper (1671–1713), the third Earl of Shaftesbury. Following the tradition of the *Meditations* of Marcus Aurelius, Shaftesbury's posthumously published work *Askemata* contains a series of reflections mostly in the form of questions and answers to himself inspired by quotations from Marcus Aurelius and Epictetus's *Handbook*, especially chapters 1 and 33. In the margins of his copy of Hieronymus Wolf's edition of the *Handbook* and the *Discourses* Shaftesbury wrote notes and later filled with comments an additional *Book of Notes Not Set Down in the Margin of My Little Colon-Edition*. In his *Sermons* Bishop Joseph Butler (1692–1750) seizes upon the description in *Discourses* 1.1 of our reflective capacity to approve or disapprove of actions to articulate his own conception of the faculty of conscience or moral sense. The clear, pithy and distinctive style of the *Handbook* made it accessible to readers who lacked formal training in philosophy, so it gained a wide readership among women in England. This popularity inspired the aristocrat, writer and poet Lady Mary Pierrepont (1689–1762) to compose her own translation of the *Handbook* in 1710 at the age of twenty-one before she married Edward Wortley Montagu. The *Handbook* was a standard school text in the Scottish Enlightenment. The economist and philosopher Adam Smith (1723–90) kept a 1670 edition of the *Encheiridion* in his library which he acquired as a schoolboy. The English poet and cultural critic Matthew Arnold (1822–88) commends Epictetus and Marcus Aurelius as 'the great masters of morals' and quotes the citation from Cleanthes' *Hymn to Zeus* in *Handbook* 53 (Long 2002, 268).

Admiration of Epictetus was at least as strong in North America. In his will, the Puritan minister John Harvard (1607–38) bequeathed a copy of Epictetus, presumably the *Handbook*, to the college he founded in Cambridge, Massachusetts. At the College of William and Mary Thomas Jefferson (1743–1826) read Epictetus with such enthusiasm that, after graduating in 1762, he ordered the entire Greek text of the *Discourses* for the library of his newly founded University of Virginia (Long 2002, 268–9). We know that the *Encheiridion* belonged to the personal libraries of both Jefferson and the polymath Benjamin Franklin (1706–90). It is easy to understand why Epictetus's emphasis on mental freedom and self-sufficiency strongly resonated with the non-conformist individualism of Ralph Waldo Emerson and Henry David Thoreau (Long 2002, 268).

Yet the most ardent fan of Epictetus among American luminaries is no doubt the inimitable poet, essayist and journalist Walt Whitman (1819–92). Whitman was deeply moved by the *Encheiridion* when he discovered it at around the age of sixteen. Throughout his life he returned to it repeatedly like a thirsty man to an artesian well, describing it as 'sacred' and 'precious'. Near the end of his life Whitman told a friend 'Epictetus is the one of all my old cronies who has lasted to this day … He is a universe in himself. He sets me free in a flood of light – of life, of vista … I do not remember when I first read the book. It was far, far back … It was like being born again' (Long 2002, 269).

At the beginning of the twentieth century Theodore Dreiser mentions Epictetus in his early novel *Sister Carrie* (1900). The influence of Epictetus can be seen in *A Portrait of the Artist as a Young Man* (1916) by James Joyce, in *Les Propos* vol. 2 by Émile-Auguste Chartier also known as Alain (1868–1951) and in *Education of the Stoic* by the Portuguese writer Fernando Pessoa (1888–1935) – under the heteronym Baron von Teive – the complement to his work *The Book of Disquiet*. Fondness for the teachings of Epictetus is a point of discord in J. D. Salinger's *Franny and Zooey* (1961). The reading of Epictetus is cited as evidence of a proper education in the novel *A House for Mr. Biswas* (1961) by V. S. Naipaul. In 1962 the psychologist Albert Ellis explicitly credits the *Handbook* when calling Epictetus a mastermind behind his Rational Emotive Behaviour Therapy. The political philosopher and Holocaust survivor Hannah Arendt (1906–75) refers to *Handbook* 1, 5, 8, 21, 30, 33.8 and 48.2 as sources of the Epictetan concept of the will. 'The Golden Sayings of Epictetus' are mentioned several times by Lydia Rowe, the narrator and prosperous mother of four in *Disturbances in the Field* (1983) by Lynne Sharon Schwartz. The theme of the novel is *Handbook* 43 while *Handbook* 3 and 11 provide its cautionary message.

In dramatic fashion the philosophy of Epictetus saves a good but hapless young man in *A Man in Full* (1998), a novel by Tom Wolfe. Conrad Hensley is a hardworking manual labourer in California whose bravery saves a co-worker from being killed in a warehouse accident moments before he is laid off due to staff cutbacks and lack of seniority. Later more misfortune makes him the victim of a bum rap, but he chooses not to bargain away his integrity in a plea deal so is sent to Santa Rita prison. By mistake, or perhaps due to destiny, Conrad receives a book called *The Stoics* instead of the book he had requested, *The Stoics'*

Game by his favourite author. Therein he finds sage teachings of Epictetus that speak directly to his dangerous circumstances. Galvanized, Conrad converts to Epictetus's Stoicism, zealously memorizing many texts from the *Discourses*. Armed with this sacred knowledge, he defeats a brawny thug and gang-leader who threatens to brutalize him. Before the thug's gang can retaliate, fate intervenes again with an earthquake that destroys the prison and frees Conrad. He makes his way to Atlanta and meets the novel's chief protagonist, the cracker and real estate tycoon Charlie Croker. Charlie is an old Georgia Tech football star whose injured knee renders him lame like Epictetus. Charlie struggles with this dilemma. He can take a deal that would save him from financial ruin at the cost of betraying an old friend, or he can reject the deal, preserve his honour, and lose his immense wealth, luxurious properties and gorgeous trophy wife half his age. When Conrad teaches the wisdom of Epictetus to Charlie, the lame, inconsolable old man is transformed. Epictetus empowers Charlie to overcome his self-made existential crisis by refusing to be coerced by the threat of losing material wealth and prestige. Charlie walks away from his former life and his corporation worth hundreds of millions of dollars to let his creditors fight over the assets. He becomes a successful televangelist with a syndicated show called *The Stoic's Hour* on Fox Broadcasting. This conclusion to Wolfe's novel anticipates the zeal with which Epictetus and Stoicism have been received the last twenty years over a broad range of media outlets, including a profusion of websites, blogs, newsletters, YouTube videos, online discussion forums and Apple's self-care app 'stoic.'

An unusual feature of *A Man in Full* is that outside of academia, the *Handbook* has generally enjoyed much greater popularity than the *Discourses*. The *Handbook*'s numerous translations and editions continue to attract practitioners of Stoicism as a way of life, those seeking self-help, life hacks and personal meaning. Within academia, however, we think it fair to say that no other text its size has exercised as wide, deep and lasting an impact in the history of Stoicism, or indeed arguably the history of Western philosophy, as the *Encheiridion*.

Part 3

Translation of the *Handbook* of Epictetus

Note on the translation

The twin goals of our translation are to present Epictetus's ideas in a fresh, contemporary idiom that reflects his brisk, direct style while also keeping close to the sense of the Greek. These goals are sometimes in tension. For example, when Epictetus refers to slaves (*Ench.* 12, 26, 33.7) fidelity to the Greek has been relaxed to accommodate his message to contemporary life, which proscribes slavery and accepts employing servants. Similar topical choices include shoe types (*Ench.* 39), currency (*Ench.* 25.3), and kickboxers, NASCAR, and sports replacing gladiators, horse-races and athletes (*Ench.* 33.2).

Some chapters of the *Handbook* are long enough that tradition divides them into subsections. In the body of the translation, subsections are indicated by square brackets: [1], [2], and so on. When cited (as in the previous paragraph) a subsection's number follows the chapter's number; for example, '33.2' indicates chapter 33, subsection 2.

The Greek text used was that of the Perseus Digital Library 4.0, Gregory R. Crane, Editor-in-Chief, Tufts University, www.perseus.tufts.edu/hopper/.

The *Handbook* of Epictetus

Chapter 1

[1] There are some things that are up to us, others that are not up to us. The things up to us are understanding, impulse, desire, aversion and, in a word, whatever acts are ours. The things not up to us are the body, possessions, reputation, professional positions and in a word, whatever acts are not ours.

[2] And the things up to us are naturally free, unhindered and unimpeded. But the things not up to us are weak, enslaved, hindered and not yours. Therefore, remember

[3] that if you think the naturally enslaved things are free and that the things that are not yours are yours, then you will be hindered, you will have grief, you will be disturbed, you will blame both the gods and human beings. If you think only what is yours is yours but things that are not yours are, as is the case, not yours, then no one will ever harass you, no one will hinder you, you will blame no one, you will accuse no one, you will not do even one thing involuntarily, no one will harm you, you will have no enemy, because you will be safe from any harm.

[4] Therefore, when considering such great things remember that it is not enough to go after them only casually, but rather to give up some things completely, and to postpone others at least for now. But if you also want these things and at the same time to wield power and have wealth, then you may not get even these latter things, because you are also going for the former, which are the only means of gaining freedom and happiness.

[5] Therefore, for every troubling impression practice saying at once 'you are an impression and not at all what you appear to be.' Then examine it and test it by the standards which you hold, but first of all and most of all this standard, whether it is about the things up to us or about the things not up to us. And if it is about something that is not up to us, then be ready to say 'it is nothing to me'.

Chapter 2

[1] Remember, that the promise of desire is success in getting what you desire, and the promise of aversion is not getting what you're averse to. And if you fail to get what you desire, then you're unlucky, but if you get what you want to avoid, then you have bad luck. Therefore, if you avoid only the things contrary to nature which are up to you, then you will not suffer anything which you are averse to, but if you're averse to illness, or death, or poverty, then you will have bad luck.

[2] So, remove your aversion from all the things that are not up to us and transfer them to the things which are contrary to nature and up to us. But as for desire, hold off from it completely for now, because if you desire something not up to us, then you're doomed to be unfortunate; and none of the things up to us, which it would be good to desire otherwise, are yet available to you. But only choose and refuse, and do so gently, with discretion and casually.

Chapter 3

With each thing that entices or is useful to you or which you're very fond of, remember to tell yourself just what sort of thing it is, starting with the most trivial of things. Should you be fond of a mug, then say, 'I'm fond of a mug,' because then, when it breaks, you won't be disturbed. Should you kiss your child or wife, then say, 'I'm kissing a human being,' because then, when she dies, you won't be disturbed.

Chapter 4

Whenever you're about to tackle a task, remind yourself what sort of task it is. If you're going to a public pool, anticipate the things that happen at public pools: people splashing, shoving, being offensive and stealing things. And so you will stick with your task to the end, if right at the start you say to yourself, 'I want to swim and also to keep my volition in accord with nature.' Do likewise with every task. Because in this way, if something happens to disrupt your swim, then you'll have this ready at hand: 'I want not just to swim, but also to keep my volition in accord with nature – but I can't keep it that way if I'm upset about the things that happen.'

Chapter 5

What disturbs people is not things, but their judgements about the things. For example, death is nothing terrible, otherwise it would have appeared so to Socrates, but the judgement *that* death is terrible, that is what's terrible. Therefore, whenever we are hampered, disturbed or annoyed, we should never blame others but only ourselves, that is, our judgements. The uneducated person blames others when he is doing badly. The one making progress in his education blames himself. The fully educated person blames neither others nor himself.

Chapter 6

Don't take pride in any excellence belonging to another. If a horse boasted by saying 'I am beautiful,' then it would be alright. But when you boast by saying 'I have a beautiful horse,' realize that you are taking pride in the horse's good. What, then, is your good? The use of impressions. So that whenever your use of impressions is in accord with nature, then be proud, because then you are taking pride in some good that belongs to you.

Chapter 7

Just as when on a voyage when your ship has anchored, if you go ashore to fetch fresh water, on the way you might collect a shellfish or a vegetable. But you must keep your mind on the ship and continue to look back at it in case the captain calls. Should he call, then you must discard all the food, so that you are not tied up and thrown back onboard like the sheep. Life is like this too. If you are given a spouse and child instead of the shellfish and vegetable, there's no trouble with that. However, if the captain calls, then discard both of them too and run to the ship without turning back. Moreover, if you're old, then don't stray far from the ship so that when you hear the call to return you aren't left behind.

Chapter 8

Don't seek to have things happen as *you* want but want the things that happen to happen as they *do*, and you'll be going with the flow.

Chapter 9

Illness hampers the body, but it doesn't hamper volition, unless volition wants it to. Lameness hampers the leg, but not volition. Say this in the face of each occurrence, because you'll find it hampers something else but not you.

Chapter 10

For each thing you encounter, remember to turn to yourself to seek what ability you have for handling it. If you see a handsome man or beautiful woman, you'll find the power of self-control to face these things. If it's pain, you'll find endurance. If it's an insult, you'll find patience. And when you get used to handling things this way the impressions won't carry you away.

Chapter 11

Never say about anything, 'I have lost it,' but rather 'I have returned it.' Did your child die? He was returned. Did your wife die? She was returned. 'But my property was taken away.' Rather, it too was returned. 'But the person who took it is bad.'

So, what do you care how the giver reclaims it from you? As long as he is lending it, take care of it as something that doesn't belong to you, like guests at a hotel.

Chapter 12

[1] If you want to make progress, get rid of ruminations such as these: 'If I neglect my affairs, then I'll have nothing to live on'; 'If I don't correct my servant, he'll be intractable.' This is because it's better to die of hunger free of distress and fear than it is to live bountifully but feeling troubled. It's better for your servant to be bad than for you to be unhappy.

[2] Therefore begin with trivial things – a little oil is spilled, a splash of wine is stolen – say to yourself, 'this is the price of mental health, this is the price of imperturbability.' But nothing comes for free. So, whenever you call your servant, bear in mind that he's quite capable of not paying attention, and if he does respond, he's capable of not doing what you want. But he's not sitting so pretty that whether or not you're perturbed is up to him.

Chapter 13

If you want to make progress, endure having the reputation of being foolish and silly when it comes to external things, and don't desire to appear to know about them. If you appear to anybody to be someone important, distrust yourself. Therefore, know that it's not easy to guard both keeping your volition in accord with nature and external things. Taking care of one of them entirely necessitates neglecting the other.

Chapter 14

[1] You're a fool if you want your children, your wife and your friends, to live forever. Fools want things which are not up to them to be up to them, and they want what belongs to others to be theirs. Similarly, if you want your servant not to slip up, then you're a moron, because you're wanting vice not to be vice, but to be something else. But if you don't want to fail to get what you desire, this you can do. Therefore, practice doing what you can do.

[2] Each person's master is the one who has power over what the person wants or doesn't want, to secure it or take it away. Therefore, whoever wants to be free

must neither want anything nor avoid anything that is up to others. Otherwise, you'll necessarily be a slave.

Chapter 15

Remember that you need to act like you're at a dinner party. Some food is passed around and offered to you. Reach out your hand and politely take some. It passes by – don't grab it. It hasn't come out yet. Don't project your desire towards it but wait until it's at hand. Behave similarly towards your child, wife, status and wealth, and you'll be worthy to dine with the gods. But if you don't even take these things when they're offered to you but instead decline them, then you'll not only dine with the gods, you'll also rule alongside them. By doing this Diogenes and Heraclitus and others like them were worthy of both being, and being called, godlike.

Chapter 16

Whenever you see someone weeping in sorrow, either over a child who is away from home or over his own stuff being lost, be careful not to be carried away by the impression that the weeper is stuck in nasty external gunk. Instead, immediately have on hand the fact that 'what weighs upon the weeper is not what has happened, but his judgement about what has happened, because what has happened doesn't weigh upon anyone else'. However, don't hesitate to support him with encouraging words, and if the occasion suggests it, groan with him too. But take care not to also groan on the inside.

Chapter 17

Remember that you are an actor in a play, of whatever kind the director wants: short, if he wants it short, long, if he wants it long. If he wants you to play the part of a disabled person, or a public official, or a private citizen, or a beggar, perform even this part gracefully. Because this is your task, to play the assigned role well, but another selects it.

Chapter 18

Whenever a raven croaks, don't let the impression of a bad omen carry you away. But immediately distance yourself from it and say, 'None of these croaks are significant for me, but rather for my puny body or my piddling property or my trivial reputation or my kids or my wife. For me every omen is good, if I want it to be, because whatever happens it's up to me to benefit from it.'

Chapter 19

[1] You have the power to be invincible if you never enter a competition in which victory is not up to you.

[2] When someone appears to have superior prestige, or great power, or some other kind of celebrity, be on guard that you're not carried off by the impression that they're happy. If the essence of the good is among the things that are up to us, then there is no place for either envy or jealousy, and you yourself will want to be neither a general, nor an executive officer, nor a governor, but to be free. There is but one road that leads to this, and that is to disdain the things that are not up to us.

Chapter 20

Remember that it is not the offensive or the abusive person that insults you, but the judgement about them that they're insulting. So, whenever someone provokes you to get angry, know that it is your opinion that angers you. Therefore, first of all try not to be abducted by the impression, since if you take some time and delay responding, then you'll master yourself more easily.

Chapter 21

Death and exile and everything that appears terrible – keep before your eyes every day, but most of all death. And then you'll never ever think sleazy thoughts nor will you yearn for anything too much.

Chapter 22

If you set your heart upon philosophy, immediately prepare to be laughed at and mocked by many people as they jeer, 'He has returned to us a philosopher all of a sudden,' and 'Where did his attitude that he's better than we are come from?' But you ought not to be stuck-up. Instead, stick with the things that appear best to you as if God assigned you to that post. And remember that if you stick to these scruples, those people who previously laughed at you will later marvel. If, however, they defeat you, you'll be doubly derided.

Chapter 23

If it ever happens that you turn outward desiring to please someone, know that you've lost your way. Therefore, in everything be satisfied just to *be* a philosopher, and if you desire to seem to be one, look like one to yourself, and you will suffice.

Chapter 24

[1] Don't let thoughts like these burden you, 'I will live without prestige and everywhere I'll be a nobody.' Because if lacking prestige is a bad thing, then ....[1] But you cannot be in a bad way on account of another person any more than you can be disgraced by another. It is not your job to win political office or to be invited to a banquet, is it? Heck no! How, therefore, is that a lack of prestige? But how will you be a nobody everywhere, when you only need to be a somebody regarding the things up to you, about which it's possible for you to be the worthiest?

[2] But, you say, your friends will be without resources. Why do you say they are without resources? They won't get some coins from you, nor will you make them Roman citizens. Well, who told you that these are among the things that are up to us, and not instead the concerns of others? Who can give to others things that he doesn't have? 'Get money, then,' a friend says, 'so that we can have some.'

[3] If I can get it while keeping my traits of modesty, trustworthiness and self-respect, show me the way to earn an honest buck and I'll do it. But if you expect me to destroy the good traits that are mine so that you may secure the things that are not good, you can see how unfair and thoughtless you are. And so what do you desire more? Some silver coins or being a trustworthy and modest friend? Well then, help me rather to be this kind of friend and don't expect me to do things which will destroy these traits.

[4] 'But,' someone says, 'my country will be helpless insofar as it's up to me.' Again, what kind of help is this? It won't have either porticos or swimming pools because of you. And what of it? For it doesn't have shoes supplied by the blacksmith or weapons supplied by the cobbler. But it's enough if everyone plays

her own part. But if you supply it with another trustworthy and honourable citizen, wouldn't you be helping it? 'Yes.' Surely you wouldn't be useless to it. 'Well then,' she says, 'what occupation will I have in the city?' Whatever occupation you can have while at the same time remaining trustworthy and modest.

[5] But if, by wanting to help your city, you destroy these traits, what use will you be to it once you become shameless and untrustworthy?

Chapter 25

[1] Has someone received greater awards than you at a formal ceremony or a warmer greeting in a reception line or being asked for advice before you? Now if these are good things, then you ought to be glad that he got them. But if they're bad, then don't be irked that you didn't. And remember that, if you don't do what others did to get things which are not up to us, then you can't be judged to deserve an equal share of them.

[2] Because how can one who doesn't keep knocking on a person's door get the same results as someone who does? Or one who doesn't wait upon a patron hand and foot compared to someone who does? Or one who doesn't brown-nose compared to someone who does? Therefore, you'll be unfair and stingy if you won't pay the price that these things cost and instead want to receive them as free gifts.

[3] But at what price are heads of lettuce sold? A dollar[2] per head, maybe. So then, since someone paying the dollar gets the lettuce, while you're not paying for it and don't get it, don't think that you're worse off than the one buying lettuce. Because, as the buyer has the lettuce, so too do you have the dollar that you didn't spend.

[4] It's the same way in this case too. You weren't invited to some formal dinner party? No, because you didn't pay the host the price of admission to the dinner. He sells it for brown-nosing, he sells it for sucking up to him. Therefore, if it benefits you, pay the price it's sold for. But if you want both not to pay the price and yet also to get these things, then you're stingy and foolish.

[5] So then, do you have nothing in place of the dinner? Well, you didn't brown-nose the host you didn't want to brown-nose, and you didn't have to endure those knocking at his door.

Chapter 26

The purpose of nature is to be learned from the things in which we don't differ from one another. For example, when someone else's servant breaks a glass, you're immediately ready to say 'These things happen.' Know, then, that when your own glass is broken, you must have the same attitude which you have when another's glass is broken. Also take this same approach concerning more important matters. Has someone else's child or wife died? Nobody would fail to say, 'It is human, all too human.' But when one's own loved one dies, immediately one says 'Oy vey! How wretched I am!' So, we need to remember how we feel when hearing this happen to others.

Chapter 27

Just as a target is not set up in order to be missed, similarly nor does nature let what's bad occur in the universe.

Chapter 28

If someone turned your body over to anyone you met, you would be vexed. But should you turn your own mind over to anyone you happened upon, so that if he abuses you, you're upset and confused, wouldn't you be ashamed to do this?

Chapter 29

[1] For each task, consider the steps that precede it and the steps that follow, and then proceed accordingly. But if you don't, you'll take it up eagerly at first since you haven't thought through the steps that come next, but later, when some difficulties arise, you'll quit the project disgracefully. Do you want to win an Olympic event?

[2] Yes, I do too, by the gods, because it's an awesome achievement. But consider the steps that precede it and the steps that follow and tackle the task accordingly. You need to be disciplined, keep a strict diet, give up sweets, train in the gym under compulsion at a set hour of day, in the heat, in the cold, you must not drink cold water or wine whenever you please – frankly, you must turn yourself over to your trainer as if he were a doctor. Then, in the contest, you need to dig into the chalk,[3] sometimes dislocate your wrist, twist your ankle, swallow a lot of sand, sometimes get whipped, and along with all these hassles, lose.

[3] After thinking over all these considerations, if you still want to, then go be an athlete. But if you don't think it over, you'll be turning from one game to the next like children do, who one minute play as wrestlers, the next as gladiators, the next play trumpets, and then pretend to be actors in a play. You too are one minute an athlete, the next a gladiator, then an orator, then a philosopher, yet you're wholeheartedly nothing. Instead, like a monkey, you ape every spectacle that you see, amused by one thing after another. Because you haven't pursued anything after thinking it through or studying it diligently, rather, you're flighty and have cold feet.

[4] Similarly, having seen a philosopher and hearing someone lecturing like Euphrates (though, who can orate like him?), some people also want to philosophize themselves.

[5] Dude! First think about what sort of role this is. Then, closely examine your own nature and whether you can fulfil it. Do you want to be a pentathlete or a wrestler? Look at your arms and your thighs, inspect your buttocks.

[6] Different people are born for different things. Do you think that you can do the compulsory exercises and eat like you do now, drink like you do now, desire the same things, and shun the same things? You must go without sleep, work your tail off, be away from your friends, be looked down upon by a lowly servant, be derided by people you meet, get the short end of the stick in everything: in honours, in public offices, in legal cases, in every tiny little thing.

[7] Think about these hassles and whether you're willing to exchange them for an untroubled mind, freedom and imperturbability. If not, then don't go near it, don't act like children, a philosopher one minute, later a tax-collector, then an orator, then a treasury officer. These things don't go together. You must be one person, either good or bad. You must either cultivate your own autonomy or material possessions, either practice the craft about what's on the inside or what's on the outside. That is, play either the role of a philosopher or that of a schlub.

Chapter 30

Duties are generally measured by relationships. He is a father. So, take care of him, defer to him in all things, tolerate his abuses and beatings. 'But my father is bad.' So, does nature make you a relative of a *good* father? No, just of a father. 'But my brother wrongs me.' Then be vigilant about your own relation towards him. Do not consider what he does, but what you'll do to keep your volition in accord with nature. Since no one will harm you unless you're willing. You'll be harmed precisely when you believe you're being harmed. So, this is how you'll discover the duty of the neighbour, the citizen or the general once you're in the habit of interpreting these relationships.

Chapter 31

[1] Know that the most important part of piety towards the gods is this: to have the right beliefs about them, that they exist, and they manage the universe well and justly, and they've put you into it to obey them, and to accept all events and obey them willingly as if they're being perfected by the best intellect. This way you'll neither blame the gods nor accuse them of neglecting you.

[2] But this isn't possible unless you separate 'good' and 'bad' from the things that are *not* up to us and assign 'good' and 'bad' only to the things that *are* up to us. Because, if you really believe that any of the things not up to us are good or bad, it completely necessitates that whenever you fail to get what you want and get what you don't want, you'll blame and hate those responsible.

[3] For every animal is naturally born to do this: to flee and to shun the things that appear harmful and the causes of those harms, and to go after and to admire beneficial things and the causes of those benefits. Therefore, it's impossible for someone who supposes he's being harmed to enjoy what seems to harm him, just as it's impossible to enjoy the harmful thing itself.

[4] For this reason, a son rebukes his father whenever he fails to give his child a share of the things that seem to be good. The belief that ruling as a despot is a good thing is what made Polyneices and Eteocles enemies of each other. This is why the farmer rebukes the gods, and the sailor, and the salesman, and those who have lost their wives and children. Because wherever there's an advantage, there's piety too. So, whoever is careful about desiring and avoiding as he should, in the same way is careful about piety too.

[5] And it's always fitting to make libations, to perform sacrifices, and to offer first fruits as one's forefathers did, with purity of heart and neither carelessly, nor by rote, nor too cheaply, nor extravagantly.

Chapter 32

[1] Whenever you approach divination, remember that you don't know how it's going to turn out, but that you go to find this out from the seer. Yet if you're really

a philosopher, you go knowing what sort of thing it is. So, if it's something not up to us, then the event is necessarily neither good nor bad.

[2] Thus, don't bring desires or aversions to the seer, and don't approach him trembling but rather discerning that every outcome is indifferent and is nothing to you, and whatever sort of prophesy it is, you'll make good use of it and no one will stop this. Therefore, go to the gods with confidence as you do advisers, and then, when some advice is given to you, remember who you've taken as advisers, and whom you'll be disregarding if you disobey.

[3] But go to divination the way Socrates thought apropos, in cases in which the whole investigation pertains to the outcome, and resources for resolving what is at hand are not provided either from reason or from any other skill. So, whenever it is necessary to share the danger faced by a friend or your country, don't appeal to divination to decide whether you ought to share in the danger. For if the seer should tell you that the omens are bad, then it's clear that death, or the maiming of some part of your body, or exile is predicted. Nevertheless, reason chooses to stand by your friend even in these situations and to share the danger with your country. Consequently, consult the greater prophet, the Pythian Apollo, who threw out of his temple the man who didn't help his friend when he was being killed.

Chapter 33

[1] Right away set up a particular character and model for yourself which you'll protect both when you're by yourself and when you're with other people.

[2] Most of the time be quiet or say what needs to be said with a few words. But rarely, when the occasion calls for speaking, speak up, but not about trendy topics. Don't chatter about kickboxers, or NASCAR, or sports,[4] or where to wine and dine, the topics that always come up. But most of all, don't talk about blaming or praising or comparing people.

[3] If, then, you can, with your words change the conversation of those with you to a proper topic. But if you happen to be among unfamiliar people, keep quiet.

[4] Don't laugh a lot, at many things, or too uncontrollably.

[5] Refuse to take an oath at all, if you can, but if you can't, refuse as much as circumstances permit.

[6] Avoid gatherings of outsiders to philosophy and ordinary folk. But if the right occasion ever arises, focus your attention on never sliding into their coarse habits. That's because you know for sure that if your companion is dirty, and you

spend time with him, then you'll necessarily get dirty too, even if you started out clean.

[7] For the things concerning the body, take only the bare necessities, such as food, drink, clothing, shelter and household staff. Cut out all pretension and luxury.

[8] Concerning sex, remain as pure as you can until marriage. If you indulge, take part only in lawful acts. However, don't offend or criticize those who do have sex, and don't frequently boast that you yourself aren't sexually active.

[9] If someone reports to you that so-and-so is bad-mouthing you, don't defend yourself against the criticisms, but reply instead, 'Ah yes, indeed, he doesn't know my other faults, since if he did, these wouldn't have been the only ones he listed.'

[10] It isn't necessary to go to contests much. But if the right occasion ever arises, don't appear to be concerned about anything but yourself. This means want only the things that do happen to happen, and want only those who do win to win, because then you won't be hindered. Completely refrain from shouting and laughing at anyone or getting very excited. And after leaving don't talk a lot about what happened, except to the extent that it leads to your improvement, because conduct like that reveals that you were overwhelmed by the spectacle.

[11] Don't go to people's lectures carelessly or casually, but when you do go guard your decency and stay calm and at the same time don't be irritating.

[12] When you are about to meet someone, especially someone regarded as a big shot, ask yourself, 'What would Socrates and Zeno have done in this situation?' and you won't be at a loss for how to make use of the occasion at hand.

[13] When you go to visit someone of great power, tell yourself that you won't find him at home, that you'll be locked out, that the doors will be slammed in your face, that he'll ignore you. And if it's appropriate to go even under these circumstances, go and endure what happens and never say to yourself 'it wasn't worth it'. For this typifies the ordinary person who blames externals.

[14] In conversations with others avoid telling long stories or gabbing one-sidedly about your own deeds or exploits, because it's not as pleasant for others to hear your stories as it is for you to narrate them.

[15] Also avoid going for a laugh, because this is the way to slip into obscenity and at the same time is enough to lower your neighbours' respect for you.

[16] It's also dangerous to use profane language. So, when some swearing occurs, if the time is right, scold the one cursing. But if it's not the right time, show your disgust at his cussing by going silent, displaying your discomfort, and scowling.

Chapter 34

Whenever you get an impression of some pleasure, as with other impressions, be on guard, don't be carried away by it. Instead, let that impression wait for you and delay for a while. Then, remember two intervals of time, both the time during which you enjoy the pleasure and the time after you've enjoyed the pleasure when you'll regret it and kick yourself. Weigh against these how much you'll rejoice and be proud of yourself if you abstain. If you think that the right occasion arises to indulge in the act, be careful that its enticement, pleasure, and allure don't overpower you. Instead, weigh against the temptation how much better it is knowing that you won this victory against it.

Chapter 35

Whenever you do something that you've decided ought to be done, you should never avoid being seen doing it, even if many people are likely to assume the worst about it. Because, if what you're doing is not right, then avoid doing the deed, but if it's right, why fear those who are not right to reproach you?

Chapter 36

Just as the propositions 'It is day' and 'It is night' have truth-value when disjoined, but no truth-value conjoined, similarly selecting the larger serving is beneficial for the body, but it is not beneficial for preserving conviviality at a banquet, as one must. Therefore, whenever you eat with another person, remember not to look only for the benefit to the body of the foods being served, but also to observe respect for your host.

Chapter 37

If you undertake some role beyond your ability, you've both disgraced yourself in that one, and you've neglected a role which you would have been able to fulfil.

Chapter 38

Just as in walking you're careful not to step on a nail or sprain your ankle, likewise be careful that you also don't harm your autonomy.[5] And if we guard against this in every task, then we'll undertake each task more safely.

Chapter 39

Each individual's body is the measure of his possessions as the foot is of the shoe. Therefore, if you hold to this, then you'll preserve the measure, but if you overstep it, then eventually you'll surely fall over a cliff. Just as with the shoe too, if you exceed what the foot needs, then the shoe becomes first an embroidered pump, then a golden stiletto, then a red-soled Christian Louboutin. For once the measure is exceeded, there's no limit.

Chapter 40

As soon as women turn fourteen, they are called 'ladies' by men. That's why when they perceive that there's nothing else for them to do besides sleep with men, they begin to gussy themselves up and put all their hopes in that. Therefore, it's worth taking care to make them understand that they are honoured for nothing other than being modest and self-respecting.

Chapter 41

It's the sign of a dimwit to spend a lot of time on things concerning the body, such as exercising a lot, eating a lot, drinking a lot, defecating a lot, copulating a lot. Instead, these things are to be done incidentally, but make your top priority the mind.

Chapter 42

Whenever someone treats you badly or speaks badly of you, remember that he acts or speaks this way believing that he ought to. Therefore, it's not possible for him to follow how things appear to you, but only how they appear to him, so that if he gets it wrong, he himself is harmed in that he's the one who has been deceived. And so, because of this, if someone supposes a true conjunction is false, it's not the conjunction that is harmed, but rather the person who is being deceived. Consequently, if you start from this perspective, you'll be gentle towards the person who abuses you. This is because you will say on every occasion, 'It seemed that way to him.'

Chapter 43

Every situation has two handles, one you can carry it by and one you can't. If your brother is unjust, don't grab that handle, that he acted unjustly (because that's the handle you can't carry it by), but rather grab the other handle, that he's your brother, that you were raised together, and you'll have grabbed the handle by which you can carry it.

Chapter 44

These inferences are invalid: 'I am wealthier than you, therefore I am better than you'; 'I am more eloquent than you, therefore I am better than you.' Rather, these inferences are valid: 'I am wealthier than you, therefore my property is better than yours'; 'I am more eloquent than you, therefore my oratory is better than yours.' But in fact *you* are neither property nor oratory.

Chapter 45

Someone bathes quickly; don't say that he bathes badly, but that he bathes quickly. Someone drinks a lot of wine; don't say that he drinks badly, but that he drinks a lot. Because until you determine his judgement, how do you know whether he acts badly? Understanding this it won't happen that you receive convincing impressions of some things, but assent to others.

Chapter 46

[1] Never call yourself a philosopher nor talk much about your philosophical principles among non-philosophers, but instead act out those principles. For example, at a dinner party, don't say how one should eat, but eat as one should. So remember how Socrates in this way so completely avoided showing off that people came to him wanting him to introduce them to philosophers, and he did. That's how easily he tolerated being overlooked.

[2] And if talk arises about some philosophical principle among non-philosophers, be mostly silent, because there is a great danger that you'll immediately vomit up what you haven't digested. And when someone says to you that you know nothing, and you're not stung by it, then know that you are making a start at your task. Sheep don't bring herbage to the shepherds to show how much they've eaten, but they digest the grass internally and bear wool and milk on the outside. And so you, therefore, don't show off your philosophical principles to the non-philosophers, but the actions that come from them once digested.

Chapter 47

When you have adapted your body to frugal habits, don't boast about it. If you drink water, don't say on every occasion that you drink water. And if you ever want to train for hardship, do it for yourself and not for outsiders. Don't embrace statues, but when you're very thirsty take cold water into your mouth, and spit it out, and tell no one.

Chapter 48

[1] The non-philosopher's position and character: he never expects either help or harm from himself, but only from externals. The philosopher's position and character: he expects all help and harm from himself.

[2] The signs of the progressor: he blames no one, he praises no one, he criticizes no one, he faults no one, he never claims to be someone or to know something. When he is impeded or thwarted by something, he faults himself. And if anyone praises him, he chuckles to himself about having been praised. Whereas if anyone blames him, he doesn't defend himself. He walks around like invalids do, being careful not to move any injured part of the body before it has firmly healed.

[3] He has rid himself of all desire and has shifted his aversion to only the things contrary to nature which are up to us. He restrains his impulse towards everything. He doesn't care if he seems foolish or ignorant. In a word, he guards himself as if he were also a plotting enemy.

Chapter 49

Whenever someone takes prides in being able to understand and interpret the books of Chrysippus, say to yourself, 'If Chrysippus had not written obscurely, this person would have nothing to be proud of.' And what do I want? To gain knowledge of nature and to follow it. I seek, therefore, someone who is interpreting it, and hearing that Chrysippus does, I go to him. But I don't understand his writings. I seek, therefore, the interpreter of those writings. And thus far there's nothing about this to be proud of. But when I find the interpreter, what remains is to apply these instructions – this is the only thing to take pride in. But if I admire this act of interpretation, what have I ended up as but a scholar instead of a philosopher? The only difference, indeed, is that instead of Homer I'm interpreting Chrysippus. Instead, therefore, whenever someone says to me, 'Read me Chrysippus aloud,' I blush when I cannot display deeds that match and harmonize with his words.

Chapter 50

Whatever tasks are set before you, abide by them as if they were laws, as if it would be sacrilegious to omit them. Pay no attention to whatever someone says about you, because this no longer concerns you.

Chapter 51

[1] How much longer will you delay judging yourself worthy of the best things and continue neglecting the power of reason to discern those things? You have received the philosophical principles that you need to accept, and you've accepted them. So then what kind of teacher are you yet waiting for that you postpone improving yourself until he shows up? You're no longer a teenager, but already a grown man. If you are now a careless slacker and always making excuse after excuse and scheduling one day after another when you'll finally get a grip on yourself, without noticing it you will make no progress and end up living and dying as a non-philosopher.

[2] So then it's time to consider yourself worthy of living as a grownup and one who is making progress, and treat everything that appears best to you as an inviolable law. And if you meet with anything burdensome or pleasant or prestigious or sleazy, remember that the contest is right now and the Olympics are right here, and you can't delay any longer, and that on a single day one action destroys or saves progress.

[3] Socrates became who he was in this way, heeding nothing other than his reason in everything he faced. And though you're not yet Socrates, you owe it to yourself to live as one who wants to be like Socrates.

Chapter 52

[1] The first and most necessary subject in philosophy is the application of philosophical principles, such as 'Don't be a fraud.' The second is that of proofs, such as why it is that we ought not to be frauds. The third subject is that which confirms and articulates these proofs, such as, how is this a proof? For, what is a proof? What is inference? What is contradiction? What is truth? What is falsehood?

[2] Therefore, the third subject is necessary because of the second, and the second is necessary because of the first. But the most necessary and the one where we must linger is the first. Yet we do it backwards, because we devote time to the third subject and entirely busy ourselves with it, while we completely neglect the first. Consequently, we're frauds, but we're ready to prove that we ought not to be frauds.

Chapter 53

[1] For everything, we must keep these reminders handy:
    'Lead me, Zeus, and you too, Destiny
    to wherever I am assigned by you.
    and I will follow without hesitation. But even if I don't want to
    and in so doing become bad, I will still follow nonetheless.'

[2] 'Whoever yields gracefully to necessity is
    wise among us and understands divine matters.'

[3] 'Well, Crito, if this is what pleases the gods, let it be so.'

[4] 'Sure, Anytus and Meletus can kill me, but they cannot harm me.'

Part 4

Encheiridion Chapter Commentaries

Chapter 1

The *Encheiridion* begins with the Fundamental Divide of Epictetus's Stoicism. Epictetus believes that understanding and always remembering this division are fundamental to proper thinking, proper desiring, proper deciding, successful acting and happy living. Epictetus divides everything in the world into the things that are 'up to us' and those that are 'not up to us'. By things 'up to us' he means things that are always, completely and by their very nature ours to control. He specifies that these things are mental faculties: understanding, impulse (to act or not act), desire (to get or experience something) and aversion (i.e. desire to avoid getting or experiencing something). He characterizes this class of mental faculties or cognitive operations as acts that are *ours*, that *belong* to us. For Epictetus, these things 'up to us' make up the real us, our self or identity as human individuals. Elsewhere (at *Disc.* iii.24.3) Epictetus explains that these mental faculties 'up to us' include our beliefs, opinions, judgements, intentions and attitudes.

On the other side of the Fundamental Divide are the things 'not up to us'. This class of things includes our own body, our possessions, reputation and professional positions (jobs, careers). He characterizes these things as *not* ours, *not* truly belonging to us. To a non-Stoic it is very puzzling that Epictetus would say that his own body is not his, or that the shoes that he owns and wears, having bought them long ago, are not his. What does he mean? In 1.2 he explains the fundamental contrast between the two classes of things. The things 'up to us' are naturally, intrinsically 'free, unhindered, and unimpeded'. Consider the faculty of understanding. Epictetus means that how a person understands, thinks or conceives is up to that person and that person alone. We are each free to understand ideas, interpret events and think about things however we want. No one can hinder you from desiring x, y or z. No one can impede your aversion to, say, cooked spinach. If you dislike cooked spinach, no one can make you like it. In the sharpest possible contrast, the things 'not up to us' are 'weak, enslaved, hindered, and not yours'. Take the body. Is a human body vulnerable to illness and injury? Yes, of course it is. Our bodies are *weak*, Epictetus explains, because a virus or a disease can do terrible things to our bodies when we don't want that. Even athletes who might seem to be extremely strong can easily be physically overpowered by water (e.g. a large wave), by ice (e.g. slipping and falling), by wind (e.g. a tornado), by earth (e.g. an earthquake) or by temperature (e.g. extreme cold or heat). Even a very physically strong person can be subdued by a group of several people of average strength. Thus, the body of any human being can be hindered, held captive and enslaved by others. Anyone's physical possessions can be stolen or destroyed by fire or flood. Anyone's reputation can be damaged or even ruined by the opinions of others, whether by word of mouth or through social media. Because of these undeniable facts, Epictetus judges that the things not up to us are *not ours*. He means that, in the most fundamental sense, such things do not constitute our real selves, our true identities as persons. We can use these things to some degree, we can exert some effect on them, but ultimately, they are not ours, they are not who we are.

Why does Epictetus believe that this Fundamental Divide (FD) is so important? The answer is that he thinks that the entire quality of our lives depends on remembering the FD and being smart about it every day. If we fail to remember the FD, then we may very well mistakenly think that enslaved things, for example, our reputation, are free. That is, we may falsely believe that our reputation, which depends on what other people think about us, is free for us to control, protect and promote. If we falsely believe our bodies are free, then we will be surprised and upset whenever we suffer an injury or get ill. If we falsely believe our possessions are truly and completely ours forever, then we will be surprised and upset when one of our garments gets stained or torn. We will get upset when we lose an important flash drive. We will get upset when a rock cracks the windshield of our car. We will get angry when we discover that someone has put a long, ugly scratch into our car door. If we falsely believe our reputation is *ours* to control, then we will be disturbed when we discover that someone is ruining our reputation on social media. If we fail to remember the FD, we will be hindered (by all these things we don't and can't control), we will be disturbed (by events not going the way we want them to), and we will blame other people or other things for our unhappiness. When a strong wind breaks a large branch from a tree that falls on and crushes our car (or our leg), a non-Stoic will blame 'the gods', or the wind, or the tree, or the branch.

Stoics, in contrast, remind themselves of the FD every day. Stoics think that only their minds (understanding, beliefs, judgements, impulses, desires, aversions, intentions, attitudes) are really theirs, and their bodies, possessions and reputation are not really theirs in this fundamental sense. The benefit of remembering the FD and orienting your thinking about events accordingly is that no one will ever harass you. This is because you will recognize that what others say is up to *them*, not up to you. No one who has a bad opinion of you can force you to agree with that opinion. No one who insults you can force you to believe that that opinion is true. No one who flames you online can harm your self-esteem as long as you refuse to base your self-esteem on what others tweet about you. A disease can hinder your body because your body is fundamentally not yours. But no one can hinder what is *yours*, namely, your mind, your freedom of thought, your freedom of desire.

Epictetus reasons that if you remember and live by the FD, you will blame no one because nothing anyone does can harm your smart understanding and proper thinking. You will accuse no one because you will take complete responsibility for your own understanding, thinking and desiring. You will not judge other people to be responsible for how you use your own mind. You will not do anything involuntarily because no one will be able to coerce you that way. You will be free to pursue only what you judge to be good, right and appropriate for you. Since you identify what is truly yours as the (mental) things up to you, no one can harm these things, and so no one can harm the real you. Your body is vulnerable, yes, but your mind is free, sovereign, autonomous and invulnerable. Thus, no one can oppose your mind, so no one can be your enemy.

In 1.3 Epictetus explains that the FD holds the promise of a life free of harassment, hindrance, harm and enemies. Such a life would be great! So, in 1.4, Epictetus cautions that such a great life – the life of an accomplished Stoic – is a great achievement, and great achievements require serious commitment. Consequently, a casual effort is not enough. Rather, one must 'give up some things completely', such as getting more wealth or power. Recall that wealth and power are things 'not up to us'. If your priority is to achieve a life free of harassment, hindrance, harm and enemies, then you must work hard to train to become a Stoic. But if you distract yourself from that goal by also pursuing power and wealth, then you are not likely to get any of these many things you pursue. Epictetus declares that the life free of harassment, hindrance, harm and enemies is 'the only means of gaining freedom and happiness'. The idea is that we will be free to be happy only if we are free of worrying about things not up to us. Our happiness can only come from what is ours, and only what is up to us is really ours.

How the world presents itself to us in impressions is not up to us. But how we interpret them and manage ourselves considering those impressions is up to us. In 1.5 'impression' translates the technical philosophical term *phantasia*. In Epictetus a *phantasia* is a sensory stimulus, a memory or a thought that occurs to us. So, if we see a person walking towards us and remember that last month that person made a nasty remark about us on social media, that memory could be a 'troubling impression'. Or if we discover that the door of our car has a new, long, ugly scratch in it that could be a 'troubling impression'. Epictetus urges us to make a practice of testing every such negative, troubling impression. The first and most important standard for testing negative impressions is the FD. So, consider the remark on social media. Is it up to us (me) or not? Clearly, remarks other people post on social media are not up to me. Since the remark is not up to me, it is not mine, and so it is not mine to worry about. Therefore, the remark 'is nothing to me'. Other people will have their own opinions, and that ought never to bother me. Any trouble I experience comes only from my own opinions, beliefs, judgements, understanding, etc. Consider the scratch in the car door. Is it up to me? Clearly it is not. My car (or bicycle) is a material possession that I use as a tool. Over time, all tools suffer wear and tear. I use my car for transportation. A scratch in the door in no way hinders the car's ability to transport me, so the impression 'the scratch is ugly and bad' is 'nothing to me'. But what if the car has a flat tire and can't be driven? Well, tires are not up to me and sometimes they go flat. So, Epictetus would tell us to keep calm and replace the tire. But what if my car is wrecked in an accident? Again, apply the FD: My car, as a tool not up to me, is weak, enslaved, hindered and not mine. My car is not me. Therefore, say to the impression 'my car is wrecked' 'it is nothing to me'.

Chapter 2

Chapter 2 opens with the injunction *to remember* a line of reasoning, which Epictetus subsequently rehearses. What needs to be remembered is what follows for how we should desire and be averse, given the FD of Chapter 1. Once we have seen things clearly, what is really valuable to us should be clear. At its core, this line of reasoning comes to a recipe for how to get what you want and how to avoid disappointment. The key is to desire only the things over which you have control. Importantly, the reasoning Epictetus presents is a series of inferences stated in Stoic logical form. Not only is the *content*, that is, the premises and conclusions, of the argument in the service of Stoic theory, but its *form* is Stoic in spirit, too.

Using the tools of critical thinking and following the rules of valid inference are hallmarks of controlling what is up to us. We control our thoughts with the tools of logic, so we guard against being buffeted about by impulse or rhetoric when we think critically. The Stoics developed a system of logic that was a precursor to what is now called 'sentential' or 'propositional' logic. This logic emphasizes the logical connections between sentence complexes, particularly those with if-then or conditional logical form. The consequence, then, is that rehearsing the argument is practice at Stoic philosophy not only in *what* one reasons about, but in *how* one reasons, too. Here is a reconstruction of Epictetus's line of argument.

1. Definition: You are *averse* to something when you desire it not to happen.
2. Definition: You suffer *misfortune* when you are averse to something, and it happens (to you).
3. If you are averse to something and it is up to you, it will not happen.

First conclusion: If you are averse only to things up to you, you will never suffer misfortune.

4. Illness and death are not up to you, and they will befall you.

Second conclusion: If you are averse to illness and death, you will meet misfortune.

5. You should avoid misfortune.

Third conclusion: You should be averse only to things up to you.

It is easy to miss that this chapter is expressly argumentative. Epictetus provides an explicit case for the conclusion that our desires and aversions should be restricted to only what is up to us; the argument proceeds from the FD in Chapter 1 and the uncontroversial definitions of *aversion* and *misfortune*. The reason why the remainder of Chapter 2 must be an argument, and a tightly presented one at that, is that Epictetus is pushing an explicitly *revisionary* ethical view. Stoicism stands apart from what passes for common sense among most people – that having wealth, status and pleasures are good, desirable things. With revisionary ethical programmes, it is not simply that one must believe and act correctly, one must also regularly reason to and around these principles. Stoicism asks us to change our lives and how we think about the things we care about. So, if a significant change in how we value and live is being called for, that change must be well-reasoned, and the quality of those reasons must be evident. So, we must not only be right, but we need to *know* we are right. We must have the supporting reasons for that knowledge easy to hand. Stoicism requires a major change in our orientation. A big part of that challenge of reorienting ourselves is maintaining that new attitude and commitment. This requires not only reminders of the views but also reminders of the reasoning for those views, including reasons against Stoicism's competitors. A life among non-Stoics will produce many opportunities to forget the Stoic programme, to lose one's way.[1] The key is not simply to remember the principles, but to rehearse the reasons, see their truth and renew one's endorsements of them. The reason why pleasure and status are tempting is because we do not, when looking at them, calculate their costs; we do not see them as things that, when we desire them, expose us. In this regard, Chapters 1 and 2 of the *Encheiridion* are instantiations of a form of *ethical intellectualism* – knowing what is of value and knowing the good are central features of a good life. That is, knowingly choosing the good is itself a defining feature of the good life, and that knowledge is what in turn makes that good life stable. Stoic intellectual exercises – remembering and revisiting the reasoning behind Stoic value theory – are a means of caring for and preserving that knowledge.

Now consider an objection to Epictetus's reasoning. It might go like this: if you don't avoid death, illness, poverty and social rejection, how do you live at all? Avoiding bad health, financial ruin, social rejection and one's death seem obviously important to a human life. The other side of the coin, too, seems curious. If you don't want life, health, wealth and acceptance, then what exactly does your life look like? Is it a *life* at all? In short, how does the Stoic live?

This objection is as old as Stoicism itself. Plutarch, a critic of Stoicism who lived at roughly the same time as Epictetus, jokes that Stoic value theory is like wine that's gone sour – one can neither drink the wine nor use it as vinegar (*Stoic Self-Contradictions*, 1047). In essence, it makes the Stoic useless. The Stoics were keenly aware of and highly motivated to answer this challenge. Their answer hangs on a distinction that comes after the FD between what's up to us and what is not. Of what is not up to us, the externals, there are things that are *preferable* and things that are *dispreferable*. Thus, one may *prefer* one's life to one's death, health to illness, belonging to banishment and wealth to poverty. So, though we are to be indifferent to external things, we may prefer some to others. Call this *the Doctrine of Preferred Indifferents*. Epictetus invokes the doctrine at the close of *Ench.* 2 when he says, as opposed to *desiring* things not up to us, 'only choose and refuse, and do so gently, with discretion and casually'. The question is how to deploy this distinction. How can we follow this advice and not fall back into the problem of desire?

One way into Epictetus's closing thought of choosing and refusing externals with discretion and casually is that some externals can coincide with our virtue but can also conflict with it. To determine which is which, we must use discretion. Health, for example, can be continuous with one's virtues. For example, when you are healthy, you can be useful to your family or your neighbours. So, you should take care of your body, like a worker cares for a tool. In the *Discourses,* Epictetus analogizes attention to externals to the attention athletes have for the ball or for game pieces in their competitions. Items of game equipment are objects of care not because they are valuable in themselves, but because with them the competitors may exercise the relevant skills (*Disc.* ii.5.21). The trouble, of course, is the chance of confusing this careful attention with valuing. Here one risks sacrificing what is truly valuable, one's virtue, for things that may only be continuous with virtue. So, one may break an oath for the sake of some pleasure. Or one may intimidate a rival to angle for a promotion. Or one may cheat and steal for the sake of wealth. Moreover, one can use those external things for bad purposes, too. What can be continuous with virtue, under the wrong circumstances and with the wrong intentions, can be discontinuous with it, too. So, the idea behind the doctrine of preferred indifferents is that one *can* have money or pursue political standing or even appreciate pleasant things, but one must be attentive to whether those things, under those conditions, are continuous or discontinuous with virtue.

What is the difference, then, between preferred and dispreferred indifferents? One answer is that this distinction is a function of two things: *nature* and *context*. First, the Stoics believed that humans were made to put the world in order, to make their home in it. *Oikeiōsis* is the Greek term for that idea of making a home in the world. Humans go about doing that by (a) taking care of their bodies, (b) fostering safe environments, (c) managing resources so that they have enough to eat and do their jobs, (d) organizing themselves in ways that minimize strife and (e) creating opportunities to improve themselves and others. So, from this perspective, we can see why, given our purpose of *oikeiōsis,* health, wealth and social connection are preferred, while illness, poverty and banishment are dispreferred. We might call this the *natural default status* for these items of attention. However, context matters, and that default status can be flipped. For example, in a society in which social status depends on casual cruelty, social standing is a bad thing. Or imagine that maximizing one's health requires destroying large swaths of natural habitats. Or consider a case in which your illness keeps you out of serving in an obviously unjust war. Anyone who can make sense of someone saying, 'I'd rather be poor than participate in that scam', can see how context matters for preferred and dispreferred indifferents.

A final consideration for the doctrine of preferred and dispreferred indifferents is how Epictetus's closing injunction of *Ench.* 2 to 'gently choose and refuse' squares with what we'd called attention to at the end of *Ench.* 1, that we 'give up some things completely'. Recall that this thesis is that if you desire great goods, you must pursue only what is up to you, and you cannot also manage multiple things at a time. So, the lesson of *Ench.* 1 is to focus only on your virtue, whether you are honest, whether you are brave, whether you are kind. Those are the things up to you. But with the doctrine of preferred indifferents you can also deal with things not up to you – so, you may attend to your health, prefer to be socially connected and manage your finances. Epictetus notes in the *Discourses* that he's not Milo, the great wrestler, but he does not neglect his body; he's not Croesus, the world's richest man, but he does not neglect his property (*Disc.* i.3.37). So, how do these two views mesh? They seem to be at odds with each other. The key is to remember how the doctrine of preferred indifferents, with its attention to context, views the question of preference or dispreference through the lens of the FD. Yes, our defaults are set on preferring health, wealth and social connection, but that is only because they are, in the natural course of living, continuous with virtue. Yet that does not make them *part* of virtue, since they can be pursued in ways that conflict with virtue. The FD attunes us to how the context question with preferred indifferents matters.

Chapter 3

This chapter, which is a greatly condensed summary of *Discourses* iii.24.84–95, builds on the emphasis on the FD made in *Ench.* 1 and 2. Here Epictetus applies the lesson of the FD to what we can call the Fondness Bond. Human beings naturally and inevitably grow fond of certain people, things and activities. We grow emotionally attached to persons, places and things. This emotional attachment bonds our fondness to such things. The lesson Epictetus imparts here is that it is wise to understand and remember the kind of thing it is to which we have bonded our fondness.

The first example Epictetus considers is a mug. A mug is a useful receptacle for holding beverages. Repeated use of a particular mug over months or years may lead us to grow particularly fond of it. Such a familiar, well-used mug may become our favourite beverage-holder. If this happens, and we have become especially fond of this mug, then Epictetus urges us to recognize this fondness bond and admit it out loud. To say 'I'm fond of a mug' is an explicit confession that I am emotionally attached to a particular kind of physical object. What is the nature of a mug? It is made of ceramic material. Ceramic material can stain over time and develop cracks. Ceramic material can *break*. No mug is indestructible. No mug lasts forever. So, to admit to oneself that one is fond of a beverage container that is subject to damage and destruction wisely prepares oneself to accept the inevitability of that favourite mug getting stained, cracked and ultimately destroyed. The advantage of ordinary beverage containers is that they can easily be replaced when they break. But the key lesson with the mug is that its fragility is not a thing that is up to us. Thus, acceptance of the mug's fragility can and ought to inform our choice to forge a bond of fondness to it. It is okay to let yourself grow fond of a mug, but never forget what mugs are and what happens to them – this is Epictetus's point about 'the most trivial of things' like mugs. If your Fondness Bond with the mug traps you into being disturbed when it breaks, then you have forgotten what mugs are and what inevitably happens to them, and that is foolish.

We can easily think of other objects we consider to be less trivial than mugs which entice us, or are useful, or which we are fond of. Imagine a favourite jacket or pair of shoes. Epictetus's advice would be to say, 'I'm fond of a jacket', or 'I'm fond of a pair of shoes'. Just like the mug, pieces of clothing are subject to wear and tear, stains, and ultimately do not last forever. What about a smart phone, a laptop computer or an automobile? These things too suffer damage and can break. No physical possessions are indestructible. The same is true of living things, like a houseplant or a goldfish. Epictetus would urge us to understand and remember that all living things are subject to illness, injury and death. This includes the cats, dogs and other companion animals we live with. It's okay to forge a Fondness Bond with them, but we can and ought to remember that they get sick, grow old and die, like all mortal beings. Their vulnerabilities and mortality are not things that are up to us. What is up to us is the ability to combine our fondness for them with our wise understanding that they can't and won't always be healthy, well and alive.

The logic of Epictetus's advice in this chapter can be reconstructed as a simple syllogism:

1. I am fond of a mug or a jacket or a car or a cat.
2. Mugs/jackets/cars/cats are fragile, impermanent things not up to us; they are subject to damage/illness/injury/death/destruction.

3. Therefore, this thing I am fond of will sooner or later suffer damage/illness/injury/death/destruction.

The most important things not up to us are our fellow human beings. Kissing our loved ones is a great way to express our fondness of them. But Epictetus urges us to remember that the same syllogism true of mugs and rugs applies to the people we hug.

1. I kiss (love) my child or spouse, a human being.
2. All human beings are fragile and mortal, subject to illness, injury and death.
3. Therefore, this child or spouse that I kiss (love) is fragile and mortal, subject to illness, injury and death.

If we rehearse this syllogism every time we kiss our loved ones, reminding ourselves of their humanity, fragility, vulnerability and mortality, Epictetus thinks we can avoid being disturbed when they die.

Is he right? The love we have for our family members and close friends is so strong, one could argue, that the Fondness Bond we have with them precludes the kind of emotional detachment necessary to avoid emotional disturbance and grief when the loved one dies. Sure, it's easy to remember that mugs break, so it's easy to avoid disturbance when your favourite mug breaks. But people are in a completely different category, aren't they? Mugs and clothes and phones don't love you back as people do.

Epictetus knows that human beings are very special to us. His point here is a simple, hard truth – namely, that the lives of human beings are just as much not up to us as the fragility of mugs, skateboards, smart phones and dogs. His advice is not that we shouldn't love our children and spouses. After all, he notes that we kiss our child and spouse; we don't kiss our mugs! His reminder is simply that we can and ought to love human beings *as* human beings, as mortals subject to illness, injury and death. Our children and spouses are not our permanent possessions. They are not ours at all (see also *Ench.* 7, 11, 14 and 15). But how we love them and whether and how we think about their fragilities are up to us. Epictetus recognizes that developing this Stoic outlook takes a lot of practice. That is why he tells us to 'start with the most trivial of things' like crockery. We must practise being wise about the Fondness Bond towards computers and automobiles before we can work our way up to companion animals. Ultimately, however, Epictetus believes we will live saner, wiser, happier lives once we learn to love people (and companion animals) while accepting that they won't always be around. Loving mortals wisely makes sense to a Stoic. Getting disturbed when the inevitable happens doesn't.[2]

Chapter 4

This chapter's exercise is a riff on a commonplace for Epictetus's audience that may not be appreciated by contemporary audiences. So, it's important to see this chapter of the *Encheiridion* in its Roman context, primarily because it targets an ambivalence Romans felt about the baths. On the one hand, the baths are a site of civilization. They are places of commerce, connection and community. The baths are public works, and they are places where one engages in public life. One gets clean, for sure, as that is their primary function. But one also sees one's neighbours, tastes an interesting cake and hears about the latest political intrigue. On the other hand, for as much as they are sites of civilization, the baths are also sites for rather uncivilized behaviour. Baths are loud, smelly, disorderly places. In *Letter* 56 to Lucilius, Seneca notes that his lodgings are above a bathhouse. Whatever convenience it pays for being a short walk down to it, he must put up with people shouting, advertising wares, pickpockets and raucous splashing in dirty water. For any Roman, these two thoughts about the baths would be familiar ones. So, a trip to the baths would need to be kept in perspective, especially as you prepare to go. You might be anticipating the warmth of the water, maybe the smell of a tasty dish being prepared nearby, and a pleasant conversation in the cooling room. But let's face facts – the water is often tepid and dirty, the food smells off, and the conversation is more like a lecture from a nincompoop who might also be trying to steal your wallet. There's our fantasy of the baths, and then there's the baths.

The Stoics held that a source of suffering for humans is thwarted desire. We want and expect something, but those desires go unmet. Also, when we picture a task, we too often paint too rosy a picture of how it will go. Epictetus's Roman audience pictures a perfect trip to the baths. We twenty-first-century denizens might picture a flawless morning commute, a well-timed and restful vacation, a socially positive dinner party. But what do we get? Gridlock, with motorists cutting us off. Vacations with travel complications that leave us feeling more worn out. Dinner parties with guests so rude that we almost resolve never to invite guests over ever again. What upsets us is the disconnect between our inappropriately rosy expectations and what reality serves up.

The key is to manage ourselves in these circumstances with exercises of appropriate goal setting. What we should really desire are the things up to us. We should be indifferent to how the externals go. If what we want when we go to a public pool is to have a quiet time in some perfectly refreshing water, we make whether our desires are met or not dependent on things not up to us.

In recognizing that pools are places of splashing, pickpockets and inconsistent water quality, we can reorient our desires – to go to a pool and in the process maintain our equanimity. The same goes for our commutes, vacations and dinner parties; desiring and expecting them to go well is a double curse when they don't – not only are we wrong, but we are disappointed.

Preparing mentally for any of our enterprises is part of the job of Stoic living guided by the FD. Think through what the job is, prepare for the trials that come with it, have a clear view of what challenges are likely. Even rehearsing how one will handle those challenges will help. So, Epictetus instructs us to anticipate what happens at public pools and be ready just to get on with our swim. We can do the same for our commutes – picture being cut off, and practise saying, 'Geez, they must be in a big hurry to have to drive like that', and then let it go. For our vacations, imagine your luggage springing open and dumping your underwear on the highway – you can now say that the skid marks have a funny story. The same goes for the dinner parties. Imagine the food coming out badly and your friend gets very drunk – you can say that at least the booze was a hit. Being ready to re-frame the circumstances is the important skill to acquire, and this requires anticipation and practice.

The philosopher-emperor Marcus Aurelius had an exercise he would perform upon waking. To prepare for his day as the emperor or Rome, he had to remind himself that he would have to deal with people who would be malicious, conniving and selfish. He was not in control of whether they were that way or not, but he could control whether he was honest and helpful in response. Preparing himself for these encounters, he would remind himself that 'none of them can hurt me' (*Med.* ii.1), because he was properly managing his desires and aversions with this exercise of anticipation. This thought generalizes to all our endeavours. Consequently, there is a sense that these anticipatory exercises make the Stoic *invulnerable*; Stoics cannot be harmed when they manage their desires and inclinations appropriately, when they properly anticipate and prepare for what they will face. But it's worth noting that many Stoics held that there are limits to these exercises of anticipation. Seneca, for example, notes that keeping one's calm in challenging moments can be helped if one is reasonably well-rested and not too hungry (*On Anger* iii.9.4–5). He further warns that if, as you do the anticipatory exercise, you find that even then you're losing your temper, you are not ready to face the circumstances. So, for example, if, when you do the exercise of imagining getting cut off during the commute, instead of remaining calm, you *pre-anger* yourself, that's evidence that you should start taking the bus. Seneca's example is that there are people who and experiences that just bug us more than others, and if you can't see yourself staying calm around them, it's best just to avoid them (*On Anger* iii.8.4).

As we saw in *Ench.* 3's exercise of the mug, building from small things to bigger things, Stoics saw that with practice, you increase your powers of control over your inclinations and emotions. The exercise of the baths is a kind of intermediate exercise of Stoic self-control. It is part of the day-to-day business of being a Roman, being part of a city, participating in the community. It takes some time to master it, and it requires that you work to *maintain* that control as you gain it. There are many things that can go wrong, so it's likely that something will happen that hadn't been anticipated. Perhaps an unruly dog gets loose, or a famous general visits and onlookers clog the entrance, so you can't even bathe. The hope is that in preparing for what has occurred, that exercise has prepared you to respond appropriately to a wide range of eventualities.

The Stoic is disburdened of worries and concerns about things she cannot control. The Stoic can plan but does not fret. The Stoic can prepare for loss but does not stand in the way of appreciating what she has when she has it. The Stoic will not be distracted by the things beyond her volition; she will judiciously choose the things continuous with it.

Chapter 5

Disturbance arises from failing to heed the FD between what is up to us and what isn't. 'Things' include the huge class of objects, people, events, facts, circumstances and everything else that is not up to us. In sharp contrast, our *judgements* about those things are very much up to us. Here Epictetus returns to the experience of being disturbed by death discussed in *Ench.* 3. Recall that in *Ench.* 3, Epictetus explains how to train oneself to avoid being disturbed by the death of one's child or spouse. Here he explains that death, as a thing that is not up to us, is not what disturbs us. In itself, death is nothing terrible. Why? Because of this syllogism in the form of *modus tollens*:

1. If death is terrible, then Socrates would have judged death to be terrible.
2. Socrates did not judge death to be terrible.
3. Therefore, death is not terrible.

Epictetus and other Stoics believed that Socrates was wise, so he appeals to Socrates as an authority about death and about what is and is not terrible. Given his wisdom, if death were terrible, then Socrates would have correctly judged it to be so. This is why Epictetus regards the first premise of this argument to be true.

Epictetus's confidence about the truth of the second premise derives from the portrayal of Socrates in Plato's dialogues, especially *Apology*, *Crito* and *Phaedo*. At *Apology* 40c–41c, for example, Socrates argues that death is nothing bad but may actually be a blessing. Socrates shows no fear of death in any Platonic dialogue. Thus, the second premise is obvious to Epictetus.

Like Socrates, Epictetus is convinced not only that the belief that death is terrible is false, but that this false belief scares (i.e. disturbs) people into doing terrible things. This is why he insists that the *false judgement* that death is terrible is actually what is terrible.

Is the authoritative judgement of Socrates the only reason Epictetus has for believing that death is not terrible? No. That all living things must die Stoics regard as a fact of nature, and they deny that nature is terrible. Rather, Epictetus sees birth, ageing and death as phases of an inevitable, endless cycle of nature. He believes that this circle of life, the rhythm of day and night, the change of the seasons and the like, are evidence that nature is orderly, balanced, comprehensible to reason, and all things considered good. Death is a part of life, and both are organic processes necessary for nature to function. Living things feed on dead things every moment of every day. So, life is impossible without death. For these reasons Epictetus judges death to be natural and necessary and neither terrible nor disturbing.

Moreover, Epictetus thinks that to judge that death is terrible is to judge contrary to nature. The Stoics argued that 'living in agreement with nature' is the goal of life and the path to happiness. Epictetus observes that unhappiness comes from feeling hampered, annoyed or disturbed. But these unhappy feelings come from us, specifically from our judging that a situation we are in or something we experience is negative, bad or terrible. People who lack an education in Stoicism suffer from the false belief that *others* hamper, annoy and disturb them. Epictetus denies that our minds are puppets controlled by others. No one can force you to make a judgement that you refuse to make. How we think, how we judge and what we believe are up to us; they are not up to others.

This chapter concludes with three tiers of progress in Stoic education. The first tier is characterized by the uneducated person. The person uneducated in Stoic philosophy is oblivious to the FD. As a result, this person will often desire things that are not up to her, and when she fails to get them, she will be frustrated and sad. She will often want what is not up to her to be up to her. Plagued by such a foolish desire, she will do badly. Not realizing that her own false beliefs and foolish desires cause her unhappiness, she will blame others for her self-imposed misery.

The second tier is shown by the person who is making progress living as a Stoic. This person has taken the FD to heart and practises focusing her desires and aversions on what is up to her while taking in stride what is not up to her. This 'progressor' works at keeping her judgements in agreement with nature. That means she works at keeping her judgements in agreement with reason. She recognizes that she is fully responsible for her own judgements. Moreover, she knows that her happiness or misery depends entirely on whether her judgements are wise and harmonize with nature, or foolish and conflict with nature. The progressor knows that if she feels hampered, annoyed or disturbed, it is because of her own foolish, false judgements. Thus, if she is doing badly, she is to blame for her own failure to judge rightly. Her self-criticism spurs her to work on self-correction.

The third and final tier of progress is characterized by the 'fully educated person'. Having upheld Socrates as a philosophical authority earlier in this chapter, Epictetus may have him in mind as such a fully educated person. In any case, we can think of this philosophically advanced student as the Stoic sage. After years of practice performing Stoic exercises, this individual has finally fully achieved total mastery of Stoic education. This amounts to achieving completely consistent, true beliefs and consistently making exclusively rational judgements and wise choices. The fully educated sage lives in complete agreement with nature, reason and virtue. Consequently, the sage is faultless. The sage is hampered by nothing, annoyed by no one, never frustrated, never disturbed, never angry, never afraid and never sad. With impregnable peace of mind, the sage blames no one.

Do such perfect people exist? For Epictetus the sage functions as a prescriptive ideal, a target for real people to aim at. While none of us are likely to ever reach this ideal, even after decades of hard work at the end of our lives, Stoics believe that the closer we approach this goal, the better persons we will be and the happier our lives will go for us.

Chapter 6

The refrain of the FD is at work here again as it is applied to the notion of excellence. Epictetus insists that a person is justified in taking pride in something only if that thing is truly *hers*. What is truly yours are the things which permanently belong to you and are always, completely, by their very nature up to you. As we saw in *Ench.* 1, our bodies and our material possessions are not up to us. The animals we keep, including, say, a horse, are external to us and so are not ours in this fundamental sense. Sure, we may own them in a legal sense. We may possess them in the sense that we routinely keep them in our home. But we do not have anything like the control over them that we do over our mental activities, our understanding, impulses, desires, aversions, beliefs, judgements, decisions, intentions and the like. Our horse, dog or cat can be stolen from us in a way that our minds cannot be.

The beauty of our horse (or dog or cat) belongs to the animal herself; it does not belong to us. The beauty of the horse is an excellence of the *horse*. But for the legal owner of the horse to boast about owning a beautiful horse is to foolishly take pride in the horse's excellence. Is ownership of a horse, or of any material possession, an excellence of a human being? No. Why? Epictetus explains: any material possession can deteriorate; break; be stolen, lost or destroyed. Ownership of property is nothing to boast about, according to Stoics. To lose a material possession is not to lose a part of *oneself*. To lose a horse or a bicycle or a cell phone or expensive jewellery constitutes no harm to oneself.

If physical beauty is a good (excellence) of the horse, then is physical beauty a good of a human being? No, Epictetus argues. Our good lies in the use of impressions. Impressions (*phantasiai*) include not only the sensory stimuli we experience through seeing, hearing, touching, smelling and tasting but also thoughts and memories we can formulate into sentences. An example would be to look at the horse and frame the thought 'This horse is beautiful'. If the horse truly is beautiful, then the impression 'This horse is beautiful' would be true. If we assent to this impression (statement), then we are affirming a true belief. To affirm true beliefs accords with nature. That is, to affirm true beliefs is to believe in accord with our nature as rational beings pursuing the truth.

Suppose that the beautiful horse is owned by someone else. In that case, we might form the impression 'I should own this horse'. Stoics would tell us to reject this kind of tempting impression, because it is a mistake to think that happiness comes from owning possessions. If I were to make the mistake of assenting to the impression 'I should own this horse', then doing so could easily invite another harmful impression like 'I will (try to) steal this horse'. If I assent to that impression, then I would certainly be using my impression contrary to nature. Why? Because I would thereby transform myself from a law-abiding citizen and trustworthy neighbour into a thief bent on wronging the owner of the horse, harming the social fabric of my community and flouting the laws of human society in general.

Using impressions in accord with nature means responding to situations with reason, intelligence and recognition that what is good for us is to be consistently good persons. Good people are truthful, honest, reliable, helpful, peaceful, just, courageous, temperate and wise. Good people are virtuous. So, when we use our impressions to form only true beliefs, we are acting in accord with our rational nature. When we use our impressions to act reliably, helpfully, generously and justly, we are acting in accord with our social, communal nature. Using our impressions virtuously is a true good. This is a good that really belongs to us since no one can take it from us. This is a good we can rightly take pride in, in contrast to having one pretty horse or fifty pretty horses in a stable. Horses can run away. Stables can burn down. Our use of impressions always, completely belongs to us.

Chapter 7

Imagine you are a sailor on a sea voyage. The captain directs the ship into a port and allows the mariners to go on shore leave. With the captain's permission, you decide to disembark and go ashore to collect some food to eat. But you realize that this shore leave is *temporary*. You recognize that, as a sailor, your role requires you to obey the captain, including the captain's command to return to the ship. You also realize that a sailor's job is to work on the ship and not sit snacking below deck. Thus, you recognize that once you're back onboard, you can't be carrying snacks. You'll need your hands free to work. Sheep, in contrast to mindful mariners, refuse to stop grazing. Sheep won't listen to commands, so they have to be tied up and forced back onboard. Sailors, unlike sheep, know their duties and obey their superior, the captain.

Epictetus uses this simile to describe life as like a sea voyage with God (Zeus) captaining the ship. While on the voyage that is your life, Captain Zeus may, for a finite length of time, give you a spouse and a child. But Epictetus emphasizes the importance of remembering your own mortality and the time of your death is ultimately up to Zeus (Nature), not up to you. That is what he means when he says, 'you must keep your mind on the ship and continue to look back at it in case the captain calls'. Captain Zeus can 'recall you to the ship' at any time. When this happens, you must be ready to 'discard all the food' and willingly return to the ship without delay. The idea seems to be that when it is your time to die, you can't take anyone (or anything) with you. Your only choices are (a) to accept your death calmly and rationally, or (b) to ignore the fact of your inevitable mortality and to foolishly, in futility, try to postpone that inevitability.

The idea that when you die 'you can't take it with you' is clear enough. Whether the 'it' is wealth, a favourite possession or a human being you love, we all know that we can't take anything or anyone with us when we die. Also clear is Epictetus's advice that if you live long enough to grow old, then you (ought to) know that your death will come sooner rather than later. So, the wise, old sailor on shore leave will know not to stray far from the ship. When the recall comes, the wise, old sailor will accept death without surprise or resistance. Resistance is futile, foolish and what we expect of sheep. Wise sailors know better than to cause themselves unnecessary grief by trying to postpone what cannot be postponed. Instead, wise seafarers accept that the end of their lives is ultimately not up to them; it is up to God (Zeus/Nature).

Comparing being alive to being on shore leave where you can collect Nature's gift of food (or loved ones) makes sense. It's harder to understand how not existing is meant to be compared with being onboard the ship. Epictetus describes the voyage as underway *prior* to the ship anchoring. He also seems to imply that the voyage will resume *after* the shore leave when the sailor returns to the ship. Is the sailor thought to be immortal? Does only the sailor's *body* die when returning from shore leave, while the sailor's *soul* continues on when back onboard the ship with Zeus?

Epictetus makes it clear in the *Discourses* that, like other Stoics, he does not believe that the consciousness of a person survives bodily death. Stoics are physicalists (*Disc.* iv.7.15). They believe that human bodies and souls are both physical, otherwise they could not causally interact. Epictetus believes that Nature recycles all constituents of animals and plants when they die, refashioning their parts and recombining them with other elements to create new living things. Thus, personal identity ends with death, Epictetus believes, but the physical constituents that make up people remain. Consequently, he does not consider disembodied souls possible. Instead, we may imagine the onboard existence of the 'seafarer' to represent this loose set of non-living physical constituents either *before* they unite to become the psychosomatic whole that is a living, conscious human being or *after* such an animate union dissolves. Epictetus does not believe in reincarnation.

It's fair to say that the idea of the onboard 'existence' of the seafarer strains the sense of this simile. But what is clear is in this simile Epictetus emphasizes that the human condition is powerfully, profoundly conditioned by Nature. None of us chooses to be born, or to be born mortal, or to be born human or to be born with any of our congenital features. Thus, we don't choose to go on this sea voyage. We discover that we are already on this voyage – the voyage of life. We learn the rules of the voyage while onboard the ship. The most important rule is that Captain Zeus is in command. Zeus decided that we would be onboard, that we would be born and alive. If Captain Zeus decides to drop anchor for a shore leave, then we are given that opportunity. We don't bring it about. What is up to us is whether to go ashore or not. Once ashore, it is up to us whether to collect a shellfish or a vegetable. If so, 'there's no trouble with that'. Moreover, it is up to us to remember that collecting such gifts in no way entitles us to extend our shore leave as long as we want. We have no power to live indefinitely. Our mortality, and ultimately the time we die, is up to Captain Zeus. (Suicide must be *attempted* because it is ultimately not up to us to guarantee success when voluntarily trying to die.) We have no power and no authority to disobey Zeus's orders. If we try to resist Zeus's command, we will be 'tied up' and forced to accept it. The ship of Earth will reclaim us, body and soul, and recycle our parts into new passengers.

Does Epictetus think that one's spouse and child are comparable to grocery items like a shellfish and a vegetable? Yes and no. Yes, other people are like food items and interesting shells insofar as neither are up to us. In time, food will spoil, and interesting shells will break even though we don't want them to. In time, our loved ones will die, even though we don't want them to. But human persons matter to us far more than some food or a curious shell. We love persons in ways we don't begin to love snacks. As we saw in *Ench.* 3, we kiss our child or our spouse to express our love for them. We don't kiss our mug. Here in *Ench.* 7, if life gives us a spouse and a child instead of a shellfish and a vegetable, when it is time for us to die, we may kiss a spouse and child goodbye, but we must let them go all the same. Epictetus knows that saying our last goodbye to a loved one is far more meaningful and far more difficult than leaving some groceries behind. But Epictetus underscores that the circumstances of our life-voyage are ultimately not ours to control. The wise course is to accept gifts, whether food or family, along the voyage while always remembering that the voyage must end for each of us. Just as we didn't get to choose when our voyage began, we won't get to choose when it ends. But what we can do is, when that voyage ends, accept it wisely and calmly. The wise seafarer knows that the voyage *itself* is the most fundamental gift from Zeus (God/Nature). Learning this wisdom will make it a good voyage.

Chapter 8

Chiasmus is a nifty ancient rhetorical device for making a call for a significant change in view. The device is simply switching out the order of two contrasting terms. Its most famous instance in ancient philosophy is Socrates' question to

Euthyphro, 'Is the pious the pious because the gods love it, or do the gods love it because it is pious?' The contrast of the phrasing can be quite powerful, as U.S. President John F. Kennedy famously challenged his fellow Americans with the injunction, 'Ask not what your country can do for you; ask what you can do for your country.' The power of chiasmatic phrases lies in the quickness of the contrast presented with the order of the terms flipped. So, when Epictetus formulates his famous chiasmatic turn of phrase in *Ench.* 8, the contrast is one with how we must change our desires and how they function:

> Don't seek to have things happen *as you want* but want the things to happen *as they do.*

The change in perspective is that of modifying how one thinks one's desires should relate to the world. The attitude to be corrected is that the world should be brought to fit with our desires. Desire, on this non-Stoic view, makes a list of things that we want to happen, things we want to have. And then with this list, people run around trying to gain as many of these things as they can – a comely partner, a big house, status, varied pleasures, healthy and admirable children, a long life, and so on. The lesson of the FD, however, is that desiring in this fashion is sure to lead to many disappointments and anxieties. To start, you can't always get what you want. Even when one temporarily has those things one wants, there are disappointments and anxieties. Those with exceedingly comely partners suddenly find themselves jealous for no reason; having a big house means having many bills and worrying about the roof; having many pleasures makes one anxious about being bored with the next ones; and children, no matter how healthy or virtuous, are objects of high anxiety for parents. Even if you have it all, you'll feel incomplete and you'll worry about losing it. That's assuming you can have it all. For one thing, you can't have it all forever. Then there's the overwhelming likelihood that you won't have it all. Desiring in this way is a guarantee for frustration, and, again, if we really do think these things are valuable, they tempt us to sacrifice our virtue and character for them.

The lesson of the FD, that matters of externals are not up to us, so they are things we should be indifferent towards, now instructs how we should direct our desires. People who do not live guided by that insight make themselves miserable. Two people can do all the same things in pursuit of externals, and one can get so many of these things while the other doesn't. Consider what not getting what you desire does to you, especially when someone no more (or even less) deserving than you gets so many nice things. One is lucky, the other not. Recall the times when you've been the unlucky one and someone else gets the promotion or the award. Recall your resentment, and how it made things worse for you in the midst of it. Not only did you not have the nice thing, so you had that disappointment, but wanting that good thing and seeing it in another's possession added to and sharpened that loss. Then there is what resentment does. Recall those times of resentment and how you were motivated in light of it. You wanted to see your rival fail, lose the thing, show himself to be inadequate to care for it. The lesson is that valuing that way not only makes us vulnerable to those losses, but after those losses it makes us shallow and now more deeply dependent on others for our fulfilment. But this time our desires are caught up with wishing for their downfall.

A better route for desire is one indexed to what is available. Instead of showing up with a list of things we want from reality, we should see what reality has made available to us and choose within those bounds. The problem, of course, with this kind of advice is that it is just hard to take, especially if one's accustomed to desiring in the other fashion. The biggest problem here is that our desires are not under our voluntary control. It is not psychologically possible to just tell yourself to stop desiring something, as anyone whose love has been unrequited can attest. Even though it would be better not to love some person, you too often find that you just can't stop. But here, Stoic training gives us a kind of indirect control over our desires. We can re-frame what is available and what is worth wanting. This requires maintaining the appropriate attitude towards objects of potential desire at all times. Even in times when things are going as we like, we must moderate our attachments in the right way. In fact, it is important to prepare for losses especially during the times when we get what we'd preferred. Recall that in *Ench.* 3, the Stoic practitioner prepares for the reality of a child's or spouse's death or absence, but the practitioner doesn't just do that when they are apart. She does that when they are together, enjoying each other's company. So, you must do so with all things in your life.

The Stoic tradition offers a few images to make sense of this mindset. A particularly powerful image is of the sports fan. One kind of sports fan cheers for one team or another; this fan lives and dies with their team's successes and losses. Another kind of fan appreciates the game as it is played; this fan wants the results to be as they are. The first kind of fan will not only face many disappointments but will often be reduced to cheering for unsporting play by their team. (Who has not appreciated a tactical foul by your team's favourite enforcer?) But notice that this has not only made this fan into someone vulnerable to the vicissitudes of a team's season, but the fan also now develops vicious attitudes, all because of a game. The second kind of fan, the one who desires that things go as they do, will never be disappointed by match results; she will never be tempted to approve unsporting play. Marcus Aurelius notes that he learned early on not to support one team or another but to cheer for the matches to come out as they do (*Med.* i.2).

Another image is that of being a soldier being given an assignment. Soldiers given tough assignments that are difficult to carry out are paid compliments by these appointments. Being given a challenging post is an honour generals give to their charges – it is a way of saying that the soldier can be trusted with dangerous missions. This is what soldiers train for, and this, by analogy, is what Stoics train for, too. Seneca famously analogizes a hard turn of fate with being given a difficult post as a soldier – he knows this gives him an occasion to display his mettle (*On Providence* 5.4).

The result is being able to *go with the flow* of life. The concept of a 'good flow of life' is central to Stoic ethics. One lives a life in accord with what is, with the will of the gods, with fate. Life in accord with it all is a life of peace, even when what reality serves up is challenges. On the soldier analogy from earlier, it helps to supplement the account of reality with the commitment that there are gods and providential plans, and they determine reality's course. So, as the soldier takes orders from a trusted general, we take our assignments from Fate and the decisions of good and all-knowing gods. Stoic theology certainly plays a role here in justifying how we can want things to go as they do, because directing one's desires to accord with a greater plan is a reasonable route only if we have reason to hold that the plan is a good one. The crucial insight here is to see the Stoics are committed to a theology according to which we are elements of something much larger than ourselves, an organic whole and complete system with a point and a purpose. Thus, desiring for things to go as they do allows us to play a harmonious role in the cosmic story.

Can the Stoic desire in this way without Stoic theology? Is it possible for a person to take the attitude that everything (even what seems bad) is all going according to plan, if she doesn't believe in a good and wise god or gods doing the planning? It's worth pausing to note that Stoicism, and particularly Epictetus's statement of it in the *Encheiridion*, is a systematic philosophical view – ethics, logic, physics and theology are supposed to come as a package. The primary way to understand each is to see it from the perspective of the others. This makes for some very developed and mature philosophical work, to be sure. But it also makes the philosophical insights in one area vulnerable to problems in another. So, if Stoic physics depends on Stoic logic, then a problem with the Stoic theory of valid inference can problematize the Stoic views of the basic workings of the universe. For sure, in this case, believing in the gods and their wise Providence makes it easier to bear the burdens of challenging experiences. But is it the only way to do so? We (the authors) do not believe so since it seems that the FD and the reasoning around it does not require an explicit theology. One can deploy the FD as an atheist or as one who might believe the gods are less than perfect. We will return to this broader question of the relationship between all the parts of the Stoic system with high points in the ethics in Part 5, in the form of the System Problem.

Chapter 9

Recall that the FD is a distinction between what is up to us and what is not. The primary feature comprising this distinction is that of whether willing something one way or the other is sufficient to make it so. On the one hand, how we direct our attention and whether we try to do what's right is up to us. On the other hand, whether we are sick or whether we are wealthy is not. The reason why this is important is that how we identify who and what we are is at stake. If we identify ourselves with our bodies, our possessions, or our prestige, not only are we vulnerable to harm, but we are not under our own control. If who you are depends on your health, a virus can control your life. If who you are is your bank account, a recession can decimate you. If who you are is your social status, a rumour can ruin you.

The following exercise can be useful in making this distinction and its consequences clearer. Think of people whom you admire and ask yourself what makes them admirable. If the list of features is possessions, status or looks, the next question you should ask is whether you admire the person or whether you envy their luck. If the list is of their virtues, their fortitude, honesty, earnestness, you don't have to ask whether you envy their luck. Because these people display those traits in the face of luck. That is, they are best displayed when their luck is bad. Who they are is revealed in the vicissitudes.

When Epictetus notes that 'illness hampers the body, but not volition, unless volition wants it to', he is observing that our self-conceptions vary, so if we identify with things that are not up to us, we make a particular kind of error. This error is one that amounts to acceding to being impeded. We participate in our enslavement to externals. It is because we accept and endorse the thoughts that we are our possessions, our appearances, or our status that damage to those things becomes damage to us.

Illness and disability hamper the body. They are impediments to its being able to do things. A sick body cannot perform at its optimal levels. A body with damaged limbs cannot do the things that bodies with undamaged limbs can do. Those bodies with illness and damaged limbs are impeded, and no amount of wishing otherwise can change those facts. We can extend this to many more externals. An empty bank account, a low social status, being ugly – those are all impediments of sorts to what we might wish to do in the world. The contrast, again, is with the things that are not impeded, the things comprising our volition. Socrates was famously ugly, poor and worked as a stonemason. But he was also courageous, honest and insightful. It was for those reasons that his compatriots rightly admired him. Epictetus was banished from Rome, poor and lame. His leg may well have been maimed from an incident when he was a child. As the story goes, one of his early masters punished Epictetus for a misdeed by twisting his leg. Epictetus warned him that any more twisting would break the leg, and when the master torqued the leg once again, it broke. Epictetus calmly said, 'I told you it would break.' Yet a poor, exiled, former slave with a badly damaged leg can be an exemplar of wisdom, peace and insight. Our bad luck cannot harm us unless we let it.

Epictetus is his own example in explaining that the Stoics' notion of the self is primarily *agential*. Traditionally ethical subjects can be viewed as either *agents* (those who decide and act) or *patients* (those who are acted upon and whom decisions affect). The crucial thing about the Stoic conception of self is that all instances of being a moral patient involve identifying with the relevant objects of being a patient. So, if *you* are harmed by illness, it is because you have identified with your body. If *you* are harmed by a recession, it is because you have identified who you are with your finances. It is the upstream identification that makes you the patient in these cases. Being a moral patient over whom others can exercise power results from you thinking you are the things over which they wield control. You choose to allow externals to control you. Thus, illness can't hamper volition, as Epictetus says, 'unless volition wants it to'.

What we must rekindle is this insight that our *choice* makes us into subjects that are acted upon and can be controlled by others and by chance. In essence, the strategy is to break the spell of externals. Illness brings pain, making our bodies function not as we wish. A damaged limb makes many tasks harder, and this often looms large for us. It's important that Epictetus's audience should have known that he himself had such a disability. Yet he is not defeated by it. The same goes for wealth and status. Notice the way these things cast shadows over our minds when we are tied up with them. When our status, for example, is endangered or when illness impedes our daily routine, it seems that it is all we can think about. The key, again, is to break the spell of these externals. The first step is to recognize our own role in allowing them to possess us. That is how they have our power: we've given it to them. The first step, then, is to shut off that initial assent.

Consequently, we must say both to ourselves and to the occurrences that they are only external hindrances. They don't harm our capacities to choose, strive and think correctly. Once we have said this in the face of these appearances, we begin to weaken their spells over us. At its core, it's entirely an intellectual task to achieve, since all the problems derive from the false premise that we are those externals. If we stay on guard against accepting that false premise, we prevent many of the downstream errors. But notice that this exercise is required in *piecemeal fashion*. Accepting the FD and being clear about the agential conception of the Stoic self are not enough to correct these errors. Instead, being clear about these things is the first step to making this correction in our lives. We must be constantly working on each judgement. We change our lives not by changing a philosophical point of theory, but rather by consistently bringing that insight to bear in our everyday judgements.

Chapter 10

An inaccurate picture of the Stoic is as a disconnected, unfeeling person. The Stoic, as this picture goes, stands aloof and feels no pain or pleasure. But this picture is incorrect. Stoics take part in their lives, they feel, and they understand the attraction of pleasures and the consequences of pain. *Ench.* 10 highlights this for Stoic practitioners. Stoicism will not make pleasure less tempting or pain less painful; rather, it will give practitioners the capacity to respond appropriately to these experiences.

Epictetus clearly holds that the bodies of others can be beautiful to the point of driving us to distraction. Whether it be in the too-long look at the jogger or in the flirtatious exchange with a customer at the store, our minds can too easily race with the possibilities. Dwelling on these possibilities tempts us with sexual desire. We halt this by redirecting our attention to what we should be doing, whether that be our jobs at the time, future matters to attend to or by simply maintaining Stoic equanimity. The same goes for pains and insults. Our bodies are vulnerable, and pain is the result of damage to a body. But do we expect anything different? We are born with bodies, so pain is a part of our story that cannot be erased. Yet we can manage how to respond to the pains in our stories. The same goes for insults. We are social creatures. Social creatures, being what they are, can get sideways with each other. Did we expect anything different? Social creatures live from their own perspectives and try to coordinate them, which yields plenty of friction. That's just what it is to be one of us. Seeing it from this perspective allows us to see it all in proper context. Perhaps there's a misunderstanding. Maybe this person is deeply confused about what's really valuable. Maybe the insult is a correct criticism. With misunderstandings, you can clarify. With those who are wrong about the good, why does their opinion hurt you? Can you teach them, perhaps? If not, then move on. And if those who insult you are right about you, you should take it as useful feedback and work on being better. In none of these cases have you really been harmed.

The structure of Epictetus's account here is that of opposing every impression that may unsettle us with a particular virtue, and each virtue is rooted in seeing the impression in the right light. So, the impression of beautiful bodies has the danger of sexual temptation, and this is answered by the virtue of self-control, rooted in our capacity to redirect our attention to more appropriate avenues. Impressions of pain can drive us to distraction and despair, and this is answered by the virtue of endurance rooted in seeing pain as a natural consequence of having a vulnerable body that must make its way in a world of hazards. Insults can drive us to vengeful behaviour but recognizing that social creatures have messy relations allows us to answer those inclinations with the virtue of patience. The ability to handle these impressions has correlate virtues that themselves are grounded by having the right beliefs and habits of mind. The primary root of virtue, according to Stoic ethical intellectualism, is judging correctly when presented with these impressions. Correct judgement prevents us from being carried away by pain, lust or resentment.

The key to virtues of self-control, endurance and patience is that we break the spell that impressions cast over us. Or better, the spell we cast over ourselves when presented with each experience. To repeat, the issue is not about the Stoic not having these experiences, but what the Stoic thinks upon having them and how she acts upon those thoughts. The training is purely cognitive, but it seems that it must be taken up in piecemeal fashion. The Stoic can grasp the principles but activating them as parts of her reasoning in the ebb-and-flow of life requires constant practice. One of the most famous Stoic exercises of breaking the spell of impressions is in Marcus Aurelius's *Meditations.* He says that for every impression, we must see it as it really is, so that we may break its spell and thereby exercise our virtues. Marcus records his exercise as follows: 'Seeing roasted meats and fancy dishes in front of you, realize: this is a dead fish, a dead bird, a dead pig. Or this noble vintage of wine: grape juice. Purple robes of royalty: wool soaked in shellfish blood. Making love: rubbing a piece of gut, a convulsion, expelled mucus' (*Med.* vi.13). Reframing our impressions keeps us safe from being carried away by them. We can say 'no thanks' to them, because, by understanding them as impressions, we make it so that they are not in charge of us. None of this is to deny that there are beautiful bodies of others, hurtful words directed your way, and painful moments when your body shudders. Stoicism denies not the existence of these phenomena, but that we must be beholden to them. The means to breaking the hold they have on our minds is to believe correctly about them, to see them the right way. When we understand our lives and our experiences properly, we live within those lives and with those experiences properly.

Chapter 11

As seen in earlier chapters, Epictetus emphasizes that how we speak about events strongly determines how we think about them, and in turn how they affect us. Here he offers instruction about the right way to speak and think about every person and every object once present in our lives.

As explained in the comments on *Ench.* 7, Epictetus believes that not only is our very life given to us by God (Zeus/Nature), but every blessing that comes our way during our lives is equally a gift from God (Zeus/Nature). In *Ench.* 7 he emphasized that when it is our time to die, we must be ready to accept it and to let go of all those gifts. In this chapter Epictetus further clarifies the status of these gifts. These gifts do not become our permanent possessions. Why? Because, as the FD teaches, not even our bodies are always, completely, by their very nature up to us. Our bodies, possessions, reputations and other people are all not up to us. So, whenever any of these things or persons come into our lives, they do so as temporary loans. Since not even our lives are permanent, we should not for a second be fooled into believing that any object, position, job or person we enjoy for a time is permanently owned by us.

So, imagine that you are gifted by Nature, that is, God, a spouse. Spouses are mortal. Mortals die. Therefore, your spouse will die. The mortality of your spouse is not up to you. You have no power to make your spouse live forever, or even for ninety years. Nature gives and nature takes back. Nature gave you a spouse. Therefore, Nature will also take back your spouse. Consequently, your spouse was only *yours* in the sense that, for a finite period, she or he was married to you. She or he was never your possession, never owned by you. You cannot lose what does not actually belong to you. So, upon death your spouse is not lost. Rather, death returns your spouse to the same Nature that gave birth to that person and then saw fit to bring her or him into your life. According to Epictetus, just as all living things spring from Nature, so too all organisms ultimately belong to Nature. That is why all things born inevitably return to Nature in the end.

Nature might give you a child. It would be more accurate to say that Nature brings a child into your life rather than that Nature has given you a child that becomes *yours*, your possession to keep permanently. Children are just as mortal as adults. So, you know your child will someday die, either after or before you do. In *Ench.* 3 Epictetus urged us to remind ourselves often that our child is a mortal human being that must eventually die. He taught us to remember the mortality of the people we kiss. So, if our child dies before we do, we must never say we lost it, but rather that we returned it to its ontological mother, Mother Nature. Speaking correctly about the child's death helps you think correctly about it too.

Property can be owned in a legal sense, but property remains something not up to you, not part of you. Thus, property can never be yours in an ontological sense. And just as property can be given to (or purchased by) you, that property can also be taken from you. The property can be taken from you by a person, an animal, legal authorities, fire, storm or flood. In the deeper ontological sense, property is given and taken back by Nature. So, Epictetus urges us never to say that our property was taken away, because that implies that it was ours in the first place, that it really belonged to us in an ontological sense. This is false. Property is given to us by Nature and will inevitably be returned to Nature. To complain that the person who took your property is a bad person misses the point. Nature is the real Giver of property, possessions and people in your life. If a thief was not the cause of your property being returned to the cosmos, it still would have been returned by some other cause—a fire, a flood, a tornado, erosion, decay or accidental breakage (like the mug in *Ench.* 3). Epictetus thinks we need not and should not worry about how the cosmos reclaims what it lends us.

What should we think about the things that Nature lends us? The simile here is that life is like being a guest at a hotel. We are not permanent residents in the cosmos. We are only travellers passing through who stay for a short time. As long as Nature lends us things, we ought to act responsibly by taking care of these things like good custodians. We don't own the persons and possessions that come our way for a finite time in life. But we are responsible for taking good care of them as long as they are loaned to us. Bad hotel guests try to take the towels with them when they check out. To try to steal from the cosmos that way would make *us* bad. Good guests care conscientiously for what is loaned to them and return what was never theirs to keep to the hotel's proprietor, God, Zeus. Epictetus implies that when we return the items loaned to us, we ought also to give our thanks to the proprietor. Why express gratitude? Because we were never entitled to these things. None of them were promised to us prior to our arrival. None were guaranteed. All were gifts for us to enjoy only for a limited time. For Epictetus, these gifts are evidence of the divine Providence steering the world. But gifts from providential Nature arrive on Nature's schedule, not when we would like to place orders for them through room service.

A final point to note is this. A hasty reading of *Ench.* 11 may suggest that Epictetus is advising the Stoic practitioner only about how to speak to himself. This would miss the fact that this chapter presents a conversation between Epictetus, the teacher, and a conversational partner, a male student. Whenever a student out loud misdescribes as a *loss* a *return* of a person or thing to the Giver that is Nature, he spouts a false belief to whomever is within earshot. Anyone who hears this untruth will be susceptible to accepting it as true and passing it along. Non-Stoics parrot this talk of losses among themselves constantly. The student of Stoicism must deliberately resist their habitual, wrong-headed talk. For his own sake, the Stoic must not speak the wrong way to keep from thinking the wrong way. But he must also not speak the wrong way around others for their sake. Otherwise, he will almost certainly reinforce their false, un-Stoic beliefs. Correct speech is thus a responsibility the Stoic in training must be ever vigilant about, both for his own benefit and that of everyone listening to him.

Chapter 12

Ench. 11 ends with an analogy, that the things in our possession for now are like items in a hotel – they are nice, but when it is time to go, we may leave them. They were never really *ours* to begin with; they belonged to Zeus, the cosmic innkeeper. *Ench.* 12 is an answer to an objection that arises in light of the attitude towards externals forwarded by the analogy. The objection runs that if we are not keenly concerned and caught up with our property and our relations, we will end up being bad caretakers of them. Call this the *Ruin Problem* for Stoicism. It is different from the lazy syllogism problem for Stoicism because the lazy syllogism is the question of whether the Stoics can live at all, but the Ruin Problem is whether Stoic value theory stands in the way of the life that the Stoics say one can nevertheless live. The Stoics allow that we can have possessions, spouses and children, households, careers and reputations. Stoicism does not ask us to forego these things, but rather to be good caretakers of them. But, as the ruin objection goes, how can we be good caretakers of these things unless we see our own well-being caught up with the well-being of these externals? We will return to the Ruin Problem in Part 5 as a major objection to Stoicism, but here we will review Epictetus's answer to a specific version of the challenge.

It is easy to see the Ruin Problem posed for the management of wealth. The challenge to Epictetus is that Stoic value theory makes for bad economics. But Epictetus's response is another economic observation: *nothing comes for free.* What the person who obsesses over every penny has overlooked is that a non-monetary price is paid in exchange for the spotless credit record, the price of placidity. Consider the person who never gets ripped off – what must he do to ensure that he never overpays for anything? Consider the person whose schooling is entirely for the sake of getting the job that will make the most money – what interesting and enriching things must she pass by for the sake of an education that is not valuable to her for its own sake, but for the sake of money that will come later? And consider money itself. It is not valuable in itself, but in what we can exchange it for. This life of managing and accumulating wealth may be successful, in that one may have many things, but one has forgotten what it all is for in the process of accumulating it all – to be happy. So again, nothing comes for free.

Thus, Epictetus asks us to consider the alternative, namely, the Stoic who can take the attitude that the wealth, like so many things temporarily in our possession, is returned. The Stoic who does not insist on getting the best (or even a particularly good) deal can refuse to be angered by the high prices at the market or that a neighbour makes more money than he does. This is the price of equanimity, the Stoic says.

Epictetus also invokes our employees and servants, or in a Roman context, slaves. Owning other human beings was a stark but everyday reality for Romans, as it was for most ancient civilizations. Epictetus's students and his readership were likely of a class who would own slaves. So, practical advice as to how to be a good person extended to how to be a decent slave owner. This fact seems uniquely trenchant with Epictetus in particular, since he himself had once been a slave, but was freed by his owner, Epaphroditus. Perhaps Epictetus's advice to slave-owners is seasoned by his own experience as a slave, or it is only a Stoic's general perspective. But it is worth pausing for a moment to note the conflict we hear in our own ears with the idea of advice as to how to be a decent slave owner.

Surely our own answer would be to say, 'Here is how to be a decent slave owner: release your slaves and encourage other slave owners to do the same.' Given that Epictetus regularly uses the metaphor of the slave as being a bad position to be in, for example, as a slave to a desire or being enslaved by depending on status, surely the fact that there are actual slaves was a matter for moral consideration.

The traditional Stoic view of slavery was that it was contrary to nature, but it nevertheless was an everyday reality. Seneca, for example, held that slavery was a failure to recognize the humanity in another, but he nevertheless owned slaves (*Ep.* 47.13). In his *Discourses*, too, Epictetus recognizes slavery as an institution that is contrary to human dignity (*Disc.* i.13.4), but he never calls for his students or readers to release their slaves or to change the polity to outlaw it. Instead, he highlights two things about the institution of slavery that can be clarified with Stoic value theory. The first is that the fact that one is a slave or not is an external; it is not something up to us. There are, however, many things that are still up to us, even when enslaved. In fact, one of Epictetus's insights is that there are ways to maintain one's dignity even when one has been put into a position that potentially affronts one's dignity. One can refuse, one can resist, one can try to highlight, even if just for oneself, the absurdity of the arrangement. Stoic value theory still can recognize the slave to be free in the minimal sense of being able to interpret and respond to the world. Though Stoicism does not abolish slavery in its Roman context, it still provides the tools for those enslaved to hold on to the things that make freedom worthwhile.

The second insight of Stoic value theory is the effects slavery has on the masters, and here we return to the reasoning at the end of this chapter. If it is part of Stoic value theory that slaves are not truly under the master's control, then Stoic theory predicts that the slaves will regularly not do what they have been bidden. If a master is not prepared for non-compliant slaves, he will react with anger. Punishments, degradations, attempts to break their will are temptations for too many masters. And so an unprepared master is upended, with his own well-being and placidity now determined by the behaviour of his servants. The master who is irate over a spilled cup of wine is one who has lost the relevant control of his life. But the master who understands that slaves must work to protect their dignity in the midst of this arrangement, the master who knows that not all tasks will be done perfectly, is the master who will not be overruled by the behaviour of the slaves. And he will be a more tolerant master.

Still, we must admit that the advice is morally lacking. A more complete criticism of the institution of slavery seems more ethically urgent than that of how to involve oneself in the institution with minimal decency. Seen from the perspective of the question of how to manage one's place in a society replete with unjust institutions, we can see Epictetus as less a radical revolutionary and more a conservative looking to mitigate harm on all sides.

Recall that the challenge of *Encheiridion* 12 is to answer the *Ruin Problem* for Stoicism, the challenge that the Stoic, in adopting that value theory, would be *worse* at the life that the Stoics hold we can live. The Stoic will be bad with money, not able to be a stern master to slaves, unwilling to cheat and connive a way to the top, too detached to be invested in the jobs that need to be done. The reply is that all of these enterprises involve a trade-off: if your well-being depends on the results, all things have a price. The price of wealth is that one must be on constant guard against being cheated; the price of totally compliant servants is that one must be the kind of master that would punish them severely. For these externals, then, one must pay with one's character and peace of mind. That is an unacceptable price to pay.

Chapter 13

Encheiridion chapters 12 and 13 both begin with the conditional phrase, 'If you want to make progress … ' The Stoic concept of progress is worth clarifying. As we noted in our commentary on *Ench.* 1, an early paradox of Stoic value theory was that the Stoics divided the world between those who were wise (the *sophoi*, or *sapientes*) and those who were unlearned and mad (the *idiōtês*, or *insani*). In effect, the value theory was that there were really only two classes of people, and not being wise was like being under water – it did not matter how far under the surface one is, since one cannot breathe in any case. The category of the progressor is one that is designed to be a subdivision of those not wise – there are those who are working on their capacity for wisdom, those who are actively improving and then there are those who are not. Of those not progressing, they may be so because of their allegiance to a competing philosophical school (Aristotelian and Epicurean programmes put one on a trajectory Stoics thought particularly unwise) or they may not be interested in philosophy at all. Either way, those who belong to this class of the unwise do not have familiarity with the philosophical insights that can help them. The key insight behind the idea of progressors is that though they are not wise, they see a path for fixing themselves. They are taking steps towards wisdom. What they need are two things: instruction in the good, so that they may know it, and practice in doing what's right, so that they may not only do it but do it without struggle or effort. Real virtue comes naturally, and this requires not only that we know what to do, but also that we've made it second nature.

The path of this practice, as we'd seen from *Ench.* 3 with the exercise of the mug and from *Ench.* 12 with the exercise of spilled oil, is to move from smaller things to bigger things. Of course, from the Stoic perspective, all of these things should seem small, but Epictetus's recommendation is in the voice of those attached to externals. We start with a broken mug, some spilled oil or a little wine stolen. These are small errors, and they do not feel costly. And then we move to larger things – a servant being disobedient, or an expensive piece of property broken or lost. Stoic progressors master not only the right perspective on these things, but they make the right reaction to them second nature as they work up the gradient of magnitude. They train themselves to keep their cool, to not let things get to them. Eventually, the progressor can take these exercises to the greatest things, one's spouse or children, and eventually to one's own life. But the important part of this progressor's practice is to resist the power that others and their opinions, illness, poverty and even the prospects of death have over us. Progressors, in mastering each of these levels, learn a lesson both about the things and about themselves. It is part of a genuine human life to have possessions and connections to others, to give and take orders, to have interests, to have a spouse and children. Humans, as humans, do those things – we are social, active beings that interact with each other and the world. But those things do not, even in our being caught up with them, have to have power over us. They can have power over us, but only if we decide to allow them to. But we don't have to give that power to those externals.

Given that externals are not up to us and given that one pays a very high price of one's character in order to have consistent success with them, Epictetus proposes an important exercise for progressors when it comes to reputation. Consider those who have a stellar reputation for being wealthy or for being well dressed, or for being good-looking, or having a vaunted position. Think of all they sacrifice in order to maintain those various status positions. Either those people are amazingly lucky, or they have shirked many other duties to have this possession. The wealthy are either lucky or they have exploited the poor. The good-looking are either lucky or they have shirked their responsibilities to others to exercise, diet and primp so that they may look the way they do. Those in vaunted positions are either lucky or they've scrambled over the backs of so many others to get their offices. Either way, with any of them the result is not quite so praiseworthy. They had to make pursuing those externals more important than pursuing virtue.

So, now consider how you should, if you appear to others for having a reputation for being well-dressed, or for having an admirable position, suspect something about yourself. You and your actions are not exempt from the universal patterns of human actions. Being virtuous is a full-time job, and it is the job of primary importance, since virtue is the only good. So if it starts seeming to others that you are important (in the sense that the unlearned would think it's worth pursuing), you should be worried that you've lost the path. This is the feedback that you may have been distracted from your primary job.

Recall that progressors will be able to not let spilled oil, an imperfect deal or a bad photo of them on social media bother them. As middle age arrives, the progressor will work to accept wrinkles, hair loss and a belly. Who would expect anything else from an ageing body? Professionally, others will scramble past the progressor, obsessed with climbing the ladder of status. Our progressor will work to accept that others will rush forward to hoard resources. But because progressors are not yet wise, they need some feedback on their progress. And it turns out that there are few perfectly wise around to give them that feedback. Epictetus has his school, and he does it for his pupils. But what do we do if we do not have an Epictetus in our lives, only his book? It turns out that, even with a shortage of wise people in our lives, we have resources for feedback – it is in others, and the unlearned in particular, that we see a resource. Feedback from the unlearned is useful. However, there is an important qualifier to how the opinions of others are relevant to how one should assess oneself. The opinions of the wise, for sure, can be seen as good feedback. So, how do the opinions of the unlearned function as good feedback? Recall that status is an external, so it is something that the wise treat as matters of indifference. But the unlearned and unwise value status. So their judgements are reverse images of what the judgements of the wise are. In essence, one should seek to be praised by the wise because they are right about the good, and one should expect to be rejected by the unlearned because they are wrong about the good. And when the unlearned praise you and think you are good, that is actually feedback that you are not pursuing the good, but rather what those who are wrong value. So, instead of taking the regard of others as a reason to be proud of oneself, their regard is in fact a marker that one has not been doing one's primary job of pursuing virtue.

The reasoning, then, is that since a progressor's primary job is attending to and cultivating her virtue, one making progress will not have a strong track record with externals – wealth, looks, status, and so on. And since progressors are not yet wise, they may not be good at keeping track of how well they have been attending to their virtue or to externals irrelevant to virtue. But uneducated others keep good tabs on the latter, and so praise from them is feedback that one has actually been attending disproportionately to externals, at the expense of one's virtue. Praise and esteem of the unwise are a negative profile of virtue.

Imagine a progressor, convinced that she has been working consistently on her virtues of honesty and fair dealing. But she is praised for being a shrewd businessperson. She should be alarmed by this – such praise ought to shatter her illusion of progress. Or consider a progressor who has been working on being present for others in need or for being reliable for his family. But he is consistently praised for how well-dressed and good-looking he is. He should take this as an alarm that he has actually neglected his duties in pursuit of his vanity.

The exercise of reputation, all told, has two moving parts. The first is one that might be called *the burden of virtue*, namely that if one is really working on one's virtue, one will not have a positive reputation with the unlearned, because one will not have prioritized being excellent at the things they value. We might say that a negative reputation here is positive feedback. The second part of the exercise of reputation is how to interpret positive reputation, and again, it is that a positive reputation is negative feedback. Being good at what the unlearned value means that one has neglected one's primary job of being good at what the wise value.

A final puzzle emerges from this insight, and it is of a piece with the problems of the lazy syllogism and the problem of Stoic ruin. Simply, it is whether a Stoic can perform the duties of being an involved person in the world. Recall that the end of *Ench.* 2 has Epictetus recommend that we approach taking care of externals 'casually', as this is a way for Stoics to manage their relations with preferred and dispreferred indifferents. Alternately, at the end of this chapter, Epictetus argues that taking care of virtue 'entirely necessitates neglecting' externals. The question is whether those two perspectives are consistent. The first seems to run that virtue can be the job of first importance, but one can pursue preferred indifferents casually. The second seems to preclude that kind of attention, even if it is casual. This is, we think an instance of a persistent tension in Stoicism between the tradition's impulse, on the one hand, to encourage active, social, familial and political lives of practitioners, and on the other hand, its impulse to promote a very stark value theory of managing and living in light of only what is up to you. Call these two impulses those of the *social Stoics* and the *hard Stoics* respectively.

The social impulse of Stoicism is that the Stoic will endeavour to be an active part of a community, striving to contribute, be reliable and be an exemplar. And so, the social Stoic will prefer having a family, being healthy, having wealth, being well-thought-of and having some status to not having those things. This way, they can do their duties more effectively and be part of the natural human order. The hard impulse of Stoicism is that virtue does not require any success in any of these endeavours, so the good life does not require it either. In fact, from the hard Stoic perspective, caring for those things, even on the level of preference, risks being lured off the path of virtue.

On their face, these two impulses are inconsistent. But there is a path to their consistency, and it comes from the shifting perspectives a progressor must manage when pursuing virtue. If externals are useful in the exercise of virtue, as good tools are useful in performing some job, one must care for the tools, but not for their own sake. One cares for them so that one's job can be done well. If the tools and their care begin to stand in the way of doing the job, one has erred with one's task. The same goes for the two perspectives. The sociable perspective is the one that one takes on when enacting one's virtues: one cares for oneself and one's interests as a human must, but one does so in order for one to enact one's human virtues effectively. A parent will give a child love, a gardener will tend to plants and think of how to make them flourish, a citizen will participate in deliberations on how to build a better city. They all participate, and they work on themselves so that they may play their roles well. But fate does not make all our paths straight, and challenges will arise. The key to these challenges is for the Stoic to remember that the primary job is maintaining one's overall virtue, not managing one external thing. The Stoic and the non-Stoic may both be wealthy. The Stoic possesses the wealth, but the non-Stoic is possessed by her wealth. This difference is revealed only when one must choose between wealth and virtue, and it is here that the hard attitude is clearest, but it has its purchase only because the softer sociable view impelled the Stoic to participate in social life to begin with.

Chapter 14

In this chapter Epictetus picks up the discussion of making progress in becoming wise addressed explicitly in *Ench.* 12 and 13. This theme was also implicit in Chapter 11 where he advised how not to speak and think about loss and the wisdom of handling blessings like guests behave at a hotel. Chapter 14 contrasts fools with those progressing towards wisdom. Fools are a kind of slave. Those progressing towards wisdom want to be free.

Epictetus begins this chapter by returning to the theme of human mortality repeated in *Ench.* 3, 5, 7 and 11. Wanting your children, spouse or friends to live forever is a foolish desire. Why? Because, as the FD made clear in Chapter 1, the mortality of human beings is not something up to you. 'Fools want things which are not up to them to *be* up to them.' Fools want to abolish the facts that constitute reality established by God (Zeus/Nature) and replace them with a fantasy of how they wish reality to be. This is impossible. To desire the impossible is foolish. Indeed, to desire the impossible is crazy.

Fools also 'want what belongs to others to be theirs'. This picks up on the lesson of acting like a good guest at a hotel in *Ench.* 11. Epictetus again emphasizes the importance of clearly distinguishing what is truly yours from what is not, the lesson of the FD. Wanting to have what belongs to others is the desire of a thief. Hence, thieves desire the impossible. Therefore, thieves are fools too. To illustrate this idea, the example is wanting your servant not to slip up. Nobody is perfect. Everyone has flaws. To err is human. Consequently, to want your servant to never err is to want your human servant to be a perfect superhuman. This desire is moronic. Human beings have shortcomings. Human shortcomings are vices. So, wanting your servant (or your employee, or anyone you have hired to do any kind of work for you) to be free of vices is to fail to grasp what human beings are. Instead of entertaining stupid desires like changing other people into flawless superbeings, what counts as a wise desire? Answer: desiring the possible. It is possible for you to get your desires in order. You are free to limit your desires to things that are up to you to bring about. Thus, Epictetus believes that the wise focus on doing the possible whereas fools trip themselves up by desiring the impossible.

The advice given in Chapter 4 is to limit your desires to things within your power to achieve, for example, desiring to visit the pool ready to be splashed rather than desiring not to be splashed when visiting the pool. Here in Chapter 14 Epictetus draws a general principle from his analysis of desire: 'Each person's master is the one who has power over what the person wants or doesn't want.' The idea is this. Who controls the things you desire? Who has the power to grant your wishes? If someone else has the power to satisfy or frustrate your desires, then that person is the master of your desires. But, if you are the master of your own desires, then you have the power to get what you want and avoid what you don't want. You have the power to secure what you want and remove what you don't want. Self-mastery is the path to freedom.

How does this principle of self-mastery apply to dealing with people who work for you? Well, instead of wanting to eliminate the mistakes that others make, focus instead on your own mistakes. It is a mistake to desire what is not up to you. So, desire instead to improve yourself. Self-improvement is up to you. Weeding out your foolish desires is up to you. Instead of desiring your worker not to err, desire to keep calm whenever others err. Instead of wanting your friends to live forever, desire to appreciate your friends while they live. Don't take them for granted. Cherish your friends, spouse and children *now* and remind yourself that they won't always be around. Moreover, accept that human mortality is not a terrible thing because to be mortal is part of being human. Thus, accept how human beings actually are instead of wanting them to be what they aren't and can't be. Do what you can to make yourself a better person – that is a goal worth desiring to achieve. Self-improvement and self-mastery are not only possible goals, they are in fact virtuous goals! Want virtue for yourself. Don't worry about the vices of others. Work to get rid of your own vices. If you limit your desires to what is up to you to get, then you can attain self-mastery. But if you desire anything that is up to others to give or take away, then you enslave yourself to them. Fools enslave themselves to others by desiring what others control. The wise are free because they have mastered themselves.[3] Mastering yourself requires mastering your desires. Desiring only what is up to you to get makes you the master of your desires. The right kind of desiring sets the wise free. Fools are slaves because they are mastered by their own desires for things belonging to others. Thieves want what belongs to others. The wise, in contrast, cherish what is theirs and what can't be taken from them: their own true beliefs and proper desires.

Chapter 15

The analogy of the banquet is a handy refrain in the *Encheiridion* which returns in *Ench.* 25. Along with the analogies of the play and the games, the banquet is an organizing image for Epictetus's picture of Stoic life. The banquet analogy differs from that of the play and the games, as they apply to your actions and your view of yourself as a participant in the world. The banquet metaphor bears on how to relate to your desires and relationships.

To begin, understanding what it is to act like one is at a dinner party is in order. First, one is a guest, and there is a host who determines what is served and when. One's role as a guest at a dinner party, then, is to appreciate what has been served and accept it when it comes at one's appointed time. A bad dinner guest requests things not at the table, demands items out of order of their service, complains about portions and critiques their preparation. Etiquette and basic table manners dictate that one express thanks for being invited, take one's appropriate portions and allow the plates to pass without holding them up. Others have plates to fill, too, and one takes short turns while others wait.

In addition, some others will receive larger portions of delicious dishes than you; a good guest can cope with this. At the end of the meal, one expresses thanks for the invitation, compliments a dish or the wine and leaves on time. The good dinner guest is, on this analogy with the banquet, a model for how one, as a progressor, should relate to one's desires. On the analogy, Zeus, as the host of the banquet, has prepared many dishes, and they come around at their appointed times. A spouse, a child, a promotion and wealth are all on the menu. But there is no guarantee that those dishes will come your way. Recall that in *Ench.* 8 Epictetus, with his famous chiasmatic phrase, urged us to desire things to be as they are, not for things to be as we desire them. By analogy, so it is with the banquet: desire what has been served, not what has not been served. So, as Epictetus puts it, 'do not project your desire towards it, but wait until it is at hand'.

Dining appropriately is a way of showing that one is justly a welcome guest, and so desiring and appreciating appropriately at Zeus's banquet show that one is worthy of dining with the gods. A common Stoic line of thought is that, in achieving virtue and the kind of placidity it provides, the Stoic becomes like a god. Kinship with the divine is a promise of the trajectory of Stoic progress.

There is a further level of progress for Stoics, that of coming to the banquet but declining the dishes. Epictetus invokes Heraclitus and Diogenes as exempla of this level. Heraclitus lived in the Temple of Artemis at Ephesus. He viewed the world as a place of impermanence, flux and strife. But he held that a deep logic functions behind this buzzing blooming confusion – the *logos*, Zeus's plan. 'Thunderbolt steers all', as he quipped enigmatically. The lesson for Stoics from Heraclitus was that there was one permanent thing in this world of transience – the *logos*, a rational and divine plan regulating the changes, and the objective of a good life is to live in harmony with that plan and principle. This required that we view many of our attachments and values, those we took on before we became Stoics, as blights we took on as sleepwalkers which we forego for deeper truths.

Diogenes's significance for the Stoics, and Epictetus especially, is that he stands as the exemplar of what we've called the *hard* Stoic impulses: spurning what is external, not merely being indifferent to it, but outright rejecting it. As we introduced him in Part 1, Diogenes was famous for being a critic of city life, confronting many for their false sophistication. He offered, instead, a 'shortcut to virtue', in practising a form of independence (*autarkeia*). He slept in a wine barrel and begged for food. His only possessions were a cloak, a sack and a walking stick. The cup he used to own he threw away when he saw a young child drinking with cupped hands. He strove to need little and want less.

When visited by Alexander the Great, Alexander stood before him and offered Diogenes anything he wanted. Diogenes said he only wanted Alexander to stand out of his sun.

Epictetus's invocation of the exempla of hard Stoics is important since it is another benchmark for progressors, and it extends our distinction between *hard* and *sociable* Stoicism. There are two kinds of guests Epictetus sketches for the banquet: a *sociable* Stoic guest and a *hard* Stoic guest. The sociable Stoic comes for the food, engages appropriately, takes her share when it comes, is appreciative of what's been offered and then leaves on time. The hard Stoic comes not for the food, but only for the company – to be with the host – and spurns all the other parts of the dinner party. On the one hand, sociable Stoics, given the analogy, participate in the human drama around them. They have spouses and children, they have wealth and status, they participate in their polity and have preferences for how things will go. The key for them is that they bear the right relation to these things that fate serves up. The hard Stoics, on the other hand, maintain a distance between themselves and those offerings of fate. They refuse to have families, wealth, possessions and even civic alliances. In this they are unencumbered, free as Diogenes the Cynic aspired to be. Their only objective is to be, as Diogenes famously said, 'friends of the gods'.

When Epictetus says that those who do not partake of the dishes 'not only dine with the gods but also rule alongside them', his insight is that hard Stoics take on the perspective of the divine, even as they are human. Humans live from the first-person perspective. Everything is *I, me, mine* and sometimes humans can extend it in the plural, so *We, us, ours,* as anyone who's married or who takes on the perspective of a team or city can attest. This is how one values, and sociable Stoicism is about managing this natural human perspective. But hard Stoicism is about foregoing one's desires, and in so doing, one takes on a wider perspective. For Heraclitus, from the perspective of the *logos,* all things are one (Fragment B 50), and all the variety of human laws are nourished by the one divine law (Fragment B 114). Diogenes, too, held that once one has renounced individual affiliations, one will no longer be a citizen of any particular state, but a citizen of the world (a *cosmopolitan,* in the true sense) (DL vi.63). From this perspective, the will of the Stoic practitioner is at one with the will of the gods, the will of fate. And so, they rule together.

There are two connected puzzles that arise from our interpretation of this chapter. The first is with the analogy with the hard Stoics as being at the feast but not partaking. The second is with what the relationship is between sociable and hard Stoicism. The first puzzle is relatively simple. It is simply that if one declines the dishes at the feast, how does one *dine* with the gods? If one declines the dishes, there is simply nothing to dine on. But here, it's best to be clear what it is to dine with the gods as gods. The gods, as gods, have no needs. They are free, and they do not feel the need to partake in the blessings they give to mortals. Dining with the gods, then, is declining all the dishes as things one not only does not need but one has no desire for. Sociable Stoicism, by contrast, allows and even encourages our partaking, as a human at Zeus's banquet should. The hard Stoic, however, like Heraclitus and Diogenes, attends Zeus's banquet as a god would. And so the hard Stoic declines the dishes.

The solution to the first puzzle required that there be a significant difference between hard and sociable Stoicism. The sociable Stoics participate in human life, but they maintain the right relationship with all the things in that life. The hard Stoic spurns those things. Earlier, in our comment on *Ench.* 3, we said the two inclinations of Epictetus's programme are dialectically related as perspectives *within* and *on* human life and all activities therein. And the practising Stoic can switch back-and-forth between these two perspectives, depending on their relationship with the activities. One is a sociable Stoic when in the midst of things – Stoic invulnerability allows one to do one's appointed job, despite the difficulties or pains. And one is a hard Stoic when the normal pathways of that life are broken – a spouse dies, one is left without a state, all seems lost. But our dialectical approach does not quite work so well with Epictetus's account here. The hard Stoicism here is not a temporary attitude one takes when faced with significant challenges external to the life of the sociable Stoic, but rather a fully different form of life. The sociable Stoic, again, has a spouse, children, possessions and a position within the state. The hard Stoic has no family, no possessions and lives without the burdens of citizenship. Epictetus says that this kind of Stoic *rules* with the gods. There are two levels of Stoic progress: the sociable Stoic is at the lower, and the hard Stoic is at the higher. What, then, is the relationship between these two inclinations?

The modest solution here is to maintain our dialectical approach. Diogenes and Heraclitus had to be hard Stoics because fate gave them paths without family, wealth or roles as citizens. So, they became consistent and persistent practitioners of the hard Stoic approach. Spurning those dishes was an endorsement of what fate had served up for them. And so, we can still see the hard Stoic inclination as emergent from sociable Stoicism, and our exemplars for this attitude are those who, by Providence, had to practise that approach their whole lives.

The more ambitious solution is to say that those two Stoicisms are divided for two different paths progressors will take. Most progressors will be given paths commensurate with the rest of humanity, so families, possessions, and civic duties and the vicissitudes of gain and loss that come with that life. Sociable Stoicism is enough for these people, and the training Epictetus most consistently offers is for this class of Stoics. But there are those whom Providence calls forth as what, in the *Discourses*, Epictetus calls a *scout* (*kataskopos*) and *messenger* (*angelos*) for the gods. Their tasks require more than those for others – they must go without creature comforts, endure poverty and isolation. These messengers display, as vanguards, that we can go without. That we can live with almost nothing, but still live well (*Disc.* iii.22.46). This life of the hard Stoic is a reminder, by Epictetus's lights, a kind of *witnessing* (*marturia*), that we may be free if we do not value externals. In this regard, Epictetus holds that the hard Stoic, in forgoing these goods, has done more good for humanity than those who take on public duties, have families or collect wealth, because they engage in a politics of genuine nobility and divinity (*Disc.* iii.22.79).[4]

Chapter 16

Making proper judgements is key to making progress as a Stoic, as emphasized in Chapters 1, 5, 6 and 9. Events do not interpret or evaluate themselves. We judge, interpret and evaluate events and situations. Our judgements, interpretations and evaluations are ours to control. External events happen as they happen and are not ours to control. In this chapter Epictetus analyses the situation of a person weeping in sorrow. Consider the situation of a parent, Chris, whose child, Dana, is away from home. Chris judges that it is bad that Dana is away from home. As a result of that judgement, Chris weeps in sorrow. Is Chris' situation bad? Is Chris stuck in 'nasty external gunk'? You might assume that if Chris is weeping in sorrow, then Chris must be suffering from a bad situation. But Epictetus rejects this assumption and argues that someone like Chris is actually suffering from a bad judgement, a false belief.

Or consider Casey. Casey has lost her ID card and judges this to be bad. Consequently, Casey cries. Is Casey stuck in nasty external gunk? No, Epictetus insists. Casey's judgement is what causes Casey's sorrow. Casey's grief is not caused by the loss of her ID. This is because other people can dispassionately judge that the loss of an ID is not a horrible event. ID cards can be replaced, after all. We can carry on despite losing an ID or keys or a wallet. So, the fact that Casey lost her stuff does not upset anyone else. Our reaction to that event is that stuff happens, people sometimes lose their stuff. No big deal. Time to persevere and problem-solve.

What about Chris? Is it really bad that Dana is away from home? No. Children grow up and travel around and lead their own lives. Children go off to college. Children become adults, get jobs elsewhere and move away. So the mere fact that Dana is away from home is not actually a bad thing. Though Chris judges it to be bad and that judgement makes Chris sad, other people are not upset by Dana being away from home. What upsets Chris is not Dana being away, but rather Chris's (false) judgement that Dana being away is bad.

Yet Chris and Casey are weeping in sorrow. Should we ignore their suffering? No. Epictetus prescribes consoling weepers. Is he being duplicitous? If the situations of Chris and Casey are not actually bad, according to Epictetus, then he must believe that their sorrow is unjustified. But if they are wrong to weep, then why would he prompt us to console them?

Epictetus urges first establishing solidarity and connection with the weeper. Everyone has wept about something or other at one time or another. So, everyone needs support when in distress. By providing encouraging words we show our care and concern for the weeper. We are trying to help Chris and Casey overcome their sorrow by consoling them. We are showing them compassion. But should we also feel bad ourselves? No, it does no good to make the error of sharing the weepers' faulty judgement that their situations are bad. There is no benefit to the weeper for the consoler to 'groan on the inside'. If the occasion suggests that it might help the weepers feel better, we can groan with them. By groaning with the weepers we signal that we care about their suffering and want to try to alleviate it. But audibly groaning with the weepers does not mean that we agree with their faulty judgement that their situations are really bad.

The callous, fake stoic offers no encouraging words to weepers as the genuine Stoic consoler does. But the consoler's role does not require taking on the emotional pain resulting from the weeper's faulty judgement (and we will comment further on these roles in our notes on *Ench.* 17). When people are drowning it doesn't help to get into the water, flail around and swallow water with them. Savvy rescuers extend a pole or throw them a rope or a flotation device and try to reel them in to safety. The consoler is not insincere or just pretending to care about the weeper. Rather, the consoler rejects the weeper's false belief and wants to correct it. Thus, the consoler is showing compassion by actively trying to ease the griever's grief and being supportive. But the consoler does not share the false belief that causes the griever grief. So the consoler does not take on the passion of sorrow afflicting the weeper. Similarly, doctors don't cure their patients by contracting their illnesses.

The timing of the treatment matters. The moment the weeper is gripped by grief is not the right time to offer Stoic philosophical therapy. We can distinguish the non-philosopher weeper from the weeper who, when calm, may be open to philosophical treatment. Both kinds of weepers ought to be consoled with encouraging words and possibly groans. But teaching Stoicism to the former person is out of place. As we learned in *Ench.* 14, Stoics focus on what they *can* do, not the impossible. In contrast, teaching Stoicism to the latter person *after* the tears have stopped may well be timely and appropriate. Once the tears have stopped, the caring Stoic has the opportunity to educate the person afflicted by the faulty judgement that triggered the tears. Gently, patiently helping others correct their faulty judgements, when they are ready to receive a lesson in Stoic thinking, enables them to gain the proper understanding and emotional resiliency that really remedy sorrow.

Chapter 17

This chapter opens with an injunction to *remember*, to hold a particular Stoic insight in mind. Stoicism is an intellectualist programme in ethics – one improves oneself with knowledge, and the best explanation for moral failing is ignorance. The key, then, is to perfect one's moral knowledge in pursuit of perfecting one's character. So, learning and then recalling the core lessons and heuristics of the Stoic viewpoint is the main job of a Stoic progressor. And it is important, especially when things may be going badly, that one remembers what one knows. The Stoic progressor may assent in the classroom or in cool reflection to some principle of Stoic ethics that provides clarity and placidity, but it is another matter to recall and live in light of these insights when faced with a challenge. But the heuristic Epictetus proposes here has a distinct likelihood of being enacted. The insight: *think of one's life as a role cast by Zeus.*

The analogy of the play, along with that of the banquet and Olympic games, is an organizing image of the *Encheiridion.* The analogy runs that our roles, as determined by Providence, are not up to us, just as the roles of actors are not up to them. We are cast into our roles, and what is up to us is to play them well. So the playwright has cast us as who we are, and it is our job to enact our roles as best we can. We are not the playwright or director – those are not jobs for humans in the grand scheme of things. Humans play the role of humans, and so we will be cast as victors and vanquished, lucky and unlucky, wealthy and poor, healthy and ill. And we know that no story has all things work out perfectly for any character. So there will come a time when our character suffers a loss and must endure a hardship. And we admire characters that make the best of their unhappy turns of fate. In fact, one might consider it a blessing for an actor to play the role of a widow, a defeated soldier or perennial loser. Such a role would be an occasion to bring dignity into challenging times. Getting to play Hecuba, the queen of Troy, now enslaved in the aftermath of Greek triumph, would be a unique acting opportunity. Or Hippolytus, falsely accused of a crime of passion, or Elektra, turned out from her father's house by her murderous and disloyal mother. Good acting can make a bad turn of fate into something worth taking on.

For those who live in contemporary liberal societies, the thought that one's role in life is determined by another is objectionable. When and to whom we are born are not up to us, but the basic thought of liberal approaches is that all the rest of our choices are our own. We choose whom to marry, what career to take, where to live, and so on. This stands in stark contrast to the illiberal arrangements of the ancient period, where one's relations were determined by the family one is born into, what the needs of the head of the household are, and so on. There is a difference to be sure, and the Roman context for Epictetus's image is clearly more posed within this model (and we will return to this issue in our comment on *Ench.* 30). But the Stoic approach to our lives as roles cast in a play still holds up in the liberal context, too. You may have a role in choosing your spouse, but that full story was still not up to you. Your spouse had to play a role in it, too. And you had to meet, which was not up to you. And you had to have had the time to develop that relationship, which required that the rest of your social relations and other obligations had to make that space. The same goes for your career. You had to be at the right place, at the right time, to get that opportunity, and your mentor had to have the right connections, and you had to have had that one experience that stood out to the recruiter. And with so many failures, the same is the case. If one thing goes differently, perhaps tragedy is averted.

The connection to make here is between the FD and the associations one has and roles one plays. What is not up to us are the roles into which we have been cast and with whom we play those roles. What is up to us is how we play them, what we bring to the role. So, when Zeus has one playing the victor for this act, one may play the victor. If so, one should play it well, namely, with grace and humility. In fact, these are excellent occasions for a Stoic practitioner to perform versions of the exercises of the mug from *Ench.* 3 – practise losing this mug, one's health, acclaim or spouse. We do not know or have control over what happens in the next act. And when the losses do come, we are, as Epictetus has instructed, prepared.

One question is whether we play the roles better if we believe we are harmed. That is: will you play a better widow if you believe that the loss of a husband is a stain on your soul? Will you play a better unhoused person if you think that wealth is a good and poverty is a bad? A core insight Epictetus has here is that regardless of the particular details of the casting for any Stoic progressor, there is one constant: they are cast as human beings. And so, Zeus has cast us primarily as rational beings, capable of reflection, judgement and self-control. We play that role first and foremost, and all other roles are played in light of that primary role. So, if you have been cast for this act as one who has lost a spouse, you should remember that you are cast as a rational creature, with the capacity for reflection and self-control, who has lost a spouse that was lent to you by Zeus. If you have lost your wealth, you have been cast as a reasoning agent faced with scarcity. In light of this, our approach to these roles looks clearer.

A further question lingers here. Is there a limit to the roles that can be cast for us? Epictetus's list is that of the public official, private citizen or someone unhoused. But can there be a role cast for thief or murderer? Can one, by hypothesis, play *those* roles well as a Stoic? Or can there be the role of the failed Stoic? It seems at first blush it would be a performative contradiction to play such a role in a way that would be successful, on Epictetus's criteria.

A promising answer to this challenge is that some roles require that we actively contribute to them for them to be permanent. So, it may be that Providence has yielded circumstances wherein one must steal to live, but one must choose to become a thief. Medea is an exemplar for many Stoics for someone who loses the track, as she has been cast in the role of betrayed wife. Medea's husband Jason cheated and abandoned her, after she had sacrificed so much for him and she bore his children. But she becomes consumed by her resentment and hate for Jason, and she kills her rival and her own children in revenge. She judges that harming Jason through these acts is more important than remaining a reliable mother to her own children. She endorses her own vice, and it is by way of this kind of error that one loses the track. One thinks, in essence, that because things have gone so badly, one is allowed to act badly. It is in this false judgement – that bad fate means that one is no longer bound by the norms of good action – that Medea fails, and too many people are tempted to terrible acts. Medea is Epictetus's example of this kind of error (*Disc.* i.28.7), but the lesson is a general one. When things go badly, those are occasions you should be most on guard against your temptations to act badly. You can be cast as a betrayed spouse, but it is by choice and false judgement that you become Medea. The same goes for any of the casting choices by the gods. They do not cast vicious roles, but you may make the casting into a vicious role by your judgements and consequent choices.

There is the final question: does this approach yield a form of endorsement of unjust social arrangements? You are cast as poor? Well, accept it and make the best of it. You are disabled? Keep your chin up. You are enslaved? Obey your master and be a good servant. Call this the *Weaponization Problem* for Stoic ethics; we will address it more fully in Part 5, when we turn to objections and replies. On this front, the Stoics had an uneven track record. They held that the institution of slavery was against nature and that its practitioners failed to recognize the dignity of other humans. Nevertheless, the Stoics themselves consistently failed to call for slavery's abolition. Many owned slaves (Seneca certainly did), and they argued that one's given role determined one's duties. Even for slaves. But, again, the issue is what this kind of acquiescence to fate's determinations looks like. The Stoics held that much of the detail of one's appropriate action must fit the circumstances, and there is no easy formula to find that fit. In the *Discourses*, Epictetus asks his students how they would handle the following challenge: they are servants who must hold a master's chamber pot in the midst of his using it. How will they handle this arrangement? Some will hold that this job will be too offensive to their dignity, and they will accept punishment for refusing to do the job. Others will disassociate themselves from the task and hold the pot without seeing themselves tarnished by the act. That criterion is one provided by one's own character (*Disc.* i.2.7).

The take-away is that though our roles in the play have been cast for us, how we can play those roles has significant variance depending on who we are and what the circumstances are. In some cases, it is best to endure the challenging turn of fate, but in others, it is best to stand up for justice and resist. Identifying the right choice under the circumstances requires judgement and insight, since some parts of the casting are clear (just from the circumstances), but others are not (since one must know oneself well enough to see how one fits with the situation). Stoicism is easily weaponized against those suffering injustice or hard turns of fate because there are many injunctions to endure and not complain. But, importantly, sometimes the role of the one who resists and criticizes is part of the casting. What's necessary is for Stoic practitioners to identify the individual roles they are to play.

Chapter 18

The Romans of Epictetus's time, including the Stoics, commonly believed in divination. Divination is the religious practice of gaining foreknowledge and foretelling events that happen by Providence. Believers in divination thought it was possible to divine (prophesy) future events by interpreting portents like the croaking of ravens, or the flight of birds, or by examining the entrails of an animal killed in ritual sacrifice to the gods. Because all things unfold according to a plan, there are hints of that plan's unfolding in surprising places. For contemporary readers of the *Encheiridion*, this kind of belief seems like silly superstitious nonsense. But before we rush to judgement, we should remind ourselves that many people today take very seriously astrology, horoscopes, the pronouncements of people claiming to be psychics, tarot cards, Ouija boards and tasseography. Many today believe in signs of bad and good luck and other superstitions. Or consider: how many times have you worried that you had jinxed yourself by saying something overconfidently before an event, or you knocked wood to ward off bad luck? The belief that there are invisible but predictable normative forces at work in the world is deeply rooted in our natures.

How did the Stoics reason their way to believing in divination? According to Stoic physics, the universe (*cosmos*) is a single living corporeal being shaped by the interaction of an active principle – also known as God, Zeus, reason (*logos*), creative fire (*pur technikon*) and spirit (*pneuma*) – and a passive principle, formless matter. Interaction of these two principles generates all living beings and objects. The active principle orders all components of the universe and provides their cohesion. Every part of the universe is seamlessly interconnected. Consequently, the active principle determines not only the causal relationships among objects but also the entire causal structure of the cosmos. Accordingly, the active principle was also called fate (*heimarmenê*). Fate the Stoics defined as the rational principle (*logos*) of the things in the world that are governed by Providence or the rational principle through which all past things have passed, all present things are, and the future will come to be. Thus, the Stoics believed in the continuity of the causal connections within the universe extending from the past through the present and into the future. The Stoics' belief in fate thereby opened up the epistemic possibility of inspecting the arrangement of objects or interpreting events in the present (signs or portents) to discern their causal connections with future events. Thus, the Stoics derived semiology as a universal scientific method from their doctrines in cosmology and physics. For them, divination was scientific, not superstitious (Man 2019).

In this chapter Epictetus insists that any bad omen (sign of bad luck) is an impression that must be judged correctly. To any omen a Stoic must apply the FD. Omens pertain exclusively to things not up to me, whether those things are my body, my property, my reputation, my kids or my spouse. Since none of these things are me, any raven's croaking out omens about what will happen can only apply to what happens to things that are not me, not mine and so nothing for me to worry about. For example, if a raven's croak is interpreted to mean that I will become ill, then I must remember the lesson of the FD that illness happens; what happens to my body is ultimately not up to me to control, and so I should cope with an ill body the best I can. From illness I can learn patience, endurance, perseverance, calm and courage. Thus, it is up to me to benefit from the omen that I will become ill.

What if a raven's croak is interpreted to prophesy that some of my property will be lost? Epictetus reminds us that the property I own is not a part of *me*. My material possessions do not constitute who I am. I can retain my virtuous character despite losing items of property I have used for a time (see *Ench.* 11, 14 and 15). The loss of property affects only the property; it does not affect me. In fact, I can judge the omen that some of my property will be lost as a good omen. The less property I own, the less I have to manage and maintain.

If a raven's croak is interpreted to portend that my reputation will be damaged, then I can remind myself that my reputation is not up to me. My reputation consists in what others say and think about me. Since I have no control over that, I should focus on being the best person I can. No person, no raven, no omen can stop me from improving myself.

What if the raven's croak portends harm to my spouse or child? Well, *Ench.* 14 insists that only fools want impossible things like their children, spouse or friends living forever. I must remember that just as my body is vulnerable to injury and illness, so are the bodies of my family members and friends. Human mortality and vulnerabilities are not up to me. What is up to me is how I respond to whatever happens to my spouse, child or friend. Since I am free to respond calmly, helpfully, constructively and virtuously to whatever happens to my loved ones, I can make every omen about them good. It is not bad if my child suffers an injury. Injuries will happen as parts of life. It is bad if I fail to help my injured child, if I fail to get the injury properly treated. I can be a good parent, a good spouse and a good friend no matter what events befall my kids, my spouse and my friends. Consequently, Epictetus reasons that really there are no such things as bad omens; there are no signs of bad luck. The croaking of ravens and the practice of divination are irrelevant to my ability to make lemonade out of the lemons I get.

The lesson of these points about divination can now be stated without appeal to the controversial Stoic theology and physics. It is this: mastering oneself guided by the FD makes one invulnerable to whatever the future holds. If divination is possible, then there are times when we find out about the future through its means. But we can often enough anticipate what awaits us (as we can with the exercise of the mug and in anticipating what it will be like in going to the baths). Either way, with the croaking of ravens or our capacity to anticipate what will befall us, we know that we will live and die, have relations that will end, and we will meet with successes and failures. Knowing exactly what, when and where these things will happen is not as important as knowing what really matters in the end: maintaining our dignity and equanimity through it all. No matter that it is fated for us; it is an occasion for us to exercise those virtues.

Chapter 19

Here a general principle is deduced from the lesson of *Ench.* 18. There Epictetus explained how you have the power to make any bad omen good by extracting benefit from anything that happens. Here he describes this transformative power in terms of a way to guarantee victory: compete only in contests in which winning is up to you and you alone.

What kind of competitions do non-Stoics enter? Non-Stoics struggle to outdo each other. Non-Stoics vie for prestige, social influence, power, wealth, fame or some other kind of celebrity. Non-Stoics believe that winning more of these things will win them happiness. There are several problems with this fantasy.

First, when fighting for any finite resource, you can't always beat others. There will never be enough for the greedy because no greedy person rests content with only a fair share. The greedy don't limit their desires to need. They always want more than they need. They are doomed because for them there is no such thing as enough. Second, even if you have success at scratching and clawing your way to get more than some other people, there will always be others who have more wealth, power, influence or fame than you do. Consequently, prevailing over everyone is impossible. Third, in trying to best others by grasping these fleeting, illusory 'prizes', you will likely have to lie, cheat, steal or debase yourself one way or another. To sacrifice your moral integrity, self-respect, honesty and decency to grasp at greater prestige or power is to play a losing game. Why? Because you are sacrificing something of real value for only a *chance* at winning a 'prize' that is difficult to keep even for a short time, and probably impossible to keep for a very long time. In other words, you are sacrificing a real good for a fake good. That is a losing game.

Epictetus believes that the essence of the good is preserving your moral integrity, self-respect, honesty and decency. Fortunately, it is up to us whether we preserve these things. We need never risk them. So long as we care more about remaining morally decent, honest, fair and trustworthy, no one can take these virtues, these true goods, away from us. As long as we care about our integrity of character more than anything else, we can never lose it. That is why there is no place for envy or jealousy. Non-Stoics envy the possessions, wealth, power, physical beauty, athletic prowess and celebrity of others. Non-Stoics are jealous of the material, social, professional or political success of others. Stoics, in contrast, care far more about being decent, honest, caring, helpful, fair, trustworthy, courageous, self-controlled, generous, cooperative, principled, excellent persons.

Could a Stoic envy someone who was more virtuous than she herself was? No. Since becoming more virtuous is up to us, no one and nothing can stop us from progressing in our self-improvement. Stoics admire and emulate models of virtue. But admiration is neither envy nor jealousy. The goal is to free oneself from faults like greed, fear, resentment, envy, jealousy, malice, pettiness, etc. Everyone has the power to liberate themselves from these faults (vices). Thus, Stoics will aspire to be neither generals, nor corporate executives, nor heads of state, nor music stars, nor movie stars, nor star athletes, nor plutocrats, nor anyone else who wields political, social or economic power. Stoics want freedom, specifically, the freedom to be happy. And the way to be free is to be good. Stoics compete against themselves to become better persons than they were yesterday. If your contest is to become better than you were yesterday, then you have the power to be invincible and to win, day after day. This is the road to freedom. To make progress on the road to freedom, you cannot be encumbered with distractions, impediments and diversions. The road to prestige leads you in a different direction to a distant destination far from where the road to freedom leads. So too do the roads to wealth, fame and political power. By disdaining the things that are not up to us, Stoics disencumber themselves of all the baggage that distracts, hampers and ceaselessly worries non-Stoics. Obsession with things not up to them enslaves non-Stoics. Non-Stoics sooner or later lose when competing for things not up to them. In contrast, Stoics guarantee victory by competing only in the contest to become better, wiser and freer.

Chapter 20

Epictetus again opens with the directive to *remember* a core Stoic lesson. The Stoic programme, as we know, is an intellectualist approach to ethics. If you correct your judgement and see the world and what's valuable correctly, most of the work of pursuing a good life is done. In short, since the best explanation for error and unhappiness is ignorance and the wrong kind of judgement, one must pursue knowledge of the world and of what is good for humans. As Epictetus had noted in *Ench.* 7, what disturbs us is not what happens, but how we judge what has happened. Seeing things from the right perspective will lead us out of the violent vicissitudes of thinking that our well-being depends on so many things that are irrelevant to it. Stoic salvation comes through knowledge; the key is keeping that knowledge active. So, Epictetus, again, directs his students to *remember.*

A long-standing problem for intellectualist ethics has been the phenomenon of *akrasia,* or weakness of will. Perhaps there have been moments in your life where you've done something you knew was stupid, or just wrong. Or you've seen this in others, where you say of them that *they know better.* This phenomenon has been widely taken to be a significant problem for intellectualist approaches in ethics. In short, the reasoning runs that if the best explanation for moral error is ignorance, then there shouldn't be any cases of *akrasia,* where people do what they know they shouldn't. But there are many. A long-standing reply to the *akrasia* problem for intellectualism is that these are instances where you don't *really* know, don't *truly* hold these truths in your minds. So, when a person does something wrong and knows better, the sense of 'knows' is too weak there. If she *really knew* better and she had that knowledge active in her mind, she would not have done wrong. So, the key for intellectualism is to exercise one's knowledge, to keep it active. That's how one will live by it. This is why Epictetus thinks that these exercises of recollection are vital. You don't just come to know the Stoic principles; you must exercise that knowledge regularly. In so doing, when you know better, you will do better.

The FD, as noted in our comment on *Ench.* 1, is a distinction arising primarily from physics. The FD reflects a difference between two classes of things in terms of their responsiveness to our volition. What is up to us is whatever our decisions can directly affect, and what is not up to us is what our decisions cannot directly affect. To be clear, our decisions can *indirectly* affect many things, but the world still contributes many things to outcomes. So, one may voluntarily contribute to one's promotions or social status by being a team-player and maintaining a good attitude; these things are directly up to you. Others must play their roles, too, in that story. Moreover, whether they do or do not is not up to us. So even instances of indirect control still require that many things beyond our control operate one way instead of another. Consequently, they too are externals.

Another thing to remember is that humans are generally not wise. Remember that *Ench.* 13 operated on the principle of indirect negative feedback: when others praise you, you should begin to think you probably have focused on the wrong things. Take the praise of the unwise as evidence that you have lost the proper path, since following that of wisdom would yield their derision and contempt. In the case of insults and those who hurl them, Epictetus's advice proceeds distinctly from these two insights. An insult can harm us only if we judge it to be a harm; that is, others can hurt your feelings only if you make yourself vulnerable to their words. You make yourself vulnerable in this fashion only if you agree with the judgements contained in the insult. The key is that insults are noise when you know that they are ungrounded and products of bad character. Think of student evaluations, for example. When they make jokes about your appearance, it is important to know that these comments really say more about the person making the comment than the target. What scholar will appear comely to the college-aged? What expectations do they have of their teachers if this is their complaint? Once you take the right perspective on these sense impressions, you can hear them perfectly, but they cause no trouble.

There are two forms of Stoic exercise: those of *anticipation* and those of *endurance.* That is, one may perform an exercise *before* facing an experience to steel oneself for what is to come. So, Epictetus reminds himself (in *Ench.* 4) of what the baths will be like before he goes, so he will not be upset when there. Or you prepare for being separated from property or family by reminding yourself that all things are finite (as in *Ench.* 3) and that, as loans, you will return them to the cosmic hotel; they are not lost (as in *Ench.* 11). You practise these 'returns' and disappointments beforehand, so you are ready when they occur. The exercise with insults here has the same anticipatory edge to it. But Epictetus also builds another feature to the exercises because there are times (given that this is advice to *progressors*) his students will actually be angered by an insult. The work of anticipation has not completely inured our practitioners to the verbal abuse from others. This is when Epictetus turns to a different kind of exercise, one devoted to *regaining control,* a special subset of protocols of what we have called *exercises of endurance.*

Epictetus is reminding his progressors how to follow what they know, how to put their knowledge to work. They are not yet perfect Stoic sages, but rather students and people who still are working on themselves. The stray comment may bother them, even if they have done the work of preparation. In this case, Epictetus allows for the fact that his student has been provoked and made angry by an insult. He proposes two stages for regaining control. The first is a purely theoretical reminder, that of the FD. The reason we get angry is because of our judgements. The problem is that one's anger over an insult is evidence one has false beliefs about whether the insult is really a harm. So, the first recommendation is, unsurprisingly, to *remember* the lesson and make the theoretical correction. The procedural problem is that one is angry precisely because one had forgotten the insight in the first place. So, advice to remember something in circumstances wherein one had clearly forgotten is thin advice. It's as useful as telling someone looking for lost keys to just *remember where they are*. That is, it's not advice one can take *in situ*. Of course, it's good to give oneself reminders beforehand to prevent forgetting, so remembering to remember is good. But assuming that this is about regaining control, this is too little too late. Yet Epictetus's advice has a second stage that is both in the service of the first stage and a stopgap for precisely this problem. He recommends *delaying action*.

The proposal of delay is a defining piece of Stoic advice. Seneca famously writes in *On Anger* that 'the best corrective of anger is delay' (ii.29.1). By putting on hold what anger impels, the Stoic allows herself to be the proper judge of the situation. This is because what anger always impels is acting to pay back the harm to the target of anger. However, once one has judged the circumstances appropriately, that is, in accord with the FD, the desires for vendetta subside. Delay prevents one from being abducted by passion. As social beings we are constantly coordinating with others, giving them feedback, and taking it. Our bodies feel pain and pleasure as feedback regarding how they are doing. So, some pleasures are feedback that one's body is functioning well, and pains mark that it needs maintenance or rest. Social feedback works similarly, and we, when we coordinate, give and get those positive and negative social vibes. But just as pain is itself not a bad thing, an insult itself is not a bad. It is only feedback from our fellows. Preferring health and its coordinate pleasures over illness and its pains is natural, just as is preferring comity and getting along with others to discord and insults. The key with insults, just as with pain, is to prevent our initial reactions to the feedback from taking over our actions. A bee may sting a progressor, and it is appropriate for the Stoic to react to being stung with a jerk of surprise, a slap on the site. But no more. An insult may sting, too. But reactions beyond acknowledging the initial sting can be postponed until one has judged the circumstances.

One strategy for enacting judgement during the pause is to pose what we call *Simplicius's Dilemma*. In his commentary on this chapter of Epictetus's *Encheiridion*, the great ancient commentator notes that one can ask the question: *is what has been said of you true, or is it false?* (2002a: 109). If the insult is true, then it is worth acknowledging this truth and taking it as feedback for better work later. The pinch of an insult, like that in one's heel, is pain that tells us that we are not fitting our circumstances quite as well as we ought. The pinch on our heels tells us that we may need to change how we tie our shoes, and the pinch of an insult may tell us that we need to, say, brush our teeth more vigorously after lots of coffee at breakfast. That's the feedback we get when someone comments on our breath. That's useful information. Simplicius even asks: how can the truth truly hurt us? For sure, there are truths that are taken to imply others – as an insult to one's looks often implies that one also can't be taken seriously on a topic. But *ad hominem* abusive arguments are correctable as fallacies. Though they ride on insults, we can pause to halt the inferences and consequences – both their effects on us (to hurt our feelings and make us angry) and on others (to have them believe on the basis of invalid arguments). Whereas if the content of the insult is false, then how can that be a bother? One can still, after the pause, correct the falsity, if it matters for the exchange, or one can let it roll off one's back. So, on Simplicius's dilemma, either they give us feedback we may need to improve ourselves, or we shouldn't be troubled by what they say because they reason poorly, or they simply believe false things. What else, again, given that their praise is a negative profile of virtue, should we expect of those who are not wise?

Maintaining this kind of cool distance between one's experience of receiving the insult and judging it properly requires significant mental energy. Given that Epictetus is presenting this advice to progressors, he concedes that these impressions have the capacity to overwhelm and abduct his students and readers. He imagines that they are sometimes provoked and angry. That's what progressors do. They follow the insights, internalize them and work on them. Then later they fail. The key is how to catch oneself in the moment of failure, to halt one's further fall. Epictetus's insight is that even after one has been angered, the strategy of delay helps one regain control. The problem, of course, is that even to follow this advice, one needs, still, enough control to delay. Anger, given its nature, impels us to hurry to reply, and if we have lost control to prevent anger, it's possible that we've lost control to delay. In this regard, the advice of delay is the last of a multi-tiered strategy of managing challenging emotions. You have exercises of anticipation to set your mind right before a difficult experience. Then, during the experience, you exercise your judgement to see through the illusions that you can too often fall for. Then, if you have fallen prey to the passion of anger, you can delay acting upon it. None of these approaches is perfect because we progressors are not perfect. Progressors need to see themselves in the right light given the fact of human fallibility and our need for wisdom.

Another Stoic preparatory exercise Epictetus does not include in this chapter, but it is worth describing. In *On Anger* Seneca acknowledges that progressors should do their best to avoid having anger at all, so there are the exercises of Stoic control and recollection of the principles that we should rely on. But given that we are progressors, they are not foolproof. Another layer to add is one that is about our own bodily propensity to react to difficult situations. Remembering your Stoic training requires energy; putting those principles into use is mentally demanding. So, it's best to not already be tired before having to do that. Having enough energy to be a good Stoic may mean that you are not hungry when you face these circumstances. He endorses the proverb that 'the tired man seeks a quarrel', but Seneca also extends it to the hungry and thirsty, too (iii.9.5). Just as your body, if it has a sore on it or is particularly sensitive, will react more strongly to a scrape or blow, your mind, if you are tired or hungry, will have more significant initial reactions to difficult experiences. Progressors, then, should sometimes prepare for difficult circumstances by making sure they're topped up with sleep and food before facing them. Of course, some people you know will push your buttons no matter how well you prepare. You should just avoid them, Seneca suggests (iii.8.3).

Chapter 21

Epictetus believes that death, exile and everything that appears terrible to non-Stoics are not, in fact, terrible. Most people believe that death is the most terrible thing of all. But in the *Discourses* Epictetus argues that no fears about death are warranted (see Stephens 2014). Therefore, he reasons that if you can rid yourself of the fear of death, you will be far less inclined to fear anything else typically regarded as less terrifying than death. Exile or deportation or becoming a refugee due to environmental disaster is for most people less scary than death. Injury and illness are also generally less scary than death. Epictetus's argument about death is the following interacting lines of reasoning:

1. We come into existence not when we choose to, but when the cosmos decides we will.
2. All things that come our way are gifts from the cosmos on loan for us to make the best of for a limited time.
3. Thus, our lives are gifts from the cosmos loaned to us for us to make the best of for a limited time.
4. All living things must die for the cosmos to recycle its elements and continue producing new generations of living things.
5. Therefore, our deaths are part of the cosmos's process of reclaiming what has been loaned for the purpose of further generation and production.
6. To be a human is to be a mortal being.
7. To be mortal, including having an end as a mortal, is nothing terrible.
8. Therefore, death is nothing terrible.
9. Understanding the nature and necessity of death frees us to live fearlessly.
10. The false belief that death is terrible grounds and motivates the fear of death.
11. The fear of death motivates vicious motives and vicious actions.
12. If one has vicious motives and acts viciously, one is not able to live freely or well.
13. Therefore, the fear of death impedes our ability to freely live well.
14. We must dispel the emotions that impede our abilities to live freely and well and the false beliefs that give rise to them.
15. Therefore, the fear of death and the false belief that death is terrible must be dispelled.

In *Ench.* 21 Epictetus urges us to think every day about what non-Stoics regard as terrible things, death being the worst of all. This strategy empowers Stoics to prepare for 'the worst'. Since things beyond our control can take us off guard at any time, it is wise to be prepared to deal with whatever happens, no matter how terrible. The lesson of *Ench.* 3 was to remember the destructibility of the things you like. Mugs can break, so remind yourself that your favourite mug can break at any time. That way, when it does break, you'll be neither surprised nor disturbed. Human beings are mortal, so remind yourself that your loved ones will die. Love them, kiss them, cherish them now and remind yourself daily that these mortals could die at any time.

Exile, deportation and extradition are 'terrible' things that most readers of this *Guide* are unlikely to face. But being forced to leave home or relocate to a distant city non-Stoics today might well regard as terrible. People's homes are often destroyed by fires, tornadoes, hurricanes or floods. Most people regard losing their homes or jobs to be terrible. Epictetus urges us to think about these 'terrible' things every day too. To most, however, death seems the most terrible thing of all. So, whether it is the death of your loved one or your own death, Epictetus advises you to look squarely at death every day and understand both what it is and what it is not. It is the end of a person's identity. It is not the end of the elements that constitute a person. Those elements nature recycles into new things. Thus, from the perspective of nature death is not annihilation but *change*. And the change from life to death to new life is neither bad nor terrible, but necessary and intelligible. Fearing this kind of change is therefore foolish.

If we understand that death is a cosmologically necessary change, then Epictetus believes that we can accept the logic of death. This understanding affords us the proper perspective within nature. Our mind, our volition (*prohairesis*), our consciousness and memories are ours. But our bodies are not up to us. Our bodies and our lives are gifts from nature on temporary loan to us and so fundamentally not ours. Nature does not belong to us. We belong to nature. To nature our bodily constituents will return.

The lesson taught in *Ench.* 17 is also at work here in *Ench.* 21. Our lives are roles the director (Zeus, God, Fate, Nature, the cosmos) has assigned us to play in the cosmic drama. How long we are on stage is up to the director. Our task is to play our roles well knowing that we must exit the stage (die) when the cosmic drama requires it. Epictetus also explains this idea using game and sport analogies (*Disc.* ii.5.1–4 and ii.5.15–21; cf. *Disc.* iv.7.1–5). Our role is to skilfully play the cards nature has dealt us (or the dice as they fall, or the ball in a ball game) in the game of life by living skilfully, that is, virtuously.

Epictetus thinks that appreciating mortality as a necessary part of being human enables us to affirm our humanity. Appreciating death for what it is and what it isn't helps us distinguish what matters from what is trivial. Yearning for a new toy, a new trinket, a trophy, a raise or a promotion at work, a new job, a fancier house – the frivolousness of these things becomes clear when we reflect on death. The lesson to learn here is to look at and think about death every day to avoid making the mistake of sweating the small stuff. Reflect on death daily and you won't make the mistake of hankering for any fleeting, flimsy, unimportant bauble too much, whether it is a drone, cell phone, laptop, big screen television, boatercycle, automobile or any other material possession. If you think about death daily, you won't be tempted by tawdry thoughts. Remembering that death is inevitable and can happen at any time will keep your mind off petty, spiteful, shameful, self-gratifying, self-aggrandizing fantasies. Being ever mindful of death and other 'terrible' things puts sharply into perspective what really matters – striving to become the best person you can possibly be before your time is up. Our lives are short dramatic roles in the vast, unending cosmic drama. Performing these brief roles well demands attention. Death reminds us to be ever alert, circumspect and focused on our task. We have no time for sleazy daydreams.

Chapters 22 and 23

Chapters 22 and 23 come as a package. In them, Epictetus addresses challenges progressors will face as a consequence of their being philosophers. Some challenges for progressors will arise from other people seeing them as philosophers. Other challenges will arise from progressors seeing themselves as philosophers. Claiming the mantle of philosopher, even claiming to be a student of philosophy, smacks of pretence. Progressor's temptation is the name we give to a set of problems that come with being interested in philosophy and actually making progress with it. One feels pride in that progress, as it is a real achievement. One is understanding things, making corrections, improving. However, that pride can be experienced and expressed in ways that impede further progress. One way is in the desire for others to see and acknowledge that progress, particularly non-philosophers and other progressors. The problem with this desire is that it is for an external, something not up to the subject. So, from a Stoic perspective, it is a failure to respect the FD. Furthermore, since these others from whom our subject wants approval are not themselves wise, they will not properly see what progress was made. In fact, for those who are not wise, actual progress on the path of wisdom will seem like folly. So, here our progressors stand, saying they are studying philosophy and progressing towards wisdom, but to those who are not wise all this will seem to be an error with the pretence of excellence. So, not only do those with progressor's temptation desire an external, but they desire an external that is practically guaranteed to elude them. Ironically, their progress towards wisdom has prompted them to an unwise desire.

Epictetus's advice here is both an argument against falling to progressor's temptation and an exercise of preparation for those who feel its pull. When one begins philosophical training, others will notice, and they will think the results are strange. Assuming that progressors are making some progress, they should prepare for disapproving judgements from others. They will think that our progressors separate themselves from the group. In a way, the others are right about this. Progressors no longer like the things others like. Progressors think the others have false beliefs about so many things and are slaves to their passions. Consequently, progressors are happy that they are no longer like the others. This is not something to apologize for or something to feel bad about. Educational experiences will change you. You will return to view your old life from a different perspective: still one of the crowd, but also very unlike it. Progress in Stoic philosophy is designed to make this change but keep one immersed in the social world. A Stoic does not retreat from society but continues to be an active member of it. Yet this change makes Stoics both members of and aliens to their social groups. Others cannot help but notice and comment on this. Stoic training is designed to make practitioners approximate the divine, so there's a sense that one should be proud of that progress and that others should marvel.

The key is not to be caught up in these judgements of *should*. Recall the Stoic Paradox that the world is divisible into two classes: the wise and the unlearned. The unlearned know only that philosophy *purports* to make one wise. But, because they are not wise, they do not know what wisdom looks like and they likely think it looks like something they already prefer – knowing how to achieve material success, manipulate others, make fortunes, and so on. So, progress in Stoic philosophy will look to them to be rather worthless. So, when a progressor announces to these folk that she is studying philosophy, she will not only be seen as putting on airs at being very important, but she will, in the view of non-Stoics, fail at it. As a result, these non-Stoics will be keen to point this out. In fact, the non-Stoics will be keen to undercut this progress, precisely because progress in philosophy puts progressors out of their realm of control.

Two lessons, then, are drawn from the matter of resisting progressor's temptation. The first is that one doesn't pursue philosophy so that one can be better than others, but so that one can be better than oneself. The second is that one isn't a philosopher so that others will look up to you or so that you can look down on others, but so that you can be wise, virtuous and happy. So, the relational gains of philosophical progress – doing better than others, not making their errors, not being tempted by their nonsense – are not the objective. Rather, the objective of philosophical training is being the best person one can be. The relational results with others are by-products of that end.

The irony Epictetus points out is that being caught up with progressor's temptation, feeling pride in philosophical progress and wanting others to appreciate that progress, not only are a distraction from philosophy, properly pursued, but make one vulnerable to being bested by others. This is why he says one will be 'doubly derided' if others and their jeering at being philosophical overcome philosophical progress. One is not only defeated by opinions of others, but one was an active participant in that defeat. Progressors, as those who have *made progress*, should know better. The philosophical showboat is the person who has learned some philosophy and believes that he thereby is wiser than others and is consequently licensed to liberally bestow that wisdom. Pretentiousness is not only taking oneself to know important things, but demanding others acknowledge those insights. In seeking that acknowledgement from others, and particularly others who are not wise, progressors not only make themselves vulnerable to disappointment but act in ways that confirm the attitudes of those who are not wise. These others think that wisdom should yield influence, power and status. So, when a pretentious progressor tries to grasp these things in the name of Stoic wisdom, these others, in quashing the progressor's claims, are also showing that Stoic training is worthless. Stoicism purports to make its practitioners invincible, but these results show them, in the eyes of others, all too easily defeated.

The key to managing progressor's temptation is to maintain singularity of focus on progress in philosophy. There are consequent external results of that progress – one will do better at managing one's life than others, one will have new intellectual skills deserving praise, and one will have insights worth sharing – but these cannot be the motivating reasons for doing philosophy. To reiterate, you pursue wisdom not so that you can do better than others and then expect them to marvel, but so that you better yourself.

Thus, Epictetus ends *Ench.* 22 with two conditionals, each reflecting the complex of motives and their consequences with progressor's temptation:

If you stick to the singular focus of philosophy, others will marvel.

If you care about them marvelling, you will be doubly defeated.

The key, to be clear, is that one's motivations to do philosophy cannot be to please others or win their approval. Seeking praise for one's philosophical insight or one's consistent practice of virtue actually undercuts the values that the insight and virtue instantiate. The correction, as Epictetus frames it, is to maintain that singularity of focus on philosophical progress in the manner of following a divine command. His direction is for progressors to stick to things that appear best 'as if God assigned you to that post'. Framing philosophical progress as a divine mission, as opposed to a strategy for social status or approval, establishes this focus.

One way to think of the illusion driving progressor's temptation and how it can be dispelled is in terms of how student motivation has so many faces. A good student may be driven by a desire to master the material, but in the process, she may find that chasing a particular grade or class rank complicated her relationship with her education. Another student may seem to others in the class to be the best, but those others are themselves in no position to know. They will think the one who speaks with the most confidence is the most knowledgeable. But the best way to achieve the grades and the class rank one wants is to avoid being motivated by those things. Rather, pay attention to the thing that grades and rank are supposed to reflect: knowledge of the material. Study and be curious about the material, and grades and class rank will take care of themselves. Chasing those other things is a distraction that undercuts the very purpose of the educational enterprise.

Importantly, the advice given here is advice students, with their complicated motives, must hear. If you are wise, you do not need to be reminded not to be a philosophical showboat or not to worry about whether others think well of your progress. But Epictetus's *Handbook* is not for the wise, but for students, those making progress. So progressors, just as any students, will have complicated motives and so feel progressor's temptation. Thus, they must prepare for those moments and correct themselves during those moments.

Epictetus closes by noting that trying to please others, particularly in philosophical work, is where we lose the thread. In some ways, this is true for contemporary academics, and not just for Stoic progressors. Think of the ways that prestige-chasing with one's publications distorts one's relationship with the discipline and the philosophical insights at stake. Ask yourself how often you've left a writing project to the side because you weren't sure it would find the right home for publication. Certainly, any early career academic can attest to this concern. We chase not only progress, but acknowledgement of that quality from our peers and (more importantly) from our deans. Or consider the fact that even when we know others in the discipline, and especially those who disagree with us, will likely misunderstand a subtle point in one of our papers, we still feel wounded by a dismissive reviewer's comments. We knew some would dislike the paper. We did not write it to please them. Yet it still stings when they get us wrong and fabricate unjust criticisms. No academic lacks a story of a hurtful judgement from 'Reviewer 2', even though we expected it.

Epictetus directs progressors to be satisfied to be philosophers, to appear only to themselves to be philosophers. Relying on others to acknowledge that progress is an error, one that risks losing one's way altogether. But at this point, a problem arises. Assuming that Epictetus is addressing progressors, who are not wise, the question is: what is it to see oneself as a philosopher, to see oneself making progress, when one is not yet wise and does not have that requisite knowledge? The Academic sceptics often challenged the Stoics along these lines. If we are not yet wise, then how is it responsible to trust our own judgement on our being a philosopher? That is, if we are not wise, then how is Epictetus's advice of trusting our own judgement better than trusting another's judgement? If neither of us is wise, then why is trusting my own judgement better than trusting the judgement of another? Let us call this problem the *progressor's paradox*. If we are not wise, then how do we recognize our own progress gaining wisdom? How do we know that we are correctly tracking our progress, or like so many unwise others, only recapitulating our errors and multiplying our vices? Furthermore, the Stoics disagreed with the Aristotelians and the Epicureans (and others) on the nature of the good life, the grounds for human excellence, and what successful philosophical progress looks like. So, there are *two levels* to the paradox.

> Level 1: How does the Stoic progressor, who is not wise, identify progress in Stoic philosophy?

> Level 2: How does the Stoic progressor, who is not wise, identify Stoicism (as opposed to other options) as the path to wisdom?

Level 1 of the paradox can concede that Stoicism is the right path to wisdom, but it locates the problem as being able to identify progress on that path. So, the Level 1 version of the paradox is *internal* to the Stoic perspective. Level 2 of the paradox is about how one who is not wise could identify the right path to begin with. So, the Level 2 version of the paradox is *external* to the Stoic perspective. It's a problem that *all progressors* (Stoic, Epicurean, Aristotelian or whatever) would have. How, unless you already know what the good life looks like, can you identify what the path of training for the good life is?

The solution to Level 1 of the progressor's paradox is that one must come upon a reliable guide to Stoic progress. In this regard, there must be a particular arrangement of facts that has come about in a way that benefits the progressor. That is, the progressor must be lucky enough to have a copy of the

Encheiridion or another user's guide to progress. But assuming that we are asking this question of Epictetus, then we have our answer literally at hand, in the very book we are reading. The necessary feedback is itself in the *Handbook*. This is why Epictetus regularly punctuates the book with the framing, 'If you want to make progress … ' and injunctions to remember the advice. Epictetus provides criteria for adjudging progress throughout his *Handbook*. In a sense it is both a set of homework exercises and the answer key. Of course, you must have had some luck being exposed to the right teachers at the right time. You must read the *Handbook* at the right stage of your life and be able to digest the lessons. Stoicism promises to make us immune to fortune by its training, but the irony is that to be a successful progressor, you needed to be fortunate enough to have been given the lessons of progress. So, Stoics thank fortune for giving them the tools to make themselves invincible to fortune.

Level 2 of the progressor's paradox is a harder nut to crack. How do we know that Stoicism, and not Platonism, Epicureanism, Cynicism, Aristotelianism or Pythagoreanism (or other school), is correct in the first place? Again, assuming we are not wise, how do we know which purported path to wisdom to take? Given that they all disagree on the nature of the good life, what is right for humans, and the nature of it all, at most one philosophy can be correct. So, even if we have a good guide to progress in Stoicism, how do we know to take that advice, as opposed to following an excellent guide to Aristotelian or Epicurean philosophy? We will address this version of the paradox later in full form in Part 5, when we turn to objections and replies, as the *Scepticism Problem* for Stoic philosophy. Here, we will sketch out the initial Stoic reply.

Level 2 of the progressor's paradox is an Academic sceptical challenge, and Stoic responses to the Sceptics start with the observation that even the unwise have the capacity for correct judgement. With practice, those capacities can be sharpened. Epictetus in his *Discourses* counsels his students to attend closely to the arguments over the good life. He says students should listen to the reasoning given by the various sides, and he tells his students to follow the best arguments and shun bad reasoning. Be a critical thinker first. Stoicism, because it survives this scrutiny and the other programmes do not, will emerge as one's commitments (*Disc.* i.27.6). The Academic sceptics pose a challenge in the abstract, but closer attention shows that some arguments are just better than others. The sceptic is paralysed by the too-broadly-stated version of the progressor's paradox. They are like people trapped and frozen by their own bad reasoning and inattentiveness (*Disc.* i.5.1). It is clear here that Stoicism, as a form of cognitivism and intellectualism, must answer the Sceptics. Knowledge, as the path to the moral good, must be defended from those who deny its possibility. The Stoic progressor, then, is not just a person who is living by a set of predetermined dogmas. Rather, the Stoic progressor is constantly working on arguments for, reasons against, challenges to and considerations favouring principles of the good life. You do not simply remind yourself of and then live by Stoicism's precepts. Rather, as a philosopher, you must endorse those precepts as items of clear and unmistakable knowledge. Stoic progressors must be enquirers, and consequently, it is in this practice that they can then see themselves as philosophers in the sense that Epictetus says they must rest content with.

Chapter 24

Exercises of anticipation are necessary for those who, as Stoics do, live with their families, participate in a society and have roles to play given those relations. Contrast Stoics with Cynics on this point. The Cynic abjures so much of social life and the values that animate it, because so many of those values are false. The Cynic stands outside society, free of its trappings, and refuses it. Diogenes of Sinope was an exile, a person without a country. He held that not being a citizen of any conventional, localized city made him truly free, a citizen of the world, instead. He had no possessions, he took no social station, he collected no wealth and he had no family. Thereby unburdened, he was empowered to be the author of his own fate on his own terms, depending on no one. He was self-sufficient, from his perspective. No baubles of illusory social goods distracted him. But he nevertheless begged for food, lived in an abandoned wine cask and seemed to demand lots of attention from those whom he criticized. The Cynics, despite their claims to stand outside society, could not break their social bond. They remain socially inflected beings. In this respect the Stoics contrast with the Cynics. They held roughly the same view of many of the social goods the Cynics spurned. So, Stoics regarded social climbing, wealth accumulation and the pursuit of status as empty nonsense. But the Stoics still participated in their societies. As shown earlier, the Stoics married and had families, they managed households with servants and possessions, they held offices and went to (and perhaps even convened) dinner parties and they consoled their neighbours in times of grief. The Stoics apparently even had favourite mugs. Stoics, then, and especially progressors, will have rich social lives. In consequence, they will have the potential for conflicted motives in those lives. Managing all these externals well carries a temptation internal to them – the temptation of falling for them, of being entranced by them. The benefit of Cynicism is that in refusing these things completely, Cynics cannot be tempted by them. But the Cynics cannot fully extricate themselves from social life. So, Stoics must manage that dual perspective of managing their lives while at the same time seeing them as full of false value.

Exercises of anticipation with social goods were, given these considerations, of regular importance. The two fronts of pull that Epictetus addresses in *Ench.* 24 are friends and civic duties. Along both lines, it is tempting to reason that, because you should be a good friend and a good citizen, you should pursue wealth so you can give generously to your friends and to the state. The more wealth you have, the more you can be a benefactor to those who need it and the more substantially you can contribute to public works and the common good. In both cases, the temptation is to suppose that the person with significant wealth and status can do her duty to and greatly benefit her friends and country. Thereby, that person can then be praised and regarded as excellent. Having honour and regard for being a reliable friend and benefactor of the state – who wouldn't want that? So, not only do we squander our chance at being rich when we take up Stoicism, but we waste our chance of being a person who can do well by others and win renown and honour. If we are Stoics, as the tempting reasoning goes, we will end up being nobodies.

Epictetus's exercise for progressors facing this temptation proceeds along two lines. The first is a reconstruction of the concept of being worthy of honour. The second is a reconception of what precisely one's duties to one's friends and one's state are. Since Stoicism is a form of moral intellectualism, having correct beliefs about these tempting matters is what makes us invulnerable to their illusions. In a way, Epictetus's strategy behind this exercise of anticipation is to prepare for illusions of social life by remembering the truths that they belie. If one can remain fixed on those truths, the illusions lose their allure. In a way, the strategy is akin to explaining how a magic trick works before one sees a magician perform it. One not only isn't taken in by the trick (as one sees that the card, say, was slipped inside the magician's hat), but one is now prepared for other similar illusions and thereby can see through them.

The illusion of honour is one that can be dispelled with two parallel lines of reasoning. Epictetus here in *Ench.* 24 provides only one line, but the second can be easily derived from it. Recall the FD, the core tenet of Stoic value theory. The only things of value are those that are up to us, so if honour is a good thing or disgrace a bad, they must be up to us. Instances of honour being improperly distributed, then, are not instances of losing out on a good, since if one is honourable but not honoured, the problem is not with the one honoured, it is with those bestowing honours. The same goes for dishonour; how can it be a bad if it is not something up to us? Here is Epictetus's argument based on the insight that we confuse being honourable with being honoured (or having prestige). But if we distinguish the two, we see things clearly:

1. Only things up to you are goods, and only things up to you are bads.
2. So, honour, if it is a good, is something up to you.
3. Being honourable is up to you, and it is a good.
4. Honour (as prestige) is conferred by others.
5. So, honour (as prestige) is not a good (and lacking it is not a bad).
6. Therefore, honour (as prestige) is not identical to being honourable. Attend to only the latter.

One way to keep this thought clearer is to highlight Epictetus's parallel reasoning with honour and dishonour in the *Discourses* (ii.22.20). The reasoning runs that if it is possible for honour to be given to those who do not deserve it and withheld from those who do, then it is unclear how honour is itself a good, because it inaccurately reflects what it is supposed to praise. That is, one receives honour for some supposed excellence (e.g. prizes for an excellent cyclist or a superb teacher), but if it is possible for those awards to be incorrectly given (e.g. to a mediocre cyclist or a negligent teacher), then what exactly is the award's value? In fact, its value is an illusion created by the bad judgements of the unwise. How can fame for being an excellent person be worth much if it is fame among those who have terrible judgement regarding such things? These judgements do not track real excellence, but rather self-promotion and general ignorance of what matters. In fact, if that is the case, then it's highly likely that 'honour' is a negative profile of being honourable. (Recall that this was precisely what Epictetus had warned of earlier in *Ench.* 13.)

The result from the first arc of Epictetus's argument is a reconstruction of the relevant notions of honour as prestige and honourability as virtue, so that they are not so easily confused. Bearing in mind the distinction between the two prevents their equivocation when reasoning in the ebb-and-flow of a life, because the terms announcing honour as prestige are those of honourability as virtue. Yet these are incorrect uses of those terms. Once the Stoic reconstruction of the terms is clarified, progressors are armed against the illusions that invariably flutter about social living.

The second arc of Epictetus's exercise of anticipation is in how you conceive that excellence as being useful to your friends and city. A cost of not pursuing status and wealth is that, if you lack them to begin with, you cannot use them in the service of helping your friends and city. Insofar as part of being a good friend and a good citizen is being useful to your friends and city, then, so the tempting reasoning goes, you must have money and status to be helpful to them.

Epictetus considers the case of a friend in need who may need money or legal assistance. If you intervene, with your largesse or position, you can set things right. Or consider a state in need; the city's building project needs financing, and you could help get those porticoes erected if you had the funds and status to organize that project. Thus, the tempting thought runs, it is for reasons of friendly and civic virtue that we must have status and wealth. It is not *for our own sake* that we must have money and social rank, but so that we can be *useful to others*.

Once stated this way, it is easy to see the reasoning here as rationalization. Consolidating wealth with the justification that it is in the service of others is an all-too-convenient fiction of the monied classes. In its stead, Epictetus runs a *hard* and a *moderate* reply.

The hard reply is, as we've seen with the notions of honour and honourable, a reconstruction of the notion of what it is to be *useful* to one's friends and city. What is it to be a good friend, a good citizen? Along both lines, Epictetus's case for reconstruction of the concept contends that it is possible to be a bad friend and bad citizen even when you have money and supply it liberally. Giving money to your friends can make for terrible results. Consider giving money to the friend who is certain to waste it all on alcohol. Giving money to one's state for gaudy ornamental building projects or for xenophobic monuments is not being a good citizen. Instead, being a good friend and good citizen requires that you enact your virtues and even try to engender them in others. A good friend is trustworthy and modest first, not rich. You can be a good friend without money, but you cannot be a good friend without the virtues. The same goes for being a good citizen. You can be a good citizen without wealth, but you cannot be a good citizen without being modest and honourable. On the reconstruction, good friends and good citizens are useful to their friends and country by being modest, honourable and trustworthy.

The hard reply, then, reconceives what it is to be useful to one's friends and city. So, Epictetus agrees that one has a duty to be a good friend and citizen, but he argues that it is different from what the tempting reasoning portrays it to be. The moderate reply follows the hard reply and depends on the thought that the progressors are enacting that reinterpretation at the core of the hard reply. The moderate reply is that even though caring for virtue is the progressor's first job (and so she does her duty to her friends and city by being honourable and trustworthy), so long as she is attending to that first job successfully, she may pursue wealth and status for that service. Epictetus notes: 'If I can get it while keeping my traits of modesty, trustworthiness, and self-respect, show me the way to earn an honest buck and I'll do it.' So long as you can preserve your self-respect while earning wealth and status, you can (and perhaps should) do so. So long as the occupation of being useful also allows you to remain trustworthy and modest at the same time, then go for it.

In this regard, Epictetus's account here recapitulates the two levels of Stoic value theory. On the first level, there is the distinction between what is and is not up to us – there are things relevant to our volition and others about which we should be indifferent. But among those indifferents, some are preferable, others are dispreferable. One way to distinguish these in the second category is to identify things which, when wielded appropriately, contribute to your capacity to enact your virtue. So, health is preferable to illness, all things being equal since health enables you to be active in your virtues. Similarly, wealth, assuming we pursue it and wield it with virtue, is preferable to poverty, again because it increases the impact of those virtuous acts.

Understanding these levels, the upshot is that, so long as you are pursuing virtue appropriately, you can rely on the distinction between preferred and dispreferred indifferents. That is, your first job is to be honest, trustworthy and modest. Being so, you are doing your duty to your friends and country, even if you lack money or status. But insofar as you can consistently perform that first job *and* gain money and status, that second job is safe to take. The vital lesson, though, is that pursuing the second job at the cost of the first (pursuing the preferred indifferent of money at the cost of honesty, say) endangers your friends and city. A powerful person with no moral integrity is precisely the picture of what Stoics are out to guard against being. Therefore, the road to trying to aid your city by pursuing wealth actually harms the city when that pursuit taxes your virtue, because it lifts a person of low character to a high position of power in the city. If the choice is to sacrifice wealth or virtue, since virtue without wealth is still good whereas wealth without virtue is vice magnified, we should sacrifice wealth.

Chapter 25

This chapter debunks the justification of envy by analysing the logic of transactions. Epictetus denies that envy and jealousy are ever justified. He holds they are never appropriate. Consider the case of someone receiving a greater award than you at a formal ceremony. Is it a good thing to be recognized with an award? To start, recall that in *Ench.* 13 Epictetus warned that we should worry if non-Stoics think well of us – their praise is a negative profile of what's truly worthy of praise. Furthermore, according to Stoic ethics, a true good is unconditionally beneficial and can bring about only happiness. Or what about someone receiving a warmer greeting in a reception line at a wedding than you get? Is it a good thing to be warmly welcomed in a reception line? What about the case of someone being asked for advice before you are? Is it a good thing to be asked for advice? If these three things are good, then you should be glad for the people who get these things, even if they are getting more of them than you or they are getting them before you. But *are* these things really unconditionally beneficial? No. Stoics insist that the only goods are virtues. Only virtues are unconditionally beneficial. Only virtues cannot possibly be abused. All and only virtues are necessary and sufficient for the kind of happiness worth having (which requires self-respect).

How is receiving a great award not a good thing? Awards are given by others. Consequently, a necessary condition for receiving an award is impressing others. But many people are only impressed by those they are predisposed to favour. Thus, award ceremonies are very often popularity contests. Many people gain popularity by schmoozing to curry favour. Many people ingratiate themselves with others and flatter those in a position to influence the distribution of awards. Many people play the game of one hand washing the other, or I'll pat you on the back if you pat me on the back. So, often awards are not given strictly as a matter of objective merit but as the result of cunningly stroking egos and playing self-serving politics. In short, Epictetus believes that it makes good sense to value self-respect over popularity. As seen in *Ench.* 19.2, envy and jealousy over externals, for example, popularity, fame, the attention of others, is out of place. In *Ench.* 23 he declares that if you turn outward wanting to please someone, then you've lost your way. You've lost your way because you've strayed from the path of self-improvement. You've lost your way because you've lost your own self-respect in seeking to gratify another.

How is being warmly welcomed in a reception line not a good thing? Well, again, this outcome results from winning the affection of the welcomers. Many people withhold their warmth from those who haven't buttered them up. If you have not previously flattered the welcomers in the reception line, then you shouldn't be surprised if those welcomers display greater warmth to those who have than they do to you. Similarly, people seek advice from those they are impressed by. If you haven't gone out of your way to impress others, then don't be surprised if they seek advice from those who have worked hard to impress them before – or instead of – asking you for advice. The bottom line is this: the approval of others, the affection of others, recognition by others, the private confidence of others and popularity are not things that are up to us. It takes time, effort and sacrifice to get these sorts of things. If you don't sacrifice what others have, and they get things you don't, you can hardly be surprised. Think hard about whether these badges of popularity are really good after all. Think hard about whether it is worth trading your self-respect for such popularity badges. If not, then such badges are not nearly as good as non-philosophers crack them up to be. Let those who have bowed and scraped and flattered and schmoozed and wheedled to get these badges have them. They have sacrificed a lot to earn them, but you haven't.

Everything has its price. You can't hope to get for free what others have paid for. Transactions simply don't work that way. 'There's no such thing as a free lunch,' as they say. Epictetus illustrates this idea with a grocery shopping example. A grocery store sells heads of lettuce, a dollar apiece. A shopper decides to pay a dollar for a head of lettuce. Transaction completed. The shopper has the lettuce and spent the dollar. If you choose instead to keep your dollar instead of buying the lettuce, then you're not worse off. You still have your dollar.

In section 4 an argument by analogy compares grocery shopping with being invited to a formal dinner party. Those who get invited to a dinner party are those who fawned on the host. Their sycophancy is the price they paid for admission to the fancy affair. You get what you pay for. But if you want not to pay the price of being obsequious and yet also to get invited to the fancy party, then you're stingy and foolish. Stingy, because you refused to pay the price of admission and no fancy dinner parties are 'free' in this sense. Foolish, because you just don't understand how transactions work. 'You have to pay to play,' as they say. For this reason, it's worth remembering the lesson of *Ench.* 19: enter no contest in which victory is not up to you. It's quite possible that flattering someone may not be enough to get you invited to his dinner party, because others may have outperformed you in obsequiousness!

If you chose *not* to brown-nose and suck up to the host of the dinner party, and predictably you were not invited to the party, are you left with nothing? No indeed! You kept your self-respect, and with it, more than likely, your appetite for a hearty meal for one. After all, obsequiousness is nauseating. Sycophants turn stomachs.

Chapter 26

Epictetus rejects the notion that nature victimizes us. His lesson is that nature's purpose can be discerned from recognizing that everyone is in the same boat, and everyone experiences the same kinds of challenges in life. We all must deal with the same kinds of events that are beyond our control. We don't differ from one another in having to deal with things breaking or people close to us dying. So, if we can preserve our equanimity when others experience the loss of property or the loss of life, then we are equally capable of remaining calm and carrying on when *we* experience these same events.

In *Ench.* 3 we learned the importance of remembering that our liking a mug won't keep it from breaking. In this chapter, Epictetus notes that it's easy to calmly accept accidents that happen to other people. When someone else's servant breaks a glass, we are quick to offer consoling words like: 'These things happen. Glasses break. Today one of your glasses broke. It's no big deal.' The challenge we face, of course, is when these accidents happen to *us*. The key to this insight is that since we can remain calm and philosophical by reflecting on the fragility of *all glasses everywhere* when someone else's glass shatters, we have the same ability to keep calm and carry on when our *own* glass shatters. *My* glass is no less fragile than anyone else's. I know that *they* can survive the loss of *their* glass. Therefore, I too can survive the loss of *my* glass. If I am right to urge them to find equanimity, then in the same circumstances I must embrace equanimity too.

As we saw in *Ench.* 11, our human loved ones are not entitlements we permanently own. In fact, we never owned them. They are not and never were *ours* in the sense explained by the FD. They are on temporary loan to us, as the hotel is for visiting guests. *Ench.* 14 taught us that it is foolish to wish your servant never to slip up. Humans err. Your servant is human. Ergo, your servant will err, for example, by accidentally breaking a glass now and again. Similarly, humans die. Your spouse and child are human. Hence, your spouse and child will die. Therefore, you're a fool if you want them to live forever – that's impossible. In *Ench.* 16, Epictetus advised us how to comfort someone weeping over the loss of possessions or whose child is away from home. In this chapter, Epictetus advises the same 'These things happen' attitude when someone else's child or spouse dies. Nobody would fail to say, 'It is human, all too human.' Death is part of the human condition. Human beings die. Your loved ones are human beings. Therefore, your loved ones will die. But nature imposes the very same mortality on one's own loved ones as on the loved ones of others. So, it is a mistake to believe that when our own loved one dies, nature victimizes us. The lesson is rather that we don't differ from one another in having to face, accept and deal with the same events that are not up to us. We can and do accept the mortality of someone else's child or spouse. Therefore, we can and ought to accept the mortality of our own child or spouse. We can and ought to show we care about the person whose child or spouse has died.

Nature never singles anyone out as a victim of death. Death – mortality, temporariness – comes with the territory of all animals, plants and the tiniest of organisms that have ever come into existence on Earth. Nature lends life as a temporary gift to *all* living things. That includes everyone we know, everyone we love and us too. No one is made wretched by nature or by events in nature. It is our judgements about events that make us wretched.

Is this Stoic attitude, that equanimity is the right response to the death of any human being, callous or cavalier? If it were, then presumably we wouldn't say, 'it is human, all too human', when someone else's child or spouse has died. Non-Stoics often respond to the death of a friend or acquaintance, and occasionally a stranger, by saying, 'it's tragic'. But Epictetus denies that anything as routine, predictable, necessary and natural as death can be tragic. This is because tragedies are instances where something that breaks the bounds of value happens, something that shakes our moral outlook. Tragedies can be avoided by forming the right judgements and making the right decisions. Mortality is part of nature's purpose. Mortality cannot be avoided. Thus, mortality and nature's purposes cannot be tragic. Tragedies occur when people make terrible judgements and terrible decisions. Epictetus suggests that the 'Woe is me!' reaction to the death of one's own loved one is unwarranted self-pity. Everyone's loved ones die. So, death does not single out our loved ones to victimize us. Understanding nature's purposes, including the purpose of death, justifies us in encouraging others to remain calm and carry on, just as it helps us to do the same. This is neither callous nor cavalier. It is wise.

Chapter 27

In this chapter, Epictetus makes an argument by analogy, one between the art of archery and the unfolding of Providence's plan. Our approach here is to explain the analogy and show how Epictetus could be arguing for either a modest result or a radical conclusion. Either interpretation, however, yields a puzzle for the notion of anything being up to us at all. This is an overarching problem about the interface between Stoic ethics and Stoic physics. We will hold that the consistent Stoic strategy of compatibilism with regard to determinism and freedom requires a major revision to the concept of self-determination.

Let us begin with the analogues in Epictetus's analogy, and then we will evaluate the breadth of the argument's conclusion. The first analogue is archery. Epictetus notes that targets are not set up to be missed. So, there is a purpose to this activity, that of *aiming* and *doing so accurately*. The archer has a goal. The point of the activity is to achieve that goal. There are skills she acquires in pursuing that goal. She learns how to stand, hold the bow, nock the arrow, draw the string, aim, correct for wind, pick her shots, release, and so on. In the process, she more consistently hits the mark. The second analogue is Nature and its lawful unfolding. What occurs in the cosmos also has a purpose: a rational development of events. Insofar as that series of events is rational, it cannot be evil.

Before we turn to developing the Stoic notion of Nature and its role in this piece of reasoning, it is worth noting that the argument by analogy is not quite perfect as stated. The fact that one sets up archery targets to hit them does not entail that one actually hits them. In fact, it is precisely what a *miss* is: it is a failure to do what one has intended to do in such an activity. So, for this analogical reasoning to do the work that is necessary for the conclusion to follow, a suppressed premise must be added. On the analogy with archery, it can be stated as follows: *Nature never misses.*

The Stoics' view of nature, their physics and their views on ethics are deeply connected. As noted earlier, the distinction between that which is and that which is not up to us is itself one provided by Stoic physics, and this Fundamental Divide is the basis for all reasoning in ethics going forward. Chrysippus, the great systematiser of the Stoa, argued that the objective is to live in agreement with Nature – doing nothing forbidden by law or reason, in accord with the harmony of the universe, and in concert with the dictates of the gods (DL 7.88). So, the life of the Stoic is devoted to understanding the nature of the universe and our place as humans in it. One of the discoveries that this project bears out is that all things in Nature are determined. There is a rational order to the universe, one that manifests a divine plan. Fate is the order of the whole emerging with any connection of events. We recognize this in seeing that, first, we cannot change the past, and further, that we can predict the future based on causes we see in retrospect. Things could not have been otherwise and taking that reasoning with our explanations into the future shows us that the same result obtains for those events. Things in the future cannot be otherwise, either. The gods, as governors of this world, are active in maintaining that determinate order, and in this, they are virtuous and worthy of human regard and piety (DL 7.187). Consequently, so the Stoics held, Nature (the divine) does not miss, and the missing premise in the reasoning in the argument by analogy is clear. *All things in Nature happen as they ought.*

The consequence is that nothing truly bad ever happens in Nature. The problem is that this directly conflicts with what looks like a pretty obvious truth: *plenty of bad things happen.* So, we have what seems an inconsistent set of commitments:

1. All things happen according to Nature.
2. Nature makes all things as they should be.
3. There are bad things.

The problem is that 1 and 3 combine to say that Nature and the divine are responsible for bad things (which contradicts 2, assuming that bad things are contrary to how things should be), and 1 and 2 combine to deny that there are bad things. Finally, 2 and 3 would seem to imply that there are non-natural causes. The most appealing solution here is to deny 3 and hold that there are no truly bad things. And, in fact, this is a consistent route Epictetus takes. This is the radical conclusion: there are no evils in Nature. Recall that in *Ench.* 5, Epictetus argues that it is not *things* that unsettle us, but our *judgement* of things. So, death, illness and poverty are not terrible, but rather it is our judgement that they are terrible that empowers them over us. That things in the world are bad is an illusion, one that arises because we fail to see how things stand together as a whole. The existence of evil is a kind of shadow created by our minds and our failures to understand the whole.

Furthermore, notice how, once you have taken on this perspective of denying the existence of evils, that all events in the world happen according to Nature, you adopt a comportment towards the whole that offers placidity. What others call 'bad fortune' is the cosmos's plan unfolding, a rational series of events that could not be otherwise and that accords with a divine plan. Part of piety, then, is understanding and accepting one's fate.

An extension of this thought is that what non-Stoics describe as 'evils' or 'bad fortune' are in fact excellent occasions to exercise your virtues. The universe puts tests before us, not as evils, but as challenges to better ourselves. So, to confuse the difficulty of the tasks the gods have given us (enduring illness, weathering tough financial times or facing social isolation) with evils is to fail to see what the universe really is: a perfect, rational order.

One challenge to this line of thought is that it radically revises how most people think of bad things. What else would a bad thing be other than pain or loss of capacity or death? That they happen in nature is undoubted, but that they are also bad things seems just as obvious.

The key is to remember that Stoicism is posited on denying the attitudes regarding value from which this objection proceeds. Stoicism requires a major revision of everyday attitudes about what is valuable. The justification for this revision lies not only in how one reasons to that view, but in how one lives by that view. That is, the Stoic revision of value and comportment of life according to Nature is one we endorse on the front end *prospectively*, based on the reasons and arguments that the Stoics give for the core Stoic theses. But it is also endorsed *retrospectively*, that is, after accepting the Stoic doctrines and living inside them. How your life is improved, how your picture of yourself is clarified and given purpose, and whether you, as a Stoic, are flourishing, are all relevant. The Stoic progressor is conducting an experiment in living, trying to monitor how she is progressing as a Stoic while evaluating whether Stoicism generally is worth pursuing. The promise of the programme is that as you progress, you will find that that life experiment also yields evidence that you made a good choice.

The key, again, is the tight connection between Stoic physics and ethics, and particularly in seeing the world as a plan of reasoned perfection. One's ethical orientation is then in living in accord with Nature and maintaining the attitude that there are no bad things. But the objection to this line of thought can be improved. So far, the thesis that there are no bad things has been limited to what non-Stoics have labelled bad – pain, illness, being passed over for opportunities, death. These things surely exist, so the Stoic reply goes, but they are not *bad*. But as goes the improved reply, what about injustice, dishonesty, cowardice, lack of self-control and dishonour? If virtue is the only good, then surely these vices are bad things. They too surely exist.

The improved objection is a serious problem for the Stoics since if all things happen according to Nature and vice happens, then vice accords with Nature too. Stoicism's call to virtue would make no sense unless there were vices in need of correction. So, whence vice?

Given Stoic ethical intellectualism, vice is a consequence of intellectual error, of false belief. This, of course, pushes the problem back a step, as now the question is what the origin of error is. Again, if all things are products of Nature, and nature never misses, then how are ignorance and error possible?

One answer is to say that error and vice are *unnatural*; this reply fits well with the thought that if the Stoic's end is to live in accord with Nature, then non-Stoics fail to do so. The non-Stoic's desire for externals and belief that they are genuine goods necessary for a flourishing life yield vices that make the non-Stoic fit poorly with the flow of the world. In fact, in the *Discourses*, Epictetus argues that this error is the source of what tragedies are; people falsely believe their good lies in the things outside of their control, and this drives them to vicious behaviour and ultimate downfall. The lesson tragedy teaches is to renounce those purported goods (*Disc.* i.4.16). However, our tragic heroes rage about honours not bestowed, or they cheat their families for what passes for love, or they think their happiness hangs on whether a family grudge is settled. For particular purposes, these actions are unnatural, they oppose the natural order. Humans are made to cooperate and be humble social partners, so instances of selfishness and dishonesty contravene that purpose. The solution in the offing, then, is that there are exceptions to the rule that all things that come to pass accord with Nature, the divine plan. So, there is evil and there is vice, but they are contrary to Nature.

Notice that this solution fits nicely with the analogy of archery. Just as there are misses in archery, it is nevertheless the purpose of archery to perfect one's skills so as not to miss, and so there are moments in the natural world that are errors which conflict with Nature's providential plan. The point is to mitigate them. That project begins and ends with one's character and beliefs, and that correcting path accords with Nature.

The problem with this solution is that it fits quite badly with the Stoic view that *all things* happen in Nature, and that Nature is a rational plan. One revision to manage this inconsistency is to change perspectives on vice, one from the inside and another from the outside. From the perspective of an external observer of human behaviour (and especially vices), bad character is easily resolvable with the fact of Providence. Again, assuming that all things happen according to a divine plan, one that explains the connection of events so that they are intelligible, the fact that people who are not wise treat each other terribly is no surprise at all. To expect otherwise is to fail to understand something about the human propensity to vice: people are ignorant. In this regard, it is reasonable to expect those who do not know what is right and good to treat each other viciously. Now take that observer's perspective upon oneself as a progressor. Progressors, as they gradually see things clearly and expect more of themselves, will experience moments when they fall short of their hopes and expectations. This is, again, because they are coming to know the good and challenge themselves to improve, but they are not yet wise. So, they expect too much of themselves. So too, often, do their teachers. Consequently, even errors and vices of progressors accord with Nature – this is precisely as we should expect of humans in this category.

Now shift to the internal perspective on vice and error. These things are up to us. We control how we interpret and respond to the world. So, from this perspective, many of our errors are not results of fate or Nature or Providence, but our own misjudgements. But this perspective neglects to take in all the antecedent causes that made us in the fashion we are in. Looking back at yourself, perhaps a decade or a year ago, you can see those prior external factors bearing on your character. This retrospection generates results in how we control what is up to us. In short, some things are up to us: our judgements, desires, aversions and intentions. But the self we bring to that nexus is not entirely up to us. It is a product of very many intersecting causal lines. Though we work on ourselves with the exercises and reminders of Stoic insight, these are correctives to years of layered habits and ingrained routine. From the internal perspective, the struggles and stumbles of Stoic progressors are cases where it seems they are out of sorts with Nature. But this attitude itself is natural since it results from slowly dawning awareness and strengthening self-control. And importantly, not only is it a natural attitude to have, but a good one, too. As a progressor, you must take on the attitude of seeing temptations to selfishness or dishonesty as unnatural, since you are retooling yourself, transforming your nature. This is the most effective perspective to have on your habits when trying to rid yourself of the bad ones. In this regard, it is an illusion, but a fortuitous one and one we, when taking the internal perspective, cannot help but work from. There are indeed things that are wholly up to us, but who we are that we bring to that nexus of volition is not wholly up to us. Focusing on the former helps us bring the latter more in line with what is right, but it is not the end of the story with Nature as a whole.

The result, as we see it, is a modest conclusion riding the radical one, a view akin to familiar forms of free will compatibilism. There are no bad results in Nature, even the vices of Stoic progressors. However, the most apt and moderate perspective to take on one's vices is that they are nonetheless instances of unnatural actions and responses. In this regard, the radical and moderate perspectives present dual views of oneself. By analogy, archers must take these dual perspectives on themselves, too. On the one hand, they must see their misses as part of the rational and apt story of archery and those making progress as archers: who expects trainees, even those much improved, to hit the target every time? Their misses, really, are as they should be. However, to improve, they must see their misses also as things to be excised and corrected, mistakes contrary to the point of archery. The result, as we see it, is that a Stoic progressor must have a kind of double-vision about herself, her progress and her errors.

On the one hand, she must see herself as simply one more person, socialized to desire things that are not truly good and taught to act in ways that are selfish and dishonest. This way, she can see her progress and her errors in light of what would be reasonable to expect. On the other hand, she must view herself and her vices as poor fits with the flow of the world and life's variances, and thus must expect better of herself.

Chapter 28

Epictetus asks us to imagine a scenario wherein we turn control of our bodies over to someone else. Perhaps it works as follows: we meet people every day, and upon shaking hands with them, they gain control over our bodies. The idea is far-fetched but is not too difficult to imagine. Perhaps on analogy with a remote-control robot or the ways players control their avatars in video games, imagine this other person now controls our bodies. Epictetus predicts that we would be vexed by this turn of events. This, we believe, is for two reasons familiar to non-Stoics and something Stoic progressors will find sympathetic.

The first reason that such an arrangement would be vexing is in the simple loss of bodily autonomy we would experience. This takes two parallel forms. The first is clearly that what should be under our control is no longer under our control, and we can see the problem here without imagining others controlling our bodies. All this requires are cases wherein we simply lack control over our limbs. Injury or disease can make it so that legs or arms don't work the ways we want. When others cause this loss of control, by some act of violence or negligence, perhaps, it is common to think a great misfortune, or even an injustice, has befallen us. When another's actions diminish our capacity for bodily control, it is objectionable.

Furthermore, consider how alienating it can be when one's body does not respond in ways one wishes. Add it to the thought that the act of another is the cause. A common reaction would be resentment. Taking these two thoughts into consideration, the power of Epictetus's image comes into sharper focus. We value bodily autonomy, and the baseline of that is in managing control over what our bodies do; cases in which that is taken away are objectionable. But Epictetus's image adds to this baseline thought, as we not only lose control of our bodies, but they are now under the control of others. That is, it is one thing to no longer have control of something, it is yet another for it to fall under another's control.

The loss of bodily control is considered a great misfortune and losing that control *to another* is yet a greater one. This is an insight as to what it is to possess something; we not only control that thing's activities, but we have control over who has access. So were another to suddenly gain control over our bodies, our sense of our bodies being our own is doubly damaged.

Furthermore, we expect that if others hijack our bodies, they will not treat them with the same care with which we treat them. Cleaning and maintaining a human body are at times onerous. Also, these bodies are fragile. One must be concerned with multiple minutiae: trip edges on floors, shoes too tight, sunburn, toothbrushing and flossing, and so on. It would be too easy to treat the body of another without the care we invest in our own. So, not only would the fact that others gaining control of our bodies be an affront to those bodies being *ours*, but we also would have reason to expect that those bodies would be *mistreated.* It would be akin to finding your neighbours have not only been taking your car for joy rides, but also finding out that they have not been careful at all with the paint and transmission.

Epictetus has arranged his analogy as follows: just as we would be outraged if others took control of *our bodies*, we should be outraged if they take control of *our minds.* Here, Epictetus asks us to consider the fact that *others do control our minds.* This passing comment upsets us, a biting bit of sarcasm deflates us, and our happiness too often hangs on praise from those we admire. Too often our thoughts of ourselves depend on the opinions of others. Epictetus provides the tools for managing one's reactions to the opinions of others in other chapters (*Ench.* 13 and 20), so we will leave comment on that task for elsewhere. However, there are four things to note about how Epictetus frames the analogy.

First, Epictetus holds that we should *feel shame* at the fact that others have this kind of control over our minds. To start, this is because, as opposed to our bodies, our own choices have given others this control over our minds. We judge them to have the insight and power to determine what we think and how we feel. So, even though we object to the result (that others and their judgements control our minds), we are the ones who made it so. You need not feel shame if another has interfered with your control over your body, as your body is not fully under your control. But your mind, by hypothesis, is. So, when others control our minds by expressing their opinions and cajoling us, not only should we protest, but the victimization is something we did to ourselves. This is why Epictetus asks if we feel shame and implies that we should.

The second item of importance here is that the line of argument is a purely cognitive approach to the challenge. Epictetus draws an analogy and then argues for a conclusion. This is different from the exercises of anticipation and endurance, strategies of comporting oneself to future or present challenges. Rather, this is a strategy of reasoning about the circumstances in general, seeing them for what they are, and then resolving to do better. You are invited to see a swath of your behaviour as irrational, feel some shame at it, and then, because of this, change that behaviour.

The third thing to take from this line of argument is that Epictetus is still addressing progressors. He holds that they should feel shame for falling short of the Stoic goal. It requires that the audience does care for their bodies, for their control over them, and that they would object to someone taking their bodies over. It requires that his audience has succumbed to the pressure of others' judgements about how they value and view themselves. For the analogy to work, Epictetus's audience must not yet be wise, and they must not have met the Stoic objectives. But they must have enough insight to see why they should feel shame in the first place. They are aware of the Fundamental Divide. They know that they can do better and resist the pressure of others' judgements. The wise, on the other hand, would not accept the premise of the analogy that one finds it objectionable that another controls one's body – it is an external, so an indifferent. Moreover, the wise could feel no shame at all over others trying to control their minds, as they would not have caved under those pressures in the first place. This chapter is useless, then, for those who are already wise, because its reasoning is entirely from false premises for them. Rather, the chapter is a set of arguments for progressors, those with attachments well beyond things relevant to their volition, still making errors, but also those who know the right path and who feel shame when they do wrong and know they can do better. Feeling shame is an intermediate state between vice and virtue. One has done wrong, so one is vicious to a degree, but one still recognizes this as a wrong and wishes to be different. So, in that regard, it is virtuous to a degree, too. Epictetus, then, relies on this emotion of moral intermediacy to spur progressors towards improvement.

The fourth and most interesting thing about this chapter is that it is an instance of what it prohibits. Epictetus's progressors are instructed that they shouldn't allow others to control their minds, and then Epictetus shames them for when they do allow it. But if the audience were to follow this advice of feeling shame, then they have allowed yet another person – in this case, Epictetus himself – to control their emotions by shaming them for allowing others to control their minds. If the reasoning succeeds, it is an instance of the kind of habit it criticizes. On its face, this seems inconsistent, since the emotional result of the passage for the progressors breaks the rule Epictetus urges them to follow. However, if we recall that the way out of the progressor's paradox we proposed in comments on *Ench.* 22 and 23 was that we must trust the judgement of the wise to evaluate our progress, Epictetus's observation is consistent. In one sense students do hand their minds over to their teachers. However, Epictetus is making an observation in accord with commitments his audience already made. He is not browbeating them to accept a conclusion or insisting they feel one way or another based on reasons they do not accept. Rather, he is noting that, given their own views, they should concede that they've done something shameful. So, this chapter is not an injunction to feel shame, but a set of reminders that, assuming our students find it fitting, urges them come to reflect on themselves and resolve to do better.

Chapter 29

This chapter repeats nearly word for word *Discourses* iii. 15. 1–13, so it may not have appeared in Arrian's original edition of the *Encheiridion*. Like *Ench.* 4, this chapter offers advice on how to prepare mentally for a task before tackling it. Epictetus believes that the roles that we have organize the tasks that we can and should undertake.

The thesis of this chapter is that authenticity of character can only be achieved by cultivating integrity of mind. The logical structure of the argument for this thesis is a series of conditionals. The chapter concludes with a command to choose between two fundamentally dissimilar roles – being a serious, educated philosopher or being an ordinary layperson, that is, an uneducated schlub. Schlubs don't reflect on their place in the cosmos, their relationships with others, the roles that suit them or their purposes in life. Philosophers, by contrast, reflect on these concerns often and very seriously.

Epictetus lays down a practical policy to guide one's selection of possible tasks. The policy is this: when deciding whether to undertake a possible task, one must first consider each step required to complete that task before it is wise to undertake it. The decision to tackle the task entails commitment to performing each step the task demands. Call this the Step-Wise policy. This policy is expressed in the following conditional:

1. If you want to accomplish project P, then you must consider the steps P_1, P_2, P_3, etc., that P requires.

The implication of this policy is the following judgement which guides the choice of projects:

2. It is reasonable to undertake P only if you commit to completing all the steps P_1, P_2, P_3, etc., P requires.

Failure to follow 1 will result in plunging precipitously into P heedless of P_1, P_2, P_3, etc. Failure to consider and complete steps P_1, P_2, P_3, etc., will result in being derailed by difficulties. Since anticipating these difficulties would have enabled one to avoid them, being derailed by them is disgraceful. Consequently, failure to practise the Step-Wise policy will result in disgracefully abandoning the project. This is classic Stoic advice. Dealing with difficulties isn't primarily a matter of gritting one's teeth and enduring them. Rather, reason requires preparing for all the difficulties that could happen before they do happen. The Step-Wise process, then, is an exercise of anticipation. It also is a point of reflection on one's capacities. Thinking through all the steps that will be necessary to reach a goal readies a person for challenges encountered along the way. Quitting a project eagerly undertaken at first is disgraceful because it shows that one has wasted one's time and energy on a project that could have been completed successfully. The choice to embark on the project ought to result from the judgement that the project is worthwhile, not that it would be easy. To quit a project is to concede too late that one is not up to the challenge of finishing it. True, it is better to gain self-knowledge late than not at all. But better still would be to accurately gauge one's ability to do a project before taking it precisely to avoid quitting on it mid-stream. That's why quitting halfway through remains disgraceful.

The example of a project that demands following the Step-Wise policy is winning an Olympic event. Epictetus is fond of examples involving athletes, athletic training and competing at the games at Olympia (see *Ench.* 51.2). He does this because a central feature of the Stoic programme is rigorous training, called *askêsis*. The Olympic training of the athlete is an *askêsis* of the body that parallels the *askêsis* of the mind of the Stoic philosopher. The many texts in the *Discourses* about athletes make clear that Epictetus greatly respects athletes committed to training for and competing in the Olympic games. Here in *Ench.* 29.2 he says winning an Olympic event is awesome. But to achieve such a feat, one must heed the Step-Wise policy. Epictetus details the habits, the sub-tasks, that the Olympian-in-training must adopt:

T_1 You must be disciplined.
T_2 You must keep a strict diet.

T_3	You must give up sweets.
T_4	You must train in the gym under compulsion ...
T_5	... at a set hour of day, in the heat, in the cold.
T_6	You must not drink cold water ...
T_7	... or wine whenever you please.
T_8	You must turn yourself over to your trainer as if he were a doctor.

The rigors of a strict programme of exercise at a set hour of the day, in unpleasantly hot and unpleasantly cold weather, are compulsory. Similarly, the food and drink of the athlete preparing for Olympic competition is strictly limited. There is much that this athlete must give up. But by exercising his freedom to aim at the goal of winning an Olympic event, the athlete must necessarily curtail his bodily freedom. The athlete must entrust his body to the care of his trainer and the strict regimen he imposes. Epictetus reminds us that the demands of Olympic competition require a physique in peak condition. By comparison, the inferior physique of a non-athlete, the condition of the person before his training has begun, needs medical treatment. Thus, if you want the role of an athlete who competes in the Olympics, you need a physician who will replace your bodily ills with robust health and strength. This kind of doctor is the physical trainer, the Olympic coach.

But the gruelling physical habits of daily exercise and the strict diet of food and drink prescribed by the trainer are only the preparations necessary to make it to the Olympic games. Epictetus imagines that the athlete is a wrestler who faces a host of further hassles, dangers and challenges during the big event itself:

T_9	You need to dig into the chalk (see Note on *parorussō*) ...
T_{10}	sometimes dislocate your wrist,
T_{11}	sometimes twist your ankle,
T_{12}	swallow a lot of sand,
T_{13}	sometimes get whipped,
T_{14}	... and along with all these hassles, lose.

The Step-Wise policy itemizes various adversities and unpleasant experiences that should be anticipated in the wrestling match itself. Anticipation of a wide range of adversities that may occur at any time helps one prepare to cope with them calmly and circumspectly. This is a common technique of psychological therapy in Stoicism.

Ingesting a mouthful of sand from the floor of the arena (T_{12}) may seem a smaller nuisance than suffering an injury (T_{10} and T_{11}) or being whipped for committing a foul (T_{13}). Yet these unpleasantries are surpassed by the greatest possible disappointment. Months of dietary self-deprivation, demanding exercise and submission of one's body to one's trainer's strictures, in addition to injury in the wrestling ring, may all culminate in defeat (T_{14}), not victory. In the end, the result of the contest is beyond your control. Any of the other competitors may simply best you on the day of the contest. This too is an important lesson in Stoic ethics. The goal of any activity that involves externals is not to achieve an external result. Rather, the Stoic's goal is to be virtuous at all times while doing everything in her power to achieve that result. This may seem counterintuitive, but to explain it the Stoics reflected on the art of archery. Whether the archer's loosed arrow hits the target depends on some factors not up to her. Her objective, then, is to do all she can to try to hit the target. Doing her best to use good form, concentrate, draw and release smoothly are up to her. The path the arrow takes is ultimately up to Fate. Fate may even break her bow string! Like archery, medicine is another art the Stoics termed *stochastic*. Doctors are not omnipotent; they cannot cure every disease of every patient. Some conditions cannot be repaired. Some injuries leave permanent damage. Some patients die, despite a doctor's best efforts. So, the goal of medicine is for doctors to do everything in their power to heal and help their patients (see Sellars 2003, 70–75).

The preparation and training of the athlete are up to her, but ultimately, winning her match is not. As long as the athlete did all she could to put herself in the best position to compete, then losing her match is an indifferent outcome without any disgrace. After all, the lost contest is a fated outcome Stoic training prepared her to accept. But note that self-deception is a danger here. Did she *really* train and compete as hard as she could have, or is she merely *telling* herself 'I gave it my best effort'? The progressor may realize, in retrospect, perhaps, that if she falls prey to self-deception, her soothing excuses are false balms blocking her progress. Intellectual honesty is indispensable to progress. So, the honest competitor knows that the gracious loser congratulates the winner for earning that win. The victor's triumph deserves praise. The sore loser, lacking the insight of the Stoic competitor, whines disgracefully.

After having detailed all these caveats in Section 2, in Section 3 Epictetus begins with the advice to think over all these considerations and only then, if the desire remains, to decide to embark on the goal of becoming an athlete and taking up this role. Failure to collect in one's mind all the necessary sub-tasks, all the challenges completing them will require, all possible setbacks, all perils to expect during the contest and, finally, the chances of losing amounts to a kind of mental fragmentation or schizophrenia. Epictetus argues that one must cultivate integrity of mind by bringing together all the many individual sub-goals constitutive of the overarching goal – a victory in the Olympic games – and recognizing the necessity of desiring the entire bundle of sub-goals at once. The seriousness and reasonableness of the Step-Wise plan is evident to adults. In contrast, failure to enact thoroughgoing, circumspect Step-Wise thinking characterizes the flaky mind of a child. 'But if you don't think it over, you'll be turning from one game to the next like children do, who one minute play as wrestlers, the next as gladiators, the next play trumpets, and then pretend to be actors in a play.' A child cannot carry through on any one of these roles. A child is not serious about any of these activities. Instead, the child only plays at them frivolously, pretending to assume one role, then another. A child has no capacity to dedicate himself to becoming a real wrestler, gladiator, trumpeter or thespian. Most children lack commitment, follow-through and earnestness. Consequently, children just fool around. To be childish is to be undisciplined and without serious purpose.

Epictetus believes it disgraceful for an adult to have the splintered mind of a child. Disparate roles cannot be conducted simultaneously, nor can they be fulfilled by dabbling briefly at one and then turning abruptly to another. Each role requires full focus when we're doing it. Though both athletes and gladiators exercise their bodies, the specific training each requires differs. Moreover, you cannot briefly be an athlete and then briefly a trumpeter. That would be like an actor switching dramatic roles during the same scene of a play. Since oratory requires its own kind of training, you cannot be both an orator and a philosopher. Performing a profession with authenticity requires whole-hearted commitment to it alone. Thus, for Epictetus, each profession requires specializing in it. You are what you do, so be *one* person excellent at your one vocation. Hopping from one identity to another displays disconnected, erratic behaviour without any stable personality.

'Instead, like a monkey, you ape every spectacle that you see, amused by one thing after another.' Mere mimicry characterizes an ape, not a human adult. Monkeys do what they feel like, moment to moment. So, if you're into fun and silly games, realize that you're not making progress as a Stoic philosopher. Letting yourself be distracted by amusing spectacles is shattering your attention. Simian silliness blocks your pursuit of your single goal of self-improvement. This is the result of a failure to think through what you do before doing it. To forge the mind of a Stoic, you must plot the route you'll need to get there, anticipate roadblocks and navigate detours. Cold feet won't carry you to your destination. Only mindful, deliberate steps will bring you closer to it. The childish, simian fool, because of his fragmented, frivolous mind, is bound to recoil in fear in the face of adversity when play time is over.

Epictetus's example of an inspired orator is the Stoic philosopher Euphrates (see Frede 1997). But to want to be a philosopher because you are impressed by the virtuosic oratory of a Euphrates is the wrong reason to undertake that role. Epictetus urges the reader to think about the demands of the role and then to objectively examine one's individual strengths and weaknesses. Pentathletes need certain kinds of arms and legs. A genuine wrestler has a distinct physical build. If you don't have the right body for a role, then it is foolish to pursue it. So, Epictetus suggests that even following the Step-Wise policy may not be enough to justify pursuing a role. You've got to have some talent at, say oratory, to make selecting that role worth your while. Epictetus thinks 'different people are born for different things'. Some have what it takes to become wrestlers, pentathletes, orators and the rest. Similarly, only some are born to be philosophers. But whereas Olympic athletes get cheers and the best orators get applause, philosophers get no acclaim. The project of becoming a philosopher is fraught with challenges. A philosopher should expect scorn, not public recognition. Part of the training to be a (Stoic) philosopher is practising losing out on all contests over the externals for which non-Stoics aggressively compete. The Stoic trainee must expect:

P_1	to change how he eats and drinks,
P_2	to change what he desires and shuns,
P_3	to go without sleep,
P_4	to work his tail off,
P_5	to be away from his friends,
P_6	to be looked down upon by a lowly servant,
P_7	to be derided by people he meets,
P_8	not to receive honours,
P_9	not to receive public offices,
P_{10}	to lose legal cases,
P_{11}	to get the short end of the stick in every tiny little thing.

Epictetus thinks these expectations of the philosophical progressor (P_1 through P_{11}) are comparable in difficulty to the expected tasks of the Olympic wrestler (T_1 through T_{14}). The wrestler's ultimate goal is to win at Olympia. But even if the wrestler successfully endures T_1 through T_{13}, there is no guarantee he will secure T_{14}. Moreover, even if he does win an Olympic victory, what then? Will he compete again four years later? What will he do if he re-injures his shoulder or knee? Should he retire from athletics and embark on a new profession? Perhaps

Epictetus is hinting that the Olympic athlete, whether in victory or defeat, must reflect on which course of action will lead to happiness in the long run, after his career as an athlete ends. Neither wrestling, nor the pentathlon, nor oratory can win a person self-control, emotional self-sufficiency or freedom from fear and anger.

What can? Well, precisely P_1 through P_{11}, the rigours of philosophical training, hassles though they may seem, can yield an untroubled mind. If you are willing to pay the price of P_1 through P_{11}, then it is reasonable to undertake the project of becoming a philosopher. Epictetus insists that one have *one* profession, not many. Success at one's chosen profession demands one's full attention, concentration and dedication. A jack of all trades can be a master of none.

But surely, an objection can be posed, we all wear *many* hats. Contemporary living is complex. To earn enough simply to pay the bills, some must hold down several different jobs. Our social groups and familial relations further multiply those jobs. So, aren't human beings perforce to have many professions?

This objection confuses professions with roles (see the comment on *Ench.* 30). While we certainly have multiple roles, Epictetus explains there is only one profession fundamental to who we are. That profession, that calling, is first, last, and always to be *human*. The most fundamental life decision is the kind of person we want to be. This choice, he thinks, is a simple either-or: to be good or bad. A good person practises 'the craft about what's on the inside'. A bad person is about 'what's on the outside'. All other professions mentioned in this chapter aim at external success. The wrestler, pentathlete and gladiator seek trophies. The trumpeter and thespian seek the audience's applause. The orator seeks acclaim and influence. All of them seek honours and fame. To maximize their chances of winning external prizes, they must be ready to sacrifice what's on the inside: honesty, decency and self-respect. If winning an Olympic contest is your top priority, you'll have to neglect your character. Epictetus concludes this chapter by pressing us to choose between two diametrically opposed roles: philosopher or *idiōtês*. An *idiōtês* is a person with no professional knowledge, an ignoramus. The English word "idiot" comes from *idiōtês*. So, Epictetus frames the fundamental choice of what kind of person to be as the choice between cultivating mental integrity or chasing external rewards and burnishing your reputation. That is, one must undertake the role of a philosopher or that of a *schlub*. A schlub may stumble upon fame, win the lottery or even steal an Olympic victory. But none of these external victories rescue schlubs from their flabby, messy minds. The Stoic philosopher's good is only available to the person who, having mastered the Step-Wise method, has built up a muscular mind. An agile, muscular mind results from wholeheartedly enacting the role of philosopher despite its putative 'hassles'. Integrity of mind brings authenticity of character. A genuine philosopher commits to becoming this Olympian of the soul.

Note on *parorussō*

In *Ench.* 29.2 the verb *parorussō* (παρορύσσω) is used to describe an activity an athlete performs during or before a contest at Olympia. The exact meaning of this term, and the purpose of the activity, has puzzled translators. The lexicon offers two definitions: '*dig alongside* or *parallel*' and '*dig one against another*' (Liddell et al. 1996, 1343). Besides Epictetus, the only other instance of this verb occurs in DL, where it is reported that Diogenes the Cynic 'would say that people compete in digging [*tou paroruttein*] and kicking, but no one in being fine and good' (DL vi.27). R.D. Hicks cites the instance of the verb in *Discourses* iii.15.4 (= *Ench.* 29.2) as evidence that 'competition in digging trenches [*en tōi agōni parorussesthai*] formed a part of the course of preparation which athletes underwent at Olympia' (Laertius 1980, vol. 2, 28–9). Oldfather, citing DL vi.27, less confidently interprets *parorussō* as a technical term 'of somewhat uncertain meaning, but probably referring to a preliminary wallowing in dust or mud before the wrestling match at the *pancratium*' (Epictetus 1928, 100).

How should we understand this term? Should we imagine, with Hicks, two Olympic competitors, side by side, rapidly digging trenches with shovels or their bare hands? Did the deeper, longer or faster trench win? Or should we imagine, with Oldfather, that the 'digging' was not a competition, but simply wrestlers rolling their whole bodies in dust to get ready for their bout? A sweaty body would be harder to grip than a dusty one. So, was the purpose of the dust bath to make each wrestler's body less slippery? Or did wrestlers wallow in mud to make their bodies more slippery? Should we envision pancratiasts as mud-wrestlers?

Neither trench-digging contests nor pre-match mud wallowing seems a satisfactory explanation. A third possibility is that the wrestlers dug a pair of small, shallow, side-by-side trenches as footholds from which to push off at the start of the match. This digging of footholds might resemble what baseball batters do in the batter's box prior to facing pitchers. A problem with this idea is that wrestlers must move their feet around quite a lot the instant their match begins. Since wrestlers need to be light and quick on their feet, it's hard to see how initially planting them in shallow foothold trenches could be any advantage.

Our translation of *parorussō* in *Ench.* 29.2 modifies Oldfather's suggestion. Modern-day gymnasts, powerlifters and athletes throwing the shot put, hammer, javelin and discus routinely apply chalk made of magnesium carbonate ($MgCO_3$) to their hands to absorb sweat and improve their grips. Gymnasts use this chalk on their legs for the high bar and uneven parallel bars. So, large trays of powdered chalk positioned beside the contest zones have been common aids for athletes for many years. We conjecture that it is not implausible to suppose that in antiquity wrestlers could routinely dig (*orussō*) their hands, arms and perhaps even legs, into a similar chalky powder or dust, available beside (*para*) the wrestling area, to ready their grips for their matches.

Chapter 30

Human beings are naturally very social beings, and so we are all connected to many other people through an extensive and robust network of interpersonal relationships. We have families, friends, neighbours, co-workers, associates, teammates, fellow club members, fellow travellers and fellow citizens. How are we to measure our duties to so many different people? Epictetus identifies the *type* of relationship we have with each person and then derives our *duties* flowing from it.

As we have seen, Stoics often think in dichotomies. Two broad categories they distinguish are *natural* and *acquired* relationships. Natural relationships are those we inherit in the course of nature rather than those we choose. These include being related as a child to our parents (grandparents, aunts, uncles), as a sibling to our siblings, as a citizen to our native-born fellow citizens and, in the big picture, as a member of the universal community of all rational beings everywhere (the cosmopolis). Acquired relationships are those we play a role in selecting and creating. These include the friendships we make. They also include the relationships we develop from the activities we choose to engage in; those we form from the groups we join; and those that arise from the jobs, professions and careers we select. So, for example, we might opt to ride a bus to work, go for a walk with our hiking club pals, dine with a friend and then meet with our book club. In doing so we would be relating to (1) fellow travellers on the bus and the bus driver, (2) our co-workers, (3) fellow hikers, (4) our friend and (5) fellow book club members. If we choose to marry, we acquire a spousal relationship. If we try to procreate and succeed, then our relationship with our newborn child is partly acquired and partly natural. If we opt to adopt a child, our parental relationship is acquired.

In this chapter Epictetus begins with our relationship with our fathers. We don't choose our father. Who our father is is not up to us. Given the FD and the role we are born into as a child of *this* parent, our only choice is whether to play this natural role well or not. Epictetus endorses the traditional view that you must defer to your father. This requirement entails accepting his stern restrictions and demanding expectations, performing the chores he assigns and even enduring his abusive behaviour. Clearly, if your father abuses you, he is a bad father. But it is *his* role to be the father. It is not *your* role to criticize how he performs his role. Your role is to be a daughter or son and to perform the duties of that role well.

What if your brother gets you into trouble, cheats you, steals, damages or destroys your possessions, deceives you or wrongs you in some other way? Again, how he behaves is up to him. You clearly do not control him. What is up to you is the kind of sibling *you* choose to be. You can treat him as a brother should be treated. You can be honest, fair, kind, generous, helpful, supportive and loyal towards him. You can show dignity, decency and integrity when interacting with him. This is what Epictetus means by being vigilant about keeping your volition (*prohairesis*) – your choices, decisions and intentions – in accord with nature. You are free to be a good sibling regardless of how your siblings behave.

The Stoic notion of harm is harm to one's real self, to one's moral character. Sticks and stones, as they say, may break your bones but they cannot harm the real you. Recall that Epictetus was born into slavery. He undoubtedly suffered abuse at the hands of cruel masters. But Stoics value self-respect without worrying about bruises or fractures. If people try to insult you, what they say can only hurt if you legitimize what they say. It's like they are throwing a punch. If you accept the insult as an accurate indictment of your failings, then you let the hurled insult land as a blow. If, however, you dismiss what they say as illegitimate, then you dodge the thrown punch and the would-be insulter's words harmlessly sail by you. You have disarmed the would-be abuser. That is what Epictetus means by saying that no one will harm you unless you're willing to be harmed. The moment you believe that the bully has harmed you, the bully succeeds in harming you. But judging whether you are harmed is up to *you*, it is *not* up to the bully.

You cannot transform a bully into a benefactor. But you can decide that a bully is powerless over your self-respect. You can resolve that a bully cannot strip you of your courage, coerce you or deflect you from your goals. As long as you concentrate on acting as a neighbour ought to act, no one can stop you from being a good neighbour. As long as you dedicate yourself to fulfilling your civic duties, no one can prevent you from being a good citizen. If you are a general or a supervisor, you should focus on being the best one you can be instead of wanting your subordinates to behave differently. Wanting others to change is a recipe for frustration. You have the power to do your job and play your roles well. It is your responsibility to do so. You have no power to make others act this way or that way. They are not your puppets. Master yourself no matter what others do or fail to do; that is the lesson of this chapter.

Chapter 31

The previous chapter outlined our duties to other mortals. This chapter outlines our duties to the divine. Given that Stoicism is an intellectualist programme, Epictetus starts with one's epistemic duties, so he identifies the core of piety as having knowledge about the gods. He then turns to the practical consequences of those cognitive attitudes with how one performs religious ritual.

To start, the three core views of Stoic theology are that (1) the gods exist, (2) they manage the universe effectively and justly and (3) our place in the universe is to be obedient to them and their plan. Knowledge of the gods, then, has a purifying effect on those who hold it. Not only does one have a clarifying view of and comportment to fate's affordances, but one bears the right attitude of appreciation of the divine at the head of it all. Piety, along these cognitive lines, is not only consistent with but recapitulates what we've called the Fundamental Divide (FD) in our comments on *Ench.* 1. This result is certainly surprising, but it is a way that Stoic value theory scales between bearing on a life for a particular individual and embracing the cosmos as a whole.

Epictetus's central insight is that false beliefs about what is good and evil create downstream errors about whether the gods help or harm, benefit or neglect us. Epictetus shows this with an analogy from relations between humans to relations between humans and the gods. To begin with relations between humans, consider Polyneices and Eteocles, the sons of Oedipus, the king of Thebes. When Oedipus stepped down from the throne in disgrace, his sons agreed to share power. They would rule on alternating years. When Oedipus visited them during this arrangement, they treated him shabbily and disrespectfully, hoping to let him know he was no longer king and had no control over their lives. He cursed his sons to be as hateful to each other as they were to him, and thereupon their power-sharing arrangement fell apart. At the end of Eteocles's year in charge, Polyneices came to Thebes expecting to be king. But Eteocles refused to hand over power, so Polyneices returned with seven compatriots to lay siege to Thebes to regain his rightful throne. The brothers met in single combat and killed each other.

The lesson of Eteocles and Polyneices is that the belief that externals such as power, wealth and status are real goods not only makes you vulnerable to fortune's vicissitudes, but also makes you resent others whom you think contribute to those vicissitudes or view as impediments to your desires. This resentment causes you to break your bonds with them. Brothers turn on their father to keep him out of their arrangement. The father turns on his sons when he feels slighted by them. The brothers turn on each other scrambling over the throne they had agreed to share. The playwright Aeschylus, in retelling the story in his *Seven against Thebes*, describes the brothers as 'children of bitterness', and observes that 'greed parts heredity in two' (935–40). False beliefs about the good incline us to resent each other and so, driven by that contempt, break trust.

In view of this point about relations among humans, Epictetus draws the analogy with our relationships to the gods. Just as the Theban brothers, because they thought that being king was a great good and being without kingship was an intolerable evil, consequently warred with each other for a throne, we are tempted to break bonds with the gods over too many externals. The farmer thinks that rain is good because it waters his crops, which will make him wealthy. The merchant thinks that storms are bad because they sink his ships full of wares, which cost him his wealth. So, when clouds gather on the horizon, one rejoices and thanks the gods, while the other, struck with fear, curses them. Why? Because they believe, just as the Theban brothers did, that these externals are the important things in their lives and that others who can bestow or withhold them are to be loved or reviled depending on which they do.

If you have the right beliefs about the gods, then you believe that all events are not merely up to the gods, but that they are up to gods who are rational and just. Consequently, you have reason neither to resent them for what happens, nor to love them more when you enjoy good fortune. Stoic theology and ethics converge here – correct beliefs about the gods and correct beliefs about one's volition overlap. Conversely, false beliefs about the gods and false beliefs about the good not only endanger our autonomy, but breed vice and impiety.

Religious orthodoxy (having correct belief), given the intellectualist programme, is upstream from religious orthopraxy (having correct practices and rituals). And the question remains: what is orthopraxy, given the fact that the gods exist, run the world rationally and our role requires obedience to their dictates? Epictetus's answer takes on a form of practical conservatism – no significant revision of ritual practice is needed. One still makes libations, performs sacrifices and even gives vegetal offerings, each fitting the gods to whom the gifts are given. The reason, first, is that this is, as we saw in *Ench.* 30, how the relationship is maintained; you treat your father as fathers are treated, and the same goes for neighbours, fellow citizens, and so on. One then treats gods as gods. That treatment is not for the sake of your onlooking friends or neighbours, but for the sake of that relationship with the god. You express reverence and appreciation in those rituals, which means that when you perform those rituals you will do so with the objective of expressing that reverence; moreover, they will be neither gaudy nor paltry, and you will perform them from the heart. In this, you maintain that relationship with the gods, just as being a good parent does so with your children, being a good citizen does so with your neighbours and your state, and so on. In fact, in the *Discourses* Epictetus pushes the idea that the analogical reasoning conducive of piety is to think of ourselves as 'sons of the gods' (*Disc.* i.9.5).

On the theological front, both with the programmes of orthodoxy and orthopraxy, it is useful to draw contrasts between the Stoic programme and other traditions. Two are worthy of note, first what we might call Olympianism, and second, that of the Epicureans.

The Olympian theological programme is at the fore with Homer, Hesiod, Vergil, and the stories of gods, heroes and monsters. Very roughly, this tradition holds that there are many gods, they are very powerful and they take keen interest in human affairs. But they fight with each other, choose sides in human disputes, cheat each other, lie to humans and abuse them. Most rituals are performed as propitiation or as transactional gifts in the service of a divine boon. So, one sacrifices, often greatly, to woo the favour of gods who are plainly not rational or just. They are powerful but since they can be thwarted (certainly by each other and it seems sometimes even by humans), they are not fully in control of the universe.

So, even though the sacrifices Epictetus endorses may not be all that different from those performed in Olympian religious practice, the Stoic approach to religious piety is very different. The Stoics envision worship and sacrifice as giving the gods the attention and appreciation they deserve, given their role as rational managers of the world. Olympian practitioners worship in order to curry favour from powerful entities easily swayed but unmoved by justice.

The Epicureans offer another contrast, as they too are practical conservatives. Epicurus holds that one should still sacrifice as others do. But he holds that the gods do not notice these sacrifices, because they live happy lives untroubled by what we do below. The Epicurean programme is posited on the view that the good lies in maintaining static pleasures, so the good life for the gods must be one without disruptions. Epicurus explicitly argues this in his *Letter to Menoeceus* (123). Epicurean gods, then, not only pay no attention to what we do or how we sacrifice (or even whether we do so at all), but they are also not troubled by having to run the universe. Such a job, by Epicurean lights, would be a major hassle that would interrupt the continuity of the gods' serenity. Cicero famously observed this in his dialogue on religion, *On the Nature of the Gods* (i.102). Epicurean religious orthopraxy, then, is more about making sure you fit in with your society and affirm the rituals of your kin. It is less about connecting with the gods. Moreover, the idea that piety involves imitating the gods is as old as Plato. But the Epicureans radically broke with other theological traditions by reinterpreting 'imitating the gods' to mean striving to emulate the gods' utterly uninvolved, eternally carefree, serene existence as much as humanly possible.

For Stoics, Epicurean theology is an absurd representation of the divine. Their gods are pictures of idleness, instead of rational diligence and duty (as argued by Cicero's advocate for Stoic theology, Balbus, in *On the Nature of the Gods* (i.102)). Epicurean ritual takes on the distinct patina of mere play-acting. One is not maintaining a relationship with the gods with such acts, but rather performing by rote for onlookers.

By contrast with Olympianism and Epicureanism, the distinct theological programme in the Stoic account of the divine is evident. However, we have a final question not anticipated by Epictetus: how might Stoic piety present in a contemporary context? Assuming the success of a broadly naturalist explanation of events in the world, from the story of modern physics, Darwinian biology and accounts of human development, there is little room for the gods to play in sustaining or explaining our world. Moreover, even were there to be such a role for a god to play, it is uncertain why worship would be an appropriate comportment. Total obedience is not the proper attitude for rational and autonomous beings, while it is unclear how sacrifices really maintain that worshipful relationship. So, what is the right Stoic theological attitude for scientifically literate twenty-first century adults? One model for such an approach is given in Bertrand Russell's essay 'A Free Man's Worship'. There, Russell identifies Stoic freedom with a non-religious but still resigned view that the world is out of our control, and we should value the virtues of right-thinking and understand Fate's affordances. Russell thinks that, ultimately, with this outlook, by understanding the whole, one appreciates it. 'To abandon the struggle for private happiness, to expel all eagerness of temporary desire, to burn with a passion for eternal things – this is emancipation, and this is the free man's worship' (1957: 114). To Russell's mind, it is Stoic moral intellectualism and the freedom one finds in the use of reason to see where things must go that constitute the heart of Stoic worship. 'Liberation is effected by the contemplation of Fate', as he puts it. The point, then, is that orthodoxy is upstream from orthopraxy. As we perfect our knowledge of the world, our acts of appreciation of Fate will change but also retain a simple nugget of wisdom: understanding and assent.

Chapter 32

This chapter returns to the Stoic approach to divination briefly addressed in *Ench.* 18. The idea Epictetus reiterates here is that divination ought never to be a cause of worry or concern for the thoughtful Stoic philosopher. Why? Because events transpiring in the world are not up to us, and Stoics focus their attention and concern on what is up to them. Thus, remembering the FD empowers Stoics who chose to consult a seer about future events with peace of mind.

In section one Epictetus explains that a philosopher – a Stoic – does not know the future. If you believe in divination, then you believe that seers (diviners) can foretell certain future events. But these are events involving externals, things beyond the philosopher's control, like what other people will do, what travellers will encounter on a trip, whether a ship will wreck during a storm at sea, who will get sick and when, who will die and when, when a child will be born, whether a child will be born healthy and whole, those sorts of things. None of these events are up to you. Therefore, none of these events are good or bad.

Understanding this, the Stoic brings no expectations about future events with her to the seer. Whatever the prediction, the Stoic knows that what is not up to her is morally indifferent, and what is up to her is to make good use out of whatever happens. This was the lesson in *Ench.* 18: no omens are bad because a Stoic can respond virtuously to every event and derive benefit from it, no matter what. Events are opportunities to exercise the virtues of circumspection, patience, resourcefulness, perseverance, endurance, tenacity, fortitude, caution and wisdom. No one can stop you from responding virtuously during delays on your trip, a shipwreck, injury, illness, theft of your property, the wicked behaviour of others or anything else. The gods send us challenges to test our virtues. If we have confidence in our resilience and our ability to cope calmly with whatever comes our way, then we'll be following the advice of our advisers, the gods.

Epictetus's most admired role model is Socrates. So, he urges approaching divination as Socrates did. Evidently, these were cases in which the seer's investigation pertained to the outcome of a situation as opposed to the intention, motivation, or available options, strategies, tactics or methods. The latter are matters for savvy deliberation, rational reflection and application of skill. As such, the latter are up to us. The former, the outcomes, are not up to us and so nothing to worry about.

Consider the first scenario. Your friend faces a dangerous situation. You can face this danger by her side. Should you? That is not a question of outcome. Consequently, that is not a question for the seer to divine. The seer cannot foretell what the right thing for you to do is. *You* must decide whether to be a loyal, courageous friend or not. If you value friendship, loyalty and courage, then you share the danger with your friend. Consider the second scenario. Your country is in danger, and you can act to defend it. Should you do so? Again, this is not a question of outcome. It is a question of your moral character, the duty of citizenship and the virtue of loyalty. The seer cannot decide for you whether you should face danger to defend your country. The seer can only prophesy whether the *outcome* of your decision will be death, or the maiming of your body, or exile. But none of these outcomes reflect whether you are loyal and courageous. Thus, not any of these outcomes are bad omens. No morally good decision results in a bad omen, according to Stoicism. Reason dictates that you stand by your friend and country notwithstanding any dangers to your body. The real danger is to your moral character, if you opt to abandon your friend or country, to be disloyal, to flee from danger, to be a coward.

Epictetus concludes that the gods are greater prophets than human seers. The gods value justice, loyalty, courage and virtues above all else. So, the gods advise us to value virtue above all else, too. The oracle of Delphi, the Pythian priestess inspired by the god Apollo, was the greatest, most revered seer of antiquity. This oracle pronounced, among other things, that no one was wiser than Socrates. Socrates showed his wisdom in valuing virtue above all else. The advice of the Pythian Apollo carries far more weight than any advice or prophesy of an ordinary seer, Epictetus insists. How did the Pythian Apollo treat the man who failed to defend his friend from murderous attack? He expelled the disloyal coward from his temple.

So, when is it right to seek a seer for divination? Only when, out of casual curiosity, you wonder how some future event will turn out. But when deciding what to do and how to act, you need only consult the role model of Socrates, the greater prophets and the gods. That is, consult reason. Consult *virtue*. Do what you can rationally justify as the loyal, steadfast, just, wise and admirable course of action.

Chapter 33

This chapter presents a medley of social rules for the Stoic progressor. The Stoic is an active participant in her family, neighbourhood and city. She also has friends and acquaintances. The rules outlined here are in the service of maintaining one's self-control, but also for being a dutiful participant in those domains. So, these rules aim at both caring for your virtue and ensuring that the bad behaviour of others with whom you must interact does not hinder your progress. Stoics are active members of their society, even when that society is rife with depravity. In this regard, then, progressors must maintain a kind of double vision. They are caring for their own virtue while being relentless critics of their missteps, but they are also participants in the social happenings around them, which requires them to extend some grace to those who are not wise. The Stoic is not a hermit who rejects her society, insulating herself from people she deems fallen and hateful. Nor is the Stoic a full participant in its political or cultural dramas and clashes. Rather, the Stoic stands both inside and outside her culture. It is worth contrasting this position with the Cynics, who not only held that most cultural practices are immoral and unnatural, but they also endeavoured to vehemently criticize and disrupt them. Diogenes the Cynic famously walked backwards coming and going to demonstrate how the city's bustle was pointless. He lit a lamp in full daylight searching for a 'true human' to confront civilization's distortions. Diogenes 'the dog' masturbated in public to protest his society's sexual norms and insistence on privacy. Since he rejected the values that drove so much culture around him, he thought that this meant that he had to defy and disrupt the *status quo*. The problem was that he was largely ineffective at convincing others to change; only a few gave up conventional living to become Cynics. So, the Dog's antics had little overall effect on his culture. The Stoic approach is to moderate the second stage of the Cynic's reaction. Instead of upsetting the apple cart, Stoics endeavour, first, to work piecemeal on reforming themselves and second, being good examples and sources of good judgement for others.

The first step of Stoic social training is to find proper *exempla*, people on whom to model one's life. Rhetoricians and philosophers trained by copying the argumentative and presentational styles of the greats, and it was a Roman commonplace to invoke the examples of civic virtue in the city's past to encourage its imitation by new generations. These exempla are useful not just for copying their great deeds or stating profound thoughts, but for all the small things that make up a life worth admiring. How would a person of excellence approach this quotidian situation or that? Mythology provides the Stoic tradition with a variety of exempla to emulate. One might model oneself after Odysseus's intelligence or Heracles' endurance. Or Thersites' plainspokenness and disdain for social rank; in the *Iliad* he chastises the Greeks for their greed in hoping to plunder Troy, which seems to be their primary motive for the war (ii.211–40). Epictetus cites him as admirable for his freedom of thought (*Disc.* iv.160). The history of philosophy also provides worthy exempla: Socrates for his wisdom and eagerness to converse with others, and Zeno for his philosophical insight and ability to synthesize many strands of argument. Even Romans of the recent past provide Stoics with exempla. Seneca argued that Cato the Younger was the kind of person on whom to model much of your life, since he carried himself with placidity and gravity right to the end (*Const.* vii.1). The lesson of exempla is that you keep good company in your mind, because you'll be going out into a world full of people who are not wise. Because these folks are not wise, they don't know any better, and they despise wisdom and virtue properly presented. A Stoic must be on guard against that but must also nonetheless coordinate with them. Too many others with whom Stoics must live are bad examples, so they must keep the exempla at the forefront of their mind as good examples.

As progressors, Epictetus's audience must take care with those with whom they will spend time. Bad habits are like colds – they spread just through proximity to others. So, if progressors are not careful, the bad habits of others will find a home in them. To repeat: it does not follow that progressors must retreat from the world. Rather, they must train at being active participants for them to do their duties, but they must also be careful not to be made worse by their companions. Epictetus's image is that of a filthy neighbour whose dirt rubs off onto others over the course of time together. In a way, the lesson is to learn your limits as a progressor. Your training makes you increasingly invulnerable to many of the world's influences, but social pressure remains very tough to resist, even for those who have made progress. So, progressors remain vulnerable, particularly during friendly exchange, like banquets, parties, public lectures, sporting events, and so on.

What follows, then, is a digest of what might be called basic rules of conversational ethics. The rules are calls for heightened alertness, since errors are highly likely. To put a more positive spin on it, call it a checklist for social and personal growth. Here are some highlights:

- Be quiet, for the most part.
- Don't make oaths.
- Don't go on and on about the games.
- Don't go on and on about nice restaurants.
- Don't be a jokester.
- Don't be crude.
- Don't be a braggart.
- Don't expect to be welcomed everywhere.

The Stoic progressor is expected to be part of ongoing conversations and social exchange, and Epictetus's advice is to be silent for the most part. This is partly because of an easy truism: the more we talk, the more likely we are to say ridiculous things. Progressors are still learning, so if they are with the wise, they should not speak so that they may listen and learn. And if they are not with the wise, they should remain silent so that they do not play along with the debasing idle talk of the unwise. The Pythagoreans required their initiates to keep silent for five years for exactly these sort of reasons (DL viii.10), but the Stoic programme, as said before, takes double vision. Progressors are working on themselves but also engaging with their culture and wider world as they are. So, though you should be quiet for the most part, you shouldn't just sit there like a bump on a log. Your duty to your culture and your neighbours is to maintain those relationships and perform in light of them. So, the progressor must be present, take part and converse appropriately.

Epictetus's finer-grained advice is about withstanding the temptations of being carried away by the activities of engagement. One will end up going to the games, being asked for a restaurant recommendation and seeking an audience with important people. The key to it all is about keeping one's dignity and self-control through every engagement. Talking sports can take over one's mind. Minutiae of the games can become an obsessive focus. So can team partisanship. Not only do you become vulnerable to disappointment in taking on such attitudes, but you are tempted to savour injustices in fouls on your team not being called or to exult over unsporting play that favours your side. The same goes for talk of fancy restaurants, as you may opine about which place serves the best dish, but others may disagree or not share that taste. Then you must defend this or that style for the dish as more authentic, savoury or complex. And now you have become a fussy gourmand, being picky about salt proportions or cooking techniques.

One shouldn't take oaths for the simple reason that one's word should be sufficient reason for credence. External guarantors should be unnecessary. But further, oath-taking condones the habit of oath-taking generally. Not only should others, too, follow the rule that their word should be sufficient, but waking Zeus to bear witness to one's claims is itself impious. Indeed, given Stoic theology, it is not the gods' role to play guarantor for one's word. Such an oath falls in with petitionary prayer and transactional sacrifice as inappropriate ways to relate to the divine. To call a god as one's witness is to misunderstand what the gods are and what they do.

Being a jokester and being crude are cases of conversational overreach. The jokester is one who has given in to the temptation to use humour to build bonds. Sharing a laugh confirms an understanding, but going overboard with it cheapens that connection. Similarly with crudity. Sharing an unsavoury detail is a gesture of frankness which confirms that you are among friends. But then there is oversharing. Crudity and jokesterism are instances of overplaying a good strategy. One reason Epictetus disallows them is that it is too easy for we who are not wise to overplay them. Just as, if there are exceptions to a rule, we are more likely to cite those exceptions when excusing ourselves, the temptations of excessive humour or crude frankness all too easily overwhelm our judgement in the first person. That is, it feels fine *for me* to spout many bad puns or off-colour observations, but less so *for you* or *for them*. Given this phenomenon of privileging oneself in these cases, it's a safer policy, especially for those not yet wise, for progressors to forego it all.

Anyone leading an active life will meet with important people. A luminary may visit our workplace, or we may need a form signed by the head of some agency or other. Societies have movers and shakers, and societal engagement dictates interacting with them. Given this reality, Epictetus reminds his progressors to keep their exempla in mind. How would Socrates handle meeting with this bigwig? How would Zeno handle having to wait for a meeting with this VIP? The contrast with the Cynics is worth appreciating again. Diogenes famously told Alexander the Great to get out of his sunlight upon being asked by the mighty conqueror what gift he could give him. The Stoic, by contrast, while seeing through the bogus values animating so much culture, is impelled to neither disrupt nor chastise them. The Stoic attends the games, opines about restaurants and appropriately meets powerful people. But neither is she swept away by it all nor does she treat it with contempt.

Another aspect of actively participating in society is managing your body. That is, our exchanges with others are both verbal and physical. So, the Stoic will have possessions, a spouse, a house, and so on. Epictetus enjoins progressors to cut out all pretence and luxury. This is an exercise of abstention: remind yourself that these things are unnecessary, that a good life is possible without them. This is both a cognitive exercise, as progressors thereby generate evidence for this truth by foregoing them, and a crafting of habits and expectations. That is, you not only know that you can do without luxury, but you come not to expect it. Thus, you are not disappointed when it isn't available. Living on less not only proves that you can, but it encourages you to keep doing so.

Epictetus's advice on sex has two valences: one we might call sex-negative, another sex-positive. The sex-negative line is that sex is an indulgence. One succumbs to the temptation of pleasure, which induces a certain madness. Infatuation and the erotic love that attends it encourage too many bonds to be broken, distracting us from our moral purpose. In sex and its pursuit, we become pictures of hedonic abandon. Since we are not wise, it is best to abstain. Sexual desire is powerful enough to overwhelm most progressors.

The sex-positive reading is that the sexual act, just as with acts of conversational engagement, is a social act. Sex affirms and deepens our bonds. In this regard, Epictetus's advice is to restrict one's sexual activity to those with whom it is appropriate to share that bond. So, just as his recommendation for conversational ethics is to remain silent and avoid conversations that degrade character (and with people who would degrade your character), his sexual advice is to abstain for the most part and be wisely picky about your partners. This is because sex has a profound effect on us as a bond-affirming and -making act. Whether that act is good or not depends on when and with whom we share it. Having the wrong kind of lovers can turn us into worse people. So, it is not about the sex *per se*, but about with whom we have it and how those experiences affect us.

A final feature of general sexual abstention worth appreciating is continuous with Epictetus's point about luxury. Abstention shows us that we not only can go without sex, but it accustoms us to not having it. A partner's availability varies. Sometimes we have no partner at all. If we are accustomed to having sex regularly, or consider having it some great good, or believe not having it is some great bad, then dry spells are dismaying. This dismay spurs desperate behaviour and overweening resentment. Exercises of abstention, then, apply not only to luxuries but to pleasures generally.

Preparing for the vicissitudes of social life is essential to being an engaged person. One will have appointments with big shots, but because they are important, they will be very busy and may not keep those times. That's a reality of life. It's something that anyone who has waited in a doctor's office or for an official to review some documents will know happens all too regularly. Epictetus's advice is to approach these circumstances along the lines we'd seen in preparing for a trip to the baths in *Ench.* 4: use an exercise of anticipation. Expect that the important person will be unavailable or will be in a mood to reject our requests. How often have we witnessed someone standing in line for something totally lose his temper over it all? Or after he has met with the important official, he bridles at the result and makes a scene? The Stoic insight here is that it is because these people arrived at those appointments with the false beliefs that things will go smoothly, quickly, and they will get their way. Even non-Stoics know that these are unreasonable things to expect. Meeting an authority over some issue means you're likely not in for an easy time or happy result. Petitioning a big cheese for her consideration is an unhappy game if you think you'll be heard all the time (or even some of the time). So, you've got to prepare yourself for these exchanges by first knowing what that situation is and then correctly setting your expectations.

A similar set of expectations should be in place for public lectures. In philosophy, it's a better bet that what you will hear is either silly or derivative. Expecting insight, tight argument and novel, worthwhile ideas on an issue is to fail to believe in accord with what we already know: most philosophy just isn't very good. So, why get bent out of shape when the lecture you attend is mediocre? The same goes for most public intellectual exercises. Most of these folks are better at self-promotion than they are at knowing things and communicating their knowledge. Again, that's something we knew already, so why do we expect differently? Furthermore, it's not worth it to make a big deal of it when it's all bad. Just as we've seen folks lose their temper at a post office waiting line, we've seen attendees react inappropriately when they disagree with a speaker. They shout or launch into a self-indulgent tirade to make a big production about raising their objection. But it's all more of the same: a ridiculous display. And it's all because they expected something else, something they had no good reason to expect. The exercise of anticipation in setting proper expectations enables us to handle the situations well.

An implication of these insights is that at some time, all these overblown reactions will come our way from others. We will need to give a comment on something, or we will be the person to whom others direct queries. These people will disagree, or they will find an inconvenience, and perhaps they will be intrusive and abusive. As people do, they will direct all this at our progressor. But, again, what else would anyone expect?

Here, Epictetus hands his progressors an exercise for enduring these turns of social fate: the technique of *repackaging the insults*. Recall that in *Ench.* 20, Epictetus argues that, given Stoic ethical intellectualism, insults harm us only if we allow them to through our opinions. So, the strategy of deflecting the harm of insults is to change your opinion of yourself and the accuracy of the insult. Recall also what we termed Simplicius's Dilemma with insults: either the insult is true or false. If it is true, take it as useful feedback. If it is false, it's noise to dismiss. In this case, the strategy modifies the dilemma by conceding the truth of the insult but adding one's other judgements about other places for growth. Epictetus reasons that if we admit our many other failings, the insult will not only sting less but will remind us that our real project is self-critical progress.

The repackaging strategy with insults is a working part of the consistent practice of double vision for progressors. Those making progress must be highly critical of themselves while being gracious to others. The progressor doesn't explicitly criticize others for their contributions to discussions or their behaviour, though there's room for expressing disagreement through silence or a well-timed frown. The primary job for progressors is that of reforming themselves and taking a light touch with others. Part of this is because Stoicism is an individually focused ethics. The key to a life of freedom is working on skills and insights you carry as an individual. But another part of this personal-individual limit is that progressors must exercise some humility about which reforms their neighbours and culture need. By hypothesis, progressors are not wise, so they can mistake behaviour by others as vice when it isn't, or virtue when it isn't. We don't know what most of those around us are facing, but given what we know about fate's vicissitudes, it's not easy for any of them. If others lack Stoic training, they are coping with what life has served up the best they know how. Their strategies likely won't be effective, but the Stoic does not compound the difficulty of others with high-browed philosopher's criticism.

Loving the regard of others is an outgrowth of our social nature. The heat of that love is stoked by praise and even more so by criticism. In this regard, this love of regard is a kind of affliction. Furthermore, it constantly tempts those engaged with others and those who maintain those relationships. This is because a standard way of gauging how one is doing and maintaining those relations is by means of others' regard. If regard is high, one is doing one's job well. If low, then not. Expressing that regard is even a way of affirming and maintaining those relations. Consequently, Epictetus warns that being a jokester or cursing too much will mean others will lose respect for us. The regard of others can be a piece of feedback on the quality of your contributions. The key is to remember that this feedback can be noise, too. How accurately, for example, do students' evaluations track the effectiveness of their instructor's teaching or their satisfaction with their grade? Sometimes they track the former, but more often the latter. So, with all expressions of regard (positive or negative) it's best to repackage them with your best judgement and the judgements of others whom you trust on where you have room to grow. Progressors should not be surprised when criticism comes their way – what else did they expect? Nor must they be carried away by praise, either.

Chapter 34

An all-too-easy picture of Stoicism is that it is only a programme for toughing it out through bad times, in that with its exercises, pain and disappointment have softer effects than usual. This picture is half-right. Stoicism is also a programme for handling good times. This thought is a more difficult one, so it's worth taking some time getting the big idea out. The big idea is that Stoics train not just to manage times when fate throws hard things their way, they train to manage themselves when fate throws nice things their way, too. This is because the nice things also affect us and our attitudes, and we must guard against many of these influences. So, just as you must prepare yourself before some challenging experience occurs and have strategies to endure it, you must have exercises to anticipate and endure (or simply abstain from) pleasurable experiences. This is because both pleasures and pains bring with them intellectual temptation. They take the general form of these inferences:

> <u>This experience feels bad.</u>
> *Therefore*, a bad thing is happening to me.
> <u>This experience feels good.</u>
> *Therefore*, a good thing is happening to me.

Call these the *pleasure* and *pain inferences*. Both inferences are, according to Stoics, fallacious because the only bad thing is vice, and the only truly good thing is virtue. Again, most Stoic exercises are devoted to heading off the pain inference, but it is important to head off the pleasure inference, too. In fact, it is in the fallacious inference that we are 'carried away' by pleasures. The pleasure does not literally pick us up and forcibly whisk us off, but rather, we hop on board with it due to the bad but tempting reasoning about the pleasures. So, through our own reasoning, we carry ourselves away.

As with all errors of reasoning, the best care for them is to be aware of where the errors are and to slow down when navigating tricky inferences. Because the errors of both the pleasure and pain inferences are tempting, they are easy to make when we relax our attention. So, the *exercise of delay* is an important tool for the Stoic progressor. Epictetus recommends this tactic in *Ench.* 20 for handling insults, but this exercise is generalizable to most circumstances, including reasoning about pleasures. When we get impressions of pleasure, Epictetus urges us to 'delay for a while'. In the midst of these delays, Epictetus poses three options for how to evaluate the pleasures. The options unfold through the process of assessing our circumstances. Epictetus opens with two possible routes as orienting thoughts. So, you are paused, exercising the strategy of delay, and in that pause, you play out two likely scenarios bearing on the pleasure at hand: pursue the pleasure or abstain from it. If you pursue the pleasure, then there are two likely stages to that story. Stage one is that you enjoy a pleasurable experience; stage two is that once the experience is over, there's no more pleasure, only its results. What these results are will depend on the pleasures. A large slice of cake results in a sugar crash. A few rounds of whiskey sours results in a hangover. A day of gambling brings consequent debt. Social media use gobbles up hours leaving little else accomplished. Moreover, we regret our decisions because we were fooled by pleasure's illusion. How is the pleasure of eating cake a good? It feels nice, but how is that experience a *good*? The contrast is to exercise self-control by abstaining from pleasure. Enacting a virtue is clearly a good, as you show that you're exercising sound judgement, that you master your desires, not the reverse. Roughly, the same goes for all the scenarios with pursuing pleasure. The result of pursuing pleasure, given this contrast, is that, as Epictetus puts it, we regret our decisions and kick ourselves. The delay, then, is a moment you take to remind yourself of the options and likely results, and you then may proceed with full awareness of just what you are choosing. So, with the delay, we find a way to halt the error in the pleasure inference.

On some occasions there is a third option: choosing the pleasurable path but not expecting to regret it. As seen in the previous chapter, social life offers many pleasant occasions, like banquets, sporting events, conversations and sex. Those are pleasurable experiences, and you can take part in them, but it is not merely for the sake of the pleasures that you have them. You do those things in the roles you have in your society, friend group and family as ways of enacting and reinforcing your relations. The pleasures, surely, are preferable in those activities, but they are not what make them choiceworthy. The temptation Epictetus warns against with this third option is that the allure of pleasure motivates rationalization. So, you may justify having too much to drink with buddies with the reason that it establishes a social bond. Or you may rationalize overeating cake with the reason that it's a way to show your appreciation and loyalty to the local bakery. But this is self-deception. Pleasure's allure has perverted your reasoning. The key insight is that there are exceptions to the rule of two paths for pleasure (pursue and feel regret or abstain and be proud) as there are pleasures that are preferable parts of our duties to others. But it is too easy for us to over-emphasize those pleasures when they are pleasures *for us*. Consequently, Epictetus's advice, especially for progressors, is to have your defaults on abstention. Since progressors are not yet wise but also have the tools of good reasoning, they are too easily tempted to rationalize their way to that third option of justifying their pursuing the pleasure. A heavy burden of proof must be placed on pursuing an activity with attendant pleasures because they are too eager to become candidates for rationalization.

A final contrast with the Epicureans on pleasure is instructive. The main principle of Epicurean value theory is that pleasure is the good and pain is the bad. In fact, an Epicurean commonplace is that even babies know this, but it takes a weird intellectual perversion of unhappy adulthood to deny it. Epicurus, too, recommends judgement when it comes to pleasures, since many are not worth the painful consequences. In fact, once properly judged, stable pleasures of relaxation and satiety win out over exciting pleasures of titillation and overconsumption. Epicurus declares: 'It is neither drinking bouts and continuous partying and enjoying boys and women, nor enjoying fish and other dainties of an extravagant table, which produce the pleasant life, but sober calculation which searches out the reasons for every choice and avoidance' (*Letter to Menoeceus* 132). The lesson, Epicureans thought, was that the most prudent way to conceive of the best pleasures is as consistent freedom from pains. So, there is considerable overlap between the pleasures Stoics and Epicureans avoid, but there is also major disagreement about their reasons for this avoidance. The issue of dispute, however, is over which pains are worth facing. The Stoic's view is that though pleasure is a preferable part of doing your duty, it is not a reason for doing it. Nor is pain a reason not to do your duty, especially when it comes to duties to your family, state, or society. The Epicurean's view, by contrast, is that because the responsibilities of these duties are so onerous, you should retreat from connections that generate to them. Epicurus enjoins that 'we must free ourselves from the prison of everyday affairs and activities' (*Vatican Sayings* 58) to ensure that we can avoid such intrusive obligations. Here the depth of divergence between Epicureans and Stoics is plain, starting with their primary views on the good in life. Once you have, as a Stoic, seen how far the error of identifying the pleasurable with the good will divert you from a life of virtue, you should be on guard against the temptations of the fallacious pleasure and pain inferences.

Chapter 35

This chapter is about the importance of resolve after deliberation leading to decision. How do Stoics decide how to act? Understanding their various roles helps them decide, according to Epictetus. Does your situation invite acting the role of a friend, or a co-worker, or a leader, or a daughter, or a sibling, or a parent, or a neighbour? Roles determine the specific tasks needed to fulfil them. Reason allows us to weigh options and consider the best means of completing each task. This is the process of deliberation, and as it was clear from *Ench.* 29, this requires looking at all of the steps required to pursue that goal and endorsing that they are to be done. Once this process culminates in a decision about what must be done, Epictetus urges us, his Stoics-in-training, *not to waffle*. Recall that *Ench.* 33 begins: 'Right away set up a particular character and model for yourself which you'll protect both when you're by yourself and when you're with other people.' Once you have decided that you ought to do something, don't second guess yourself. Don't allow yourself to be distracted. Don't let others deflect, deter or delay you from doing what you decided you ought to do. Don't fail to do your duty.

How does a Stoic know whether what she has decided to do is right or wrong? A good heuristic approach to answering this is to consult your reactions to publicly doing the action, so: if you would be embarrassed *to be seen doing it*, then that is a sure sign that you decided to do something shameful that ought *not* to be done. Whether you are invisible to others or in their plain sight, the rightness of your action remains unchanged. Having 'set up a particular character and model for yourself' of the kind of person you want to be, integrity demands fidelity to that public model in every action. If anyone who sees you act could legitimately criticize what you did, then that indicates you chose a disgraceful deed. But if you are confident your decision conforms with your roles and relationships with others, and aligns with the model of your best self, then you have no worries about being faulted for doing it. You are free to act without fear, doubt or hesitation. Actions express and reveal one's character. A good person has nothing to hide when she acts because all her acts are good. Indeed, if you act as a good role model, others are benefitted by watching you in action.

Call the principle behind our reasoning here the *sunlight principle*. It runs roughly that if you are acting rightly, not only would you not object to others seeing what you are doing, but you can also share your reasoning and motives with others. Furthermore, it may even benefit your reasoning for it to be shared in many cases, since others recognizing motives and reasons may create more comity. The sunlight principle is one of the reasons why Stoic exempla matter so much to progressors; not only can we see their actions, but we can inspect their reasons and be improved by that reflection. However, there is one complication with the sunlight principle for Stoics. It arises from the fact that Stoic practitioners share their lives with and relate to non-Stoics. The problem is that all too often sharing the details of philosophical reasoning with those uninterested in philosophy (or those who outright reject Stoic principles) can alienate them. Recall that in *Ench.* 16, Epictetus tells his students to vocally grieve along with a neighbour who has experienced a loss, but not to grieve inside. In *Ench.* 46 Epictetus will instruct progressors never to call themselves philosophers and to remain silent when philosophy is discussed with non-Stoics. The reason, in both cases, is that Stoic philosophical insights will sound absurd to non-Stoics, and that will offend them. It will sometimes be simply out of place to share Stoic insights (as one might err in telling grieving parents about the exercise of the mug after they've lost a child), and there are other times when it would be simply hopeless.

The key to the Stoic approach as to when and how to follow the sunlight principle is that the cases in which to override the principle should themselves be able to pass the test of the principle. So, returning to the case of the Stoic practitioner grieving along with neighbours, the Stoic does not explain her motives in the situation because that explanation would ruin the relation. But that suspension of the sunlight rule itself seems to pass the sunlight rule – if asked why they cried, but not inside, our progressors can say that a philosophical imposition would have destroyed the relation and the actions it required. And this reasoning can be endorsed by all on whom the decision bears. In this regard, the perfection of resolve is downstream from the perfection of judgement.

Chapter 36

This chapter is another of Epictetus's arguments by analogy. In short, the case is that one should handle logical complexes of certain forms in particular ways, and these patterns resemble how one must proceed in social settings. That is, there are many circumstances where both logically and socially, we cannot have both of two things. We must approach those circumstances with understanding of that fact. The argument is rooted in familiarity with some concepts from Stoic logic, and Epictetus clearly expects his readers to have mastered these concepts and their function. Understanding these facts essentially depends on understanding the logic of the situation.

Stoic logic proceeds from the insight that logical complexes have functional properties. Most of these complexes are built with connectives, such as *and, not, or* and *if-then*. Their functional properties emerge from how they interact with other propositions and other complexes. So, you could reason from *A or B*, and *not-A* to infer that *B*. Alternately, you could reason from *A*, and *if A then B* to infer that *B* is true. Patterns like these are writ into the structure of reality, so grasping logical rules is a way of seeing the plan of the universe. The duty of the wise person is to reason well, see the world as it is and grasp the truth so as to be able to live by it. So, the route to wisdom necessitates mastering the tools of logic. We reason to truths about what's the case, what our duties are and what the right path forward is. Thus, we owe it to the truth, each other and what's right to gain complete mastery of these skills. A necessary part of being a good person is being a good critical thinker – that is a crucial consequence of Stoic ethical intellectualism.

The two logical complexes Epictetus takes as his proximal analogues for his argument by analogy are *conjunctions* and *disjunctions*. Conjunctions are complexes made by two propositions joined together with 'and'. The new complex (the conjunction) is true when and only when both joined propositions are true. So, the conjunction *A and B* is true when and only when both A and B are true. The complex built by the connective 'or' is called disjunction. A disjunction is true when either of the propositions in the complex is true. So, all it takes for the disjunction *A or B* to be true is for either A or B to be true. One of them being false doesn't make the whole thing false for disjunctions, since the other can make the complex true. This is not the case for conjunctions, by contrast, since *A and B* is made false by either one being false. A final concept must be in place regarding relations between propositions. Two propositions are *contradictory* or are *mutually exclusive* when they must always have opposite truth values. That is, if one is true, the other will be false. And if one is false, the other will be true. Putting all these concepts together, then, yields the following insights. A conjunction of two contradictory claims will always be false, since if one is true, the other will be false (and thereby make the conjunction false). And any disjunction of two contradictory propositions will always be true, since one or the other will be true (and thereby make the disjunction between them true). Those are interesting results, and they emerge from basic insights about logic that the Stoics considered indispensable to mastering one's mind.

Given these two patterns of how the form of the propositional complexes and the relations between the propositions in them bear on the truth or falsity of the complexes, Epictetus asks his students to consider the contradictory propositions 'It is day' and 'It is night'. Assuming that they are contradictory, they always have opposite truth values. So, any conjunction of the two will always be false, but any disjunction of the two will always be true. In short, you will always have one, but you can't have both. This result is no random accident; it emerges from the logical relations between those propositions and what those propositions are about. Failing to grasp this, then, can result only from either failing to understand the logic of the relations between day and night or from not understanding what day and night are. Expecting for there to be a time when it is both day and night at the same time would be silly. We can get only one or the other at a time, never both. That's just how day and night work. Logic and our knowledge of what we are reasoning about capture all that. Epictetus expects his student progressors to get all this and to understand it given the logic of the circumstance. Finally, now, imagine someone who is upset by this result. Perhaps she wishes for some time when it's both day and night. Not only would we think that this desire is out of whack with what's possible, but it's also genuinely incoherent. So, the only cure for this day-and-nighter's desire would be a little bit of logic and a better understanding of what exactly she is desiring. Once we have clearly recognized the situation, not only does the desire for both at the same time vanish, but we would also see it as mostly nonsense.

Given that the Stoic approach to everything is to see each event as the result of the rationality (*logos*, logic) written into the universe, all desires that things be otherwise than how they are or have been are incoherent in the same way as the desire for day-night. Fate is the logical unfolding of truths and their implications. Desiring otherwise can be possible only if one fails to grasp the relevant truths or see their implications. But once one sees those truths and their logic, the desires should not only go away but should be revealed as incoherent on reflection.

So far, we've analysed the proximal analogue in Epictetus's argument by analogy: logical complexes and contradictory propositions. Epictetus's distal analogue for the argument is options for how to behave at a banquet. You must choose between making sure to eat your fill and being a convivial guest. Taking the analogical reasoning into this choice, Epictetus argues that, in the fashion of propositions that are mutually exclusive, making sure to eat your fill at a banquet has a way of making it impossible to be a good guest or good company. Insisting on a second helping, making sure you get the choicest cuts of meat, angling for the first slice of pie – all these behaviours alienate the diner not only from other guests, but also from the host. The point of a dinner party is not merely to fill bellies but to create and sustain camaraderie. If you are focused on the former, you cannot focus on the latter. Earlier, we called a version of this decision point 'the all-in thesis' – that your singular motive must be your duties and your progress, and if you are focused on other things, your primary duty is undone. Realistically, you cannot tightly manage your finances while simultaneously working on being a person who doesn't let the world get to her; these two orientations clash. This thought was originally about looking out for your own moral progress, but it now applies to behaving as a social creature. Looking out for benefits that accrue to yourself, in this case your body, gets in the way of attending to the needs of others and fostering a community.

The lesson generalizes, as pursuing your private interests with externals, whether they be accumulating wealth, pursuing status or focusing on your diet, comes at the cost of fulfilling your social duties. Takers are the poison of community. Consider any time that resources are short. If someone in the group is inclined to hoard, community dissolves. But if everyone takes proportionate shares in times of scarcity and nobody hoards, then even though there may not be much, solidarity is maintained. Making sure others get their share sets a good example; it also preserves the bonds that make each a member of the group. Being a taker severs those bonds.

So, the analogy runs, then, just as with contradictory propositions, you cannot have personal interest in both externals and community-building. For the latter, you must proceed as though there is only one respectable choice. Given that virtue is the only good, virtue demands doing your duty, and your duties are defined by your relations, it follows that you must support your community.

All this said, an objection looms. The analogy posits that there is an apt similarity between the proximal analogue of contradictory propositions and the distal analogue of the choice between eating your fill or being a modest guest. The logic is supposed to be that you simply cannot have both. It seems clear with Epictetus's example, it being day and it being night, this analysis is accurate. But it is not obviously correct with eating your fill and being a good guest. You can *never* have both? That simply seems wrong. Consider the case of the grandmother who fixes a dinner too big for her visiting family. Not to eat your fill would be a failure to be a good guest, and in fact, it may be required that you eat well past your fill. But the counterexample need not be so extreme, as it seems clear that you *can* be a good guest at a banquet and properly honour the host and one's fellows while at the same time eating to satiety. Epictetus's analogy with contradictory propositions just seems too strong, because in the case of the dinner party dilemma, you can at least sometimes have both. And this is enough to show that they are not contradictories. Furthermore, given that nourishing her body is a preferable thing (to not nourishing her body), not only would a Stoic practitioner accept results with full bellies, but she should positively prefer them to instances when they are not full, so long as the bellies were filled while fully adhering to proper guest etiquette.

The result reiterates what we'd observed earlier as the challenging fit between Epictetus's all-in thesis and the Stoic doctrine of preferred indifferents. Our approach to this fit has been to manage the tension with the objective of generating compatible approaches, but compatible in terms of order of importance. You should proceed according to the all-in thesis, on the analogy, so you should proceed as though banquets are occasions where you can't have both full bellies and comity. You then choose comity over the full belly, since it's your duty. Now, it's best to proceed with the expectation that the two are mutually exclusive, since we won't be distracted by looking for larger and tastier servings. If they do end up coming, it won't be because we were distracted by them, since we were doing our duty. They are salutary results of how the resources happened to be distributed. So, the all-in thesis expresses our default approach, just as we see with the thought that we cannot have both. We set our expectations appropriately so that we can do our duty, not be disappointed if we end up still a little hungry at the end of the meal, and we can still accept the result of satiety if it comes.

The key is to concede, as Epictetus does at the end of the passage, that there are cases where we can have both. Those are cases when we may pursue the preferred outcome. Epictetus urges, however, that we first observe respect for our hosts and only then may we look to benefit our bodies. Personal interest is secondary and allowable only if we've achieved the higher priority of establishing and maintaining our relations with others. So, look to eating your fill only after ensuring others got their proper shares and your host has been duly honoured. And, just as we think the primary lesson generalizes, this coordinating lesson does too. So, the injunction *Don't be a taker* still obtains, though there are situations where one may take. But those instances occur only after the communal goods have been secured. The *taker* has reversed these defaults by looking after herself first and then turning to communal goods only after having fully sated herself. The Stoic prescription here is to proceed as though having both isn't possible and reminding oneself that virtue requires putting the duties of courteous association ahead of one's appetite.

Chapter 37

As we have seen, Epictetus frequently illustrates how Stoics figure out how to handle the many situations we find ourselves in by identifying, and then virtuously carrying out, our many roles in the drama of life.

In *Ench.* 4 Epictetus urges us to act the role of a calm swimmer at a public pool who is mindful of its predictable shenanigans. In *Ench.* 6 he distinguishes our human role as beings who can take pride in keeping their use of impressions in accord with nature from a horse who is proud of her looks. *Ench.* 7 urges us to accept our role as mortal, obedient passengers on the ship of life commanded by Captain Zeus. The message of *Ench.* 11 is that we ought to act as travellers at a hotel aware that we don't own its amenities, which are provided only for a limited time. In *Ench.* 24.4 we read that 'it's enough if everyone plays her own part'. *Ench.* 29 is a lengthy explanation of the rigorous training demanded of those who dedicate themselves to the role of philosophers aspiring to be Olympians of the soul. *Ench.* 30 describes how duties are measured by relationships; for example, the role of a parent differs from the role of a child or a sibling. *Ench.* 31 explains that the role of a pious person requires expressing gratitude to the gods.

We thus have many kinds of roles. Some we are born into, as a child, a sibling, as female or male, as a member of a family with a certain amount of social prestige and wealth, or as an orphan, as a neighbour, a citizen of a particular country, etc. Other roles are to varying degrees up to us to choose, like whom to associate with, whom to befriend, sometimes perhaps whom to marry, our job or profession, etc. In this chapter, Epictetus makes a simple but important point. Your talents and abilities ought to guide your chosen roles. If you are a slow eater, you ought not to enter a pie-eating contest. Doing so is literally biting off more than you can chew. If you cannot run fast, you ought not to undertake the role of a sprinter. You ought to know both your weaknesses and your strengths, and then accordingly make graceful choices of roles. Choosing a role that you cannot successfully perform is a double mistake. You disgrace yourself by failing at the chosen role. But you also disgrace yourself by failing to have chosen a role you could have successfully performed.

Does Epictetus mean that if you're not good at something, then it is wrong to do it and try to get better at it? It seems that here he is not talking about undertaking a particular skill 'beyond your ability'. Rather, his advice is about undertaking a *role* that involves a whole set of skills. Reading, writing and speaking clearly, for example, are skills. Every citizen is obliged to develop competence in these skills to contribute to the civic good of the community. To fail to gain the necessary abilities to do your part for your community is to fail to fulfil your role as a citizen. But citizenship is a role most people are born into; they don't choose it. In contrast, chosen roles include writer, teacher or transit worker. Not everyone is suited to excel as a writer (journalist, reporter, novelist, poet, etc.) or a computer programmer or a gardener or a bus driver or a singer or a firefighter. These are the sorts of chosen roles that Epictetus seems to be talking about.

How do you know whether a role is 'beyond your ability'? A good amount of self-knowledge is needed. Epictetus thinks you should pay attention to what the role of Olympic athlete, for example, requires before you plunge into such a demanding role. If you lack the physique and discipline to be able to endure the deprivation that athletics demands, then you ought to know that about yourself. A very ancient Greek maxim that Socrates lived by was: 'Know yourself.' As we noted in Section 1.1, Socrates was a big hero for the Stoics and Epictetus's favourite role model. He was, as regularly (and paradoxically) noted, a Stoic before Stoicism. Socrates' insight was that self-knowledge is essential to wisdom. Self-deception about one's ability to fulfil a role is real foolishness, the opposite of wisdom. People have different talents and different weaknesses. Knowing your limitations is a crucial step towards gaining wisdom. Honing your raw talents so that you can fulfil the right roles, the roles that suit you, indicates moral progress and personal growth.

A final consideration in our careful deliberation about our roles is that of opportunity costs we incur with our choices, especially our bad choices. Given finite resources of time and energy, even were we to succeed in taking on some inapt role, that comes at the cost of not taking on one that is just as important but more suitable (and so less costly to perform). And if we are unsuccessful, the problem is magnified – not only have we failed to achieve the good in our chosen role, but we have neglected another set of duties that we could have completed. So much is squandered. Consequently, knowing yourself requires not only knowing your capacities and which skills you have and can perfect, but you must also know which roles are within your purview. This allows practising Stoics to choose roles that are not only fitting for them but are fitting in the sense that they do not leave other important jobs undone.

Chapter 38

In this chapter, Epictetus again argues by analogy. Here the analogy posits a similarity between taking care of one's bodily health and caring for the health of the soul (mind). This analogy is typical in the Classical and Hellenistic philosophical periods. Philosophy was billed as a kind of medicine for ailing souls that promoted psychological health. Plato's *Republic*, for example, suggests that inculcating justice and rationality in one's soul encourages its harmony and health (*Rep.* 445a). Epicureanism was touted by Philodemus as prescribing a fourfold cure to life's ills: that one should fear neither death nor the gods, that what's good is easy to get and that what's bad is easy to manage; from this arose a medical model of philosophy's relevance (*Against the Sophists* iv.9–14). Diogenes of Sinope compared himself to a doctor lancing boils of social pretension in the culture around him. He explained why he spent so much time in the city he disdained by saying he is like the doctor who must live near the sick (Stobaeus, *Anthology* iii.13.43). The analogy between philosophical work and maintaining health is a mainstay of the rhetoric of explaining the value of philosophical training. The Stoics continue this tradition. In his letters, Seneca argues that sometimes medicines are bitter, but philosophy's medicine is bitter only if you are truly ill. As you get better, taking the medicine becomes more pleasant and edifying (*Ep.* 50.9). Elsewhere, Seneca notes that philosophical training is analogous to physical training, as it is in challenges that strength grows (*Ep.* xiii.3). Musonius Rufus, Epictetus's teacher, argued that philosophical arguments are a particular kind of powerful medicine, and so must be dispensed proportionately for the particular illnesses and their extremity (Stobaeus, *Anthology* ii.32.125).

Epictetus is an inheritor of this popular medicinal model for philosophy shared by the Platonists, Epicureans, Cynics and Stoics. But he inherits the distinctive Stoic take on the analogy by conceiving of health not merely as a state of mind (perhaps as harmony or pleasure) but as ensuring discrete capacities. So, it is a uniquely Stoic approach to health that Epictetus takes with this analogy.

The proximal analogue for the argument is a commonplace for beings with bodies: we care for them. This care takes the form, first, of avoiding damage to them. That is, if you are regularly walking, you should take several precautions to care for your feet. Don't step on sharp things. Avoid uneven ground that strains your joints. Second, you can wear shoes that provide good protection and support. If your foot is injured, you might wear a bandage, apply some ointment or rest and heal. Epictetus holds that it is appropriate to care for our bodies in this fashion because a healthy body is a natural preferred indifferent.

Not only is health pleasant, but further it facilitates doing our duties. You take care of your body the same way you take care of the tools for your job. Epictetus notes that just as artisans care for their implements (oiling them to prevent rust, sharpening them when they get dull), we should care for our bodies. They are our tools for our actively pursuing duties in the world (*Disc.* iv.11.13). At times, Epictetus uses the metaphor of the *little donkey*. Our bodies are little donkeys loaded with packs and ready to haul goods. We use them for the jobs necessary. The donkey, too, needs to rest and to be fed. We cannot expect a donkey to perform the things we ask of it if we don't care for it. So, we must care for that donkey. We can, of course, lose that donkey. It can be injured or grow old. But while we have it, that donkey is under our care and supervision. So, we owe it to the donkey, due to the tasks we ask of it, to do right by the donkey while it's ours (*Disc.* iv.1.79–80). Our bodies are little donkeys, so we must treat them similarly.

Finally, with bodily care, you not only avoid harms but look to improve capacities. Soldiers engage in hard winter training to prepare for war's hardships. Olympic pankratiasts train to be strong enough to win in the ring. Artisans train their hands to craft objects with skill. Thus, care for the body consists in not just avoiding its degradation but also seeing to its development.

On the analogy, care for the mind takes a similar form to care for the body: we not only look to avoid things that would injure it, but we should also look for ways to improve it and perfect its capacities. So, the question is, on Epictetus's analogy, what things damage the intellect, and what things improve it? What are the things that are for the mind like stepping on a nail or twisting an ankle? And what things can we do to improve our minds?

Starting with things that degrade or injure our intellect, we should look first to erroneous judgements. According to Stoic intellectualism, the main explanation for vice and moral error is false belief. So, guarding against temptations of false value is essential. Wealth, pleasure and status all have the power to pervert our judgement when we're in their thrall. Those distortions yield passions like jealousy, contempt and anger. Even the pleasures we feel in judging others harshly, or enjoying their errors and downfall, distort our moral purpose. Love, too, tells us a false tale about what's good for us, what we can and cannot live without. These, when we give in to them, create a cloud of bogus narratives about ourselves and what matters. Consequently, habits and modes of thinking coalesce from this cloud of falsity. Consider the damage you do to yourself when you seethe over a slight from a colleague. Anger over the insult, the desire to extract retribution and focus on their vices – all these are frequent results of this reaction. But, through the Stoic lens, they are all unwarranted reactions which poison our virtue. The vice of others is not a reason to be vicious oneself. Your job as a proper colleague is to highlight and promote the virtues of your fellows. Expecting others, especially others you know are not wise, to behave well is a baseless attitude. So, a correction is in order, not simply for the sake of salutary emotional regulation, but also for the sake of maintaining your virtue and doing your duty. Those beliefs and the emotions they spawn damage us.

Further, just as with our bodies, we should look to promote our intellectual capacities. So, again, the wrestler trains to grow stronger and the soldier trains to build endurance and focus. Stoic progressors train to perfect their judgement and critical thinking. Reminding themselves of the Stoic principles, they work diligently to see their justification and application. So, the care of the mind, in both protecting and improving it, is rooted in judging things correctly and then motivating oneself to continue to see things clearly. That means you consistently work to shun easy dogmatisms, remaining curious about how you could be wrong about something or how your information or inferences could be corrupted. You work to be a better critical thinker, sorting out as much bullshit as you can and keeping what you can see best as truth.

Epictetus's handbook is precisely the kind of training manual to use in the project of perfecting judgement. The *Encheiridion*, as we've tried to show, is not only a set of reminders of Stoic precepts but also a resource of Stoic argumentative exercises. Not only does its reader recall the commitments of Stoic progress, but she reasons out how these theses are true and applies them to the relevant circumstances. This, again on the analogy with physical exercise and promoting bodily health, is philosophical exercise and it promotes the reader's mental health.

It is worth pausing to appreciate how apt the medicinal model is for articulating the value of philosophy. Philosophy is a corrective and care for a set of ailments that plague humans. It both eliminates bad health and fosters good health. However, a cost to this model involves how to view those who are not properly philosophical. If the model is right, then those who are uncured by philosophy's medicine still suffer from psychological illness. As a result, non-Stoics are pathologized. Consequently, criticism of the Stoic programme is interpreted through this lens of pathology. An early version of this approach was discussed in section 1.4.4 regarding the Stoic Paradox that all who are not wise are insane, i.e., suffer from *mania*. All criticism of the Stoic programme from non-Stoics has the potential to be construed as the kind of noise that those who suffer from mental illness make when prescribed therapies. They rationalize, complain and opt out. They are in love with their symptoms; this is the worst part of their illness. Taking non-Stoics' challenges seriously is not an urgent matter for a Stoic, as the interpretive line for objections such as these is that they arise from illness, not rational scrutiny.

The line of thought outlined here regarding competing philosophical programmes yields an uncompromising dogmatism and insular approach to philosophy for the Stoics. The world is divided sharply between the wise and the mad, so accordingly, proceed with caution. A consequent problem is that, given that it is very hard to become wise, and that progressors are obviously not wise, it follows that progressors, too, suffer from psychological illnesses that degrade their souls. How can they, then, trust their own judgement about their progress? What about their judgement about who is wise (and so a beneficial teacher) to begin with? In his *Discourses,* Epictetus observed that sceptical challenges like these have the effect of paralysing your mind and eliminating your confidence. This effect makes it impossible to have the clarity and strength of commitment needed to be a Stoic (*Disc.* i.5.2).

The reality is that these are exactly the stakes for any philosophical programme that must revise common sense and challenge the status quo. The Stoic idea is that our lives too often, seemingly by default, ride the rails of false values that make us miserable and then induce us to rationalize away that misery. To correct course, we need a radical break, and Epictetus's programme offers it. But a radical break has high stakes, the biggest of which is that the person making the break cannot do it half-heartedly. Rival programmes, if Stoicism is right, propagandize false values wrapped up in tempting paths leading away from excellence. In short, they are bad for us. Even worse, they distort our intellects so that we cannot see it once we are stumbling along their erroneous, downward sloping paths. Surely anyone who has made a clean break with a lifestyle, addiction, religion or relationship knows this: you must do it fully and completely. Half-measures won't cut it. That's what it takes to escape those false values, whether the appeal be drugs, alcohol, a cult, gambling or a bad boyfriend. Merely cutting back won't do it. Rather, they must be banished from our lives because they are not only bad for us, but we are too tempted to rationalize our jumping back in fully. So, the stakes are high for thinking of those non-Stoic programmes as unhealthy. They are akin to the version of you addicted to drugs and explaining how they make you feel free, or you in love with your abusive boyfriend telling stories about how cool he is. Those stories we tell ourselves about them are more fever dreams of minds tortured by their illusions than made happy by them. This is why the medicinal model for philosophy with the Stoics yields such stark results. It is also why the Stoics must be so tough with those who stray off the path.

Note on *hêgemonikon*

The Stoics theorized that the human soul (*psuchê*) is composed of eight parts: the five senses (touch, taste, smell, hearing, vision), the faculty of reproduction, the faculty of speech and the central 'commanding' faculty (ἡγεμονικόν = *hêgemonikon*). All higher cognitive functions and cognitive experience occur exclusively in the *hêgemonikon*. Its four basic powers are impression or presentation (*phantasia*), impulse (*hormê*), assent (*sunkatathesis*) and reason (*logos*).

We chose to translate *hêgemonikon* 'autonomy' in *Ench.* 38 to emphasize its operation as a command centre of cognition that establishes the laws (*nomoi*) or rules for one's own (*autos*) conduct. Admittedly inexact and undoubtedly imperfect, 'autonomy' we preferred as more natural and suggestive than a literal phrase like 'ruling part' or a stilted 'command faculty of the soul', either of which would likely puzzle first-time readers of the *Handbook*. Here in *Ench.* 38, Epictetus's analogy more strictly regards the *hêgemonikon*, which we have proceeded with our argument to apply to the more broadly construed soul.

Chapter 39

Stoics believe that human beings flourish when they focus on developing their minds, rather than pampering or beautifying their bodies. Consequently, Stoics endorse frugality, simplicity and a kind of minimalism when it comes to material possessions, clothing, shelter and food. Functionality matters, not fashion. This minimalism rejects the materialism that motivates amassing possessions you don't really need, including fancy or expensive apparel. Stoics, as minimalists, oppose consumerism: the social and economic order that glorifies acquiring goods and services in ever-increasing amounts.

So, how many pairs of shoes do you own? And how many pairs of shoes do you need? The answer to the first question may well be more, perhaps a lot more, than your thoughtful, honest answer to the second question. Do you own more shirts than you really need? More pairs of slacks, more socks, more jackets? If you have two feet, then you only really need one sturdy, functional pair of shoes, Epictetus implies. A set of clothes that fits your body and protects you from being too hot, cold or wet is a fair measure of need. What about when that set of clothes gets dirty or smelly? Okay, so one set of clothes to wear when you launder the other set seems justifiable. But if we want to argue that we need one set of clothes for the spring, another for the summer, a third for the fall, a fourth for the winter, a fifth for exercise, a sixth for travel, a seventh for the evening, an eighth for special occasions, and so on, then Epictetus cautions that this multiplication oversteps the measure of the body. One pair of shoes have now multiplied into eight pairs or more.

In January 2020, sisters Ariana, Dresden and Dakota Peters were reported to have collected more than 6,000 pairs of sneakers (Wright and Parisi 2020). Is it admirable to stockpile thousands of shoes that you will never wear? A new pair of shoes created by the French fashion designer Christian Louboutin go for $700 to $4,000. Famous rappers collaborate with Nike to make diamond-studded Air Jordan basketball sneakers that sell for up to $100,000 or more. In 1984 the US basketball team, led by Michael Jordan, won gold at the Olympics in Los Angeles. His Airness signed the Converse Fastbreaks that graced his feet in that game and those shoes fetched $190,373 at auction. Stoics conceive of shoes as apparel to wear on feet, not commodities to collect in warehouses. What about handbags? Hermès Birkin bags range from $40,000 to $500,000. A Birkin appreciates in value on average 14% a year (Houston and Kim 2021).

One way to interpret the message of *Ench.* 39 is that being seduced into consumerism triggers a slippery slope of desire. Once you exceed what your body really needs, you succumb to greed. There is no way to slam on the brakes and stop your greed from relentlessly pushing you over a cliff to your financial and personal ruin. Those gripped by consumerism do not own their possessions; they are owned by them. In contrast, a master of her desires strictly disciplines herself to want only what she truly needs. This keeps greed in check. Stoic practitioners strive to eradicate the vice of greed that fuels consumerism.

But what about possessions you don't wear? Recall the story we discussed in section 2.1 of Epictetus replacing his stolen iron lamp with a cheaper one made of terracotta (*Disc.* i.18.15–16). In his role as a teacher, Epictetus will sometimes, perhaps often, need to read and write up lectures at night. So, he needed a lamp, but not a fancy one.

Another case of measuring possessions is described by Seneca. In one of his letters (*Ep.* 87.1–4), he explains how a two-day road trip with a friend showed him that much that we possess is superfluous and eliminable. Seneca recounts that they took along only a few slaves (one wagonload), a mattress, a rug to lie on, another to sleep under, bread and figs. Their vehicle was a farmer's wagon (*rusticum*) pulled by plodding mules whose drover had his shoes off but not because of the heat. Seneca confesses that his embarrassment made it hard to persuade himself to let anyone catch sight of him in such shabby (modest) transportation, a trial of the sunlight principle. 'It's perverse, but I'm still ashamed of doing what is right, and whenever we meet a snazzier caravan, I blush despite myself, which proves that the habits I approve and applaud are not yet firmly established. He who blushes riding in a shabby carriage will boast in a fancy one' (*Ep.* 87.4–5). Seneca challenges himself to limit his possessions to what he truly needs by testing what he can do without. Minimalism, as we said, is the Stoic's target. Seneca scolds himself for worrying about non-Stoics deriding his humble wagon because he knows that modest possessions bring no shame at all to those who value virtue above all.

Nonetheless, we might feel a tension between this chapter's blunt, almost Cynic-styled, approach to possessions and the tenet that we must play roles in our societies. This problem can be stated with a series of examples bearing on how our roles influence our material needs. To start, during the COVID pandemic of 2020, many teachers found they needed better computers to produce video content and hold virtual meetings with their students. Correlatedly, many students found they too needed similar upgrades. Or consider the fact that many occupations have standards for professional attire. So, for many to play their roles, they must assemble wardrobes of suitable attire, including clothes for 'casual Fridays'. Or think of scholars and their books. Does one *need* the new translation of and commentary on an ancient text? In a sense, no. Epictetus sees reading books as preparation to act well in life, to exercise your motives to act and not to act, to manage your desires and aversions, to go about this vigilantly, to apply yourself to it energetically, to prepare conscientiously and to act in harmony with nature (*Disc.* i. 4. 13–17; cf. iv. 4. 8–14). His point is that books don't make someone a good scholar, let alone a good person. Yet it seems that some scholars need certain books, insofar as their scholarly work keeps them in conversation with other scholars. The key, we think, is how the particularity of the cases bears on what it means, using Epictetus's metaphor, *to go beyond the foot*. Every case will be different. So, given the roles we play and duties we have, our material needs will likely vary. But we must remember to resist the temptation to rationalize our desire for nice things as needing them for our social roles.

Chapter 40

Epictetus opens this chapter with the cultural observation that once girls start being recognized as women, they become objects of sexual interest. Consequently, they are tempted to be swept up and away by such attention. To be sure, it can be exhilarating to be admired and wanted. It is a familiar enough story. When they are found to have curves, young women become intensely interesting to young men. Consequently, they become intensely interested in maintaining young men's interest. This is the story of the genesis of the cosmetics industry. The industry promises those coming into womanhood that they will become more interesting using its products. It promises those who have been women for some time that they will not decline in being interesting to men, provided they adequately apply various products. Women are acculturated sex objects, observes Epictetus, and given that they appear to have no other means to find self-worth in their social circles beyond playing that role, they become beauty-hounds.

In fact, Epictetus goes further than this point about beauty and its admiration. He notes that being an object of sexual interest isn't only about being eye-candy but being a sexual plaything. Women recognize, given the social norms, 'there's nothing else for them to do besides sleep with men'. These women have internalized the way the men around them see them. They are seen, both by the men looking and by themselves in reflection, as sex objects.

This acculturation has consequences, even for those who are given other opportunities. This is not a phenomenon restricted to the ancient world, either. Consider the fact that there are women who go to college not for the sake of educational opportunities, but to find husbands. It is profoundly sad that college education, an instrument of self-awareness, self-realization and liberty, is used as a final grade in finishing so as to find the right mate. Flippantly, no specific academic degree is sought, but only the 'M.R.S'. Of course, the irony is that college provides an alternative way for women to conceive of themselves. College is not an alternative to marriage per se, but an alternative to thinking of yourself as having only one role entirely determined by your gender, specifically, being the thing that a man goes to bed with. College offers a world of critical reflection, of intellectual growth, of knowledge. You invariably learn to see yourself differently, as an inquirer, thinker, knower. Consequently, the way you value yourself changes, too. A woman may still go to bed with a man, and get married, too. But thereafter, her hopes are not all tied to those two aspirations. That is the change, or rather, transformation.

Ench. 40 ends with a similar contrast, as Epictetus's last sentence offers what he sees as another way. Epictetus tells his audience of (male) progressors that it is of value to be attentive to the sociological patterns just reviewed, so that an alternative can be made clear to these women. Women are rightly honoured not for their beauty or for how well they've married, but for their modesty and self-respect. This is to say, the right condition upon which to hang your hopes and self-regard is the virtues of being in control of yourself, being orderly, being self-aware. In short, it is worthwhile to understand the sociological problem of the sexual objectification of women and how it is internalized, because these young girls seem to internalize it far too readily and, as a corrective, they need to know about and be offered alternatives.

It is worthwhile to pause to note Epictetus's cultural observation that the views of oppressors about the oppressed become the oppressed's self-conception. So, sexism and oppression are internalized as members of oppressed groups are acculturated. Clearly Epictetus is criticizing both edges of the oppression – both the institutions of it and the internalized judgements of the oppressed. Equally clearly, he offers an alternative. But there are two competing interpretations of how to read the alternative. One is a misogynistic view on women's capacity for reflection on these matters. The other is a more progressive view.

The misogynistic interpretation grants that Epictetus criticizes social norms, but faults him for criticizing the women who accede to them. Elsewhere, Epictetus takes a dim view of women. In the *Discourses*, he addresses a visiting student who dresses finely and sports an elaborate haircut. He asks, 'Whom are you trying to impress? Frail womankind?' (*Disc.* iii.1.22). In other words, why should a man try to impress *women*? He analogizes someone who yearns for possessions and contact with friends to a 'worthless woman' who overreacts to everything (*Disc.* iii.24.3). Given this pattern of harsh judgements about women, it is harder to see Epictetus as offering a full version of Stoicism as the alternative to these women's current roles. Instead, he may be offering simply a comparatively less vicious set of cultural norms that may mitigate the harm to their souls. The interpretation of *modesty* and *self-respect*, then, are admittedly alternatives to *sexpot*, but they are more traits of a *serviceable wife* than virtues of a *philosopher*. Simplicius, the fourth-century commentator on Epictetus, thinks that it is best to provide young women with the message that lasting respect from men will come from being the sort of women who 'have subordinated themselves to their husbands' (2002b, 109). These qualities better serve women than mere beauty, because housekeeping, child-rearing and caring for their husbands are their long-term social roles (2002b, 109). Their beauty will surely fade, so they need to develop the virtues of being good wives and mothers.

The trouble with the misogynistic interpretation is that it is, well, misogynistic. Epictetus's advice to these women is that the best alternative to playing the sexpot is to play the devoted wife and mother. This advice smells strangely un-Stoic, as, again, the advice consigns women to a position where their well-being depends on the regard of others. They still, in the end, trade their sexuality for cultural capital. But instead of it being merely sex, it's the relations that sex yields – husbands and children. Further, note that the tone of this misogynistic line seems to be that of blaming the victim, by casting Epictetus as focusing a greater deal of his judgement on women and how they are complicit with the sexism of the age than he is on the men who perpetuate it. This seems upside down, since it is also in the power of those who benefit the most from these oppressive relations to revise them. Namely, the primary target of blame is the men who perpetuate these inequalities and reap their benefits.

However, there is still an identifiable Stoic hue to the misogynistic interpretation. The Stoic view is that you can't control the roles into which you are cast. Given the arrangement of Roman society, women have few roles they can play. Once the role of being a sex object for men is taken on, there are nevertheless better and worse ways to play it. Epictetus is simply pointing out the more choiceworthy of the two options.

As an alternative to the misogynistic interpretation, the progressive view is that Epictetus is enjoining his students to find ways to bring the lessons of Stoicism to all, even young women stuck in the social doldrums of being objects of desire. Epictetus sees himself as playing a role in Nicopolis like Socrates' in Athens, one stationed by God on a divine mission to engage in philosophical discussion (*Disc.* i.9.24–5). He is a messenger, witness and apostle for the Stoic perspective. He hopes to save the souls of the lost. Epictetus enjoins his students to bring the peace of the Stoic life to those who need it the most. In this case, it is young women who are viewed, and who view themselves, as little more than sexual playthings. Given that his students are the very same young men who will be these women's primary points of contact on this issue, they must be educated about and motivated to change the oppressive norms. That is, feminism is not just for women; it's for future husbands, brothers and fathers, too.

In taking this progressive view, that even women have the spark of rationality in them and so can appreciate philosophical analysis, Epictetus extends Musonius Rufus's views that women have the same intellectual essence and basic dignity that men have. Consequently, they too deserve opportunities to develop and perfect their rationality. They can be philosophers, too. Such views were also expressed in Plato's *Republic*, when Socrates says that women can be philosopher-kings (*Rep.* v. 456a–b). Epictetus elsewhere even remarks that it is good for women to be aware of Plato's views on the matter, noting that the educated women of Rome regularly point to Plato's *Republic* as evidence that there should be more opportunities for women to pursue philosophy (Stobaeus, *Anthology* iii.6.58). Epictetus's teacher

Musonius Rufus was part of this proto-feminist movement in Rome (Stobaeus, *Anthology* ii.31.126). Epictetus explicitly takes Socrates as his model for philosophical virtue, and Musonius's influence is evident. The progressive view is an appealing line to take, then, with Epictetus's closing injunction.

How successful did Epictetus expect the project of bringing philosophy to the young women to be? It is unclear. Some may not expect much success at all. As we have noted, the prospects of successfully bringing philosophy to anyone are dim since the whole project is a kind of cultural de-programming. Few are going to be interested. But it seems particularly challenging with young Roman women, given cultural expectations. Imagine how such a discussion perhaps might go: the philosopher making the case about rationality and dignity, but with the young woman operating on the background assumption that the philosopher is actually trying to take her to bed by teaching her philosophy. Stories of sexual harassment in philosophy departments even today persist in darkening these prospects. But regardless of the prospects of success, it nevertheless remains the philosopher's duty to try to discuss philosophy and work to promote virtue. Socrates, too, changed few minds in Athens, but he did what the gods tasked him to do. So, it may go for Epictetus and his students.

A limitation of Epictetus's proposals is that it's still women who will be the students when philosophy is taught. That is, Epictetus teaches his (male) students to teach philosophy to the young women in their lives. But the next step is never thought through completely – that afterwards, *women* can teach philosophy. To other women, for sure, but even to men. So, even on the progressive interpretation, there is a significant limitation to how progressive it really is. Women are encouraged to pursue philosophy, but it is still at the behest of and under the tutelage of men.

The two interpretations are not inconsistent, and elsewhere, Aikin and McGill (2014) call this the 'uneven track record' for Stoics on women. We ourselves prefer the progressive line for its philosophical vision and its extension of a vital tenet of Stoicism: that all humans have the spark of rationality within them, so all deserve dignity and opportunities to develop their rational capacities. But this fundamental Stoic view also leads us to the misogynistic view, as there is a special kind of revulsion to take in seeing a person's rational capacities perverted by complicity in the false consciousness of an age. Moreover, even on the progressive view, what persists is a misogynistic assumption that women must be saved by men, even from false consciousness.

A final point should be made about *Ench.* 40, though it is not about what Epictetus explicitly says in this chapter. Rather, it is about what he could reasonably have expected for his students to have experienced in taking his advice. He enjoins his students to help make women aware that they are more than sexual playthings. Surely this message is not only for the females his students address, but also for the students, the males, too. The trouble is that it is overwhelmingly young men who perpetuate the culture of objectifying women. One step towards challenging that isn't just changing the women's self-awareness, but having men positively change the ways they take up with the women in their lives, namely by treating them as modest and self-respecting and by offering them opportunities to develop those capacities. Epictetus's insight is that though the feminist message is in its first instance one for women, it is essential that it be heard and believed by the men in their lives, too. Feminism, Stoics hold, is not just for women. It is for men, too. In fact, once one sees the critical insights and the critical response Epictetus proposes, it releases men from the bonds of their culture's expectation of sexual conquest. In this regard, *Ench.* 40 has indirectly communicated the message of proto-feminist cultural critique to the young men who ought to hear it and live by it.

Chapter 41

Obsession with the body and bodily functions is unhealthy. Overeating, for example, can lead to obesity and its attendant health risks. Overeating also causes excessive defaecation. Spending a lot of time on the toilet is certainly an unhealthy habit. Excessive concern with bodily appearance can also drive people to exercise compulsively to lose weight. Compulsive exercise, sometimes called exercise addiction, often accompanies eating disorders. Someone with bulimia may exercise a lot to compensate for binge eating. Some believe they can achieve an impossible ideal body type by exercising more and more. Neither injury, nor illness, nor socializing with friends, nor bad weather deters those who exercise compulsively. For the sake of our mental health, Epictetus urges us to steer clear of exercising or eating too much. Elsewhere he also advises against exercising and eating too little (*Disc.* i.2.37 and ii.15.4–13).

What if one of your roles is being an athlete? Doesn't Epictetus often praise athletes because they are very serious about physical training and exercising quite a lot? While it's true that athletes take physical training to a higher level than non-athletes, it's also true that even athletes can exercise too much and get injuries resulting from overuse of muscle groups or ligaments. Moreover, athletes very much need mental toughness to excel in their athletic roles. So, Epictetus's advice in this chapter applies just as much to wrestlers, runners, skaters, cyclists, swimmers, rowers, discus throwers and athletes in all other sports as it does to non-athletes.

Drunkenness makes sober thinking impossible. Excessive drinking of alcohol often indicates depression or alcoholism, which robs one of positive personal relations, physical and emotional health, and happiness. Excessive consumption of alcohol and drugs often spurs people to shed their inhibitions and engage in overly casual, even reckless, sexual activity. Compulsive sexual activity, also known as sex addiction, also harms one's mental health. Failure to practise safe sex risks catching sexually transmitted diseases which harm one's physical health. Epictetus does not demand total sexual abstinence. Rather, he urges developing the virtue of temperance or moderation. Temperance enables us to control our eating, drinking, sleeping, exercising and sexual activity in healthy ways that promote our well-being.

Our minds must be our top priority. If we work to strengthen our minds, exercise our minds by learning to reason logically and critically, feed our minds by reading good philosophy (in particular, the writings of Stoics), literature, history and science, then our strong, wise minds will take good care of our bodies. The body won't be sound unless it is ruled by a sound mind.

A question remains: how much of these things (exercise, eating, sex) is too much? The answer is to start with the individual and her relations and duties. Second, the person must consider what those activities of eating, exercising and sex are for. Further, we must keep in mind a third question: what other activities do these people sacrifice for the sake of pursuing these bodily activities? Returning to the case of professional athletes, their lives are managed so that their roles are restricted to developing physical excellence. But it is still appropriate to be disappointed with them if they neglect to also work on their minds. Or consider the couple that has lots of sex. If it is for the sake of deepening their bond or for the sake of having timely progeny, this is appropriate. But if it is mere pleasure addiction at the cost of them being able to do their duties for others, it is a problem. Again, it is fitting to be disappointed with them if they fail to develop their minds. In the end, we all have roles in our communities, and we must pursue them in varied and individually tailored ways. But we all share the same role of being rational beings. We must pursue excellence in that role without exception.

Chapter 42

Epictetus returns in this chapter to methods for enduring insults and abuse from others. Recall in *Ench.* 20 the exercise of reframing insults by considering harsher judgements one could make about one's shortcomings. This chapter proceeds in the same spirit of reframing an insult or perceived injury, but this time, the reframing is done by interpreting others through the lens of the Stoic intellectualist approach to ethics. The intellectualist approach, again, is captured by the basic commitment that to know the good is to do the good. The two main applications of that principle are that moral improvement comes through cognitive improvement and that the only explanation for vice is ignorance. In short, people are bad because they don't know any better. Therefore, the only escape from moral badness for them and for us is knowledge. So, when people do bad things, they do not do them intentionally as bad things. Rather, they are doing what seems right to them to the best of their knowledge. But they, in fact, are simply wrong about what's really good. They don't deserve our resentment or blame, then, because they err solely out of ignorance, and nobody wants to be ignorant.

Applying this theoretical view to cases of others insulting us or abusing us requires some well-developed confidence in the Stoic intellectualist approach. It is no accident that this purely theoretical piece of advice appears later in the *Encheiridion*, since it is a highly intellectual response, as opposed to the sturdy practical one in *Ench.* 20, earlier in the handbook. This is because the progressor readers are expected to be further along in controlling their reactions, preparing themselves for challenging experiences, and thinking through and applying Stoic principles. So, *Ench.* 42 is indeed a highly theoretical exercise, but if successful, it is widely applicable.

The key is that one must interpret others' insults through the intellectualist lens, seeing their insults in the service of something the insult-giver perceives as good. It may be that they are in error about what actually serves that good, or they may be in error about what the good really is. Either way, their moral wrong is explained by their upstream cognitive error. They were doing what they thought best, but they did not have all the information or they slipped up when thinking things through.

Epictetus's analogy is to logic and evaluating logically complex claims. In this, he makes it clear that the issue is a cognitive matter. The analogy is that someone who judges it appropriate to hurl an insult at you is like someone making an erroneous evaluation of a complex logical formula. Both are errors, and both should be appreciated in the same spirit. With the logic case, because it is an error of evaluating a complex claim, Epictetus holds that the harm is really to the person doing the insulting. Epictetus says that those who think that a true conjunction is false do not harm the conjunction. Rather, they harm themselves by believing something false. The analogy is supposed to show that the error lies in making mistakes in thinking through implications of statements. That is, there are two ways to err in reasoning: to have bad inputs, and to err in making inferences from those inputs. Epictetus is focusing on the ways we can do one well but if we err with the other, we make that error hard to detect. So, to complete the analogy, consider how we think through implications of logical complexes. Conjunctions are propositional complexes best conceived as linking two claims together with the connective 'and'. So, the conjunction of the claims 'Socrates was an Athenian' and 'Caesar was a Roman' makes the complex: 'Socrates was an Athenian and Caesar was a Roman.' That complex claim is true when and only when both component claims are true. Conjunctions, then, are easy to make false, since it takes only one of those claims being false to make the whole conjunction false. So, if we wrongly believe that some true proposition is false (perhaps that 'Socrates was an Athenian' is false), we will then reason further that any conjunction with it as a component will also be false. Errors on one level then lead to larger errors on another level, even when we are reasoning well between levels. And, importantly, what makes the error hard to detect is that the reasoning around the bad input is itself good.

The result, then, is that when we think others are doing something morally bad, being vicious, or trying to harm us, we need to remind ourselves that they are nevertheless doing right by their own thinking, even though they are wrong. They harm not us but themselves by doubling down on and amplifying their errors. These are people deceived by the noxious bullshit of their culture, by their bigoted broadcasters, by their teachers or by themselves. They are victims of lies. So, when they insult philosophers for being poor, or not being useful, or not being good employees, or for being strange or badly dressed, they have reasoned to this commitment, and then to the notion that it is right to say things. They have reasoned from false premises about value that money, status, fitting in and having nice clothes are gravely serious things. From that, they have seen it necessary to insult those who lack those things. But now progressors should see this commitment in the context of the fragility of these externals. A twist of fate can take away their looks, status or money. Then *they* will be the laughingstocks they revile, and by their logic worthy of contemptuous treatment. Surely, they too can see this. Surely, they tremble with fear at what their lives would be like were such turns of fate to come to pass. But they are wrong about what's good and what's bad, and they suffer for it. Even though they insult us, they don't deserve our contempt in response. Rather, they deserve a gentler reply. We can now totally understand how they got to their insults, and in understanding that, we defang them. We have neutralized the sting in their words. Seeing their barbs through the lens of upstream intellectual errors renders them powerless over us.

Ignorance, then, is the problem for the Stoic programme. Given this, we must wrestle with two attendant questions. The first is how this insight bears on the way progressors must view themselves. The second is whether attributing ignorance really mitigates blame in the way it must for Epictetus's reasoning to follow.

First, with the knowledge that the best explanation for moral evil is cognitive error, all moral disagreement boils down to the question of what is truly good. In this chapter, all the judgements of ignorance have been *outward looking*. That is, it is always *others* who are judged to be in error or otherwise deceived about the good. This is a natural way to approach disagreement on first blush: 'I believe what's true and they are just wrong.' However, any reflective person has had the extra thought: 'What if I'm the one who's wrong?' Surely Stoic progressors have had this thought since they own up to not being wise. The insight that humans are error-prone comes home and should yield some humility. A part of wisdom, especially for those making progress, is to recognize the limits of one's knowledge.

The second question attending the problem of ignorance is whether seeing others who try to hurt us as blameless actually follows. For sure, holding that someone acted out of ignorance mitigates the blame for their actions, but it seems that another kind of blame can be placed on them being ignorant. That is, we may not blame them for intentionally doing something bad, but we can still hold them to be blameworthy for being negligently ignorant. So, with those who insult us, we may not blame them for their insults, since they proceed from their not knowing better. But it seems we can still blame them for not knowing better, because they should know better. On this issue, Epictetus and the Stoics break with Socrates' version of the intellectualist approach. Socrates famously believed that since to know the good is to do the good, ignorance mitigates blame. But he also held that there is *blameworthy ignorance*, namely thinking that you know something when you don't know (*Apology* 29b). We can certainly see the merit of endorsing this thought, as believing you know when you don't gets in the way of correcting your ignorance. This blameworthy ignorance impels you to act on and share your ignorant beliefs. Thus, it looks like a product of unreflective dogmatizing. We can do better, and we ought to. Those are the commitments which drove Socrates' withering criticism of his fellow Athenians, and which led to his execution, too.

How does one make sense of the Stoic break with the Socratic commitment regarding blameworthy ignorance? We think the best way to conceive it is in terms of the grip that ignorance has on us and others. Stoicism is a radical break from the common-sense modes of thinking of those in the dominant culture. Accordingly, and as we explained in Part 1, the Stoics admitted that their fundamental views were *paradoxa*, i.e., contrary to common sense. The tenets of Stoicism are strange, counter-intuitive commitments. Can we really blame people for not believing things that seem to them are patently false? To reiterate, they are victims in all this. Pernicious propaganda has deceived them about the good. By endorsing so many false views, people participate in deepening this deception, and as a result they suffer for it. In the end, they have been duped into being ready participants in enculturating themselves into a lifestyle contrary to human happiness. How they treat philosophers who break with these pathological patterns is only a deeper symptom. So, instead of blaming them for their insults or abuse, the Epictetan line is to say: 'it seemed that way to them.'

Chapter 43

As we have seen, the Fundamental Divide teaches us that it is imperative to focus our mental energies on what is up to us rather than on what is not. One thing that is up to us is correct thinking that aligns with reality. An example of such correct thinking is accepting what is not up to us rather than deciding to get upset about it. How others behave is not up to us. But doing our part to fulfil our roles is up to us. It is up to us to carry out our roles the best we can.

An important role that many people have is being a sibling. Imagine Ann has a brother named Bob. How Bob treats Ann is up to Bob, not Ann. Similarly, how Ann treats Bob is up to Ann. Suppose that Ann believes that Bob treats her unjustly (cf. *Ench.* 30). How Ann forms her beliefs is ultimately up to her. Her belief that Bob treats her unjustly may be true or false. Ann ought to base her belief on the best available evidence. But even assuming that she does, the possibility remains that her belief that Bob treats her unjustly is false. What is certain is that nothing should stop Ann from being a good sister. That's the handle she should grab to 'carry' her duty as a sibling.

What if it is true that Bob treats her unjustly? Doesn't intellectual honesty compel Ann to declare that Bob treats her unjustly? If Ann judges that Bob treats her unjustly, then doesn't justice dictate that she seek redress for Bob's wrongdoing? Shouldn't Ann focus her energy on correcting Bob's unjust conduct? Epictetus argues here that the answer to these last three questions is NO. Focusing on the mistakes of others is the wrong handle to grab. Why? Because Epictetus believes that you are not your brother's corrector. Siblings are peers. Your sibling is not your subordinate, not your pupil to teach, not a perpetrator whom it is your job to punish. You are neither a judge nor a juror in a court of law. Ann's role is not to play the District Attorney who arraigns Bob to be a defendant on trial. Ann is not a prosecutor. Ann is Bob's sister. So, her responsibility is to concentrate on fulfilling *her* role well, not to criticize Bob for poorly performing his role. The idea is that each of us must 'carry' our own responsibilities holding onto 'the handle by which we can carry' them. Be a good sibling, Epictetus instructs us, since that is a burden we can carry. If Ann focuses on her own role as a sibling, as a thing up to her, then she can hold the correct handle and carry that role successfully. Improving herself is an attainable goal. Improving Bob is ultimately not up to her. Ann is like a passenger in Bob's car. If Bob is driving, then it would be very bad for Ann to grab the wheel away from him and try to steer the vehicle. Bob is responsible for how he drives his own car. Ann must accept this. She is not Bob's driving instructor. Her role is to concentrate on being a good passenger in Bob's car.

What if Bob really is unjust and treats everyone unjustly? Don't unjust actions demand reprisals? If Bob is undeniably unjust, this does not release Ann from her duty to be a good sibling. Epictetus says that Ann should remind herself that she was raised with Bob as close kin, in the same family. Thus, Ann can and should do her best to be supportive and understanding of Bob despite, or especially because of, his missteps. If Bob commits crimes, then it is the duty of the police to arrest him. It is the duty of the District Attorney to arraign him. It is the duty of prosecutors to try him. It is the duty of jurors to convict or acquit him. It is the duty of the judge to sentence him. If Ann were a District Attorney, she would not be permitted to decide whether to arraign her own brother. Ann can act justly and be a good sister regardless of Bob's unjust deeds. This is the lesson of the two handles: get your own house in order instead of trying to remodel your brother's house.

A question lingers. It is simply whether this rule of two handles has any exceptions. Is there any variance to its application? Further, one could pose the question another way: what if those who are unjust deploy that reasoning on us? Imagine Bob knows that Ann is a practising Stoic and, during the act of treating her unjustly, reminds her of the rule of two handles. He may say, 'It doesn't matter whether I'm unjust to you. What matters is that we are siblings, and you should still treat me as your brother.' Not only does the rule of two handles make Stoic practitioners doormats for others, but in the hands of others, the rule becomes a weapon for worsening unjust relations. Given that the rule of two handles encourages us to endure abusive treatment, it is easily weaponized against those who object. We will address the broader form of this objection, what we call the _Weaponization Problem_, in Part 5. Here, we will provide some tools to manage this particular challenge, what we call the _doormat problem_, for the rule of two handles.

We think the rule of two handles has two different strengths, so we offer two answers to the worry. The strong form of the rule is exceptionless – if we have relations, we should give them their due, regardless of how they treat us. The weak form of the rule is that we should give those with whom we have relations their due until doing so impinges on our other duties. So, it should be our defeasible default, one with exceptions.

On the strong interpretation, a brother who consistently mistreats his siblings still deserves to be treated as a brother. But what is the proper treatment for a brother? To give him what he needs. In this case, the consistently unjust brother may need a trip to rehab, a class on money or anger management, support for proper medications, and so on. What siblings owe to each other varies by the individuals in the relationship. So, in the case of consistently bad behaviour by one sibling, we have reason to think they need help. In the end, it is that kind of support that siblings owe each other, not to be each other's doormat.

On the weak interpretation, if the work supporting one relation makes it so that you cannot do your duty to others, you must make a choice. Many decisions are not only decisions to do something, but they are also decisions not to do something else. So, supporting a sibling with money problems also means not contributing to your child's college fund or not making a down payment on a house for one's family. Time devoted to unravelling a sibling's legal troubles is also time not spent studying philosophy or serving a worthy social cause. All commitments have opportunity costs, so it is fair to ask whether some are worth the correlate sacrifices. Our defaults should be on doing those sibling duties, but we must also be open to acknowledging how costly doing them can be.

On either interpretation, the doormat problem for the rule of two handles can be mitigated. On the strong interpretation, the duties of the relation can change in light of how one's relations behave. On the weak interpretation, some duties can override those to our relations if the latter become excessively onerous or impose unfair, unrelenting demands. So, on either interpretation, Stoics may need to be their brothers' keepers, but they need not be their doormats.

Chapter 44

Eliminating errors of inference is a necessity if one is to have a clear vision of the world. Valid inference leads a reasoner from true premises to true conclusions. That is, with valid reasoning, it is impossible for the inputs to be true and the outputs to be false. This feature of valid inferences makes them very valuable since they perfectly guarantee transmitting truth. Consequently, if one makes an inference that is *invalid*, it's possible to have true inputs but false outputs. In making such inferences we open ourselves to the possibility of errors being introduced into our cognitive systems, even if we've been very careful about what our inputs are. Given the Stoic intellectualist programme in ethics, this is not merely an intellectual risk but a moral risk. So, you must introduce only true premises into your reasoning, and you must reason in ways that don't squander those truths. According to the Stoic theory of cognitive impressions, when we attend correctly to the world, we can have impressions that are caused by what is true and that cannot be confused with what is false. Basing our commitments on these provides that initial guarantee of truth. We will have more to say about these cognitive impressions later in the comments on *Ench.* 45. Stoic logic was devoted to what one does on the other side of having those impressions – which inferences one can aptly make from them. Stoic logic was developed as a systematic account of how to reason validly from those commitments. Wisdom is conditioned on not making input or processing errors in reasoning. So, when Epictetus identifies invalid forms of reasoning, he not only identifies inferences that can lead us from truth to falsity, but he does so to undo the sway they hold over us as reasoners. These are fallacies, pieces of reasoning that seem valid but are not. In criticizing them and showing their invalidity, Epictetus is out to dispel the illusion of their apparent validity. This is what the skills of critical thinking should do for a mind: inure it to bad reasoning by making the errors manifest and thereby avoidable.

The two invalid inferences reflected on here are: (1) I am wealthier than you, so I am better than you; (2) I am more eloquent than you, so I am better than you. To see these inferences as invalid, all we need to do is think of counterexamples to them – cases wherein the premises are true, but the conclusion is false. The task is not so difficult with either. With inference (1), consider the rich person who became wealthy by theft or by exploiting others. That person is not better than an honest poor person. With inference (2), consider a very charismatic and popular lecturer who is in fact not at all knowledgeable about what he speaks. He goes on and on, spreading falsehoods and garnering acclaim. This person is not better than the knowledgeable but socially awkward scholar. Now that these inferences are clearly shown to be invalid, the hope is to find ways to avoid their appeal. One way to do so would be to find valid inferences to replace them.

From those two inputs Epictetus proposes valid inferences as corrections for the sake of a lesson. They are: (1*) I am wealthier than you, so my property is better than yours; (2*) I am more eloquent than you, so my oratory is better than yours. These are not very informative inferences, but this is precisely Epictetus's point. There's not much to infer about a person based on how much property (or money) she owns or how eloquent she is. Moreover, it is a fallacy to identify someone and her value with these externals. Such an inference may seem, in too many situations, valid, but it is in fact invalid. These are intellectual illusions that must be dispelled. We need these reminders because the spell of the value of externals is hard to break, as is preventing that spell from being re-cast.

The target of Epictetus's criticism of these two invalid inferences lies in mistakenly tying our values as individuals to the externals we possess. The error is to think a person's value consists in accumulating money or in being a polished talker. The Stoic principle is that virtue is the only good, so it is not in these externals that value resides. The error of identifying oneself with property or the skill of oratory has two coordinate risks. The first is that if you have made the error of seeing your value hang only on these things, you will be motivated to ignore virtue and pursue these things. So, you will cheat to get money, or you will argue for absurdities to burnish and show off your rhetorical skill. The second risk is that a person is maximally vulnerable in these pursuits. Fire, flood, storm or earthquake can destroy property. An economic downturn can rob the affluent of their money, but it will also rob those who identify their value with wealth of seeing meaning in their life. An injury to a speaker's voice can take away her capacity to speak with the rich, rousing tones that move audiences, but for the orator for whom all of who she is depends on this, the injury wrecks her life. Again, the lesson of *Ench.* 1 and 2 is that the Fundamental Divide clarifies how to thrive safe from fortune's vicissitudes. But a further insight can be gleaned here about identifying how we value *ourselves.*

We are neither our material possessions nor our acquired skills. It is not what we have that matters for our virtues. Rather, it is how we *use* what we have that matters. So, Epictetus is not saying that we should spurn money or the skills of oratory, since these are clearly preferred indifferents. What matters is not that we have wealth or a powerful voice. But if we do have them, it matters what we do with them. Do we use our wealth to contribute to the well-being of our community? Do we use our powerful voices for causes of justice?

It is worth lingering over Epictetus's invocation of eloquence as an external in these cases of self-concept. The Stoic views on wealth are familiar enough, but eloquence and oratory are new arrivals in the *Handbook*. That this communicative skill arrives at this later stage in the manual is, we think, another indication of the developmental structure of the *Handbook*. Stoic training, with logic, rhetoric, physics and ethics as foci, will equip progressors with both impressive argumentative skills and substantial insights. Progressors will look at themselves and each other and begin to adjudge their progress in terms of how well they fare compared with other speakers. Consider how scholars can get caught up with having a public reception for their work. Or consider how students think they excel at philosophy because they are comfortable talking often in class. Of course, neither is a good criterion for discernment. Much public philosophy is more the selling of thoughts that people already think back to them as profundity. Too many students think that volume of verbiage is a measure of quality of class discussion. A reality for philosophers who are thinking through things that are difficult and worth figuring out is that they will have to risk being boring. A tedious logic lesson may need to be rehearsed before they can proceed. Or they may end up being cast as hectoring needlers in their society. Too many critics of culture are more likely to be reviled as killjoys than embraced as inspiring orators. Or they will simply be judged to be weird losers. Certainly, arguing that money, status and good looks are not goods will sound like sheer nonsense to the vast majority of audiences. Philosophical progress may not be the sort of thing that is easy to sell. Plus, even if you have some rhetorical skill, the appeal should really be in the argument. If you win over folks with jokes or cool turns of phrase and not something that gives them knowledge, then what exactly have you really accomplished?

Chapter 45

The previous chapter was about eliminating errors introduced by our inferences. This chapter is about ensuring that we provide ourselves with correct information before we start drawing inferences and passing judgements. In this regard, *Ench.* 44 and 45 come as a package: 45 is about taking care not to pollute our inputs by prejudging them, while 44 is about making sure to draw reliable inferences from that information.

Stoic ethics is based on a theory of knowledge. If to know the good is to do the good, then it is important to have a clear picture of what it is to know. In the

Discourses, Epictetus makes an analogy between sorting beliefs and appearances and identifying straight lines and right angles. To cut straight lines and right angles, a well-trained artisan uses a carpenter's rule – a criterion for these things brought to the hurly-burly material to impose order (*Disc.* ii.11.14). The same goes for a subject with beliefs and impressions – she must bring a criterion to her impressions to identify the true ones and distinguish them from the false. The proposal is that *cognitive impressions* do this work. A cognitive impression is caused by what exists in a way that accurately represents it and cannot be caused by something else. So, a subject has a cognitive impression when she sees what is as it is and couldn't mistake it for something else. We have knowledge when we have many of these cognitive impressions and reason rightly from them to construct a systematic network of information. The result is something that isn't merely correct about things, it also explains those things and identifies how we know them in the first place. Stoicism's founder, Zeno of Citium, to explain this view, said that a cognitive impression is like a hand tightly grasping a piece of information, and knowledge is like another hand tightly grasping that first hand (Cicero, *Academica* ii.145). The key to it all is having these cognitive impressions in the first place and not getting in our own way in gaining them. The primary way we occlude these cognitive impressions is prejudging circumstances. So, we show up with a prejudice or faulty expectation, or we hastily draw inferences from too little information. The best habits, both for our cognitive health and our moral development, are to make sure to stick to what has been given.

Epictetus cites examples of hastily inferring something about someone based on only a little information. So, we might see someone who bathes quickly, or we might see someone who drinks more alcohol than most. What is important for Epictetus is that we assent only to what we've seen in these cases. In the first case, the bathing was done quickly. In the second case, the drinker drank a lot. But in both cases, we might feel tempted to say that they did so badly. So, the bather bathes *too hastily*, or the drinker drinks *too much*. The lesson is that since we don't yet have all the facts, we mustn't be too hasty with those judgements.

What makes bathing good or bad is the virtue or vice the bather enacts while doing it. The same goes for drinking. In both cases, we must know the judgements that the bather and drinker employ when they undertake their tasks. Only once we know what they are thinking can we judge whether their actions were bad or good.

To be sure, there are duties of cleanliness and moderation. With cleanliness, we should care for our bodies as our instruments for doing our duties. In caring for our bodies, we honour the god for those gifts by beautifying and caring for them as we can. Further, we owe it to our fellows to be clean for social interaction. Being cleanly dressed and properly groomed expresses respect for our cohorts. And comity requires that we not smell in ways that offend. Drinking, too, is an activity with duties, and in this case, they involve moderation. A great deal of alcohol can impair our self-control and ruin our health, while the right amount can induce conviviality. As social beings, we have found our own paths for most effectively living up to these duties. A certain time allotted to bathing and grooming is needed to meet the standards we hold. Also, there is a limit to how much we can drink before we've passed the limit. Some self-knowledge is perfunctory; most adults reach it. How long does it take you to get ready for the day? How much is too much to drink at a dinner party?

To start, answers to these two questions will vary widely across individuals. Bathing times depend on what needs to be washed. For example, those who are bald don't need long hair-washing regimens. So, their showers will be shorter than most others. Dinner parties, too, will have some variance with how much wine goes down. Those with larger bodies and who've eaten quite a bit will require more alcohol to feel the right cheer that others can get after only a drink or two. So, we may have someone who showers more quickly and drinks more than most, yet neither is a vice; both are in fact appropriate for who he is. Once we know the facts, our judgements can be accurate.

Just as we had seen in *Ench.* 44, we must look at what others do through the intellectualist lens. That is, we must account for their judgements of what's good, since in those judgements we find their motivations. It applies here in evaluating behaviour that may initially appear vicious. In the previous chapter, the key was reconstructing an account of why others would think it appropriate to hurl insults. In this case, it is about reconstructing why they might bathe so quickly or drink so much. So, instead of judging that they bathe or drink badly or viciously, we should first ask why they bathe so quickly, or drink more than others do. If we see which considerations are upstream for them, we can identify their reasoning and motives. Then we can adjudge whether these are badly performed actions. This requires that we identify an error in those reasons. Our bather may not care about how his smell impinges on others, or he may be unaware that it does. Our drinker may think that he is better company when very drunk or that being intoxicated will dull the pain of being socially anxious. However, in both cases, the error is not primarily in the bathing or in the drinking, but in the judgements that motivate these actions.

Epictetus's insight is that we cannot properly assess these circumstances if we allow our judgements to rush ahead of our cognitive impressions. The proper procedure should be first to describe the situation in neutral terms, with the objective of identifying why people do what they do. Only then can we judge that they've done what they've done as appropriate or inappropriate. This is not only the method of correctly judging the moral situation with others, but it's the only technique for wisely navigating the social world. In short, the wise do not judge beyond what their cognitive impressions support.

The rule that the wise should assent only to cognitive impressions provoked vigorous debate between the Stoic and Academic (sceptical) schools. The Academic sceptics argued that there are either no or vanishingly few cognitive impressions to assent to. Recall that a cognitive impression is an impression caused by what is that represents it accurately and is fashioned such that it couldn't have been caused by anything else. This last qualifier the sceptics challenged by posing a series of *indiscernibility cases* to the Stoics. For example, many eggs are indistinguishable. Imagine you are shown two eggs from a grocery store and then later asked to say which was which. Or consider identical twins. Most people seem to have a very difficult time telling them apart, else they wouldn't be called 'identical'. Further, consider the fact that the gods often send visions that are indistinguishable from real experiences. Heracles was tricked by Hera into thinking that his family was robbers. Hector was tricked by Athena into thinking he had help in his duel with Achilles. How do we know we are not now facing such illusions? One cannot point to any feature of our experiences to say so, since those features can be replicated in the illusions. The sceptical challenge yields the result that there are likely no cognitive impressions because any impression could be identical to an illusion or could be caused by something not identical to what we think it is. Consequently, the requirement that the wise assent only to cognitive impressions entails that the wise assent to no impressions.

The radical sceptical result of the argument from indiscernibles was intolerable for the Stoics. In the *Discourses*, Epictetus commented that these sceptical arguments were instances of people using their intellects to abuse their own intellects (*Disc.* ii.20.8). The main Stoic reply was to point out that with skill and care, people do develop the capacity to tell twins and even eggs apart. These similar pairs are distinguishable, but for us to do so, we must attend with focus and care. To the challenge that the gods can deceive us, the reply is that nature equips humans with the measures and skills to discover truth, and to attribute deceptive motives to the gods is impious (*Disc.* ii.20.22). The sceptical challenge, according to Stoics, is an instance of clearly self-refuting reasoning. The sceptic argues that we cannot reason well or come to see anything clearly, yet they take themselves to have offered an excellent set of reasons for a view that they believe clearly follows. What, to a Stoic's mind, could be more absurd? All of this, Epictetus holds, is not only reasoning that shows its own falsity, but is a waste of one's time and intellectual energy (*Disc.* i.27.21).

One thing that emerges from the Stoic-Academic exchange on cognitive impressions is the persistent question of how to identify them. The upshot is that the demandingness of the Stoic requirement is obvious. Insofar as the reply to the Sceptics is that one must be like the person who is acutely aware of her surroundings in a way that resembles one who can distinguish two very similar eggs or two identical twins, the wise person, on the Stoic model, must be extremely perceptive and painstakingly careful.

Chapter 46

Three lines of thought converge in this chapter. The first is a return to the issue of how progressors should comport themselves when keeping company with non-philosophers. The second is how progressors, in appreciating their progress, can get in their own way. Finally, the third is how Stoicism's primary objective as a philosophy is as a way of life. Stoicism for Epictetus is a practical philosophy, so we have here a picture of what might be called a *Stoic pragmatism*.

Epictetus has already discussed the problem of talking philosophy with non-philosophers, and the highlights of this advice are reprised here. Not putting on the highbrow of the philosopher among non-philosophers returns, as does making peace with the thought that non-philosophers won't appreciate well-founded philosophical insight. These two thoughts are important enough to be said twice, because much of our lives will be spent around non-philosophers and being a philosopher is a full-time job. The problem is that the non-philosophers around us are not wise, but they likely think they know a lot. They won't be interested in hearing the Stoic views on things, or if they are, they will likely be dismissive. Or worse, they will want to know the views of popular nitwits that will in turn make them nitwits, too. Moreover, given that the non-philosophers who are interested in philosophy are not wise, Stoic insights will sound like noise or nonsense to them despite their purported interest in philosophy. So, you shouldn't go on and on about philosophical principles with them. Further, even if they are talking about philosophical issues, you shouldn't be tempted to think that they are really doing philosophy. Joining a philosophical discussion with non-philosophers is a recipe for disaster. Too many of our acquaintances think they like philosophy, but what they really like is to hear themselves talk or to have their own views said back to them approvingly. The true criterion for being philosophical is how you handle an objection or a problem with your view. Too often those who say that they love philosophy will turn defensive and resentful upon even the slightest critical response. This isn't philosophy proper, but self-indulgent theoretical talk masquerading as philosophy. Making a habit of playing along with this practice is bad for progressors. Best to just avoid it.

Finally, there is the simple fact that you will likely be drawn into these discussions, even if you have not jumped in on your own. In those cases, you will need to manage the overt but baseless judgements of rejection others will have about your contributions. They will say, because we don't know about the latest bloviator about culture or opinionator about the gods, that we are irrelevant. Or because we are not up to date on the most recent fashionable theoretical nonsense, we are clueless about where things are happening, even in our own discipline. Or, given that it takes careful reflection on things to construct a responsible philosophical view, we lack hot takes on current affairs. Consequently, it is judged that philosophy cannot 'keep up' with a fast-moving world by opining on everything that happens to have popular attention.

Notice that the default attitude here is a harsh elitism about philosophy and philosophers. Even people who discuss philosophical principles can be non-philosophers. Apparently, it takes quite a lot of skill and commitment, on this programme, to be a proper *philosopher*. Consider this term 'philosopher' as denoting an aspirational concept which can have deficient and widespread use but can also have a very demanding use. The term 'flat' is like this. There are contexts where, say, a card table is *flat*, perhaps for a game of gin rummy or setting a simple meal. But there's a sense that the card table is not *flat* at all. It has many bumps and ridges and is certainly not level. What would it take for that table to be *really flat*? Or consider terms for our enterprises. Being a 'soccer player' is one that admits this variance. In one sense the six-year-old next door with the shin guards and muddy cleats is a *soccer player*, since some Saturday mornings she runs around and kicks at a ball. But compare that with what's required to play the game at a competitive level; what the six-year-old does isn't enough even to qualify as doing it badly. There are players for the best teams in the world whom fans doubt can even play the game. (For example, Shkodran Mustafi, Arsenal's astoundingly often wrong-footed centre back from a few years ago, was jokingly judged by fans to belong in the category 'can't play football'.) The concept of *philosopher* functions similarly. Those unfamiliar with how the standards ramp up steeply beyond the bullshit sessions in dorm rooms or in bars are often surprised at how different things are for experienced, trained philosophers. Once seen in this light, Epictetus's elitism makes more sense. There are skills and principles one must master to make the progress necessary, but those unfamiliar with the purpose of those requisites will see learning them as unnecessary or wrong-headed. Too many parents at children's soccer games object to seeing the ball passed backward, out of tight defences, thinking that the only way to make progress on the soccer field is to advance the ball. The same kind of thing happens when well-run philosophy is witnessed by non-philosophers.

The second theme at the forefront in this chapter is that progressors get in their own way. In this case, they inhibit and even derail their own progress when they are around non-philosophers. In *Ench.* 22, the progressor's temptation was to seek approval from others for their philosophical progress. To reiterate, there are two errors in this. The first is it puts value in an external, in this case, by seeking acclaim from others. The second is that it is a losing proposition to ask non-philosophers to appreciate progress in a philosophical programme that is explicitly devoted to contravening common sense. This is why the analogical argument Epictetus gives with Socrates is essential. Socrates was arguably the greatest philosopher in the ancient world, yet in his own time, he was routinely overlooked when people were hoping to pursue wisdom. At the opening of the Platonic dialogue *Protagoras*, Hippocrates asks Socrates' help in getting the sophist Protagoras to teach him. In the *Meno*, it is the sophist Gorgias who is declared to be the real bringer of insight and skill by Socrates' interlocutor, Meno. In neither case is Socrates put off by the interest his associates have in hearing wise things from others. For progressors, this lesson is a tough one since they will think their insight to be worthy of interest. Even if it is not yet perfect, progressors will think their insight better than that of some popular charlatan or grandstanding buffoon. But this is precisely what should be expected from audiences made up of those who are not wise. They will ask those who are wise to take them to those who will miseducate them. For the most part, the wise can only look on. The philosopher, then, must learn to tolerate being overlooked, not just by non-philosophers but even by those who might pass for philosophers. Again, consider the resentments roiling among so many of our colleagues in philosophy departments or in the profession as a whole. Someone wins a prestigious award or a hefty grant, and the first thing we're tempted to do is ask how our own work is not similarly recognized. Or consider the pull of deflation you feel when a student talks glowingly about how interesting another professor's course is.

These twinges of jealousy and resentment are products of what we've been calling progressor's temptation. It is the temptation to be taken in by and overvalue one's own philosophical progress and insight. In the first instance, one should feel some pride in philosophical progress, because it is a true good. But one should not be side-tracked by that pride. This is because that pride in our progress impedes further progress. In this case, that pride in progress can yield the expectation that others will recognize it and value it accordingly. When that expectation is not met, we are disappointed. The key is to see that this disappointment is evidence that there is yet more progress to be made.

The third theme of this chapter is what we might call *Stoic pragmatism*. The pragmatic vein of Stoicism emphasizes that it is a practical philosophy with the primary good of living a life of virtue and so, happiness. All other endeavours that neither contribute to nor are components of that end are unnecessary. So, the theoretical work of Stoicism is devoted to clarifying that end and its means. One may think that Stoicism and the philosophy associated with the American pragmatists is a bad mix, since the pragmatists emphasize the efficacy of action, while Stoics focus on grinding out what Fate has given us. But we've argued that the view of Stoicism as utterly passive is incorrect. The Stoic programme is, like that of the pragmatists, focused on how to most effectively play one's role in one's social nexus and as the natural being one is (see Lachs 2012 for a case for this synthesis). One's end is a life according to nature, so we must clarify what *nature* is and our best means to *live in accord* with it. That's the objective of Stoic theory. The theoretical programme is not the end, but in the service of the life one lives guided by it.

Epictetus makes an analogy to illustrate his pragmatist mode of thought. Sheep eat and digest their food, but the valuable products of that consumption and digestion are their quality wool and milk. Philosophers study their principles and refine their arguments, but the valuable products of that study and argument are their lives of virtue. Philosophical digestion is a process of three stages. The first stage is understanding philosophical doctrines and reasoning. The second stage internalizes the commitments and reasoning skills. The third stage perfects what has been absorbed in practice. The product of this digestive process is making this set of Stoic commitments a kind of second nature in action. Thus, to launch into a lecture about these principles with non-philosophers, as Epictetus puts it, is to 'vomit them up' undigested. Principles without practice are undigested food, on the analogy. They are mere words, parroted mindlessly, but not put into motion in one's life.

To call this orientation *Stoic pragmatism* is to highlight the goal of Stoic theorizing, namely, to live rightly. A basic pragmatist doctrine is that theoretical difference without practical difference is either not worth attending to or is negligible to the point of irrelevance. Epictetus's Stoic agenda conveys the same comportment. The point of eating the grass and digesting it is to yield wool and milk with the sheep. They process it all internally, since showing it all off is not the point. This process operates internally, in your soul and on your own, as your own work. Your foremost goal is one you must always keep in mind, in all circumstances: to live a life of virtue.

Chapter 47

Stoics take self-improvement very seriously. Self-improvement is measured by progress in developing a virtuous character (as noted in the previous chapter's comments on Stoic pragmatism). Good character is promoted by frugal habits. So, the point of adapting your body to frugal habits is self-improvement, not to goad people into praising you. The goal is to improve yourself, not your reputation. The goal is not to win applause. The goal is not to inspire others. Wanting the admiration of others is arrogant. Arrogance, vanity and boastfulness are vices, defects of character. So, if you abstain from alcohol, Epictetus says, it is unseemly to report to people every chance you get that you only drink water. Boasters fish for compliments. Compliments don't make you a better person. Frugality and self-discipline make you a better person. You aren't performing to hear an audience cheer. If you decide to train to become austere and tough, then do it for yourself; don't do it to recruit fans. Tough physical training was termed *askêsis*, from which the word *ascetic* derives. Historically, asceticism has been practised in religious traditions as various as Buddhism, Christianity, Hinduism, Jainism, Judaism and Islam.

The original ascetic of ancient Greece was Diogenes of Sinope. He became known as the Cynic, the dog-philosopher. The Stoics greatly admired him. To toughen himself up and learn how to endure hardship, Diogenes was said to have rolled in scorching sand in the summer, and in the winter to have stripped naked to embrace snow-covered metal statues, and to have walked barefoot through snow (DL vi.23, vi.34). Diogenes engaged in many dramatic stunts like these to shock others out of their complacency. His aim was to conspicuously challenge their false beliefs about comfort and conventional norms. In *Ench.* 47

Epictetus cautions Stoics in training not to be show-offs like Diogenes. Epictetus is emphatic in the *Discourses* that the calling of a Cynic is a very special vocation that exceeds the abilities of virtually everyone (iii.21.19). For a beginner Stoic in training, aspiring to become a Cynic is far too lofty a goal. For nearly everyone, it is a role beyond one's ability (see the comment on *Ench.* 37 reminding us to have knowledge of what we can do before we start taking on tasks beyond our abilities). Instead, Epictetus urges the very thirsty Stoic trainee to take some water into her mouth and then spit it out *without* telling anyone. The message: a Stoic thirsts for self-improvement, not showers of praise.

The problem we've been calling progressor's temptation takes a specific form in this chapter. Most forms of the temptation thus far have been cases of seeking attention for one's intellectual progress. Progressors are tempted to prattle on and on about their philosophical views or to show off a new argumentative technique. In this case, even the practical results of one's progress can be traps of temptation. So, showing off one's hard-won Stoic capacities for endurance becomes a point of pride one wants others to observe and marvel at. Despite the temptation having a new locus (practical results instead of theoretical skill), the form is the same: taking a good (progress in developing virtue) as a reason to expect adulation and admiration. Once again, the problem is that an external is valued and replaces the focus on what is worth valuing.

The implicit contrast with Diogenes the Cynic deserves to be expanded, especially along these lines. This chapter is one text in Epictetus's work where he is not unswervingly positive about Diogenes as an exemplar. Progressors are instructed *not* to do as he did. The key is that Diogenes's exercises were overtly public. They were not only for the sake of his own progress, but performed for onlookers, too. His Cynic way of life was not only about being independent from civilization and its groundless norms, but about showing to others that one could live this way. So, Diogenes was a deliberately performative iconoclast. His ascetic stunts legitimized the pillories he barked at people, proving that he walked his talk. In this way he strove to break free of and confront the false values of his society. On meeting Diogenes, Plato famously commented to him that 'your lack of pretence would be admirable, were it not so pretentious' (*Gnomologicum Vaticanum* 445). The problem Plato observed was that despite the fact that Diogenes was working to make himself independent of his culture, he seemed to want very much to be noticed by it. This seems a tension. Epictetus's solution was to identify Diogenes's particular role. Diogenes was, in Epictetus's eyes, a scout and messenger of the critical approach to a host of false values, so he had to employ overtly subversive, exhibitionist tactics. Stoic practitioners, however, don't need to play the role of Diogenes. They just need to be themselves, enacting their own relations and duties. Diogenes, in this regard, was unique. He was literally a man without a country, with no occupation, no family, and only a single obligation: his divine calling to be messenger to humanity. So, he could act in ways that were rude, confrontational and demonstrative. Not so for most Stoic practitioners. They still have relations, vocations and cities to serve. Best for them to just get to their jobs, practise exercises of endurance, do their many duties and not worry about being evangelists or philosophical showboats. Those Stoic responsibilities are plenty challenging enough. The Cynic's daring shortcut to virtue's summit is too steep a route for Stoic trainees to climb. Theirs is the longer route.

Chapter 48

The contrast between philosophers and non-philosophers is a frequent theme for Epictetus. In this chapter, he presents benchmarks for progressors between the two classes. A significant feature of these benchmarks is that many are about the progressor *not* doing things: not blaming, not praising, not defending oneself and not actively desiring. There are two ways to assess one's progress: *positively* and *negatively*. Positive progress is measured by how close to your goal you are getting. Negative progress is measured by how far you have gotten from where you started, often by having corrected or eliminated errors. Often, these metrics coordinate, so when you walk directly somewhere, how close you are to the destination also measures how far you are from the starting point. But since not all paths are linear, eliminating vices doesn't guarantee that you have replaced them with fully cooked virtues. In these cases, progress can be assessed only negatively; this bad habit has been broken, or that problem has been eliminated. So, a progressor gauges her progress in terms of how well she lives by the Fundamental Divide (*Ench.* 1) – she doesn't live committed to or entangled with valuing externals. The objective is for progressors to see the new habits they have acquired by living in light of the Fundamental Divide as a kind of progress – they are no longer doing something they see as unwise, and they have replaced those habits with something better. But this does not mean that these new habits are unproblematically perfect. The threefold division between non-philosophers, progressors and philosophers is supposed to remind progressors that they should try to maintain a kind of beginner's mind with Stoicism. That outlook entails always trying to detect where one needs to improve, remaining open to discoveries and growth. This is a vital insight since this chapter appears near the end of the *Encheiridion*. Progressors, even if they have made plenty of progress, are still progressors, so they can become complacent in their development. This is a common theme for aspirationalist philosophies. The goal will ultimately exceed the grasp of most, if not all, mortals. Stoicism is an aspirational philosophical vision. So, those who have made great strides in practising this programme should remember that even if they are doing better than their pre-philosophical past selves, there is always room for improvement.

From this aspirationalist perspective, Epictetus's positive recommendations to chuckle when complimented and to be on guard against oneself as if against a plotting adversary has distinct significance. The reason why you should chuckle when complimented is not because the compliment is inaccurate or silly. The reason is that you should always remember how much more work you have to do, no matter how much progress has already been made. It should be the chuckle that you have during a stopover on a long road trip. Our friend may say that we've made good time for this first seventy miles, but we know that it is a multiple-day journey. One may chuckle at this, not to deny the progress but to put it into perspective. The chuckler sees progress relative to how far she still must go.

The same aspirationalist perspective bears on the recommendation to guard oneself as if against a plotting enemy. The key is that the impediments to your progress as a Stoic are entirely a matter of you and your consistency. That is, every progressor is her own greatest obstacle to progress. One site of this vulnerability is what we've been calling the progressor's temptation (we will say a lot more about it in the closing chapters of the *Encheiridion* in 49 and 52). At this stage, the temptation is to take pride in your progress and it being recognized, and then to rest on your laurels. This attitude is correct in one sense, since philosophical progress, even negative progress, is a good of sorts. The progressor is changing herself by eliminating her vices, rooting out her errors. Also, she is developing a virtue of reflection, both in managing the skills of self-control in living in accord with the Fundamental Divide but also in assessing her progress in doing better over time. Take it on analogy with health, as the medicinal model of philosophy consistently conveys. You don't simply *get healthy* once and for all, but you commit to the project of *maintaining your health*. This means that you will allow wounds to heal, you will eat right, and you will exercise sensibly. Being healthy requires constant work. Some of it may be easy and perfunctory, like regularly bathing and brushing your teeth. The hard part is being consistent about it. No one part is difficult, but the whole, as it turns out, is. You cannot become complacent once you enjoy a good run of good health. In fact, when on a run of good health, it is a good time to focus on how to improve and perfect oneself. The temptation is to take progress as a reason to let up or rest satisfied. But given the task of progress towards virtue and resisting vice, the opposite is true. There is always more to refine and correct.

Chapter 49

This chapter is devoted to addressing a new problem for progressors. Some temptations to fall away from Stoic principles arise from sources outside the philosophical life. Thus, even as a progressor, one could still be tempted by externals like pleasure, fame or wealth. In the first instance of what we call progressor's temptations, these externals are tempting distractions common to both non-philosophers and those making philosophical progress. Progressors might think they deserve higher acclaim as philosophers or that others should appreciate their pronouncements more. One can imagine a popularizer of Stoicism fretting over whether her next book will be a best-seller or suffer scathing reviews. In these cases, philosophical progress is taken as a means of getting the same old externals as before. So, progressors should vigilantly guard against these temptations. However, other instances of temptation for externals are unique to progressors. In these instances, the temptations arise from within the philosophical tradition, because they are not about the standard externals that appeal to non-philosophers (wealth, pleasure, status and the like). Rather, these temptations range over things that are coordinate with being a practitioner of a long-standing philosophical programme. They are temptations unique to belonging to intellectual traditions. Stoicism, as an intellectualist ethical philosophy, requires intellectual work. So, the externals of the life pursuing that intellectualism become temptations to progressors.

One pride of intellectualism is that things that are cognitively difficult for most are easy for the intellectual. A riddle is solved, a puzzle fixed, all with little time or effort. This is because these intellectuals have specialized skills, training and background knowledge. Now consider the fact that status among intellectuals is determined by how they handle those puzzles. The philosophy professor who can interpret the cryptic writing of one of the greats is lauded as an excellent expositor. Status even comes from being inscrutable, too. The American academic John Searle tells the story of how in a conversation with the French philosopher Michel Foucault, Foucault asked him why he writes so clearly. Searle could enjoy much greater stature were he to adopt a more obscure style. Verbal obscurity erects a kind of fortress of interpretation and criticism. If a critic identifies a problem in a turgid author's argument, the plausible reply is always that the critic misinterpreted the main point. Interpreters, then, become gatekeepers not only for access to the tradition's insights but also for what might count as a legitimate criticism or relevant contribution.

Epictetus's target is those who are impressed with interpreters of Chrysippus, the Stoic tradition's great, but stylistically obscure, systematizer (see Section 1.1). Chrysippus was the third head of the Stoic school, after Zeno and Cleanthes before him. It was said of him that without Chrysippus, there would have been no Stoa. He was committed to defending the Stoic philosophical programme from the criticisms of the Academic sceptics, so he worked to find solutions to problems that consistently plagued Stoic views. He was a leading light in developing the notion of preferred indifferents, for one. Much of his work was dialectically intricate. Since he wanted to answer all the critics, his replies often required many subtle distinctions and qualifications. As a result, Chrysippus was, at least in the opinion of the ancient historian of philosophy Diogenes Laertius, a writer with an 'unsuccessful style' (DL 7.180). His legacy, then, is a philosophical school and scholarly tradition of reading and interpreting a notoriously difficult but astute corpus of texts. Understanding these books is worthwhile because they clarify the principles of right thinking and living well, and they defend these principles from trenchant criticism. In fact, one might even say that, because of Stoicism's intellectualist bent, it is of utmost importance to master these texts. Consequently, skilful interpreters are good to have around; their skills are useful.

The key to Epictetus's insight in this chapter involves preventing a confusion. The two things which are confused are the instrumental value of an interpreter's role and the value of the wisdom the interpreter is supposed to make accessible. Being good at interpreting Chrysippus is an achievement only because his writing is very turgid. Were he to have written in a different fashion, we would not need interpreters. But appreciating their skills is part and parcel with progressing in this tradition. The Stoic progressor strives to have wider knowledge of the Stoic tradition, because it deepens her understanding of the wisdom on offer. A progressor works on the tools of logic to better understand how arguments, objections and replies function. So, bringing those skills into, and exercising them upon, Chrysippus's texts is a fitting application of them. Finally, a progressor works to internalize the principles of the programme. Seeing and appreciating defences of the principles against objections and understanding their development is a central facet of a progressor's orientation. So, excellent expositors of Chrysippus embody many of the skills that progressors should aspire to cultivate and perfect. This fact is what makes this a sly temptation for progressors. It is in so many of the inclinations and accomplishments internal to the philosophical life that the progressor encounters these distractions.

The problem with the objects of progressor's temptation is that the instrumental value of a tool is confused with the value of its end. To start, the value of a tool is conferred only by its contributing to that final goal. The value of being an excellent expositor of Chrysippus is in understanding his views on the principles. These principles are themselves valuable only if the knowledge imparted by them facilitates optimal living. And this knowledge is valuable only if one puts it into action by living well. Earlier, we'd called this comportment towards philosophical value a form of Stoic pragmatism, according to which the value of theory is found in the difference its successful practice yields. The analogy from *Ench.* 46 was that between progressors and sheep. The sheep show they have digested their grass and water by yielding high-quality wool and milk. Progressors show they have digested their philosophical arguments and principles by living well. And it is not in 'vomiting up' those nutrients for others to appreciate that one should search for value. Expositors, then, are not identical to practitioners. In fact, one can envision an expositor of Stoicism who does not practise the philosophy at all. The expositor may just find it a rewarding exercise, like reading a tricky section of Homer (as Epictetus suggests) or solving some other mind-bending puzzle. One can be a shrewd expositor without believing any of what one is explaining. The job, however, is not just to explain Stoic philosophy, but to believe it and then to live it.

The crucial contrast for Epictetus here is between philosophers and mere scholars of philosophy. Epictetus's Greek term for such a scholar is *grammatikos*, literally 'grammarian'. The mere scholar may be very knowledgeable but has little to no wisdom. The scholar can explain the details of a complicated passage from a text of wisdom. She may trace a line of influence, show how it replies to a certain worry or how a turn of phrase is a reference to something otherwise unseen. Plus, it all may be clear what was meant by the author. But the mere scholar treads no further. She is interested in the cult of personality around the author, so she attaches herself to the adoration of Chrysippus, Homer or another writer. She is out to build herself into a bastion of that fortress of interpretation. The philosopher, by contrast, is out to know and thereby change her life. So, when the interpretive work is over, the philosopher asks, 'Is this true?' Only if the proposal passes this test does she endorse that principle and live by it. The prime objective, on the pragmatic orientation, is to philosophize for the sake of living better. The mere scholar asks whether this or that interpretation of Chrysippus is right about Chrysippus. The philosopher asks first whether Chrysippus was correct, and second how to live nourished by that insight. Sticking with Epictetus's image of the *grammarian*, the mere scholar values only the words. The philosopher values what the words are about. Philologists love words. Philosophers love wisdom.

It is no accident that the warnings against this form of progressor's temptation come at the end of the *Handbook*. Progressors who have read their way to the end, even of this short manual, will be the ones likely to struggle with admiring great interpreters of Chrysippus. Only much later in their philosophical training will this form of progressor's temptation emerge. Only later in one's development as an intellectual will admiration grow for scholarship or outstanding exposition of an opaque writer. These are still externals, just as oratorical skills were in *Ench.* 44. It is still fallacious to infer that explicative skill is worthy of moral admiration from the fact that it has a use. These are externals, but externals closer to the core of the intellectual programme, temptations one will feel only once progress in philosophy has begun.

It is worth lingering over this thought that new temptations will emerge for progressors as progressors. They will face the same appealing externals as potential distractions which they faced before devoting their lives to Stoic practice. But engaging in Stoic practice itself brings its own tempting externals that non-philosophers won't find tempting at all. This is exactly why we've called them progressor's temptations. Yet the significance of this phenomenon is not to be understated. Marcus Aurelius admits that he was not taken seriously when he began as a young man to wear the philosopher's cloak, a simple garment signifying a commitment to a simple life. But it did not matter in the end whether others appreciated it. Imagine someone taken with the romantic picture of being a philosopher who acquires the right clothes for the role: a philosopher's cloak, a black turtleneck, or a tweed jacket, depending on the locale and period. These are distractions, but they also announce that a person is (if but confusedly) committed to the philosophical project. Because progressors are not wise, we should expect them to make such errors. But we should also expect them to be able to catch these errors and correct themselves when given the opportunity. So, with students, we should have a pretty high tolerance for philosophical posers among the sophomores, but less so for the graduate student in our orbit or our colleagues. A final point is worth appreciating here. Institutional credit and professional advancement in academic philosophy clearly favours mere scholars over philosophers. So, even if you got into the pipeline for philosophy based on the right motives of living philosophically, there are so many points wherein perverse motives infiltrate your mind and derail your progress. Living well does not directly yield peer-reviewed publications in the best venues, but scholarship is precisely the model for that. So, stature in universities and the philosophical community ironically conflicts with the pragmatic orientation and the impetus behind the philosophical enterprise, properly considered. The key for the Stoic progressor is not to fall for the illusions of value that intellectual life creates, even if those illusions are direct consequences of one's commitment to that life.

Chapter 50

Stoics take their responsibilities, duties, roles, jobs and tasks very seriously. Each role, job or profession involves performing many different tasks. Some tasks we set for ourselves, knowing we need to do them to fulfil a role we have. Other tasks are assigned to us by others. Here Epictetus may assume that any task we choose to undertake we will automatically take very seriously. What he says explicitly is that if a task is set before you, you must handle it as if it were a sacred law to obey. Shirking your task is not an option. Approaching the task in a careless or lazy way is not an option. Treat it as if the god assigned you the task, so that skipping that task would violate divine law and defy the god's will. Defiance of a divine law would be flagrant impiety – sacrilege.

What if performing the task stirs up gossip about you? What if doing the task makes you unpopular? What if completing the task provokes criticism from someone? None of those consequences matter, Epictetus insists. If you do your job and do it well, that's all that should concern you. What others do, as we have read again and again throughout the *Handbook*, is not up to you, and so no worry of yours. Procrastinating about your task is totally your irresponsibility. Doing your task carelessly is on you. So, pay attention to doing your task as if it were a sacred charge, Epictetus teaches, and give no thought to what people say about it.

The categorical nature of these tasks and our singular focus on them is highlighted by the religious language Epictetus uses to describe failure: *sacrilege*. But notice something important about the way this language is qualified: one acts *as if* it were a sacred duty given by the god. The question is: why is it *as if*? Given Stoic providentialism, the entirety of one's life is ultimately a dispensation of fate, every bit a product of divine reason. The result should be a simple and clear *is*, not the conditional and qualified *as if*.

The puzzle of the *as if* can be answered in two forms: one conservative, the other concessive. The conservative solution starts with the point that *as if* is still consistent with *is*. Epictetus's framing concedes that we must switch perspectives among the quotidian obligations that arise in our relations and events of the day. That is how we attend to them one by one. But we must see all of this from the perspective of the divine and recall that the god has cast us into these roles (as noted in *Ench.* 17). So, on the conservative line, Epictetus calls attention to the shift in perspective needed to attend to the roles in the proper way. The qualifier shows the shift one must make. Instead of weakening the commitment to Stoic theology, the qualifier highlights the shift in levels one must make when attending both to the duties specified by the situation and the divinely dispensed roles that define them.

The concessive interpretation is that Stoic theology makes it easier to take on the roles and perspectives, but it is unnecessary. You can proceed *as if* the gods have determined your role and planned the events of the world in providential fashion. But you don't have to believe it, and it doesn't have to be true. Viewing it all through this lens is a useful heuristic, and it can provide motivation. But that is all these commitments are in the end. The question in the background here is: how much does Stoic ethics depend on Stoic theology? The conservative Stoic answer is that one cannot have Stoic ethics without Stoic theology; it all comes as one systematic philosophical package. In Section 1.3, we reviewed this take on Stoic philosophy as the commitment that logic, physics and ethics all have organic internal relations (as, for example, parts of an egg: the shell, white and yolk). But a plausible position is that Stoic ethics can be practised without all the details of Stoic theology or Stoic logic. We will review the options for this puzzle of how connected the parts of Stoic philosophy must be in what we call the *System Problem* in Sections 5.7–8. The point here is that the concessive interpretation of *as if* here in *Ench.* 50 is a form of Stoic Minimalism, the view that Stoic ethics can be practised without commitment to other substantive Stoic doctrines in physics, logic or theology (see Chakrapani 2022 and Gill 2022 for outlines of the minimalist line with Stoic ethics). The *as if* on this line is a mere heuristic, like the injunction to live *as if* you are being watched by a wiser version of oneself, or to philosophize *as if* you are explaining everything to an alien. The lesson, as we see it, is that the interpretation of this *as if* depends on how systematic Stoic philosophy must be.

Chapter 51

In this chapter Epictetus conducts a candid review of the lessons he has imparted to his adult students. He urges them to reflect on what they have learned, to honestly assess their own progress, and to take accountability as adults. He expresses impatience with their progress and urges them to buckle down and redouble their efforts. Laziness and excuses will never free them from the mental weaknesses and character defects afflicting them. We could also read this as Epictetus reflecting aloud on his own educational history, as a Stoic who has taken Socrates as his teacher and his favourite role model to emulate (see *Ench.* 5 and 46.1).

Epictetus has undertaken the role of a Stoic teacher instructing his students in the philosophical principles, the ethical lessons, they must master and live by in practice. The implication is that his students have learned these lessons because Stoic principles are easy enough to learn, eminently intelligible, and make good sense. Stoicism is not rocket science. After a few years of learning, rehearsing and memorizing the tenets of Stoicism, his students have matured from adolescents into adults. Stoicism is not for children, and his students must now take accountability for being adults. He expects them to walk (eat, drink, act) like Stoics now, not just talk like Stoics. By now they should have made sizable progress in shedding the false beliefs that cause worry, anxiety, fear, disappointment, frustration, anger, resentment, envy and grief. If they can't by now, after spending years learning to be Stoics, get a grip on themselves, then there are no excuses left to make. By now they should have become masters of their desires. If they can't at this point control their appetites, keep calm no matter what happens, keep cool no matter what anyone else says or does, then they have only themselves to blame. If they haven't mastered their desires yet, then they are likely going to die as philosopher-wannabes.

Adult philosophers, that is, real Stoics, don't procrastinate or make excuses for their failures. They take accountability for themselves and for their rate of progress towards their goal. That goal is *never* to get angry, *never* to be afraid, *never* to resent or envy anyone. That goal is *never* to be arrogant, spiteful, unfaithful or greedy. That goal is *never* to be intemperate, unfair, ungrateful, cowardly or foolish. To take this goal seriously, Epictetus urges his students to 'treat everything that appears best' to them as an 'inviolable law', echoing his advice in *Ench.* 50. Trust your judgement of what appears best to you and then pursue it without letting anything deflect you from it.

Many things can distract a Stoic from her goal, like, for example, the *difficulty* of certain tasks. Some tasks demand a lot of hard work over a long period of time, thus requiring great endurance and persistence. This makes many duties 'burdensome'.

A second powerful distraction is *pleasure*. Pleasures tempt us to take a break from our work, the longer the break the better. Pleasures invite us to procrastinate. Pleasures condition us to forget that the job isn't done yet. So, pleasures and creature comforts are very pernicious to the challenge of making continuous progress as Stoics.

A third thing that can deflect a Stoic from her goal of self-perfection is *prestige*. Fame, acclaim, awards, applause and popularity are all useless in a Stoic's quest to become the best version of herself. The desire for prestige can seduce a person into doing sleazy stuff. Sleaze includes compromising one's moral integrity to please others. Debasing oneself to gratify another is sleazy. Stoics avoid sleaze like the plague. How? By thinking of the goal of Stoic training like victory at the Olympic Games. Olympic athletes train for hours, every day, week after week, month after month and year after year. Stoics are mental athletes with full-time jobs and no vacations. Every day, even every hour, a Stoic strives to put into practice her philosophical (ethical) principles.

Why does Epictetus think that 'on a single day one action destroys or saves progress'? Well, imagine that you are prone to losing your temper. You resolve to dedicate yourself to ridding yourself of this character defect. Your course of progress is like a chain in which each act of keeping your cool is a link. If just one link snaps open, if you lose your cool once, then the chain breaks and your progress is destroyed. So, when anyone tries to provoke you, say, by hurling an insult at you, you must remind yourself that his criticism is either true or false. If it is false, then it is a mistaken opinion that does you no harm. If his criticism of you is a true judgement, then you ought to thank him for bringing to your attention a defect you need to correct. Either way, anger is not a justified response (see *Ench.* 33.9 and comment).

Now imagine that you've gone two months without getting angry. One day while you're carrying heavy packages someone runs by you, steps on your foot, and knocks the packages to the ground. You immediately judge that the person was 100% to blame for injuring you and breaking the contents of the packages. You hastily judge that he wronged you and you must retaliate against him. So, you curse the 'wrongdoer' or, worse, strike at him. This single act of blowing your top erases the progress you have made in successfully controlling your temper for two months. On the other hand, if you can keep a grip on yourself, remain patient (see *Ench.* 10), pause to think and recognize that the person's *apparent* recklessness (see *Ench.* 42) cannot be a fault of yours, then you can justifiably take pride that his apparent error (possible recklessness) need not cause you to commit your error (anger). You didn't let it halt your journey towards consistent calmness (see *Ench.* 28). That is what Epictetus means by 'saving your progress'.

Other examples of a single action that destroys progress may include taking credit for someone else's excellence (as in *Ench.* 6); lusting after an attractive person (*Ench.* 10) or debasing yourself in pursuing sex instead of doing one's duty (*Ench.* 33.8); quitting a worthwhile task because it is painful or tiring (*Ench.* 10); tackling a role you can't pull off instead of one you can (*Ench.* 37); instead of introspecting about improving yourself turning outward in a desire to please another (*Ench.* 23); flattering a big shot (*Ench.* 25 and 33.12–13); criticizing the gods (*Ench.* 31); professing to be a philosopher or lecturing non-philosophers about how to behave (*Ench.* 46.1); boasting (*Ench.* 47).

Stoics believe that failures of reason lead to mistakes, misdeeds and excuses. Epictetus believes that Socrates consistently listened to and followed reason in dealing with every situation he faced. In the *Discourses*, Epictetus borrows from Platonic dialogues and Xenophon's *Symposium* to sing copious praises of Socrates. Socrates loved his children in a free spirit and remembered his first duty was to be a friend to the gods (iii.24.60). He fulfilled his duties as an assemblyman and soldier (iii.24.61). He easily resisted sexual temptation (ii.18.22). He said, Epictetus reports with approval, 'One man rejoices in improving his farm, another in improving his horse, but I rejoice every day in following the course of my own improvement' (iii.5.14). Socrates urged people to examine their lives as he did (i.26.18; iii.12.15). He never boasted he had knowledge (iii.23.22). He scoffed at death, calling it a mere 'bugbear' that frightens only unsuspecting children (ii.1.15). With great skill and clarity in dialectical reasoning (ii.12.5), committed to rational argument, Socrates was ever respectful of his conversational partners (ii.26.6–7). When alone he tested and examined himself in a practical way, trying out precepts and thinking as a *philosopher* (ii.1.32–3). (See the distinction between philosopher and mere scholar in the comment on *Ench.* 49.) Socrates faithfully kept to the post assigned to him by the god, to philosophize in Athens with others and help them improve their souls, thereby honouring his duties to his kin, his neighbours and his fellow citizens (iii.1.19–22). By refusing to abandon his divinely appointed role to philosophize under threat of imprisonment, exile, execution by poison, and so losing his wife and leaving his children orphaned, Socrates knew how to 'play ball' in the lawcourt (ii.5.18–20). Facing the judges, he spoke truth to power (ii.13.24). In prison he was considerate to his jailer (i.29.65). His commitment to his God-given mission is what it means, Epictetus says, for a human being to truly be kin to the gods (i.9.22–25). This kinship with the gods was evident when he identified his country as the cosmos (i.9.1). Socrates calmly withstood being reviled, always wearing the same expression on his face (i.25.31). He never got riled up during an argument, and never used any terms of abuse or hubris, but instead endured the abuse of others and put an end to strife (ii.12.14). Epictetus marvels at Socrates' power, in every kind of social setting, to bring those in his company over to his own side (iii.16.5). Obviously, Socrates brought people to admire and emulate him (iii.7.34). In Epictetus's judgement, Socrates succeeded in everything befitting a good man (iii.24.61). He lived so nobly and died so nobly (ii.16.35), accepting his fate as pleasing the gods (i.4.24; i.29.18).

For Epictetus, then, Socrates is the paragon of virtue, a model of Stoic intellectualism, and the ideal philosopher. Socrates is the Polaris of Epictetus's Stoic aspirationalism. In the *Discourses* Epictetus says that he will not be better than Socrates, but if only he is not worse, that is enough for him (i.2.33–7). Nor can Stoic progressors be the next Socrates. But what they can do is work hard at becoming the best possible versions of *themselves*. They can aspire to that challenging ideal and *make progress towards it*. Because progressors have earned the progress they've made, they deserve due credit for it. In the closing sentence of *Ench.* 51 (notice, on the last page of the *Handbook*), Epictetus gives his Stoic trainees a gentle slap on the back as a modest gesture of approval. He congratulates them for getting this far. But the slap is also a friendly, encouraging nudge to propel them forward, a signal to *keep going*. Were they to stop where they are, they would cheat themselves out of any future progress they stand to make. So, Epictetus urges his progressors to judge themselves worthy of continuing their programme. They are not yet Socrates, not yet wise, but they owe it to themselves to see how close to being wise they can get. That is their noble mission. Every progressor deserves to and can 'live as one who wants to be like Socrates'. This means wanting to achieve Socrates' wisdom, epistemic humility, calmness, courage, affability, and his other virtues. The extreme difficulty, or even impossibility, of reaching that goal in no way undercuts the possibility of approaching it.

Chapter 52

Epictetus poses a metaphilosophical paradox for progressors with this chapter. There are two progressions outlined, but they contain a conflict. The first is the progression of value. One becomes a philosopher to be wise, to be excellent, to live well. That is the point of the Stoic programme. The central feature of Stoicism is its intellectualist outlook: knowledge is the key to living well. Consequently, one strives to gain knowledge and understanding of the principles of living well, and to acquire that knowledge and understanding one must master the reasoning to and from those Stoic views. But to understand those arguments, one must master the logic for explicating them, and the canons of logic contain many details and technicalities that one must get just right to do it all properly. So, the order of value puts a life of virtue at the top and the technicalities of logic at the bottom. But the order of study and work is flipped. This is the second progression since the person making progress must first master the logical principles to fully understand the ethical system which puts them on a path to a good life. So, one must do the least important things first to grasp the most important things at the end.

This flipped order is not all that paradoxical, when viewed with a particular philosophical view of ethics in mind. We can clearly see that it is a direct consequence of Stoicism's intellectualist programme. It might be ironic at best, but it is fully consistent with what Stoic ethics entails for progressors. The result is that the most important thing is delayed so that it can be grasped properly. One's training in logic and critical thinking is an ethical project, even if this is not made obvious as one attends to technical details. The genuine paradox arises because the delay of ethical conclusions and practice is a delay for those who are not yet wise. Those who are making progress, in this circumstance, are subject to another form of progressor's temptation, but one that is unique in form and unique in difficulty to resist. Recall that progressor's temptation is a distraction from the life of wisdom and Stoic principle that emerges from within the philosophical tradition and philosophical work. It is a distraction that tempts only those making progress. Those temptations can start off as standard distractions, but in philosophical dress. One may expect non-philosophers and other progressors to appreciate and honour one's philosophical insight. That is simply the philosopher's version of the desire for acclaim and status. But then (as shown in *Ench.* 49) one becomes inspired by the skills of an expositor of challenging philosophical texts. This could still be admiration of someone's status, this time as a gatekeeper for a tradition. Yet it might take a different valence. That is, it could be that a progressor grows enamoured with a tool of philosophical progress, and in being impressed with it, forgets the valuable thing it is supposed to be instrumental for. So, in *Ench.* 49, the progressor is impressed with an expositor's skill, but loses sight of the wisdom the exposition should make accessible. This temptation afflicts only philosophical progressors; they risk becoming distracted by the tools for acquiring wisdom.

The paradox of *Ench.* 52 arises from the fact that in putting logic and its technicalities first, the order of Stoic education delays teaching the insights that lead to wisdom. As a consequence, unwise progressors will be distracted by the technicalities of the logic they learn. Due to this distraction, they neglect to progress to the ethical knowledge and practice which the logic should have clarified. So, our progressors will revel in debating a fine point about conditionals or wrangling over a puzzle about self-reference. But by focusing their vision on mastering these subtleties, they've lost sight of the point of the broader enterprise. And note that this is a feature of how philosophical progress must be – we are giving the tools of wisdom to the unwise to use on themselves. They may use those tools wisely, but we really should expect them to use those tools unwisely.

Epictetus's example is that of the prohibition on being a fraud. Do not be false; do not tell lies. There are good reasons not to be a fraud. To borrow the distinction in *Ench.* 49 between the *philosopher* and the *mere scholar*, these reasons open two paths to a progressor, as we see it. The philosopher, having mastered the concepts of good inference and proof, will evaluate these reasons, and survey the dialectical situation with other thinkers to scout out any objections. If the argument is good and no standing problems are found, the philosopher endorses the rule and obeys it. In contrast, the mere scholar will be distracted by the details of the argument. Perhaps the scholar will identify the variety of forms of inference that make up the argument, compare it to other inferences of similar type, and try to ascertain whether one basic tactic of argument underlies them all. Surely, this project is interesting. It may even be worthwhile. But it can come with an opportunity cost: no one comes to live by the conclusion of the argument because we were distracted, ironically, by the argument's details. So, we have a mere scholar who can wax academic about why the proof that we not be frauds is an excellent proof, but who is not made better by it.

Anyone who is a philosopher will feel the tug of this type of progressor's temptation because it involves the very tools of the philosopher's trade. Appreciating scholarship is not uniquely philosophical, so the mere scholars of *Ench.* 49 need not themselves be practising philosophers. This is why Epictetus invokes scholarship on Homer as an analogue. But the temptations of the progression outlined in *Ench.* 52 are uniquely philosophical. The constituent temptations lie near the heart of those who love wisdom. Wisdom requires the capacity to appreciate and draw fine distinctions, to follow and evaluate long lines of reasoning, and to understand the point of arguments and disputes. The tools of philosophy sharpen these capacities. A joy also accompanies exercising them. Like muscles, agility and speed being developed, one delights in those capacities. But too narrow focus exclusively on honing the skills distracts from what they are for. It is like athletes who enjoy some training exercise so much they think more of it than they do about the game they train for. There are so many fine athletic skills for which players ruin their overall games to single-mindedly master. Take the tennis player who has concentrated so intently on her drop shot that the rest of her game crumbles. Or the soccer player who can juggle the ball impeccably but is clueless about how to pass or tackle effectively. So, we have our progressor who has gotten so tangled up in the trappings of philosophy that mere scholarship monopolizes her intellect. This progressor can give a detailed analysis of the proof that one ought not be a fraud, but she is nevertheless a fraud.

This is the highest-grade form of progressor's temptation, so it should be clear why the *Encheiridion*'s closing chapter in Epictetus's voice bears on this issue. By the end of the manual, the greatest temptation for a progressor will stem from philosophy itself. Even if our progressor has overcome the temptations of the untutored (for pleasure, power or wealth), and has overcome the temptations of intellectual life to be a gatekeeper for a tradition or to brandish impressive interpretive skills, or the temptation to flaunt her Stoic powers of endurance, a final temptation in the skills conducive to wisdom confronts her.

How can this last temptation be resisted? Recall that the other temptations are dispelled by re-describing the object of desire in a fashion that makes clear precisely what it is. Consequently, the desire for that object dwindles or disappears. Philosophical skills, on the other hand, are not of that kind. In fact, the skills that become distractions are themselves the means which allow one to do that re-describing in the first place. The more clearly one sees and appreciates them, it seems the stronger the temptation they pose. This, then, makes the progressor's temptation in *Ench.* 52 unique.

In the *Discourses*, Epictetus complains that the works of his fellow Stoics are 'full of quibbles' (i.29.56). Getting hung up on these tiny details of a logical puzzle or a fine distinction, they are 'diverted from the study of morality' (i.8.6). The exercises of these books written by these mere scholars are works of 'conceit and vanity' (i.8.7) which, because of the distractions they promote, are 'disgraceful' (i.29.60). The result, we think, is that one can view this temptation in the right light. But in this case, it is not the items of value that are deflated but the way one values them.

One trouble emerges from this solution to the problem of progressor's temptation, namely, that though the progressors are now certainly motivated not to be distracted by quibbling, the problem remains of distinguishing pointless quibbling from matters of import. No one engaged in quibbling recognizes it as quibbling as they're doing it. Rather, quibblers believe they are making a significant point. Such is the nature of all rationalization. For it to have the effect of rationalization, it must at the time feel astute. The result is that Stoics require a double vision along these lines. They must see their philosophical work from the inside, but they must also see it from the outside. In a way, this is a special version of what we called the progressor's paradox in our comments on *Ench.* 22 and 23. The progressor's paradox was the puzzle: how, given that they are not wise, can progressors ascertain their progress or identify where they need more work? In the case of *Ench.* 52, the question can be framed like this: how can progressors, given that they are not wise, know whether their work is making progress on matters of import or mere quibbling? Our solution to the progressor's paradox was that the *Handbook* itself sets clear benchmarks for that progress with Epictetus's feedback in the form 'those who are making progress will … ' One can hit these marks and others like them, and thereby keep tabs on the track record of one's ethical advancement. But this is a different matter with the progressor's temptation version of the paradox in *Ench.* 52, since the question is: how do you know whether you are quibbling or philosophizing, if you are not wise and the tools of both are the same? To deepen the problem, it seems that too many Stoic authors set poor examples, since Epictetus complains that they are quibblers, too.

An appealing, but very non-Stoic, solution would be to agree with Aristotle about the necessity of having good friends. A genuine friend is someone who, in parallel pursuit of virtue, gives one the feedback needed to make corrections. You cannot see the back of your own neck. But others can. So, you need reliable friends to provide you constructive critique (see Aristotle's *Nicomachean Ethics* ix.1169b.35). The problem is this solution requires that we not just have friends but that they be virtuous, or at least worthy progressors. However, these are external factors Stoics cannot count as up to them. Consequently, Stoics must hold that this Aristotelian move cannot solve the problem. To do so would undo Epictetus's Fundamental Divide.

A more Stoic, but less immediately effective, solution is to find ways to enact what is done by others for oneself. Granted, you cannot, when quibbling, see it as quibbling. But you can consistently do so *in retrospect*. That is, you can recognize your errors in hindsight and thereby learn from them. This is certainly a common experience for many philosophy professors. When they began their career in the profession, they learned an argumentative move or a pertinent detail and grew monomaniacal about it. Thereby, they became quibblers or mere scholars about those things. But as they matured, these thinkers saw the devices and nuances in the right light, and thereby learned a lesson that generalizes. So, keeping track of their thoughts can be a way for Stoics to guard themselves against progressor's temptation. They can recognize it best in themselves only in retrospect, but even this allows for living forward and correcting their mistakes. This won't guarantee that they can eliminate all the vices, but it does supply a way to mark their progress. It is, as we've noted earlier, a *negative* marker of progress, but this is as one should expect from an aspirationalist philosophical programme.

Chapter 53

The *Handbook* concludes with four quotations. The first (*Ench.* 53.1) is from the *Hymn to Zeus* by Cleanthes of Assos, the second head of the Stoa (see Part 1.2, p. 5). The Stoics defined the goal (*telos*) as 'living in agreement with nature'. Their rich concept of 'nature' included (1) the things that happen in the world, that is, the course of events, and (2) the constitution of each living organism. Stoics believe that the special endowment the world gives human beings is reason (*logos*). Thus, 'living in agreement with nature' for us means above all 'living in agreement with reason'. According to Epictetus's theology, reason demands that we identify the course of events with the will of the gods, God, or Zeus. Zeus's will is identical with fate, destiny and Providence. Zeus (destiny) gives us our innate abilities, talents and characteristics, and assigns us the circumstances we encounter in life. We inherit many, though not all, of our roles from destiny.

A Stoic believes it is eminently reasonable to embrace all assignments she is given by destiny and thus to align her will with that of God. To resist or reject the will of God is a flagrant failure of reason, utter folly. So, opposing destiny is seriously vicious. To refuse to follow God's lead is thus both crazy and impious. It is irrational because to fight fate is reckless futility. It is to want the impossible. What destiny decrees for nature's course is inevitable. Moreover, to oppose God's will is impious because it defies the wisely ordained plan of the cosmos. Spurning how the beautifully designed universe unfolds is downright ungrateful. So, whether we choose to comply with destiny or to struggle against it, we will follow it either way.

This understanding of fatalism is captured in a famous simile sometimes attributed to Cleanthes. 'When a dog is tied to a cart, if he wants to follow, he is pulled and follows, making his spontaneous act coincide with necessity, but if he doesn't want to follow, he'll be compelled anyway. So it is with humans, too. Even if they don't want to, they'll be compelled in any case to follow what is destined.' Wise dogs and wise humans opt to walk closely behind the moving cart of fate instead of being unpleasantly dragged along the ground by it. That Epictetus offers this excerpt from Cleanthes' *Hymn to Zeus* as a reminder *for everything* underscores how essential the Stoic doctrine of fatalism is to his philosophical, theological and ethical outlook.

The second quotation (fragment 965 in J. A. Nauck, *Euripidis Tragoediae*, 1854) scholars attribute to the great Athenian tragedian Euripides (*c.* 480–*c.* 406 BCE), a contemporary of Socrates. *Ench.* 53.2 reinforces the imperative to accept destiny. A Stoic conceives of the acceptance or, even better, the *affirmation* of destiny as graceful yielding. If an event is necessitated, then it is smart to affirm it and stupid to deny it. Grasping the truth of this conditional shows an understanding of 'divine matters'. Grasping the truth of this conditional demonstrates wisdom in the ways of the world, specifically insight into the divine order of the cosmos. The wise align their desires with necessity and thereby are reverent. Resisting necessity is an irreverent rejection of the good possibilities the divine provides. Thus, walking (behind the rolling cart of fate) can be done gracefully and gratefully but being dragged on the ground is disgraceful and foolish. Stoics believe that the cart of fate, nature, the cosmos, is a beautiful, well-structured, intelligent, living macro-organism, basically the body of God.

The third quotation modifies a text from Plato, *Crito* 43d. In this dialogue Socrates has been lawfully convicted and sentenced to death. As he awaits execution in a jail cell in Athens, Socrates is visited by his old friend Crito. Crito reports that the return of a ship on a sacred voyage is expected later today, and so the postponement of Socrates' execution will terminate tomorrow. So, his execution will proceed. Socrates replies 'Well, Crito, if this is what pleases the gods, let it be so.' Socrates, however, goes on to doubt that that will be the day he dies, because of a dream he had which he interprets to mean that he will die the day after tomorrow. In the remainder of the dialogue, Crito tries to persuade Socrates to escape prison and flee Athens. Socrates argues that were he to do so, he would break a just agreement with the Laws of Athens to abide by them and their judicial verdicts. So, he reasons that breaking the law would be both unjust and unholy. Instead, he must submit to the lawfully rendered verdict and punishment from his trial. He must submit to execution. Socrates believes that since his argument is sound and Crito voices no objections, reason has led them to a decision that the god also wants. The dialogue ends: 'Then, Crito, let it be and let us act in this way, since it is in this way that the god leads us' (*Crito* 54e), thus echoing 43d. Epictetus greatly admires Socrates' commitment to pleasing the god by using reason to guide every action and embracing every destined outcome.

Epictetus uses the fourth quotation, from Plato, *Apology* 30c–d, to deny that death inflicts personal harm. Non-Stoics consider this Stoic view to be wildly counter-intuitive, so it calls for explanation. Socrates can be executed because he is mortal. As we have seen, Epictetus recommends daily reflection on the inevitability of human mortality (*Ench.* 21; see also 3, 5, 7, 11, and 14). Mortality is a permanent feature of all organisms. Nature's cycle is birth, maturation, death, decomposition and rebirth. Every generation is replaced by a new one. Life and death are thus necessary, reciprocal phases in the operation of nature. Epictetus believes that death is not an annihilation but a change, a recycling of organic matter into new lifeforms. Consequently, Stoics do not regard death as a permanent loss or a kind of damage. Rather, death is a natural necessity, not a change that harms nature.

But what about the *person* who dies? Doesn't Socrates' death harm *him*? Epictetus applauds Socrates' view that the real self is the mind or soul, not the body. (See *Ench.* 28 for an implication of this view.) Thus, bruising your foot does not harm you, it only damages a part of your body. So, only harm to Socrates' mind (soul) is real harm to Socrates himself. Since virtue is the good condition of the self, true harm to the self is vice. Harm to Socrates would therefore be harm to Socrates' moral character or personal integrity. Socrates' prosecutors Anytus and Meletus can get him executed, but execution only destroys his body, it cannot touch his moral character. As long as Socrates keeps his own courage, justice and wisdom intact, he is unassailable. The virtuous are invulnerable to the wicked deeds perpetrated by others. No one can rob Socrates of his virtue. So, no one can victimize him. The executioner's poison can remove life from his body, but nothing has the power to remove the goodness of a good person. So, Epictetus enjoins us to preserve as a handy reminder for dealing with everything that our moral goodness is *up to us*. Consequently, our personal harm and deliverance are also ultimately up to us, not up to others. This paramount lesson in Stoic ethics, which harks back to the Fundamental Divide in *Ench.* 1, concludes Epictetus's *Handbook*.

*

Part 5

Critical Responses to Epictetus's Stoicism and Replies

In this closing part the broader lingering concerns with Stoicism, and Epictetus's particular statement of it, must be addressed. Many have been given voice and developed in our commentary on the chapters of the *Encheiridion,* but here we present them as fully articulated objections to address. Six broad classes of criticisms require replies. Here they are in short form.

The Inaction Problem: Stoicism makes no room for any motive to act.

The Ruin Problem: One's duties are determined by one's relations but living as a Stoic ruins one's relations.

The Practicability Problem: Stoicism is psychologically impossible. We lack the control over our minds that is required to practise Stoicism.

The System Problem: Stoic ethics is supposed to be a part of an organic and systematic whole with Stoic physics and Stoic logic, both of which are implausible.

The Scepticism Problem: Stoicism requires that we know many things with utmost assurance in order to properly live as Stoics, but we lack that kind of knowledge.

The Weaponization Problem: Stoicism is too easily turned into a programme for rationalizing unjust arrangements or victim-blaming those who oppose injustice.

Our objective with this part is to review these six critical responses, give them all a fair hearing, and lay out the Stoic replies we consider most plausible. One upshot of our replies is that revisions to the ancient programme are necessary, and this opens a broader question of what the proper limits of revising Stoicism are. How much can Stoicism be revised before it becomes something else? We will contend that Stoicism is a living philosophical tradition, not a dead dogma. Living traditions can keep the spirit of their founding alive without being shackled by every word (or even what are thought to be the most important words) of their founders. Stoicism, as a tradition that places the use of reason at its core, must be responsive to the reasoning of those who maintain and adapt it. The story of the Stoa in antiquity displays this developmental picture, whether it be with Chrysippus's proposal of preferred indifferents or the imperial (and distinctly Epictetan) proposal of the category of progressors, the Stoic programme has shown flexibility about its central commitments, finding ways to integrate the insights of critics and innovators into the system. Even Stoicism's founder Zeno revised his theory of knowledge in light of Arcesilaus the Sceptic's criticisms.[1]

Most of the objections we survey here were familiar to the ancient Stoics, as their rival schools regularly raised them. In fact, it is the great philosopher, historian and priest at Delphi, Plutarch, who sets the stage with most of these objections. He compiled extensive objections to Stoicism into three books titled *On Stoic Self-Contradictions, On How Stoics Speak More Paradoxically than the Poets,* and *Against the Stoics on Common Conceptions.* These works have been excellent sources of both material for our knowledge of Stoicism and pointed criticisms of the Stoics' system. The Pyrrhonian sceptic Sextus Empiricus also devotes considerable space in his *Outlines of Pyrrhonism, Against the Logicians* and *Against the Ethicists* to criticizing Stoicism. But neither Plutarch nor Sextus Empiricus anticipated the problems that developments in psychology and the natural sciences pose for today's Stoics. So, these latter challenges deserve their own treatments. Further, the cultural role philosophy plays has changed since its ancient practice. This brings us to the fact that the current popular reception of Stoicism among many who present the philosophy as a 'life hack' for getting ahead seems to lack any moral thrust. Given this fact, a worry arises that Stoicism's tools for self-control can be abused. This is not a new phenomenon, as Seneca himself seems to have been both a practising Stoic and a predatory money lender, but it is a concern that calls for our contemporary response.

5.1 The Inaction Problem

Stoicism, according to the Inaction Problem, leaves no room for motives to act. We are, on the Stoic's view, utterly passive in the face of the world's variances. This objection takes two forms. On the one hand, there is the *value* version of the inaction objection, which is that, given the distinction between what is up to us and what is not, our lives drastically constrict to the tiny realm entirely within the ambit of what is up to us. So why care about one's body, one's children, or anyone or anything beyond one's mind? All these things are externals, so whether they thrive or not is not a concern that touches our *prohairesis* (volition, real self). On the other hand, there is the *fatalist* version of the inaction objection, which maintains that if the Stoic view of the world as determined by Providence is right, then one's actions can make no difference in any outcome. So, even if one ought to perform some duty or try to become a Stoic, it is predetermined whether or not this will come to pass. But a fundamental presumption behind every motivation to do anything is that our doing makes a difference. Fatalism robs us of that possibility because things can't be otherwise. And since things can't be otherwise, we can't make a difference. So, fatalism robs us of the grounds of motivation. On either the value or the fatalist version, the inaction objection is that Stoicism undercuts our natural motives to act, and so it is a form of do-nothing-ism.

Both versions of the inaction objection are very old. In fact, they are as old as Stoicism itself. Plutarch famously analogizes the Stoics' self-congratulation of invulnerability to the names inscribed on boats found wrecked on rocky coasts – names such as 'Providence' and 'Good Journey'. By valuing in this way Stoics make the things we naturally value which function as springs of motivation into empty, impotent 'indifferents' (1057e and 1060e). As a result, we are robbed of any reason to act to avoid ruin or pursue good things.

The value version of the Inaction Problem depends on what seems a relatively clear principle: you're motivated to do something only if you think you doing that thing brings about a good or prevents a bad thing. If nothing of value to an agent depends on the act, it is hard to identify what would motivate her. Of course, nothing deters the agent from acting either. But that's in some ways worse. The problem is magnified, since there is not only no reason to do anything, but also no reason not to do anything, either. On the value version of the inaction objection, it's just unclear why anything matters at all to the Stoics.

The fatalist version of the Inaction Problem also depends on a clear principle: you're motivated to do something only if doing it has a different result than not doing it. One has motive only if acting makes a difference and, if fatalism is true, nothing makes any difference. What will be will be. So, if you are ill, you will recover or not, and that result is fated. So, what you do to remedy your illness (seeing a doctor, taking medication, or resting) will make no difference. There then is no point in trying, planning or even holding each other accountable for what's done. If it's all fated, then not only are the results set, but even our actions around those results are set too. We praise or blame people for what they do based on the belief that they *could have done otherwise*, but it seems that Stoicism's view of the world has made even that impossible. Instead of being an advancement in ethical theory, Stoicism seems to destroy it.

5.2 Reply to the Inaction Problem

The Stoic reply to this collection of objections, often called the Lazy Arguments, is to make a few distinctions and provide some reminders of what is of value in light of Stoic ethical theory.

To the value version of the inaction argument, there are two lines of reply: the argument from the virtues and the argument from preferred indifferents. These are logically distinct arguments, so one can be true while the other is false. But they are logically consistent and in fact can be considered mutually supporting. They provide what we think is, on the whole, a plausible response.

The argument from the virtues runs that your motives can still be activated by goods or bads hinging on your actions, even if externals are not truly good or bad. This is because you can be motivated to be a good person. That is, you can be motivated to act one way or another by the simple fact that your actions have effects on your character – you are enacting and reinforcing your virtue (or vice) depending on what you do. So, a good or bad does hang on whether you act or not, but that good or bad is not external but internal to you. Consider the person who tells the truth. Basing her motives on whether or not others will consequently have true beliefs puts her in a position where the good done is not up to the truth-teller. But if the good resides solely in enacting the virtue of honesty, then she has the motive to be truthful and that good is invulnerable to how her statements are received. The same might go for any other ethically significant action – one's motive is rooted in enacting that virtue, not in bringing about a particular external circumstance. Notice that this is why we might judge to be praiseworthy principled truth-telling even when the prospects of being believed are slim, or bravely taking a stand even when there is little likelihood of success – the good is located in the virtue enacted, not in how any external results shake out.

The argument from preferred indifferents begins with the observation that there are externals that are useful to doing your duty. You can best care for your family, all things being equal, if you have health, money and status. If you're sick, you cannot attend to important tasks as well as a healthy person can. A person with fewer funds cannot provide food and shelter for those in her care in the way a richer person can. And a person whose word has weight can speak up in ways that a person who is not respected cannot when the situation is desperate. Of course, the fates can change things significantly, as a city may suddenly need healthy people of wealth and standing to go on an expedition, and so only the ill, poor and lower classed can remain to care for their families. Moreover, those means themselves can be misused. They can pervert our relations to each other, given that we can pursue those means instead of pursuing our duties to each other. But, again, under the right conditions and for the right reasons, these externals are useful to have. Consequently, a minimal revision to Stoic value theory is in the works and it bears on the principle of motivation. The revision now applies not just to *goods and bads* but also to what's *preferable and dispreferable* with the externals with which we must engage. So, a person has motivation to do something only if she thinks that her doing so will bring about a good *or preferable* result or prevents a bad *or dispreferable* result. With this revision to the principle of motivation, the Stoic theory of preferred indifferents makes significant progress in seeing Stoics engaged in the world and its results. Epictetus in the *Discourses* agrees by saying that the god makes us so that we naturally choose these things (*Disc.* ii.6.9).

A lingering problem remains for the doctrine of preferred indifferents. It is simply that if these externals are part of the effective exercise of virtue, then it turns out that we should be worried about them. That is, they are no longer indifferent to our happiness. If virtue is the only good and preferred indifferents are the means to be properly virtuous, then they are goods by extension. Cicero famously posed this challenge to the Stoics on preferred indifferents in his magisterial dialogue *De Finibus*: 'How can you have greater inconsistency than for the same person to say both moral worth is the sole good and that we have the natural instinct to seek the things conducive to life?' (iv.70). Famously, Aristotle had held that for a person to fully develop and exercise her virtues, she needed a minimum of wealth, standing, good looks, health and family stability (*Nicomachean Ethics* I.1099b.1). For Aristotle, one could not count, for example, people lacking means as truly generous, since they had nothing to share. Accordingly, on Aristotle's model, externals are required for completely developed virtue. Thus, the question is how Stoicism, with its doctrine of preferred indifferents, is now so different. Stoicism is supposed to be an alternative to Aristotelian ethical theory, as Stoicism promises a form of anti-elitism regarding the good life and virtue. Aristotle's ethics makes it so that only the privileged (and so the lucky) have genuinely happy lives, and the Stoics waged an anti-luck campaign against that view. But the doctrine of preferred indifferents seems to be a significant concession, if not capitulation, to Aristotle's common-sensical view that luck with externals (wealth, family, looks and standing) can drastically change whether a life is virtuous, and thereby happy, or not.

The objection, then, is that in refining the clean break with the common sense take on things, we have circled back around to common sense. But we don't consider the objection to be as devastating as is commonly thought, because the issue is not that Stoics and Aristotelians engage with things in the world. Rather, the issue is how the respective philosophers really value the items they deal with. Stoics have returned to the world having seen through the illusory value that animates too much of our social lives, but Aristotelians have never seen the *illusion as an illusion* and so remain stuck in its trap. Both Aristotelians and Stoics still inhabit the world perpetuated by that illusion, with its petty squabbles and dramas. And they both, given their roles, will participate in its contests. But the Stoic has viewed it from the outside. The Stoic knows that even if all her prized externals are stripped away, room remains for virtue and self-possession. This is because there will always be other people with whom she can share her life. The Aristotelian needs good health, vision, hearing, a sound body, a prosperous family, a well-run city, status, and so on. In contrast, the Stoic can exercise virtues and lead a life of active goodness even when things all fall apart. The Aristotelian will worry in a different way over ruin, even though both the Aristotelian and the Stoic will try to avert it. The Stoic knows that opportunities for virtue and happiness are still open even if ruin comes. It is in this comportment to externals that Stoics and Aristotelians crucially differ.

The fatalist version of the inaction argument is that if all is fated, then there is no point in trying to accomplish or avoid anything. One has motive to act only if one's actions make a difference, and since all outcomes are fated, one's actions can make no difference. The Stoic reply to the fatalist's lazy argument begins by denying the assumption that one's actions make no difference.

Consider the situation of the parent of a very sick child. Again, we can all agree that the child will recover or not, and whatever results will have been fated. But given that recoveries from severe illness are possible only with proper treatment and care, then if the child in fact recovers, there must have been treatment administered and care given. The same goes for all events – you cannot pass a test unless you study, you can bake a cake only if you mix the ingredients and put it all in the oven, you cannot achieve wisdom without applying yourself, and so on. So, it seems, your actions *do* make a difference, even if the results are fated. This is because they are necessary conditions for the fated outcomes.

If the actions did not occur, the results they are necessary conditions for would be impossible. Consequently, given that the results are fated, and the actions are necessary for the fated results, the actions and their results are, as Chrysippus puts it, *co-fated* (as Cicero reports it in *On Fate* 30).

Importantly, even if fatalism is true, our actions matter. This is because they are the things that make possible (or not) the outcomes fated to be (or not). We do not yet know what was fated to come to pass, as we can see those things only in hindsight. So, our actions are part of the unfolding (but already written) story of everything. We and our actions, as it turns out, *do* make a difference. So, instead of making us lazy, belief in fatalism should make us active in our duties, since it integrates our actions with the whole Providential plan.

The solution of considering our actions to be co-fated with their results certainly shows that they make a difference, yet another problem lingers. It runs like this: that our actions also are fated now makes the problem of motive worse, not better. This is because now not only are the results of our actions not things we can alter, but our actions are also fated to be what they are, and they too can't be otherwise. Tad Brennan puts the objection in this way: 'Chrysippus's response is intended to make it look as though the big event is in my control after all. But its real effect is to show me that things are worse than I had thought; along with the big event, there is another event, the co-fated one, which is not under my control' (2005: 278). So, even though our actions do make a difference, another requirement of motivation is missing: that we could do otherwise. What, then, is it to think about whether to do something or not? When deliberating about taking measures to act one way or another, we do so on the assumption that our deliberations could go one way or the other, and so we will act differently as a result. But this belief, on the co-fatalist line, is false. Rather, deliberation is more a matter of arriving at the reasons that will move us to do what we were already going to do. Yet this is not what deliberation *feels like*. As Brennan puts it, 'this fails to distinguish deliberation from discovery' (2005: 287).

On our view, the fatalist's reply must concede this point. Nevertheless, there are good ways to make it less counter-intuitive. One way to consider it is according to perspectives we take on our own reasoning. When we reason from the first-person perspective, as an 'I' in the present tense, it feels like an exercise of free acts of mind. We could go one way, another or just do nothing. However, when we reflect on our own reasoning in the past, perhaps on decisions we made years ago, we can see how those reasons motivated those younger persons, given all the things that mattered to them. So, we view our own reasoning in the third person in the past tense, a 'them' who thought things through then. And we can, from this perspective, say things like 'of course this moved them'; how could it have been otherwise? The fatalist line is an unwavering third-person perspective on our reasoning and motivation which coheres with the perspective we must take on our Stoic training. In order to be moved by the reasons that constitute Stoic philosophy, one needs training and understanding. Without them, the reasons will be ineffective. So, one trains one's mind to be sensitive to those reasons. We can take that third-person perspective on ourselves even as we reason and deliberate. We do so by reminding ourselves of who we want to be and the exemplars we aim to emulate. These exercises play determining roles for us and this is why deliberation is really discovery of which reasons motivate us. That is a surprise, in a way, but it is not quite as alien a thought as it initially seemed.

Another option for Stoics is to modify their fatalism. William Irvine proposes a modest form of fatalism wherein our perspective should be that the past and the present are as they are and cannot be otherwise, but the future is not set. 'In their advocacy of fatalism, then, the Stoics were advising us to be fatalistic, not with respect to the future but with respect to the past and present' (Irvine 2009: 106). Irvine reasons that approaching the future as determined is an incorrect orientation. We should want things to happen as they do, but not as they must. He reasons that we cannot welcome visitors before they arrive, so we cannot experience fate's weavings until they have been tied up.

Irvine's tame type of fatalism is surely more congenial to our sense of difference-making with our actions and our feeling as though we can do otherwise. It also saves the intuition behind Brennan's point earlier that fatalism objectionably turns deliberation into inquiry. There are, however, two problems with Irvine's modification. The first is that it breaks with the Stoic orthodoxy on fatalism being about the future. Otherwise, Chrysippus's earlier point about co-fated events would not need to be posed. Moreover, Epictetus's reasoning about seers rests on the Stoic belief that portions of the Providential plan can be revealed in advance (as we comment on in Chapters 27 and 32, and as Cicero explains in detail in *On the Nature of the Gods* ii.7-12). But the second problem with Irvine's modification is that fatalism cannot hold only for past and present events. If the past and present are inflexibly as they are and couldn't have been otherwise, then it follows that the future is just as inflexible too. Time does not change anything with regard to what is possible and what is necessary. We can see this simply by noting that every event now in the past was, at some time prior to it, a future event. Insofar as past events could not now have been otherwise, they, before they occurred, could not have been otherwise either. That is why they came about by the events that caused them. Only if the facts around those events were different could they have been otherwise. It's the *arrangement* of those facts that makes it possible for things to be otherwise, not *when* they are so arranged. So, time is simply the mode in which those events play out. If an event is necessitated, it doesn't matter whether it is in the past or the future. The passage of time in no way alters how things are necessitated.

Regardless of whether one adopts the full fatalist view or Irvine's modest version, a consequence is that *blaming* results from a kind of confusion. Epictetus promises in *Ench.* 1 (and cf. 48.2) that Stoics will blame no one. Now we understand why – those whom we might be tempted to blame cannot do otherwise. It does not follow from this that punishment is baseless, since it can still be part of a social nexus of deterrence, public expression of disapproval, and even a means of restitution, when performed appropriately. But the *resentment* that animates the desire to blame and punish should dissipate when one adopts the fatalist perspective on human wrongdoing. This, again, is why Epictetus promises in *Ench.* 1 that a Stoic will not blame others – not only are the goods required for her happiness out of others' reach, but she cannot help but see them in the grips of a world they do not understand.

5.3 The Ruin Problem

The Ruin Problem for Stoicism is simply that, if practised consistently, Stoicism ruins our relations. Given that Stoics see their duties as determined by their relations, the significance of the problem is dire. One way to appreciate the Ruin Problem is through a common reaction to the exercises Epictetus recommends in *Ench.* 3. You remind yourself, to start, that your favourite mug is finite and fragile. That way, when it is broken, you have done the preparatory work so that its destruction does not surprise (and upset) you because you are emotionally prepared for it. You then apply this exercise of anticipation progressively to other increasingly precious things, finally to your spouse and children. In the midst of appreciating them, you remind yourself that you are kissing mortal, mobile and fallible human beings. This is done so that when they leave, get injured or sick, die, move on or simply disappoint you, you are prepared. The Ruin Problem is that this attitude significantly undercuts that relationship. Imagine that, while embracing your spouse, she or he knows you are contemplating her or his death. Or that you are constantly preparing for your child to leave or to disappoint. Your spouse or child may complain: 'Am I really just like a mug to you?'

Another way to appreciate the Ruin Problem is through a more theoretical lens. The Stoic insists that virtue is the only good. But a reasonable challenge is that virtues are good because they are stable relations with other goods. On this view, virtues are really second-order goods that depend for their value on the first-order goods they reliably produce. For example, honesty is a valuable virtue. But its value is grounded in the fact that honest people tell the truth and are believed by others. So, it's because honesty is a reliable means of producing true beliefs that it's valuable. Or consider the virtue of being a good parent in providing a stable and nurturing environment for one's children. If children were not reliably made healthy and well-adjusted by those efforts, they would not be coordinate with being a good parent. We can give a similar analysis with any virtue – what makes the virtue a good thing is its stable relation to some other good beyond the virtue. Thomas Hurka puts it like this: 'virtue [is] a higher-level good, one that involves a certain relation to other intrinsic goods and evils. Its being so means that virtue can't be the only intrinsic good. There need to be other values it responds properly to' (2011: 122).

Given that Stoicism is committed to a theory of value that locates the only good in the virtues, there's nothing left to explain what makes the virtues good. And, again, given that the virtues are traits that are rooted in being oriented beyond mere exercises of the virtues, Stoics face a very strange puzzle. Stoics must say that these virtues are determined by our relations and are about acknowledging and maintaining them, but the goods that are presumably in the relations doing the work of determining the duties of virtue are denied to be goods at all.

Notice that this ruin objection is not that a Stoic does not act, but that her actions, both from her Stoic perspective and from the perspective of those with whom she lives, become a pantomime of care. The Stoic proceeds *as if* it is morally important that some external good is preserved. Yet the value resides exclusively in the action aiming at the objective, not the objective. So, the good Stoic parent proceeds *as if* the health and welfare of her child is a matter of importance, but only *as if.* The Stoic citizen behaves *as if* the safety of her republic is crucial, but only *as if.* Once she sees the problem clearly, she may still act, but it seems like an empty charade. The nineteenth-century German idealist G.W.F. Hegel observed that the Stoic's approach yields a detachment from her own life, so that she does merely what reason demands, not what she actually cares about in the circumstances. 'The True and the Good, Wisdom and Virtue, the general terms beyond which Stoicism cannot get, are therefore in a general way no doubt uplifting, but since they cannot in fact produce any expansion of the content, *they soon become tedious*' ([1807] 1977: 200, emphasis added). The upshot is that

Stoicism's focus on virtue and the commitment that virtue is the only good can make a practitioner immune to fortune and even provide her motive to act in the world, but the distance created scuttles her life and makes it a bore – both from the inside for the Stoic and from the outside for those with whom she lives. For a theory of how to be happy, Stoicism turns the life it prescribes into something desperately dreary.

5.4 Reply to the Ruin Problem

To escape ruin the Stoic reply requires two lines of argument. The first must address the Ruin Problem from the inside, from the perspective of the practitioner. The second must address the problem from the outside, from the perspective of those with whom the Stoic has relations.

The argument from the inside holds that the Ruin Problem is simply wrong about how virtuous motives work and what the consequences of anticipation have for practitioners. Starting with the exercise of the mug in *Ench.* 3, first notice that the Stoic practitioner will have a favourite piece of dinnerware. In addition, the Stoic will feel affection for her spouse and child. At no time in the exercise is the Stoic urged to *eliminate* those connections or the feelings that accompany them. Rather, the exercise prompts the Stoic to see what precisely that connection is with – in all cases, a finite, impermanent thing. Any parent or lover can attest that knowing that a moment is fleeting does not rob that moment of its meaning. In fact, reminding oneself that we are mortal and fallible beings makes those moments all the more poignant. We recognize it, on occasion, in non-Stoic life, but it often takes a funeral, wedding or graduation ceremony to bring it up and jostle us enough to savour it. The Stoic exercises allow practitioners to take that perspective of poignancy without any more prompting than doing the work of practising one's skills in seeing things as they really are.

Instead of facing a problem of ruin, the Stoic approach opens a variety of avenues of appreciation and joy for Stoics. When seeing the world from the Stoic perspective, natural moments leap out with vibrant significance. Marcus Aurelius remarks:

> Nature's inadvertence has its own charm, its own attractiveness. The way loaves of bread split open on top in the oven … Or how ripe figs begin to burst. And olives on the point of falling: the shadow of decay gives them a peculiar beauty. Stalks of wheat bending under their own weight … And anyone with a feeling

for nature – a deeper sensitivity – will find it all gives pleasure … He'll look calmly at the distinct beauty of old age in men, women, and at the loveliness of children. And other things like that will call out to him constantly – things unnoticed by others.

(*Med.* iii.2; Aurelius 2003: 27–8)

The point is that these exercises do not numb a person's sensitivity to beauty and things worth connecting with, but, to the contrary, they instil in her a unique appreciation of these things. The Stoic appreciates poignancy and the thought that our loves must be savoured, because she remembers that they all will end. Impermanence makes them special. Instead of something boring, tedious or dreary, a Stoic's life is animated by the rhythm of the world with its distinct traces, tones and textures to which she attunes herself.

The problem, still, is the theoretical difficulty in explaining how the virtues can be good if only the virtues are good. How can relations generate our obligations unless they have some good in or dependent on them? The Stoic's answer is that these relations are all expressions of nature; acting in ways pursuant of affirming and maintaining them is life in accord with nature. That, in the end, is both the happy and the good life. So, when Epictetus analogizes the roles we have to the roles given to actors in a play (as in *Ench.* 17), the best way to think of the good is as the entire drama, the whole play, as scripted. The good of virtue as dutiful action is that it is the actor playing her part in the drama of existence unfolding as planned. There are the roles of family member, spouse, citizen, and so on, but they are all subordinate to the role of rational being in the world (see Johnson 2014). One's roles and one's virtue, then, are grounded in nature and Providence being as they are. Our rationality's primary goal is to orient us appropriately, and that in every instance involves identifying whom one is related to and then determining one's duties accordingly.

The external argument is slightly more difficult to give, since it must account for the variety of responses non-Stoics will have to announcements of Stoic valuations. To be sure, Epictetus recognizes that there are right places and right times to share pearls of Stoic wisdom, just as there are certainly times not to share those principles, too. When one's friend is grieving, one does not recite the Fundamental Divide between what is up to us and what is not. Rather, one laments aloud with the friend (but not internally). Epictetus also seems to give regular advice to refrain from going on about one's philosophical views with non-philosophers. This can be precisely because of a version of the Ruin Problem in the external form. Others may find Stoic ethics, when it is stated directly and clearly, to be offensive and alienating. Epictetus tells progressors to 'tell no one' about their Stoic exercises (*Ench.* 47) and to be 'mostly silent' about philosophical principles (*Ench.* 46). Instead, progressors are supposed to only live out their philosophical work. It is in enacting our virtues and doing our duties that we affirm and maintain our bonds with others. Thus, progressors need not tell their children or their spouses that they do their best by them *as Stoics*. Stoics just need to do their best by them.

The problem, of course, is that this keep-it-to-yourself reply seems to concede the external version of the Ruin Problem. Stoic valuing, if others are aware of it, risks alienating them. So, even if you've been an exemplary spouse on the whole and in the details, it's still possible that the mug exercise will actually destroy that connection when it is made explicit. 'Am I really like a *mug* to you?'

Remember that Stoicism is a revisionary ethical programme. Further recall that one of the Stoic *Paradoxa* is that those who are not wise suffer from mania, utter loss of emotional control. This, too, is probably something that non-Stoics will not hear positively; moreover, if the Stoics are right, these non-Stoics will react very negatively. So Stoic value theory, if said aloud, has the distinct propensity to ruin the relations it means to affirm and maintain. That's the price of the paradoxes. But that the Stoics predict this result seems to make it all so much worse.

Perhaps one reply here is that these dark thoughts are based on expecting too little from non-Stoics. Any Stoic practitioner can attest that before she became a progressor, there were proto-Stoic insights she could think about and appreciate on her own. Non-Stoics can understand and endorse a Stoic principle or line of reasoning. It may take the right circumstances, and they need to have an open mind about it. Others, perhaps, will be less inclined to follow. Surely anyone who has knowledge others lack will understand that sharing that knowledge risks alienating them. But consider things from the perspective of the Stoic's spouse, now, in terms of what he would reasonably want. Would he want his loved one to be utterly broken by his death, or would he hope that his spouse would carry on and, indeed, flourish? That is, assuming their relationship is about love and regard, why would one partner hope for greater harm when their relationship ends? The mug exercise might be, after sober, unselfish reflection, just what they would endorse.

The last version of the challenge is that loving relationships seem to thrive when both people are swept away by the magic of the moment. Given the power of romance, Stoic exercises in the midst of those thrilling times break their spell.

The Stoic's reply here is that this final objection gets wrong the nature of properly loving relationships. To start, let's distinguish *natural affections* from *passions.* A natural affection is the kind of commitment one has to care for other beings and even some things. As we've seen, Stoics will have their favourite mugs and will feel deeply about their spouses and children. These affections befall us, just as sensations do. A person simply feels good around some people and some things. Stoics rationally consider whether and how to act on those feelings. Moreover, our innate sociability generally supports building connections. Stoics are not unfeeling. But the passions are quite different. The passions behind pictures of love, the kind of feelings that overwhelm us, Stoics oppose. The Stoic view is that those kinds of feelings are ultimately bad for us, as they make us not only vulnerable but in consequence motivate us to be bad people. It is due to passion that lovers may embrace, but that same passion drives them to fits of selfishness, jealousy, rage and worse. The Stoic exercises are designed to break the spell of those kinds of destructive feelings, for sure. But this is not bad news. Rather, it's good news. If love really were a passion, an utterly overwhelming emotion, we should just avoid it, and Stoicism is a secure path to maintaining control. But love can also be a relation of mutual regard and appreciation, an ongoing opportunity to cultivate what is good in one another. If love is like that, it's worth pursuing and preserving. It is this second kind of love that the wise value (Stephens 1996). It requires no illusion or overpowering passion, but rather appreciation, respect and honesty. The first kind of love as passion creates a form of emotional bondage wherein one feels at the mercy of another's inclinations. She who is a passionate hostage has turned her judgements over to the captor of her passion. In sharp contrast, the second kind of love is one wherein our rational capacities are recognized, our autonomy is respected, and we are free to pursue and cultivate what's best.

5.5 The Practicability Problem

The problem of practicability for Stoicism is simply that it seems impossible for a human being to be a Stoic, so described. In short, it is psychologically impossible to control one's mind so as to think, desire and live as Stoics want to. On this objection, Stoicism is all theory, unmoored from the reality of practice. Given that ethics should be bound by the rough principle that *ought-implies-can*, then it is doubtful whether Stoic ethics really is *ethics*.

Perhaps the best place to start with this objection is with the first chapter of the *Encheiridion*. There, Epictetus introduces what we call *The Fundamental Divide* between what is up to us and what is not. First, he gives examples of each class. Our understanding, impulses, desires and aversions are up to us, and our bodies, possessions, reputation and professional position are not up to us. Next, Epictetus gives us criteria for sorting these things. The things that are our own are *free, unhindered* and *unimpeded*. Things that are not up to us are *weak, enslaved, hindered* and *not ours*. In the *Discourses*, the relevant marker is whether things are unhindered (*akōta*) (*Disc.* 3.24.3). The question is whether this division, and Epictetus's sorting, is correct: are our mental states really under our direct control?

Let's start with *understanding*. One cannot simply decide to understand something and then understand it. Understanding doesn't work that way, which is the reason why good teachers are vital. They facilitate understanding that clearly can be hindered. Now consider *desires* and *aversions*. Surely resolving not to desire something is ineffective at eliminating the desire, and the same goes for aversions. Fear does not go away when one wishes it to. And desires, too, are the kind of things we cannot just decide to have. Beliefs, too, are not voluntary either. No matter how much money you're offered, it would be impossible for you to believe that Socrates is the current President of the United States. Thus, our mental states are not fully under our control.

Moreover, it seems our beliefs, desires, aversions and our understanding can be under the control of others. What else is advertising and propaganda? Or try this one: don't think of a pink elephant. You just did, didn't you? Or consider the phenomenon of the earworm, a snippet of a song or saying that you can't stop playing in your head. Thought-insertion is a robust psychological phenomenon wherein one's thoughts are not under one's control. It presents prominently in schizophrenia and obsessive-compulsive disorders, but it manifests in cases of depression and anxiety too. There are also instances of non-disordered thought-insertions. The earworm cases, again, are clear. But there are other cases where one's thoughts, independently of one's inclinations, return to particular things. So, any time someone says 'I just can't stop thinking about … ', she is experiencing this phenomenon of not being fully in control of her thoughts. Observing this robust limitation on our control, a Christian critic of the Stoic tradition wonders: 'If the *hegemonikon* is an unassailable acropolis, why do we have a hard time sorting impressions?' (Rowe 2016: 77).

Another way into the Practicability Problem is this. Recall that Stoic ethics proceeds from the axiom that virtue is the only good and vice is the only bad. The problem here is whether this view is something that a person can consistently maintain. Cicero tells the story of a student of Zeno of Citium named Dionysus of Heraclea who tried to live by the Stoic doctrines. But when he suffered through passing several kidney stones, he announced that he would no longer be a practising Stoic because pain is clearly a bad thing (*Tusc.* ii.25.60; also reported in DL 7.37 and 167). Ancient critics of Stoicism often told similar tales – of practising Stoics who, once they got a taste of the pains they had said were indifferent, promptly changed their minds (Plutarch cites many; see *The Stoics and the Poets* 1058c-d). A simple survey of recent work on happiness shows that consistent pain and social isolation significantly impact whether people report that they are happy (Peterson 2006).

All of the impracticability arguments proceed from a principle that if one is establishing an ethics, it must be practicable. Thus, *ought implies can*. On this principle, if we can ascertain limitations to human capacities, it is silly to assert that we ought to do things beyond those limits. Especially if the programme of ethics offers practical advice, the advice must still be something a person can act on. If the advice is only good for non-human creatures, it's worthless as a prescription for human beings.

5.6 Reply to the Practicability Problem

The Stoic reply to the practicability objection works on two levels. The first addresses the *ought-implies-can* principle. The second responds to the question of whether people can put Stoic principles into practice.

To start, Stoics must reject the *ought-implies-can* principle. Stoicism is a philosophical programme that upholds an ideal of perfection as its target of aspiration. The objective is mightily ambitious – to make oneself akin to the gods, to be better than oneself. The tradition of aspirationalist ethics, particularly that of remaking oneself in god's image, has a hallowed ancient pedigree. Plato and Aristotle held that the project was a recipe for perfecting human life by making it into something superhuman. The Stoics extended this project with the model of piety conceived of as making oneself worthy of kinship with the gods. This is why Heracles the demigod is the Stoic (and particularly Epictetus's) frequently invoked exemplar for living out the virtues. Heracles is superhuman. Aspirationalism, by these lights, is an uncompromising view on the task of self-perfection. The aspiring Stoic will always have flaws, weaknesses and bad habits that need work, so dialling the criteria for how one ought to live modestly within the bounds of what one can do now sets too low a standard. One must raise high the target as a kind of true North by which all of one's improvements can be measured and towards which they can all be oriented. So, Stoics reject the *ought-implies-can* principle in favour of the ought-implies-aspire precept.

Given aspirationalism, the fact that the Stoic objectives are beyond present human capacities is exactly the point. In fact, the aspirationalist would agree with a good deal of the practicability challenge as a description of the serious difficulty of the path ahead for the Stoic practitioner. But our prospects for progress are not all so grim because a better way to read the Fundamental Divide is as another target to achieve by means of Stoic practice.

A practical programme for reading the Fundamental Divide is to take it as something one establishes and maintains with Stoic exercises. Sure, one does not have *direct* control over one's beliefs, desires, understanding or aversions. But one does have *indirect* control. So, the tools of critical thinking bring one's beliefs under control in the sense that the skills help us direct our beliefs towards the truth. So, we search out high-quality evidence, try to get as total a picture of what's the case before we judge the matter, and we suspend judgement when matters are unclear. That's how we incrementally gain control over our beliefs. We control how we pay attention to sorting good and bad reasons.

The same goes for our desires and aversions. We try to see things for what they are and judge whether they're worth wanting. Even when we judge them worthy of preferring, we can still withhold them from ourselves to exercise further self-control (as Epictetus recommends in *Ench.* 34). Some desires and fears disappear when we see through them. The infatuation with a person may dissipate when we see that he is terrible to his siblings or children. Fear of a medical procedure may recede when we see others recover easily from it. Yet others can persist. What Stoic exercises of preparation and endurance do is give us a shrewd perspective on those experiences. Further, when we postpone a pleasure or endure a pain, we gain insight about ourselves – namely, we learn that we can still be happy when we don't get what we might prefer. We can be content without satisfying desire. The desire may never go away, but we no longer crave to satisfy that desire, and thereby we take control because the desire does not control us.

Pleasures and pains are impressions over which one exercises no control, so Stoic strategies cannot mitigate them. Stoicism will not make food taste better or worse, nor will it make hunger pangs hurt more or less. The challenge is whether knowing that these are mere impressions will soften their impact on us. In particular, as the example of Dionysus of Heraclea showed, the more pointed version of the challenge is whether a Stoic exposed to consistent pain can maintain his Stoicism.

The reply can begin with the fact that Cicero follows his story of Dionysus of Heraclea with a story of the Stoic Posidonius who, amid pains of gout and joint failure, philosophized with Pompey the Great and took particular care to remark that pain is not a bad thing (*Tusc.* 2.35.61). Many others have given accounts of how Stoic training provided a path to endure to those facing nearly unendurable hardships. Vice Admiral James Stockdale recounts how his Stoic training gave him the skills to endure a prisoner of war camp after he was shot down over Vietnam in 1965 (Stockdale 1998). Nancy Sherman's *Stoic Warriors* (2005) recounts and analyses stories of how Stoic exercises were instrumental in helping veterans recover from the traumas of war. Stoicism doesn't make pain less painful, but it plots a path through it.

William Irvine proposes a model for coping with challenges and pains he calls the 'Stoic test strategy'. The heuristic is to approach every challenge as a kind of puzzle with the objective that 'we must not only come up with effective workarounds to setbacks but also, while doing so, avoid the onset of negative emotions' (2019: 75). The strategy is to regularly step back and appreciate both the challenge the world has served up (and how difficult it is) and also view oneself as able to navigate that hazard. This technique requires not just living in those moments but stepping outside of them to view them (and oneself) from a third-person perspective. Irvine holds that a third category arises from the dichotomy of control. This third class is comprised of 'things over which we have some but not complete control' (2009: 89). His example is winning a tennis match. How assiduously a player practises and prepares is up to him. The type of shots he tries is up to him. How energetically he moves on the court is up to him. How hard he competes is up to him. Gusts of wind are not up to him. Nor is how his opponent prepares or plays. Nor are the net cords, when a ball clips the top of the net and trickles over. This means, he concludes, 'the possibility of restating Epictetus's dichotomy of control as a trichotomy' (89).

We find useful Irvine's subdivision of what is not up to us into what is completely not up to us (e.g., the weather, a co-worker's mood upon arriving at work) and what is partially up to us (e.g., one's tennis match, one's grade in a course). This distinction guides us in conceiving of what it is to do rightly by others and to do our duty. A person exerts what control she has to do what she ought, but that guarantees no results. However, our issue has been not with subdividing what is not up to us, but with the domain of what is up to us. Which things are contained in that domain? And what exactly are our means of control within that domain? Our result is that the domain of what is completely up to us is quite limited in scope, yet it is possible to expand what is *indirectly* up to us. Achieving this expansion takes training and a redirection of one's mind.

The result, we think, is that the Fundamental Divide's line separating what is and is not up to us is not rigidly fixed for Stoics (or anyone), but another objective of aspiration. It is something we work to establish and maintain. Pierre Hadot rightly observes here that 'Stoic philosophical life consists essentially in mastering one's inner discourse' (1998: 50). The point is precisely that our inner discourse is not under our direct control. Moreover, it is only by means of various strategies and exercises that we bring it under our indirect control. We cannot, just by telling ourselves to, eliminate a desire, beget a belief, create understanding or be indifferent to a pain. Commanding oneself to do those things doesn't work. But working to see things clearly and carefully reminding oneself of the goods of self-control indirectly shepherds those mental states bit by bit, over time, to where they should be. This is an indirect and gradual process.

A lingering question, though, is whether the fact that completing the process of Stoic perfection lies ever beyond our grasp constitutes a real problem for Stoicism. Epictetus revised the Stoic paradox that there are only the wise and the mad by adding a third class of progressors. But once we have this third option, it is unclear whether the class of the wise is populated at all. The Stoics who thought there were sages held that they were 'rarer than the Phoenix'. A few candidates from classical myth are mentioned. Heracles tops the list. It seems that Odysseus is also included. From ancient Greece Socrates and Diogenes of Sinope are mentioned. Perhaps the founder of the Stoa, Zeno of Citium, makes the list. Seneca regards his countryman Cato as a good candidate. But this list is very short. Only two of them are arguably practising Stoics. Of the two mythic figures, one is a demigod. More fundamentally it can be doubted whether any of these individuals actually belong on the list, since each can be criticized for one failing or another, whereas sages never err. And even if Socrates never erred, he denied his own wisdom, which seems inconsistent with being fully wise (Brouwer 2014 holds that this is a different kind of wisdom). So, what follows if no one is truly wise? Would it prove that the Practicability Problem sinks Stoicism? We think not.

One way to mitigate the sting of the objection (that no Stoic sages exist or have existed) is to note that degrees of progress can be identified within the class of progressors. Advice in the *Handbook* is clearly indexed to those who have progressed from where they started. Early chapters of the *Handbook* provide exercises to master basic Stoic intellectual skills and apply its doctrines. Later chapters offer advice on dealing with particular circumstances, facing very specific challenges, and even advice on how not to get carried away by one's own progress. The *Encheiridion* is a developmental book. Its sequential agenda lays out a programme of exercises, tips and insights at the end that are for the kind of student who reads attentively all the way to the end. So, even if there is no point at which one becomes an unerring sage, Stoic practitioners can still make progress. They can always improve. And improvement is a kind of victory.

5.7 The System Problem

From its inception Stoic ethics has been promulgated as a part of a larger system of philosophy dependent on a Stoic theory of physics and logic. The problem with this is that Stoic logic and physics are as controversial as, or even more controversial than, Stoic ethics. This magnifies the challenge to the tenability of the programme. Call this the System Problem.

The early Stoics approached philosophy as a system integrating their insights into three parts: logic, physics and ethics. In their ancient context, these areas were broader than they are in contemporary usage. Logic extended from formal logic to argumentation theory and rhetoric, to philosophy of language, to epistemology. Physics spanned the topics of basic physics, metaphysics, ontology, cosmology, theology, philosophy of mind, and a theory of human nature and development. Ethics included theories of human relations and virtues, ethical principles and meta-ethics, and a theory of human flourishing. Ancient Stoics thought these three domains (logic, physics and ethics) were organically connected, like parts of an egg (the shell, the yolk, the white), or a fertile field (the surrounding fence, the soil and trees, the fruit), or even an animal (the bones, the muscles and sinews, the soul) (DL vii.40). This implied that logic, physics and ethics are interrelated disciplines; one cannot, for example, do ethics without knowing what kind of animal we are finding norms for, and we cannot know those norms without a clear picture of good reasoning. A virtue of systematic philosophies is that they can be robust and useful accounts which practitioners may live by. They are ways of life. A problem for systematic philosophies is that they are highly vulnerable to being undermined, since if everything is essential to the system, the whole can be unravelled by a single patch of controversy. The recent interest in Stoic philosophy is exemplary since the attention has been almost exclusively on Stoicism as an ethics. Comparatively little attention to Stoic logic and Stoic physics in their popular instances has been seen. For scholars, as controversial as Stoic ethics is, Stoic physics and logic have even steeper hills to climb with philosophical critique and defence.

That Stoic ethics intertwines with Stoic physics is obvious. Most prominently, many of Epictetus's exercises are designed to work within a Stoic Providentialist worldview. So, that one *gives back* loved ones or possessions, as Epictetus argues in *Ench.* 11, assumes an antecedent divine owner-giver. Epictetus analogizes having so many things as having been loaned to us or as things that ultimately belong to another. Further, the perspective that each of us is an actor in a play, as in *Ench.* 17, requires that we think that there is a playwright and director who directs everything for the best results. Without this perspective, it surely would be fair to object to a casting choice in the play; if you think it's a farce scripted and directed by an idiot, your disagreement is morally relevant.

Stoic logic, too, plays a central role in Epictetus's programme as a touchstone for successful thinking. Thus, practitioners must think that particular logical forms (such as conjunctions, disjunctions and conditionals) have particular logical functions. Consequently, a disjunction of two contradictories is true, but a conjunction of them is false (as seen in *Ench.* 36), and true conjunctions remain true even when people may believe they're false (as seen in *Ench.* 42). Epictetus's point is that perspicuity in logic (and in seeing how the world works) yields a view of how to live rightly. We work to see the world and ourselves correctly so that we may live correctly.

The problem, again, is that central theses of Stoic physics and logic are so controversial that, if the Stoics are right about the systematic nature of all the views being interdependent, they make Stoic ethics deeply problematic. Providentialism is the view that things are not only determined but that they are determined to be rational and best according to a divine plan. But Providentialism collides headfirst with the problem of evil: the world is full of unnecessary suffering, injustice and wickedness. Surely, *that* can't be the plan, could it? If it is, we are at a loss as to what it would mean to call the divine plan 'just' or 'rational'. And if it's not, then Providentialism is false. Further, until we can say for sure what that plan is or how it is rational, we are not justified in holding that Providentialism is true. As for Stoic logic, while it's good at what it does (which is handle deductions derived from the connectives, such as *and*, *or*, and *if-then*), it cannot address inferences with quantifiers (like *all*, *none* and *some*) or relations between objects (like *taller*, *darker* or *fastest*). Stoic logic is woefully incomplete as a theory of good inference or rationality. These are only the simplest challenges for Stoic physics and logic. Others can be posed quite easily. According to Stoic physics the world is periodically consumed in a cataclysm of fire (called the *ekpurosis*), and the human soul is warm, fluid breath (*pneuma*). Stoic logic denied that one could know on the basis of inductive evidence – knowledge derives from either infallible 'graspings' of truth (called *kataleptic* impressions) or inferences from those graspings that could not be undone by new information. The sage, the only true knower, cannot err. Surely one can disagree with these few (rather exotic) doctrinal commitments yet maintain that Stoic ethics is, in all other respects, true and defensible. But, again, if the Stoics are right about the systematic nature of their philosophy, one cannot do that.

Our point in this brief overview of the controversies of Stoic logic and physics is to show two things. First, we wish to demonstrate the stakes for and scope of the System Problem for Stoic ethics. If you're committed to Stoic ethics and the coordinate systematicity view that ethics, physics and logic are inextricably interdependent, you must defend the physics and logic to defend the ethics. Plus, there is a wide variety of commitments to defend. The second point is to highlight the fact that there is something right about the system challenge: Epictetus's reasoning and exercises are best appreciated and enacted within the broader system of Stoic philosophy. Without that systematic set of commitments, much of Stoic ethics seems indefensible or at least undermotivated.

5.8 Reply to the System Problem

The Stoic reply to the System Problem has three moving parts. The first concerns whether the systematicity thesis is true: can Stoic ethics be intelligible, defensible, and practicable without commitment to Stoic physics and logic? On this issue Stoics fall into two camps, *minimalists* and *systematists*. Stoic minimalists hold that Stoic ethics is independent of Stoic logic and physics, so they reject the systematicity thesis. Stoic systematists embrace the systematicity thesis, so they contend that defending Stoic ethics requires also defending Stoic views about logic and physics, too. We will survey the cases for these views shortly.

The second question is whether Stoic physics and logic can be revised and updated to meet contemporary challenges. So, we may not think the human soul is warm, breathy *pneuma*, or that there is a divine plan for all events, or that first-order propositional logic is the best model for human reasoning, but we may ask whether there are contemporary analogues of these views that are defensible.

The third question is how much revision to a philosophical tradition is too much. For example, is a Stoicism that gives up the hard division of what is up to us and what isn't, abandons Providentialism and the view that the world is periodically destroyed in a fiery *ekpurosis* and then re-coalesces, and denies that the wise never err, still genuine Stoicism? Or is it something else, something not *Stoic* but merely *Sto-ish*?

This final question raises further questions about traditions generally, which we will tackle presently before we turn to the Stoic tradition in particular. Carrying on an intellectual tradition is a Janus-faced enterprise. Like Janus, the Roman god of transitions, one must look both forward and backward. To start, a tradition must have a causal continuity with its past. The texts and debates from its crucial figures must be carefully preserved and interpreted; distinctive themes must be kept alive, insights appreciated, habits and approaches refined, and founding arguments clarified. That said, living intellectual traditions are not museum pieces. A viable tradition must apply to contemporary circumstances. Contemporary practitioners must demonstrate the relevance of their tradition by importing its characteristic principles, practices and arguments into the fray of debates today. Naturally, this will prompt new challenges for the tradition. Contemporary critics of the tradition will marshal innovative lines of objection, and material arrangements will change in ways that the founders did not (and could not) anticipate.

Thus, a tradition's distinctive insights will need updating and revision. Sometimes, more drastic measures will be necessary. Given that any tradition will have had internal debates at its founding or in its early development, those who seek to carry on that tradition must be open to the possibility that errors were made at its inception. After all, if the tradition's founders disagreed, at least one of them was wrong; maybe all were. The formative moments of a tradition are animated by debates over how its most worthy insights can be fortified and perfected while discarding its dross. Accordingly, those who seek to keep a tradition alive must engage those debates anew by answering challenges from external critics and by addressing internal disputes among adherents. Without this forward-looking face open to transitions and revisions, the tradition degrades into dead dogma.

Those who uphold traditions must look both ways, like Janus. But this raises a difficulty involving what philosophers sometimes call the *problem of vagueness*. Although small modifications don't undo a tradition, small changes can aggregate into significant deviations. For example, if Zeno is tall, then if Zeno were half a millimetre shorter, he would still be tall. A minor change is minor. But small changes can add up: say, if we aggregate 400 of those small changes with Zeno, that's now 20 centimetres lost, and our once tall Zeno isn't quite so tall any longer. But if each change didn't make a significant difference, then what happened? Or take the famous Ship of Theseus problem. A museum has replaced parts of Theseus's ship over time because they've rotted away. Replacing an oar or plank is only a minor change, but because all the pieces eventually rot and are replaced, a problem arises: Is the ship now Theseus's ship?

One way out of the vagueness problem is to deny the initial premise that small changes make no significant difference. So, if a single plank is replaced, the ship is no longer Theseus's ship. This move may have some plausibility with the ship's identity in a very strict sense, but it seems implausible with other concepts – surely there is room for half a millimetre to not make a significant difference as to whether Zeno is tall. Thus, the question lingers: what does it take to continue an intellectual tradition and when do adjustments and deviations amount to abandonment?

The temptation is to retrench to the tradition's canonical expressions, that is, to go originalist. This is what drives the intuition behind rejecting tolerance for replacing even a single oar on Theseus's ship – if it's Theseus's ship, then we've got to have all and only Theseus's oars, spars and planks. Not only is there some plausibility to the retrenchment strategy, it provides clarity that brings consequent institutional power. Retrenchers function not only as demarcators but also as gatekeepers. They interpret the founding documents and then judge whether contemporary expressions preserve orthodoxy.

The other strategy to take is to embrace a 'big tent' conception of the tradition, one that accepts that the ripples from the founding need not stir us now. There is a causal continuity, and some similarities, between the new and the old, and that's enough for the tradition to endure. So long as the tradition is current and relevant, that's what matters. If certain views of the founders have lost relevance or demand massive revision, so be it.

The trouble is both strategies seem incomplete. For the retrenchers, the canonical views become dead dogma. For the big-tenters, it's none too clear which tradition is being preserved. The former sets the tradition in historico-cultural concrete, dooming it to irrelevance. The latter strains to keep the tradition supple but sheds its distinctive features.

It should be clear that our commentaries on the *Encheiridion* and our work with objections and replies here in Part Five have been informed by the Janus outlook for living traditions. We feel the pull of the two trends. We are trying, as we write a guidebook to Epictetus's *Handbook*, to look both ways. The texts of the ancient Greek and Roman Stoics are founding documents for the Stoic tradition. It is a great irony that most of the earliest documents of that tradition are lost.

In their place what we have of the ancient writers is what survived over many centuries. The Stoic tradition was itself a target of considerable controversy over what exactly its distinctive insights were. Was Stoicism primarily a physicalism? Or was it chiefly a pantheism? Was its demanding requirements for knowledge its defining feature? Or was it a theory focused on a unique vision of virtue and the good life? Or a set of therapies to achieve a sound mind?

Given the variety of options for argument, three significant movements have emerged on the System Problem when applied to Stoic ethics.

- **Stoic Minimalism**: Stoic ethics is free-standing; it depends on no particular physics or ethics, or, if it does, only on modest claims about human psychology.
- **Stoic Systematic Conservatism**: Stoic ethics depends on Stoic physics and logic; an understanding of the ethics requires a clarification and defence of the whole system.
- **Stoic Systematic Revisionism**: Stoic ethics (sadly) depends on Stoic physics and logic, which must be revised considerably to be defensible.

Versions of these positions were staked out by the ancients. Aristo of Chios famously held that one should concern oneself only with ethics and leave physics and logic aside (DL vii.160). Marcus Aurelius held he was bound to his (quasi-Stoic) ethics whether there was Providence or random atoms in the void (*Med.* ix.28). Cicero reports that Stoic ethics needs only simple truths about human nature, namely that we are rational and can endure hardship (*De Fin.* iii.42). The systematic conservative approach is represented by Chrysippus's view that the point of the system of philosophical education is to be able to harmonize with the world in all things (DL vii.88). Epictetus too sees his ethics from the perspective of the larger system, emphasizing that one must learn logic in order to reason properly in ethics (*Ench.* 52). In contrast, Seneca states a version of the revisionary perspective when he asserts that the heads of the Stoic school 'are our guides, not our masters' (*Ep.* 33.11). Seneca also liberally quotes Epicurus on points about which he thought Epicurus was right (*Ep.* 8.8) whereas Epicurus's views are rebarbative to Epictetus (*Disc.* i.12.1; i.20.17–19; i.23; ii.20.6–20; ii.23.20–2; iii.7.1–23; iii.24.38). The objective of adopting a philosophical viewpoint is to have a true, defensible and systematic take on things, not to take on a school or simply choose a team.

The two best lines of defence we see for Stoicism are to argue for either minimalism or a revisionary programme for the system. Both strategies have fairly significant drawbacks, but that is the fate of those trying to defend any ancient philosophy in any contemporary context.

The case for minimalism, again, is that Stoic ethics is free-standing and independent of any substantive views on the nature of reality or the structure of rationality. Stoic ethics can proceed, minimalists contend, without any controversial Stoic views in physics or logic. The case for minimalism can be made along three lines:

- **Independence:** Stoic ethics is intelligible without a commitment to Stoic physics or any particular theory of inference. (For example, the Stoic theory of duties is not based on anything about the universe being consumed in a fiery *ekpurosis*.)
- **No Implication:** It is not clear how theses in Stoic physics or logic uniquely imply theses in Stoic ethics. (How does the Stoic theory of valid syllogism inform the doctrine of preferred indifferents?)
- **Practice:** Many contemporary (and some ancient) Stoic practitioners successfully practised Stoic ethics without commitments in Stoic logic or physics. (The fact that people have no substantive views in physics or logic yet practise Stoic ethics shows the latter is separable from the other two branches.)

If any of these lines of argument have any plausibility, the minimalist view is a good way forward for Stoics. Certainly, a view of human nature and the capacities we have for rational self-control is necessary for practising Stoic ethics, but these commitments are not more substantive claims than that we are capable of reasoning well about things and we are capable of enduring challenging times. The minimalist reasons that since there are no clear implications running from Stoic physics to Stoic ethics or vice versa, they need not come as a package.[2]

The cost of minimalism is that it is thin. Providentialism, for example, provides considerable support for so many Stoic perspectives because one can rest assured that all things are part of a rational plan. What is more, the commitment to the cosmos-destroying *ekpurosis* is a commitment that nothing lasts forever. Also, the Stoic commitment that the sage never errs is a cognitivist version of the Stoic aspirationalist thesis. Ethical Stoicism without these commitments seems flimsy or arbitrary. One may practise Stoicism without these challenging commitments, but the minimalist programme on the other side seems weakly motivated and lacking a complete view of the context of what Stoic action is. A picture of the whole is needed in order to harmonize with it.

To the criticism of thinness the minimalist will reply that this is precisely the point of minimalism: minimalist ethics makes it so that one's ethical principles can be the same even if one must regularly revise one's theory of how the world works. That is the insight behind Marcus Aurelius's 'Providence or atoms' alternatives – it's best to be a Stoic in either world.

The revisionary programme for Stoicism is posited on revising Stoic theses in light of the best criticisms. So, for example, one can concede that Providence is implausible because of the problem of evil, but one can still maintain a form of fatalist determinism which skirts the problem. As a consequence of axioms of logic, fatalism invokes no notions of the good or justice but offers a picture of the world amenable to Stoic ethics: all things are determined, so not up to us. Yet this type of fatalism leaves out the divine plan.

Is this revised version still Stoicism? Yes and no.[3] Yes, because it is a form of minimal alteration to a tradition devised by people doing their best to keep what's worth keeping and discard what's not. If Stoic theology is not worth keeping, fatalist determinism is what's left of a world still amenable to rational inquiry without divine purpose. The same goes for the Stoic doctrine that the wise never err; revise it to say that the wise correct and learn from their errors and therein lies their wisdom. This alteration keeps the aspirationalist edge to the idea without making wisdom an impossible ideal. Indeed, this tradition of the Stoic ethics of belief is alive and well as evidentialism, the view that people should believe only on the basis of evidence, which was advocated by the philosopher and admirer of Epictetus, W.K. Clifford.

On the other hand, there is another sense in which, no, this revised version is no longer Stoicism proper. The issue is whether the result of these revisions is Stoicism improved or are they really just modern appropriations of Stoicism yielding something more Sto-ish than Sto-ic. Those sympathetic with the revisionary programme argue for 'big tent' conceptions of traditions which are wild and unruly intellectual and cultural movements.[4] It is testament to a tradition's purchase that it swells beyond its original bounds. But the gatekeepers must make peace with the fact they are no longer the sole heirs who can claim the programme for themselves. Big tent philosophers appeal to our sense of intellectual autonomy, again invoking Seneca's insight that the originators are not our masters, by announcing that *we* are the Stoics, now. The revisionists hold that insisting on a philosophical school being irrevocably defined by its founders is like expecting the dead to drive our cars.

The problem of vagueness for traditions returns. If we are really big tent Stoics, then might it happen that someday someone will, in the name of Stoicism, argue that pleasure is a good? Or hold that virtue isn't all it's cracked up to be? Or deny that rational self-control is the key to happiness? Big-tenters will have no principled answer. And indeed, Seneca's big-tent approach stretches the fabric with liberality so great that he approvingly quotes Epicurus's line 'The beginning of well-being is awareness of wrongdoing' (*Ep.* 28.9).

The remaining response to the System Problem, Conservatism, embraces with nostalgia the classicism of a 'back to Zeno' movement. On this view, we make no changes to ancient Stoicism by our lights but rather preserve it *in toto* as the Hellenistic philosophy it was. A concern to raise is whether, for the Systematic Conservators, the ideas of the Roman imperial Stoics already strayed uncomfortably far from the doctrines of the earliest Greek scholarchs Zeno, Cleanthes and Chrysippus. Conservators could try to dismiss this as a worry for only historians of ancient philosophy and designate Marcus Aurelius as the last of the bona fide Stoics. But even if we grant this, what is the advantage of Stoic Systematic Conservatism? It certainly preserves the Stoic programme and delineates clear criteria for what makes a programme Stoic or not (just like those who have no tolerance for the slightest variation to Theseus's ship). But with that comforting clarity comes a stark implausibility for modern practitioners. Much of modern science must be jettisoned as incorrect, advances in logic must be dismissed as minor or discounted as inessential to the task of reasoning well, and one must affirm a theology of a god sustaining and maintaining all according to a just and perfect plan. In short, one must pretend to be an ancient Roman, even amidst a contemporary world. As we've said above, this playacting turns Stoicism into a musty museum piece, a specimen under glass in the gallery of the history of philosophy to be viewed but not touched, rather than a living, practicable philosophy. The result, we think, is that if Stoicism is to answer the System Problem, it must be either minimalist or revisionary. Both programmes have their benefits, but they have their drawbacks, too.

5.9 The Scepticism Problem

Scepticism is the view that knowledge in some area isn't possible. Someone is a sceptic when she thinks that we cannot be justified in saying something is or isn't the case in one domain or another. Scepticism comes in many forms because there are many things we can fail to know and there are many ways we can fail. Scepticism in ethics takes two scopes: general and particular. General ethical sceptics are sceptical of any claims to ethical knowledge. Particular ethical sceptics see problems for claims to knowledge in particular programmes in ethics. So, the sceptical problem for Stoic ethics takes two faces: the general and the particular. The general problem for Stoic ethics, which is best framed as a problem of disagreement, can be stated thus: because disagreement abounds among camps claiming (quite plausibly) to have ethical knowledge, we are in no position to know. Not only can at most one of those many camps be right, but even those folks cannot explain how they are right. The particular problem for Stoic ethics is that the requirements for knowledge for Stoics (and how it undergirds their ethics) are something no one can achieve. Consequently, if one is not already wise by Stoic standards, one cannot know that Stoicism is the right ethics. First, we will expound these sceptical objections to Stoic ethics. Then we will turn to three levels of Stoic answers.

The general Sceptical challenge to ethical knowledge comes in two forms, each posited on the fact of disagreement over moral norms and the nature of the good. The key datum in the argument from disagreement is simply that there is widespread, persistent controversy over virtually every item of moral judgement. Take lists of virtues. Aristotle, for example, lists greatness of soul (magnanimity) as a central virtue, but many regard it as mere braggadocio of privilege. Plato insists that knowing one's place and limits, *sōphrosunē*, is a cardinal virtue, but liberal societies are based on the possibility that a person can improve her life and standing. Moreover, even over the nature of the good disagreement reigns. Epicureans held it to be pleasure; Aristotelians claimed it to be the full social, political and intellectual flourishing of a human being who wasn't ugly and had a good family; and Stoics declared it to be self-control and following nature. What is more, a bounty of moral puzzles looks to defeat our systematic moral understanding. For example, is it *really* best to hang an innocent person to appease a violent mob bent on burning down a town? Or is it *really* morally defensible to lie under oath out of loyalty to one's family? The fact of reasonable and persistent disagreement on all these fronts means we should have serious concerns about knowledge of ethics.

The first general argument from disagreement is that, assuming there are reasonable disagreements, we have a problem of sorting who's right. Take disagreement over the nature of the good. Epicureans say it is pleasure and have reasoned carefully over that matter. They appear to live quite well by their own standards. And they've reasoned to those standards with some weighty philosophical arguments. In fact, they seem to be just as good at philosophy as most anyone else. So, can we know so easily that they are just wrong? This uncertainty applies equally to so many of the alternatives. How can we determine who's right, given that Plato, Aristotle and Epicurus weren't obviously better philosophers than each other? For example, if you're not an Aristotelian, then what makes you think you know better than Aristotle about these things? (This challenge can be run with any philosopher – Plotinus, Buddha, Confucius, Lao-tse or whomever.) The result, then, is that since all these disagreements look like ties, we can't settle who's right. Therefore, we can't have knowledge.

The second general argument from disagreement runs that if we could know things in ethics, we'd surely have more robust agreement by now. That is, if there were a knowable good for humans, we'd not only know it, but those who deny it would be correctable. But disagreement seems to be deep and persistent while correction seems less likely than people digging in on their respective sides. Given this scenario, it looks like ethics isn't an area amenable to knowledge for humans.

Let us now turn to particular sceptical arguments that target Stoicism uniquely. Recall that Stoicism is an intellectualist and cognitivist programme in ethics committed to the following claims: (a) there are ethical truths; (b) to know them is to be motivated to follow their dictates and (c) the best explanation for moral failure is ignorance. Knowledge is the key for Stoicism. Further, Stoicism is a revisionary programme in ethics. Stoicism impugns so much of what passes for common sense. Many of the core commitments of Stoicism diverge sharply from how people around us think and live. That was why the Stoic *paradoxa* reviewed in Section 1.5 regularly needed to be defended and kept in mind: virtue is sufficient for happiness, only the wise are sane, and only the wise are rich.

Given these two things about Stoic ethics (its intellectualism and its radical divergence from common sense), it is reasonable to require that we be really sure we are right if we are to be Stoics. That is, if common sense were right about the good life (or if it was good enough), then Stoics are walking away from something good to what denies it. Recall that Stoics have to deny that pleasure is a good, pain is bad, being shunned by others is a harm, health is a matter of moral concern and having wealth is a central feature of a full life. Stoics insist that virtue alone is sufficient for happiness. The costs are very high if you are wrong about those things. So, Stoics must be absolutely, positively sure they are right.

The Stoics saw that they needed an account of knowledge to answer this challenge, so they conceived the theory of *kataleptic* impressions. Kataleptic impressions are caused by and accurate about what is true, and they cannot not be caused by what is false (DL vii.51). If we have our knowledge on the basis of these kinds of impressions, then we should be able to answer the sceptics. If we build our house of knowledge on unshakeable foundations, then we will have the kind of stable knowledge needed for life.

The problem, as the Academic sceptics observed, is that we don't ever seem to have those kinds of kataleptic impressions. Two eggs, identical twins, similar things far away, and decisions between what seem equally good options, all give us impressions we cannot distinguish. Since they all look equally good and right, they're all equally bad and wrong. Furthermore, the Academics argued, the gods can trick us, our fellows dupe us, and we're consistently fed misinformation, half-truths, propaganda and lies. Consequently, we can't be sure we've got kataleptic impressions or reasonable facsimiles (see Sextus Empiricus's arguments in *M* vii.254 and Cicero's reports in his *Academica* ii.20 and 89). Given that ethics is a battleground for controversy, it is ground zero for a multiplicity of errors. Which is more likely, given this state of affairs? That you have kataleptic impressions and everyone else is wrong, or you, like everyone else, merely think you know better? The honest answer, surely, is the latter.

The problem for the Stoics is deepened by the fact that they hold that only the sage fully knows anything. So, until you have wisdom, you can't really know what wisdom is. Consider this: how did you know Stoicism was the right philosophy to follow in the first place? Furthermore, how can you know whether you're making progress in that school of thought or not? If you are not wise, you're more likely than not to mistake your vices for virtues! In our commentaries on *Ench.* 22 and 23 we called these the progressor's paradoxes – how do we find wise teachers of wisdom and keep track of our progress on that path? Sextus Empiricus raises these challenges explicitly in his *Outlines of Pyrrhonism* (iii.259–64) and concludes that ethics is an enterprise in which we should never be sure when we think we have the truth, and Stoics in particular should be more modest.

Notice, finally, that this sceptical problem scales depending on how one has handled the System Problem. Recall that the System Problem is that if the Stoics are right about how their philosophical views come tied together into one big package account of the nature of reality, rationality and how to live, then that system must be evaluated as a whole. One cannot do Stoic ethics without Stoic theology and theory of knowledge. As stated, the sceptical challenge is only a problem for Stoic ethics. Yet if the systematicity thesis is right, then scepticism about Stoic fatalism and Stoic logic simultaneously undermines Stoic ethics. As a result, the System Problem amplifies the Scepticism Problem because there is simply more to be sceptical about as one gets more systematic. Stoic Minimalism dodges this amplification since it divorces Stoic logic and physics from Stoic ethics. Stoic Systematic Revisionism, in contrast, only manages this problem since it seeks the most defensible versions of Stoic (or, as we conceded, Sto-ish) theses. But it will not entirely avoid the problems of controversy we reviewed, because controversy hounds virtually every philosophical view. Finally, Stoic Systematic Conservatism converts the sceptical challenge to the single branch of Stoic ethics into a global challenge. For the systematic conservator, persistent disagreement and sceptical problems in any one area of philosophical reflection (logic, theology, metaphysics, theory of knowledge) can undercut the entire system. To our minds, this extreme vulnerability yields yet another compelling reason for defenders of Stoic ethics to favour either minimalism or systematic revisionism. Regardless, an independent reply to the sceptics in ethics is in order.

To review, the sceptical challenge advances on three distinct levels. The first is the general sceptical challenge that because of the many deep and abiding disagreements in ethics, we must ask: is knowledge of the good really possible? The second and third levels comprise particular sceptical challenges. On one level, the Stoic model of knowledge required to meet the burden of proof for the radical break with common sense seems to demand too much of us. Either there are no kataleptic impressions or we'd never know for sure we ever had them. On the other level, even if Stoic knowledge is possible for us, given our lack of wisdom, we cannot tell what counts as progress toward that knowledge. That is what we called in our comments on *Ench.* 22 and 23 'the progressor's paradox'. Additionally and ironically enough, as Epictetus observes in *Ench.* 52 with what we called the 'progressor's temptation', even if progress is possible, our progress in philosophy can actually stand in the way of our ability to progress further. Training in philosophy might give us the tools to be wise, but we're more likely to use them to rationalize excuses and veil our vices. The result, the sceptical challenger concludes, is that the project of knowledge in ethics in general, and Stoicism in particular, is hopeless.

5.10 Replies to the Scepticism Problem

The Stoics' prescribed treatments for the virulent spectre of scepticism come in three dosage strengths: strong, modest and weak. The strong reply is that all the sceptical arguments can be answered directly. The modest Stoic reply is that the sceptical challenges are not really the kind of challenges one must answer in order to have an ethics. This reply avoids the problem. The weak Stoic reply concedes to the sceptic that there is no knowledge in ethics, but Stoicism nevertheless out-performs competing ungrounded theories. Thus, Stoicism is, as it were, the best of a bad bunch. We will survey these three responses in order.

5.10.1 The strong dose reply

The strong Stoic reply to the sceptical challenge has two parts: the offensive and the defensive rebuttals. The offensive rebuttal is one that undercuts sceptical arguments as promoting intelligible theses. The defensive rebuttal of the strong Stoic reply is to say that the core parts of Stoic ethics can survive sceptical scrutiny.

The Stoic offensive against scepticism is simply that scepticism is itself hopelessly futile. For one thing, sceptical arguments are clearly self-refuting. The sceptic has paradoxically proved that proof is impossible. The sceptic has shown clearly that nothing can be shown clearly. The sceptic has knowledge of ethics that we cannot know truths about ethics. Thus, scepticism amounts to a counterexample to itself. Epictetus argues that sceptical conclusions have the same self-refuting form as 'No universal statement is true' (*Disc.* ii.20.5).

Furthermore, scepticism offers no alternative to the ethical knowledge it criticizes, leaving us with no recourse. Thus, it is not at all clear what we are supposed to do after the sceptic attacks our norms. Ought we to suspend judgement and do nothing? To prescribe inaction would land us back in self-refutation territory. How does the sceptic live after delivering sceptical critique? As Cicero reports it (in his *Academica* ii.22–29), the convergence of this self-refutation and *apraxia* (inaction, no practice) arguments was thought by many ancient Stoics to be a pretty powerful offensive anti-sceptical line of argument.

The defensive versions of the strong Stoic reply to scepticism rebut the sceptical arguments from disagreement. First, the central premise of the argument from disagreement seems overstated. There is not as much disagreement as the sceptic makes there out to be. Despite some points of disagreement about listing virtues, most agree that wisdom, justice and honesty are virtues whereas cruelty, ignorance and cowardice are vices. Moreover, the commitment to justice, in particular, as treating like cases alike is widely shared. Yes, disagreement about the exact nature of the good exists, but we can recognize better and worse insights with the cases. Seneca, as we observed earlier, was able, as a Stoic, to make use of Epicurus's insights as a tool to cultivate virtue (e.g. at *Ep.* 12.11). The simple fact that we can still argue about these disparate views means that we can wield criteria for good judgement. Consequently, reason enables us to bridge the debate.

Stoics contended that it was with *kataleptic* impressions that these stalemates of reason are to be broken. But, as the sceptical challenge goes, do we really have them? The Stoic reply is that, yes, we do. Consider the challenge of indiscernibles like twins, eggs, and so on. For sure, identical twins are hard to tell apart, but their parents and friends learn to differentiate them. As familiarity increases, the capacity to differentiate develops. As with so many hard things, it works this way: with a little experience, we discern features we otherwise would miss. Cicero reports in the *Academica* (ii.54–7) that this was the going Stoic reply, in essence that, if the items really are distinct, we are able to see them as such with some exposure and attention. The same goes for any of those other indiscernibility cases. With the proper skills, attention to detail, and experience you can detect and correct for illusions and distinguish contraries. That's what critical thinking and collecting evidence is all about. Epictetus pauses to answer sceptical challenges in the *Discourses* by noting that it is the business of the educated person to hit the mark, but sceptical 'education' seems to make a person incapable of even seeing it (*Disc.* i.27.2). The upshot is that with practice, experience and refinement of our skills, we show that sceptics are simply wrong about our capacity for knowledge.

The sceptics were not terribly impressed with the strong Stoic reply. The first problem, as noted by Sextus Empiricus (*PH* ii.188), was that the offensive argument shows that Stoicism, too, suffers from the self-refutation and *apraxia* problems since the sceptical results were drawn from premises the Stoics themselves accept. The second problem was that the argument that we can improve our capacities to judge situations, argue with each other, and even find points of agreement, fails to establish that we have knowledge. Rather, it merely shows that we satisfy local worries about coordinating with each other. Those results, the sceptics argued, were more the effects of our socializing than achieving knowledge.

5.10.2 The modest dose reply

The modest Stoic reply to the sceptics is to show that, even if we cannot reach the height of unassailable knowledge, we can obtain stable, rationally acceptable commitments with which to live our lives. Scepticism is a challenge to a different kind of objective: to know like a god. As far more humble creatures, we really only need to know like human beings. So, Epictetus asks the sceptics, who deny they know anything, whether, when they are hungry, they cannot figure out into whose mouth to put pieces of bread. When they want bread, do they ever grab a broom instead of the loaf? When they want to go to the baths, do they arrive at the mill by mistake? (*Disc.* i.27.18–19).

The Stoic reply to many of the sceptical arguments is that they arise against a background of generally competent knowing. Even the vaunted puzzles of ethics (like choosing between hanging an innocent man to pacify an angry mob or letting the mob violently riot) may not have obvious right answers, but they certainly have obvious wrong answers (like, for example, hanging everybody or secretly hanging the innocent person without the mob knowing). Philosophizing begins with using those puzzles to test our background competencies. The puzzles are not the end of philosophy. In fact, Epictetus observes that our ability to recognize difficult cases as difficult shows that we have plenty of well-formed judgements (*Disc.* ii.11.13). Furthermore, the simple fact that we can live together and reason our way through challenging differences shows that nature has given us criteria for discovering and sharing the truth (*Disc.* ii.20.21).

The modest Stoic reply to scepticism has the virtue of making the objectives of knowledge more achievable, which puts the Stoics on friendlier terms with other philosophical schools. Usually, the focus is on what divides them but acknowledging significant points of agreement matters too. Nevertheless, an important thread has been lost with the modest reply, namely what the Stoic's burden of proof is with a revisionary programme in ethics. Recall the Stoic Paradox that only the Stoic sage is sane while everyone else suffers from *mania* (an emotional disorder of 'madness' wherein one has no control over oneself or one's judgements). Recall that Stoicism demands that we break radically with common sense and its defenders. Any revisionary programme that emphasizes the similarity of Stoicism to rival philosophies instead of their dissimilarities undercuts Stoicism's radical agenda. Diluting Stoicism in this way is possible but comes at a very high cost. This emendation saves Stoicism by making it less identifiably Stoic. Alternatively, note that if Stoicism is going to be the radical philosophy it is supposed to be, its practitioners should know better than all their competitors. As remarked above, if you're going to be a philosophical revolutionary or radical, especially in ethics, you've got to be really sure you are right. This is because the error costs are very high when selecting a theory of the good life. If that arrangement with the burden of proof is right, then choosing the modest dosage in responding to sceptical ailments amounts to giving up on the game.

5.10.3 The weak dose reply

The weak Stoic reply to scepticism is to concede that persistent disagreement in ethics and philosophy cannot be answered. The Stoic admits that problems of knowledge for Stoic ethics are insurmountable. But then we note that this is the case for *all* ethical views. All the competitors' views will have the same general problem and roughly similar particular problems. Yet life goes on. We nevertheless continue to live, which means questions of how to live remain. It turns out, after we've reached this point, that Stoicism remains the most appealing of the various views. This is because Stoics offer a good path to walk despite the lack of perfect knowledge. Stoicism also satisfies some inclinations we might have as individuals.

Cicero famously announced that, though he was an Academic sceptic first, he was a Stoic second. He declares that the Stoics are the only real philosophers (*Tusc.* iv.53), because they are the only ones who take sceptical challenges seriously and work to answer them. Furthermore, Cicero thinks, the Stoics are the only ones who clearly see the stakes for their views. Only the Stoics argue for transforming ourselves into admirable people. This is not so for the other views. Common sense leaves us alone and complacent. Epicureanism degrades us into pleasure-seekers. The more plausible, probable, or reasonable, after a rigorous examination, is the criterion left standing at this stage. Stoicism satisfies that humbler criterion. In *On Duties*, Cicero contends that this is as good as we can hope for in ethics (ii.8). Elsewhere Cicero concludes his debate over the nature of the gods noting that even as a sceptic he finds himself agreeing with the Stoics, because they 'approximate more nearly to a semblance of the truth' (*On the Nature of the Gods* iii.95).

Alternately, one can account for one's commitment to Stoicism as it being a philosophy that suits one's temperament. Here one's philosophy is conceived of as the best expression of personal attitudes and inclinations. Massimo Pigliucci notes that its focus on the self and its social emphasis was what drew him to Stoicism. He explains that Stoic views on practice, nature, happiness and death 'resonated with me' (2017: 3, 7). This thought is extended by Ryan Holiday, a popularizer of Stoicism who packages his brand of it as capturing certain individual values. Holiday gives examples of successful people, not all of whom were familiar with the Stoic tradition, but who faced adversity and applied themselves to their tasks (George Washington, Walt Whitman, Frederick the Great, Adam Smith, Thomas Jefferson, Theodore Roosevelt, Anna Kendrick and Tom Brady). Holiday explains, 'knowingly or not, each individual was a part of an ancient tradition, employing it to navigate the timeless terrain of opportunities and difficulties, trial and triumph' (2014, xv). According to Holiday it was not their philosophical or reflective knowledge that made them exemplary, but that they 'were people who flipped their obstacles upside down'. They are Stoics, 'even if they'd never read them' (2014: 4). On Holiday's judgement, the academic exercises of answering all these challenges are distractions. Stoic wisdom has been, as he puts it, 'taken from us, co-opted and deliberately obscured by selfish, sheltered academics' (2014: 184). Getting bogged down in these details isn't philosophy that counts, because the true philosophy makes one 'a person of action' (2014: 183). Holiday draws a similar contrast: 'While academics often see Stoicism as an antiquated methodology of minor interest, it has been the *doers* of the world who found it provides much needed strength and stamina for their challenging lives' (Holiday and Hanselman 2016: 2). The result, then, is a form of pragmatism with Stoic ethics. The goal is to have an approach that fits one's temperament and fuels an active and successful life.

The weak reply, as one might expect, is open to the challenge that not being interested in addressing sceptical challenges does not make them go away. Nor does dismissively declaring that the people who take them seriously by trying to answer them are inferior in some way. However, pragmatism does provide a different kind of justification for philosophical views, one that emerges from successfully living them from the inside. Yet, we must note, here the challenges posed by the sceptics return. Can you *really* live Stoicism as described? – the Practicability Problem redux. Can you *really* live as a Stoic without alienating yourself from your relationships with others? – the Ruin Problem redux. Can you *really* adopt Stoic ethics without becoming a passive participant in your world? – the Inaction Problem redux. How much Stoicism do you need to believe to earn those successes, and how much of it must be true? – the System Problem redux. Indeed, the simple fact that Holiday begins his stories of successful 'Stoics' by displaying their worldly exploits on the other side of their practising the skills seems to betray something about a distortion of Stoic value theory.

Pragmatism in philosophy is too often deployed as an indifferent shrug at what might be called 'high theory'. But a consistent lesson of the pragmatist tradition has been that high theoretical questions can be posed as matters of practical, personal interest. In his essay 'The Present Dilemma of Philosophy' William James observes that commitments of high theory have expressive and practical results. They are instances of the deeper conflicts in our natures between our tough- and tender-minded inclinations (James 1975, 13). Seeing our theoretical commitments as expressions of who we are and our plan of life is of deepest importance.

Is the indifferent shrug at challenges also an expression of the kind of person we want to be? Cicero admired the Stoics not just because they were good citizens, brave soldiers and faithful friends, but because they were smart arguers and shrewd thinkers. Since all errors are also occasions for moral slippage, Stoics feel obligated to answer objections and solve theoretical problems. Focusing exclusively on the active dimension of Stoicism ignores the intellectual work necessary to consistently endorse those actions. For sure, one can be side-tracked by high theory (as a version of what we'd called progressor's temptation in our note on *Ench.* 52), but that's no reason to neglect the theoretical work. In fact, that risk is a reason to do it well. Doing it well includes being clear when the time for action comes. Some people may just be naturally inclined to be Stoics – call them *congenital Stoics*.[5] Bearing misfortunes may come easy for them. They may have a talent for dodging the turmoil of interpersonal nonsense. But for their courage to really be courage, they must know what they are doing and why. For their justice to really be justice, they must know what they are doing and why. For their virtue to really be virtue, they have to know what they are doing and why. Thus, for them to know what they are doing and why, they need the wisdom to find good answers to the sceptical challenges.

The upshot is that the best way forward is for practising Stoics to keep wrestling with the sceptical questions. Not all obstacles that block the way are iron doors, mountains, or gruelling training; some are intellectual difficulties, critical questions. To be sure, sceptical challenges needle Stoics. But sceptical needling is actually medicine that builds resistance against intellectual laziness. The disease is a smug dogmatism which stubbornly turns a deaf ear to the medicine. We believe Stoicism's revisionary programme is the best hope for a theoretical approach that will pass muster with the sceptics. But this remains an open question.

5.11 The Weaponization Problem

Some object that Stoicism's value theory is too easily made into a weapon that rationalizes unjust arrangements, makes us complicit with them, and blames victims of injustice when they protest. Stoicism makes its practitioners callous. Stoic vocabulary is too readily appropriated by the powerful to justify their power. Stoic writings often inspire those willing to ignore the consequences of their actions. Call this the Weaponization Problem.

Samuel Jackson was a communications worker for the European budget supermarket chain Lidl. Jackson was a self-identified practitioner of Stoicism who thought he 'must adhere to the truth, without fear of offending people' (reported in McCulloch 2020). Jackson publicly called Asian people 'greasy' and refused to apologize for it. After offending his colleagues, he was fired. At his dismissal hearing he explained that, as a Stoic, he does not concern himself with externals, including the consequences of his words and actions. 'The realization that the consequences of what I would say would cause offence would not stop me from saying it' (McCulloch 2020).

The classicist Donna Zuckerberg observes that a reactionary movement of men sharing resentments against women, immigrants, people of colour and the liberal elite has coalesced into an online community. This group goes by many names and has many faces – the Alt-Right, the manosphere, Men Going Their Own Way – but it can be broadly termed The Red Pill Movement. The name derives from the choice the protagonist Neo faces in the film *The Matrix* (1999) between swallowing a blue pill (which would return him to servility in a comfortable illusion) or a red pill (which would transport him to freedom in a harsh reality). Neo chooses the red pill. Members of the Red Pill movement claim to be inspired by Neo's choice. The Red Pillers also claim to see through the illusions of much of the liberal, progressive and feminist programmes. Zuckerberg observes that Stoicism is regularly discussed on Red Pill websites, whose contributors commonly invoke 'Stoicism to justify their belief that women and people of colour are not just more emotional than [white] men, but morally inferior as well'. It is important for those interested in Stoicism 'to understand how Stoicism's tenets can lend themselves to the perpetuation of systematic injustice' (2018: 7). Red Pillers use Stoicism as a 'self-help tool' which easily blends with the personal gain objectives of these communities. Their notion of self-improvement as self-gain shifts blame for consequences of oppression onto the oppressed. Zuckerberg observes that many share the view of the oppressed that 'their oppression would bother them less' were they to be more Stoic (2018: 80). The result, Zuckerberg believes, is that 'these men are weaponizing ancient literature and philosophy, not to become more virtuous, but to gaslight women' (2018: 88). Furthermore, Olúfẹ́mi Táíwò agrees with this troubling application of Stoic thought. He argues that it 'has not come from the pro-feminist left but rather from the "pro-Western" and often racist and antifeminist elements of the center and reactionary right' (2020: 3). Stoicism seems to too closely resemble a form of 'emotional compression' that recapitulates 'patriarchal mores that make men unable to provide emotional care for themselves and others' (2020: 16).

The Stoic view of living harmoniously with fate is illustrated with the striking image of a dog tied to a cart. This analogy is drawn from Hippolytus's overview of Stoic fatalism, which he explicitly attributes to Zeno and Chrysippus: 'When a dog is tied to a cart, if it wants to follow it is pulled and follows, making its spontaneous act coincide with necessity, but if it does not want to follow it will be compelled in any case' (*Refutation of All Heresies* i.21; *SVF* ii.975). We humans are effectively down on all fours with the dog. Fate determines both our paths and everyone else's. If you want to live harmoniously, you must choose to trot along in pace with the cart. The only alternative is to struggle in vain against the cart and be dragged along, nonetheless. But given the manifest injustices of the world, the prospects of resisting injustice, if fated, seem bleak. Lee McBride III observes, with pragmatist inflection: 'At best, this Stoic view justifies and advocates a caste system … Efforts toward social mobility are depicted as inherently juvenile and perhaps insolent … We are asked to accept this as divine providence' (McBride III 2021: 113). The inequalities rampant in society, including slavery, are not only divine institutions decreed by Providence but are irresistible and unchangeable. But this justification and consequent political quietism only worsens the injustice. McBride's reply is sharp:

> I cannot callously shrug off the systematic oppression of women, the poor, and racialized groups … I do not believe that these things were/are fated … To the contrary, I believe there are better explanations for our present conditions. I believe the present order of things bears the markings of egregious human manipulation and greed … I will not accept or embrace 'my role' as a silent, timid, swarthy grandson of fieldworkers, stage left.
>
> (2021: 114–15)

The skills of Stoic mindfulness can offer a balm to endure one's oppression, but this, as the objection runs, short-circuits activism, resistance and criticism.

As a tool not only for rationalized self-justification but also for deflecting the energies of reform, Stoicism's programme of self-control and endurance looks like too neat a fit. Jacob Rosenberg, writing for *Mother Jones*, observes that 'in an era of massive inequality, it was only a matter of time before someone found a way to rebrand the oligarchs' retreat from their social obligations as timeless hard-edged virtue' (2020). Rosenberg recounts his interview with Ryan Holiday:

> 'At the core of it,' Holiday, a former marketer for American Apparel, is telling me, 'I think there's something in Stoicism that connects to the philosopher mindset' – he catches himself – 'or, sorry, the entrepreneurial mindset.' Zeno is 'an entrepreneur,' Holiday explains, 'a person trying to make their way in the real world.' Then he begins to rattle off the new mantras of the philosopher-entrepreneur.
>
> (2020)

Holiday's Stoicism is a productivity hack for those who've already made it or have had it handed to them. Even worse, it excuses passive acceptance of the injustices that in turn benefits the already privileged. Rosenberg concludes wryly: '[W]hat's so baffling about rich people seeing the solutions to the world's problems as a matter of individuals honing their own resiliencies? What's so incongruous about a ruling-class philosophy that says that things are as they were fated to be, so just deal?' (2020). Through this lens Stoicism deforms our adaptive competencies into maladaptations. Becoming overly tolerant of a bad environment morphs you into an apologist for what makes the environment so bad. Weaponizing Stoic philosophy is the main worry on this front. Here's how the criticism is framed. Whenever challenges befall a populace, the most vulnerable are the most adversely affected. They seek help or oppose the arrangements, but their pleas and protests are heard by too many as irrational complaining. Those unharmed by the status quo offer the advice that Stoic value theory provides the inner strength necessary to endure. Hence, Stoicism becomes a tool for rationalizing the status quo and for inaction when things go badly. Consider a company that offers Stoic mindfulness exercises for employees facing economic insecurity instead of paying them a living wage, providing decent health care coverage, and assigning reasonable hours. Philosophical views are tools, but some tools are too easily turned into weapons by the powerful and unscrupulous.

In sum, the Weaponization Problem has three distinct forms: the complicity problem, the victim-blaming problem, and the appropriation problem. Though related these three forms have distinct presentation. The complicity problem is a special version of the Inaction Problem that seems to endorse unjust arrangements that cannot be changed. The victim-blaming problem ascribes to Stoic ethics the belief that those suffering oppression ought to adjust their attitudes and quit complaining since they fail to see the world aright. The appropriation problem is that even if proper Stoicism does not inevitably fall victim to the other two problems, it has not been formulated carefully enough to avoid being taken to endorse them. Stoicism is too easily weaponized for those unjust purposes, so it's a bad tool for reformers seeking justice.

5.12 Reply to the Weaponization Problem

The Stoic reply to the general Weaponization Problem begins by noting that Stoicism was a philosophy designed to appeal to all humans, regardless of their social status, profession, physical (dis)abilities or identity. The Stoic model for virtue is not gendered. The Stoic theory of happiness does not depend on sexual orientation, ethnicity or class. Stoic practitioners hailed from all walks of life – from the enslaved and later manumitted (Epictetus), to the manual labourer

(Cleanthes), to the mercantile (Zeno), to the equestrian rank (Musonius Rufus), to the senatorial rank (Cato the Younger) and emperor (Marcus Aurelius). Probably the greatest virtue of Stoicism is that it is a programme for maintaining one's dignity through the toughest times. The centre it provides no one can harm or take away.

In the *Discourses*, Epictetus argues that 'the reasonable and unreasonable are different for different people' (*Disc.* i.2.4). Since we must adapt to different situations, who we are and what our roles are in those situations vary. Epictetus describes a difficult scenario designed to show how Stoicism is a theoretical but also practical method of handling even the most degrading moments. He asks us to imagine a particularly degrading job: a servant ordered to hold the master's chamber pot. On the one hand, you could stand up for yourself and refuse to do it, and so keep your dignity when punished. On the other hand, you can introspect and realize that what's up to you is how you handle this challenge, not whether you have to face it. Responding like this, you may still come through with your dignity intact. The lesson is that Stoicism's tools do not tell a person what's right but enable her to ascertain what's right *for her* in her own circumstances. So, there's no one correct way for a Stoic to face degrading or unjust treatment. The Stoic may endure the treatment, or the Stoic may object to it, resist and endure the consequences. The decision depends on the Stoic and how she assesses her obligations at the time. Epictetus tells the story of Helvidius Priscus, a senator told not to object to the emperor's motions during senate meetings. Priscus replied that, as a senator, 'I must answer what seems to me right,' thereby risking his life speaking truth to power (*Disc.* i.2.23). Stoic endurance is a tool for either enduring an injustice (for now, in this situation) or for enduring the hardships of opposing it – which choice you make is up to you and the circumstances of your choice.

The point is that the contextualism of our duties in Stoicism means that there is no one universally applicable answer to injustice and oppression. Stoicism equips those who think they must endure with the armour to endure. It also gives those who find they must protest and resist a means of making themselves invulnerable in their pursuit of what is right. Stoic ethics, as an account of enacting one's virtues in light of specific obligations at specific times, is a programme that admits of wide flexibility. That flexibility, however, is both a positive and a negative for the philosophy. It is a positive, because it is wisely attentive to all the unique choices we must make as individuals. Even if we face choices that are generally similar, we must make them in particular situations as individuals with unique histories, relationships, affiliations and sets of strengths and weaknesses. Take, for example, the decision between staying home with one's family or facing an enemy. This dilemma confronted Hector the Trojan hero in the *Iliad* as well as the existentialist philosopher Jean-Paul Sartre's student during the Second World War. The decisions share similar elements but occur in different situations. The decider chooses to stay (or leave) *this* family, *this* city, at *this* time, with *this* enemy at the gates. The key for the Stoics is that we perfect our reasoning so we can figure out the right decision for *us* under *our* circumstances. This is why, with all the various cases, Epictetus insists that we must improve our intellects. We 'need education, so as to learn how, in accordance with nature, to apply our preconceptions of what is reasonable and what is unreasonable to specific instances' (*Disc.* i.2.6).

On the flip side, however, Stoicism's flexible approach to performing duties is also a negative. The problem is that it depends on Stoic practitioners exercising their best judgements without any one universally applicable or certifiably correct answer to calculate for each individual moral decision. There are certainly bad choices. For instance, Epictetus harshly scolds a father who leaves his young, suffering child because seeing her suffer unsettles him (*Disc.* i.11.1–4). But the appropriate is often particular. Here the wide berth of individual fit for Stoic ethics can be a cover for vice or for at least rationalizing not being truly virtuous.

Recall from our commentaries the progressor's temptation – the idea that the tools of wisdom, in the hands of the unwise, are likely to be misused. One's own progress towards wisdom can be an impediment to wisdom. This phenomenon assumes many faces. Progressors will want others to acknowledge their status as philosophers. They will obsess over their role as interpreters of difficult texts. They will be distracted by exciting technicalities in pursuit of fine-grained theory. All these traps will either slow, stall or undercut their progress. Another temptation is a kind of elitism reflected in the Stoic paradox that all who are not wise are *insane*, i.e., *manic* (have lost emotional control). We must see so many of those around us as, in a way, hopeless and lost. This certainly may help with not blaming them when they behave badly or it may help block the sting when they insult us, but it also breaks a bond that we would need to sympathize with them or to feel truly obliged to them.

Weaponization, then, can be construed as a version of the progressor's temptation, at least in its primary form. We will turn to the more developed forms shortly. The primary form is that since practitioners of Stoicism are not wise, they misuse the tools for wisdom, thereby inhibiting their own progress. Thus, those who are proper targets for the complicity objection have tried only one of at least two possible responses to challenges of injustice: they opt merely to endure the hardship. For some the appropriate option is to endure. But for others the right choice is active resistance. Sometimes the cart we are leashed to is a cart that carries us to the front lines of the fight against tyranny, or to a desk-writing campaign, or to rooms where decisions are made.

The victim-blaming problem can be answered, then, by noting that even if externals are not goods, being just still is. Being just requires acting justly. To start, just action means ensuring that those who say injustices are being done are permitted to use their voice. Second, just action requires ensuring that those voices are heard. As noted with the complicity problem, enacting a Stoic virtue manifests in both enduring mistreatment and the courage to call it out. So, with the victim-blaming problem, we must see the same dual face to Stoic virtue. We must hear those who protest as bravely speaking truth to power. The point is that the complicity and victim-blaming problems are mirror-images of a misunderstanding of Stoic virtue, namely that it consists only in enduring misfortune. Once Stoic virtue is understood to encompass also opposing an unjust status quo, both the complicity and the victim-blaming problems dissolve.

The appropriation problem calls for a different approach. Certainly, this problem is partially answered by the progressor's temptation reply since part of that reply is to acknowledge that ethics can also be a source of rationalizations. But the appropriation problem alleges that Stoicism tends to turn too easily into rationalization; Stoicism too often offers cover for bad behaviour. Samuel Jackson, the Lidl worker who said that as a Stoic he did not care about externals, thought that this view justified him in not caring about how his racist remarks were received by others. Red Pill Stoics hold that Stoicism is a good means of justifying their views that white men are morally better than others. Stoicism, as much of its rhetoric claims, makes its practitioners exceptional, so many of the norms that bind others should be suspended for Stoics. This, again, is reflected by the Stoic paradox that all non-Stoics are mad. So, as was said above, even if the paradigmatic Stoics of old never argued along these lines, their texts lend themselves too easily to baneful appropriation.

The first step in replying to the appropriation problem is to reiterate that Stoicism was, at least by the ancient Greek and Roman standards, a positively progressive philosophical programme. The second step is to point out that the progressive angle to Stoicism can extend to contemporary contexts. To start, Stoicism was not only cosmopolitan in its stated views (that we are citizens of the same world as well as citizens of different countries), but it was cosmopolitan in its history and composition. Zeno of Citium was from Cyprus and many of the leading Stoic philosophers were from the Near East or were Phoenician, and so Semitic, in heritage (as noted by Sharpe 2018: 108). Stoicism is thus an early form of multicultural philosophy. Hierocles's model of concentric circles of concern acknowledges our debts and obligations to those close to us but also enjoins us to expand our moral domain to include all of humanity, and perhaps more. Hierocles observes that we start with caring for ourselves, then our families, then our communities, and then find that we share kinship with all other humans simply due to our gregarious natures. We form bonds easily, just by sharing a meal or sitting together. Kai Whiting and Leonidas Konstantakos gloss Hierocles' lesson as follows: '[W]e should aim to draw circles of concern inward, thus bringing the whole of humanity closer to our sense of self until we are able to recognize ourselves in all humanity and all of humanity in ourselves' (2018: 82). Whiting and Konstantakos believe that the exercise of the circles extends beyond the human world to that of the animals and environments we inhabit, especially if we are moved by Stoic theology. We shall return to this idea shortly. The point is that Stoic philosophy is supposed to generate a form of other-interest and concern for humanity generally that would be inconsistent with sexist, racist, nationalist or any bigoted applications.

How to explain the appropriation problem, then? It is easy to see misogynist interpretations as perhaps too tempting. In fact, Stoic philosophy, despite its proto-feminist orientation, regularly uses *femininity* as a term of abuse. Seneca, even amid making the case that women can do philosophy, be virtuous and deserve civic standing, uses terms like *womanly* to mean weak-minded and emotionally compromised (*Helv.* xiii.14.2). Epictetus famously calls those who neglect caring for their virtue in favour of pursuing pleasures 'worthless women' (*Disc.* iii.24.5). In addition, there is the built-in gendering of the classical languages for terms denoting excellence. Virtue (*virtūs*) in Latin has *vir* (= man) as its root; courage (*andreia*) in Greek has *anêr* (= man) as its root. Thus, both languages effectively make the term for excellence equivalent to 'manliness'. Yet this was a problem for ancient philosophy generally, a problem for Platonists, Aristotelians, Epicureans and Stoics alike. Surely, we can distinguish the philosophical programme from an objectionable language used to articulate it. But we can also see how the objectionable rhetoric of this ancient philosophy, as well as how comfortable their proponents were with its tropes, has tainted its interpretation.

Consequently, two points must be made. The first is that a good deal of misogynist rhetoric was part of how Stoicism was articulated in the ancient texts, but this was more a feature of ancient Greek and Roman intellectual culture than the philosophical programme itself. Just as we can extract the arguments from Greek texts and state them in English, we can capture the force of the rhetoric without the sexist overtones. This isn't to exonerate the blameworthy attitudes of our forebears. Rather, it's a way of seeing their virtues not being entirely overwritten by their vices. All Greek and Roman philosophical texts were stated in this linguistic and rhetorical idiom, but it was Stoicism (and sometimes Platonism) that explicitly resisted its misogynist influence with argument.

The second point, which is a consequence of accepting a revisionary view of Stoicism, aligns with how we outlined options for addressing the System Problem earlier. Stoicism offers tools for developing a progressive agenda. Emily McGill argues that Stoicism provides 'insights for a feminist conception of autonomy' given the notion that our faculty of choice and our relevant choices are constituted by our connections with others (McGill 2022).[6] Whiting and Konstantakos think that Stoic ethics, in tandem with Stoic theology, encourages us to live in accord with nature, which requires that we pursue 'unity with the natural world, by extending our care to animals, plants, and their habitats' (2018: 118). One of the authors of this book argues that Stoic value theory compels food-secure people to be vegetarians (Stephens 2022a). Stoicism offers tools for criticizing and correcting the egregious moral errors that have made so much of moral life problematic. It is incumbent on contemporary Stoics to continue the discussion with Stoics and non-Stoics alike so that with our shared reason we can resolve our disputes and solve our problems.

The take-away of the second point in our reply, then, is that Stoicism is a tradition still evolving. The debate over what exactly it prescribes also remains ongoing. The fact that progressive and not-so-progressive interpretations of the philosophy exist speaks to the fact that there is more work to be done to hone the tradition into a univocal tool for justice. Such a hope may be misplaced, however, since a consistent lesson of the progressor's temptation is that, assuming that we are not wise, even the best designed tool for wisdom can be misused and inhibit wisdom. Such is the fate of rational but fallible creatures and their tools for correction. Any philosophy promising otherwise sells a false hope of making us into something we are not.

Notes

Part 1

1   Erected during the fifth century BCE, the *Stoa Poikilê* sat on the north side of the Agora, the marketplace of Athens. A stoa is a covered colonnade, portico or porch. Early stoas were open at the entrance with regularly spaced columns. The Painted Stoa, renowned for the paintings and war loot it displayed, was a popular spot.

2   DL vii is the source of most of the details reported here on Zeno of Citium, Cleanthes, Aristo and Chrysippus.

3   This and the other examples above are instances of the Stoic paradox that all bad deeds are equal just as all good deeds are equal; see section 1.5.3.

4   This argument supports the sixth Stoic paradox that only the sage is wealthy; see section 1.5.6.

5   Epictetus appears to defend the Stoic paradox that all errors are equal at *Disc.* i.7.30–3 where he relates the story of a logic lesson with his teacher Musonius Rufus. Rufus criticized Epictetus for missing one omission in a syllogism they were studying. Epictetus replied 'Well, it's not as bad as if I had burned down the Capitol,' to which Rufus retorted, 'Slave! The omission here *is* the Capitol.'

6   Marcus Aurelius rejects this Stoic paradox. He agrees with the Aristotelian Theophrastus who said that moral errors committed out of desire are worse than those resulting from anger. Marcus describes the angry man as turning his back on reason out of a kind of pain and inner convulsion. The man impelled by desire, in contrast, is mastered by pleasure and so seems more self-indulgent in his mistakes. So, the moral error committed out of pleasure merits harsher criticism than one committed out of pain. 'The angry man is more like a victim of wrongdoing, provoked by pain to anger. The other man rushes into wrongdoing on his own, moved to action by desire' (*Med.* ii.10; Aurelius 2003, 19–20). Marcus may have endorsed this outlier stance because Stoics view anger as a kind of temporary insanity, and so for that reason he judged it less culpable than errors resulting from wanton pleasure-seeking.

7   Diogenes the Cynic is Epictetus's second favourite hero and Heracles his third. Epictetus expresses qualified admiration for Odysseus while criticizing Agamemnon and Achilles.

8   Notice that this wording essentially restates the second Stoic paradox; see section 1.5.2.

9 As Plato relates in Alcibiades' speech in praise of Socrates at *Symposium* 215A–222B. Alcibiades epitomizes an un-Stoic fool enslaved by his desire for something not up to him when he confesses at 219E 'But how could I possibly win him over? I knew very well that money meant much less to him than enemy weapons ever meant to Ajax, and the only trap by means of which I had thought I might capture him had already proved a dismal failure. I had no idea what to do, no purpose in life; ah, no one else has ever known the real meaning of slavery!' (Plato 1989, 71).

Part 2

1 This period is suggested by *Disc.* iii.7.3 and iii.7.10, where Arrian recounts Epictetus mentioning the inspector Maximus whom Trajan sent to the seaport Cassiope on the island of Corcyra (present-day Corfu). This Maximus is probably the governor to whom Pliny the Younger addresses *Epistula* 8, 24 *c.* 107–110 CE.
2 Though our account below owes much to Brandt, our goals include situating the *Encheiridion* within the Stoic argumentative tradition.

Part 3

1 We surmise that the consequent of this conditional statement has dropped out of the text, so we take this argument to be an enthymeme. The omitted consequent is 'you can be in a bad way on account of another person'.
2 Obol.
3 For a discussion of this phrase see the Note on *parorussō* after the comment on *Ench.* 29.
4 Gladiators, or horse-races, or athletes.
5 For a discussion of this term see the Note on *hêgemonikon* after the comment on *Ench.* 38.

Part 4

1 See MacGillivray (2020) for an account of Epictetus's recommendations for 'selective engagement' with people not interested in philosophy. In fact, as we will show in comments on subsequent chapters, interactions with 'laypeople' or *idiōtês* (which we translate as 'fools' and 'schlubs') is something Epictetus takes to be rife with intellectual and moral temptation.

2   One of the most famous references to this exercise of anticipation is in
     Shakespeare's *Julius Caesar*. Brutus, upon hearing the news that his wife Portia has
     died, says, 'Why farewell, Portia. We must die … With meditating that she must die
     once, I have the patience to endure it now' (Act IV, Scene iii).
3   This expresses the fifth Stoic paradox, discussed in section 1.4.5. In *Disc.* ii.1.23–5
     Epictetus argues that all and only the wise, i.e., educated Stoics, are free. In *Disc.*
     iv.1.1–5 he argues for the corollary that no bad person is free.
4   See Schofield (2007) for an extended discussion of Epictetus on the Cynics.
     Epictetus himself has a long account of the influence of Diogenes and the Cynic
     tradition on the Stoics at *Disc.* iii.22.

Part 5

1   See Frede (1999) and Schofield (1999).
2   Recent statements of minimalism have come in two strengths. On the one hand, a
     strong version of Stoic Minimalism, presented by Chuck Chakrapani (2022), holds
     that Stoic ethics is independent of any particular theses of physics or logic. On the
     other hand, Christopher Gill (2022) argues for a modest version of minimalism,
     according to which Stoic ethics requires a few substantive views of human nature
     (that we are rational and capable of withstanding substantial hardship), but little
     beyond that. See also our review of Stoic mimimalisms in our introduction to a
     special issue of *Symposion* devoted to Contemporary Stoicism (2022).
3   See Aikin's 2022 overview of a revisionary programme for the Stoic theory of
     knowledge, one that must straddle the thought that insofar as one revises the
     system, one must ask whether one retains the same philosophical programme in
     the end. Again, the concession can be that the result isn't *Sto-ic*, but rather *Sto-ish*.
4   See Alyssa Lowery (2022) for a discussion of 'big tent' Stoicism and an account of
     the troubles that come with an expansive approach to a philosophical school.
5   Stephens (2022b) has termed these 'stoical' figures, people who naturally have a
     calm, austere fortitude.
6   McGill and Aikin (2014) argued earlier that there is space for a Stoic model of
     feminist autonomy, one that starts with the requirement that we recognize the
     Fundamental Divide being deployed by others.

References

Ahbel-Rappe, Sara (2006), 'Philosophy in the Roman Empire', in David S. Potter (ed.), *A Companion to the Roman Empire*, 524–40. Oxford: Blackwell.

Aikin, Scott (2017), 'Seneca on Surpassing God', *Journal of the American Philosophical Association*, 3 (1): 22–31.

Aikin, Scott (2022), 'The Stoic Sage Does Not Err: An Error?', *Symposion*, 9 (1): 69–82.

Aikin, Scott and Emily McGill-Rutherford (2014), 'Stoicism, Feminism, and Autonomy', *Symposion*, 1 (1): 9–22.

Aikin, Scott and William O. Stephens (2022), 'Introduction: Contemporary Stoicism', *Symposion*, 9 (1): 7–10.

Aurelius, Marcus (2003), *Meditations*, trans. Gregory Hays, New York: The Modern Library.

Boter, Gerard (1999), *The Encheiridion of Epictetus and Its Three Christian Adaptations*, Leiden: Brill.

Brandt, Ulrike (2015), *Kommentar zu Epiktets Encheiridion*, Heidelberg: Universitätverlag Winter.

Brennan, Tad (2005), *The Stoic Life*, Oxford: Oxford University Press.

Brouwer, René (2014), *The Stoic Sage*, Cambridge: Cambridge University Press.

Čelkytė, Aistė (2020), *The Stoic Theory of Beauty*, Edinburgh: Edinburgh University Press.

Chakrapani, Chuck (2022), 'Stoic Minimalism: Just Enough Stoicism for Modern Practitioners', *Symposion*, 9 (1): 11–29.

DeBrabander, Firmin (2007), *Spinoza and the Stoics: Power, Politics and the Passions*, London: Continuum.

Epictetus (1925–1928), *The Discourses as Reported by Arrian, the Manual, and Fragments*, trans. W.A. Oldfather, 2 vols, Cambridge: Harvard University Press.

Frede, Michael (1997), 'Euphrates of Tyre', in Richard Sorabji (ed.), *Aristotle and after* (*Bulletin of the Institute of Classical Studies, Supplement* 68), 1–11. Oxford: Oxford University Press.

Frede, Michael (1999), 'Stoic Epistemology', in Keimpe Algra, Jonathan Barnes, Jaap Mansfeld and Malcolm Schofield (eds), *The Cambridge History of Hellenistic Philosophy*, 295–322. Cambridge: Cambridge University Press.

Gill, Chrisopher (2022), 'Stoic Ethical Theory: How Much Is Enough?', *Symposion*, 9 (1): 31–49.

Hadot, Pierre (1998), *The Inner Citadel*, trans. Michael Chase, Cambridge: Harvard University Press.

Hegel, G.W.F. ([1807] 1977), *Phenomenology of Spirit*, trans. J.N. Findlay, Oxford: Oxford University Press.

Holiday, Ryan (2014), *The Obstacle Is the Way*, New York: Penguin.

Holiday, Ryan and Stephen Hanselman (2016), *The Daily Stoic*, New York: Penguin.

Holowchak, M. Andrew (2008), *The Stoics: A Guide for the Perplexed*, London: Continuum.

Houston, Jack and Irene Anna Kim (2021), 'Why Hermès Birkin Bags Are so Expensive, According to a Handbag Expert', *Business Insider*, 30 Jun. Available online: https://www.businessinsider.com/hermes-birkin-bag-realreal-handbag-expert-so-expensive-2019-6 (accessed 27 May 2022).

Hurka, Thomas (2011), *The Best Things in Life*, Oxford: Oxford University Press.

Irvine, William B. (2009), *A Guide to the Good Life: The Ancient Art of Stoic Joy*, Oxford: Oxford University Press.

Irvine, William B. (2019), *The Stoic Challenge: A Philosopher's Guide to Becoming Tougher, Calmer, and More Resilient*, New York: W.W. Norton & Co.

James, William (1975), 'The Present Dilemma in Philosophy', in *Pragmatism and The Meaning of Truth* (Works of William James), 7–19. Cambridge: Harvard University Press.

Johnson, Brian E. (2014), *The Role Ethics of Epictetus: Stoicism in Ordinary Life*, Lanham: Lexington Books.

Lachs, John (2012), *Stoic Pragmatism*, Bloomington: Indiana University Press.

Laertius, Diogenes (1980), *Lives of Eminent Philosophers*, trans. R.D. Hicks, 2 vols, Cambridge: Harvard University Press.

Liddell, Henry George, Robert Scott, Sir Henry Stuart Jones and Roderick McKenzie (1996), *A Greek-English Lexicon*, with rev. suppl., Oxford: Clarendon Press.

Long, A.A. (2002), *Epictetus: A Stoic and Socratic Guide to Life*, Oxford: Clarendon Press.

MacGillivray, Erlend (2020), *Epictetus and Laypeople*, New York: Lexington Books.

Man, Andrei-Tudor (2019), 'The Role of Divination in the Stoic System', *Hermeneia*, 23: 155–74.

McBride, Lee III (2021), *Ethics and Insurrection: A Pragmatism for the Oppressed*, London: Bloomsbury.

McCulloch, Adam (2020), 'Dismissed Lidl Worker Claims to Follow Ancient Hellenistic Philosophy', *Personnel Today*, 24 Sept. Available online: https://www.personneltoday.com/hr/dismissed-lidl-worker-claims-to-follow-ancient-hellenistic-philosophy/ (accessed 11 May 2022).

McGill, Emily (2022), '*Prohairesis* and a Stoic-Inspired Feminist Autonomy', *Symposion*, 9 (1): 83–104.

Miller, Jon (2015), *Spinoza and the Stoics*, Cambridge: Cambridge University Press.

Peterson, Christopher (2006), *A Primer in Positive Psychology*, Oxford: Oxford University Press.

Pigliucci, Massimo (2017), *How to Be a Stoic: Using Ancient Philosophy to Live a Modern Life*, New York: Basic Books.

Plato (1989), *Symposium*, trans. Alexander Nehamas and Paul Woodruff, Indianapolis and Cambridge: Hackett Publishing.

Rosenberg, Jacob (2020), 'Why Silicon Valley Fell in Love with an Ancient Philosophy of Austerity', *Mother Jones*, Jan./Feb. Available online: https://www.motherjones.com/media/2020/01/silicon-valley-stoicism-holiday/ (accessed 12 May 2022).

Rowe, C. Kavin (2016), *One True Life: The Stoics and Early Christians as Rival Traditions*, New Haven: Yale University Press.

Russell, Bertrand (1957), 'A Free Man's Worship', in *Why I Am Not a Christian*, 104–15. New York: Simon and Shuster.

Samuelson, Scott (2018), *Seven Ways of Looking at Pointless Suffering*, Chicago: The University of Chicago Press.

Schofield, Malcolm (1999), 'Academic Epistemology', in Keimpe Algra, Jonathan Barnes, Jaap Mansfeld and Malcolm Schofield (eds), *The Cambridge History of Hellenistic Philosophy*, 323–51. Cambridge: Cambridge University Press.

Schofield, Malcolm (2007), 'Epictetus on Cynicism', in Theodore Scaltsas and Andrew S. Mason (eds), *The Philosophy of Epictetus*, 71–86. Oxford: Oxford University Press.

Sellars, John (2003), *The Art of Living: The Stoics on the Nature and Function of Philosophy*, Aldershot: Ashgate.

Sharpe, Matthew (2018), 'Into the Heart of Darkness; or: Alt Stoicism? Actually, No …', *Eidos: A Journal for Philosophy and Culture*, 4 (6): 106–13.

Sherman, Nancy (2005), *Stoic Warriors: The Ancient Philosophy behind the Military Mind*, Oxford: Oxford University Press.

Simplicius (2002a), *On Epictetus' 'Handbook 1–26'*, trans. Charles Brittain and Tad Brennan, Ithaca: Cornell University Press.

Simplicius (2002b), *On Epictetus' 'Handbook 27–53'*, trans. Charles Brittain and Tad Brennan, Ithaca: Cornell University Press.

Stephens, William O. (1996), 'Epictetus on How the Stoic Sage Loves', *Oxford Studies in Ancient Philosophy*, XIV: 193–210.

Stephens, William O. (2014), 'Epictetus on Fearing Death: Bugbear and Open Door Policy', *Ancient Philosophy*, 34 (2): 365–91.

Stephens, William O. (2020), 'Refugees, Stoicism and Cosmic Citizenship', *Pallas. Revue d'études antiques*, 112: 289–307.

Stephens, William O. (2022a), 'Stoicism and Food Ethics', *Symposion*, 9 (1): 105–24.

Stephens, William O. (2022b), 'Midwest Stoicism, Agrarianism, and Environmental Virtue Ethics', in Ian A. Smith and Matt Ferkany (eds), *Environmental Ethics in the Midwest: Interdisciplinary Approaches*, 1–42. East Lansing: Michigan State University Press.

Stockdale, James Bond (1998), *Courage under Fire*, Stanford: Hoover Institution.

Táíwò, Olúfẹ́mi O. (2020), 'Stoicism (as Emotional Compression) as Emotional Labor', *Feminist Philosophical Quarterly*, 6 (2). Available online: https://ojs.lib.uwo.ca/index.php/fpq/article/view/8217 (accessed 3 May 2022).

Whiting, Kai and Leonidas Konstantakos (2018), *Being Better: Stoicism for a World Worth Living in*, Novato: New World Library.

Wright, Erica and Ray Parisi (2020), 'Inside One of the World's Largest Sneaker Collections, Worth Millions – and It's Owned by 3 Women', *CNBC*, 31 January. Available online: https://www.cnbc.com/2020/01/31/photos-sneaker-collection-worth-millions-owned-by-chicks-with-kicks.html (accessed 27 May 2022).

Zuckerberg, Donna (2018), *Not All Dead White Men: Classics and Misogyny in the Digital Age*, Cambridge: Harvard University Press.